D0946845

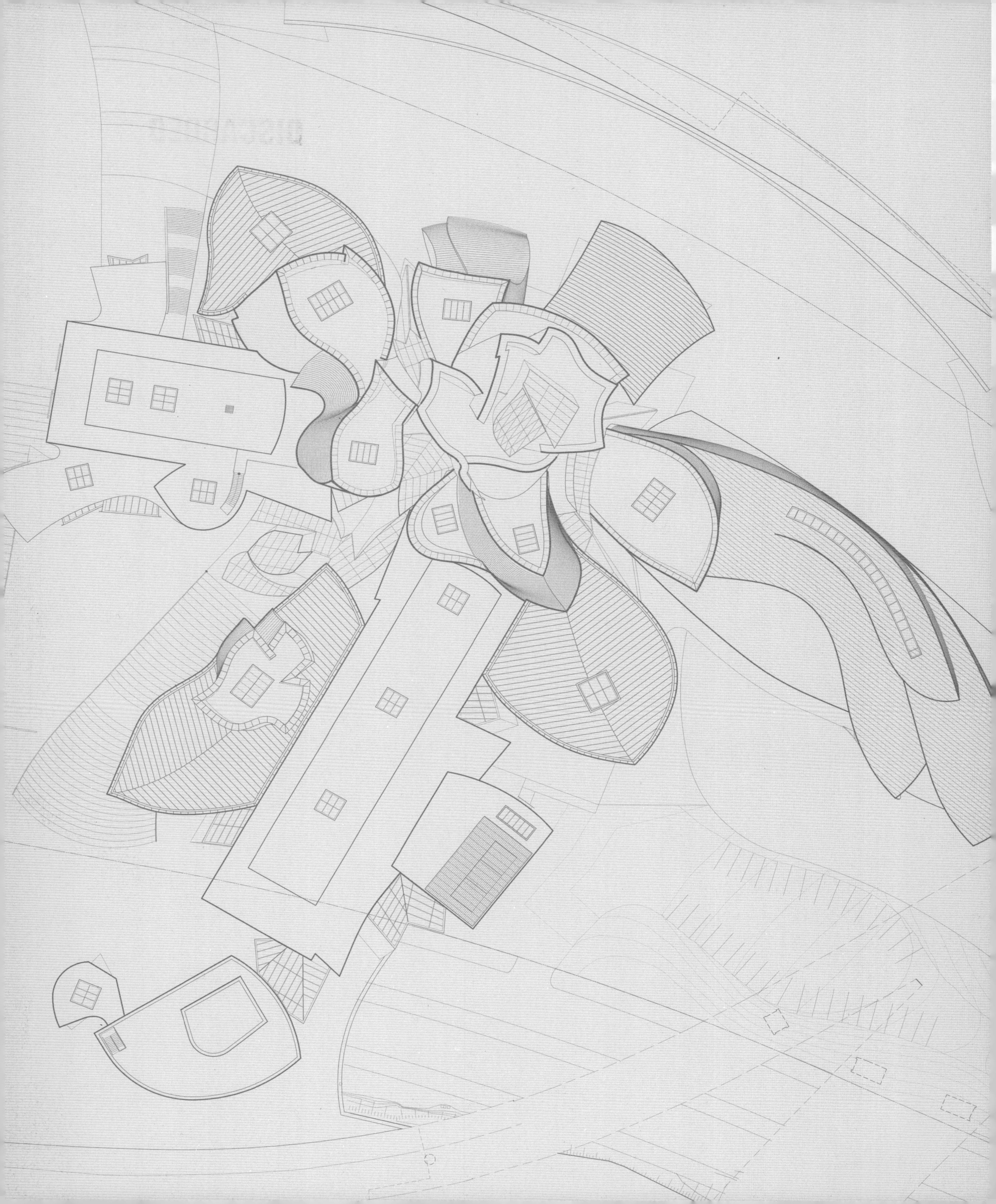

GREAT MODERN STRUCTURES

NOTE

This book contains over 70 structures, each of which is characterized by dozens of weights, measures, dates and other pieces of data. This book, therefore, contains many hundreds of "facts". We have endeavoured to get them all right.

However, in researching this book it has often been difficult to find sources that agree on what would appear to be simple, incontrovertible truths. One would imagine it is relatively easy to find out how tall or long a structure is, or when it was completed, or how much it weighs. But it is not so simple. There can be considerable time lags between the practical completion of a structure, its "fitting out" and its official opening. The height of a building can be measured from ground level, from basement level or from the top of a "plinth"; it can be measured to the altitude of its roof or the tip of its antenna, or merely to the height of the highest inhabited floor. In recording the length of a bridge, do you measure the gap that is spanned or the distance between one end of the structure and the other (for example the anchor points of a suspension structure)? Does the weight of a structure include its foundation or the weight of a building's contents? Surprisingly, it has even been difficult pinning down how many storeys a tall building contains – do the figures include uninhabited levels, such as machinery zones and basement car parks? We have often encountered conflicting "facts" in relation to the simplest of enquiries and it is not unusual to find wholly reliable sources using different data. We have endeavoured, however, to check our facts with as many sources as possible and make a judgment about which are the most reliable or meaningful.

THIS IS A CARLTON BOOK

Published in 2007 by Carlton Books Limited
20 Mortimer Street
London W1T 3JW

A catalogue record for this book is available from the British Library.

ISBN: 978-1-84442-814-4

Project Editor: Gareth Jones
Copy Editor: Kate Michell
Senior Art Editor: Gülen Shevki-Taylor
Design: Smith Design
Picture Research: Claire Gouldstone
Production: Lisa Moore

Printed and bound in Dubai
10 9 8 7 6 5 4 3 2 1

Previous page: Centennial Hall, Wroclaw, Poland
Opposite: CargoLifter Hangar, Brand, Germany
Overleaf (clockwise from top left): Glasgow Tower, Glasgow, UK; Channel Tunnel, UK to France; Esplanade, Marina Bay, Singapore; Space Needle, Seattle, USA; Gateshead Millennium Bridge, Gateshead, UK; Environment Canada Biosphère. Montreal, Canada; Thunder Horse Oil Rig, USA; Great Court, British Museum, London, UK; Farnborough Wind Tunnels, Farnborough, UK; Maitreya Project, Kushinagar, Uttar Pradesh, India; Falkirk Wheel, Falkirk, UK; Frauenkirche, Dresden, Germany; Petronas Towers, Kuala Lumpur, Malaysia; 30 St Mary Axe, London, UK; Bilbao Guggenheim Museum, Bilbao, Spain; Golden Gate Bridge, San Francisco, USA.

GREAT MODERN STRUCTURES

100 YEARS OF ENGINEERING GENIUS

DAVID LITTLEFIELD & WILL JONES

CARLTON
BOOKS

CONTENTS

FOREWORD SARAH BUCK, ISTRUCTE PRESIDENT 2007–2008

As President of the Institution of Structural Engineers during the celebrations of its centenary year, I feel very privileged to be asked to write a foreword for this magnificent book, which celebrates the best of modern man-made structures throughout the world.

In most people's minds famous locations are defined by their structures. Sometimes these structures are formed by nature, such as Mount Everest, the Grand Canyon or Uluru (Ayers Rock), but more often the allusion is to something man-made. And for perhaps as long as man has been able to write or remember lists, there have been lists of "wonders". These lists indicate an enduring curiosity about remarkable structures. For example, Byzantine mathematician and traveller Philon listed the Seven Wonders of the Ancient World in 150 BC. Even more remarkably, the Great Pyramid was 2,000 years old then, and some 2,000 years later it still impresses. *Great Modern Structures* follows a proud tradition of listing wondrous structures.

David Littlefield and Will Jones have organized the structures under a number of categories: Height, Span, Volume, Surface and Power. In doing so they have recorded how structural engineers have pushed the boundaries of the possible and have developed form and materials to build higher, longer and with more complexity than ever before. This book not only describes and illustrates the structures, but it also explains how key developments made the advances possible. Steel frames enabled buildings to go higher; lifts allowed people to use the buildings; intricate damping systems permitted higher and longer structures to be built in earthquake areas; and finite element analysis and complex graphic packages have enabled very complex shapes to be analysed with confidence.

For many of the illustrated structures, structural engineers showed great ingenuity, beyond innovative design, to enable the construction to take place. For example, the London Eye required careful lifting arrangements while the 850-tonne (940-ton) Gateshead Millennium Bridge was floated up the River Tyne and lifted into place by one of the largest cranes in the world.

Most of the structures required effective teamwork to bring the projects to fruition. The collaboration of the structural engineer and architect is well illustrated in the Surface section. The complex organic shapes of the Guggenheim in Bilbao; the geometric shapes of the Sagrada Familia in Barcelona; the hyperbolic paraboloids of the Philips Pavilion in Brussels; and the seemingly random structure of London's 2002 Serpentine Pavilion all required such teamwork. To achieve the vision, careful and complex structural modelling was required to prove the adequacy of the structural form and to ensure that the structures could be built.

A considerable number of the structures take their essence from nature. Structural engineers and architects have been joined on many of the projects by sculptors to assist in the design. The geodesic domes at Eden, the timber gridshell at Downland, the Beijing National Stadium and the Atomium in Brussels all illustrate the influence of nature in design. The combination of these talents has created structures that sit comfortably in the landscape and have a natural feel to them.

Two main elements of modern focus are safety and sustainability. It is sobering to read that in building the Panama Canal, which opened in 1914, an estimated 25,000 people lost their lives. When the Golden Gate Bridge was built in 1937, nets were erected below deck level to catch anyone who should fall. Nineteen were saved in this way, but still a total of 11 died during construction. Safety has now become integrated into the design and construction of modern structures, and these days any loss of life is rightly viewed as unacceptable. Sustainability is also of vital importance as society reviews its collective environmental impact. For instance, in the Maitreya Project in India, natural stack ventilation is being used to avoid the need for air conditioning. Water will be harvested and recycled, there will a waste management system and pollution will be controlled. This is a trend which will continue and is likely to make the biggest impact on construction in the near future.

This book strikes the right balance. There is enough detail for the professional, yet it is written plainly and it is beautifully illustrated for the general audience. Above all it celebrates those visions that have become solid realities which stir the imaginations of all that see them. I can thoroughly recommend this book to the reader.

SARAH BUCK

FOREWORD SUNAND PRASAD, RIBA PRESIDENT 2007–2009

There is a Russian tradition, probably mythical, whereby at the exact time the first vehicles cross a newly-built bridge, its engineers have to take up position directly underneath it. Mythical or not, the notion vividly captures the visceral thrill of the moment when a structure, entirely reliant on the human mind for its existence, is first fully tested by physical forces. Not all the fascinating structures in this book are about suspending weight in such a way, but all have this in common: they were conceived by extraordinary feats of the imagination, shaped through a fusion of science and art, and constructed with will and daring. That must be one of the reasons for the enduring power of great structures to excite and move us, but perhaps there is something more fundamental. We are children of nature and in awe of its expanse, its might and its beauty. Spans that cross seas, towers higher than clouds, interiors as large as caverns, dams that create new lakes and surfaces with the captivating intricacy and sensuality of leaves and crystals: they make us feel more significant; they suggest that we have the measure of the world.

These structures have more than just a visual presence. Some of them are almost hidden, like the tunnels or the submerged gates of flood defences. Unlike the Øresund Bridge which connects Denmark and Sweden, we cannot actually see the Channel Tunnel which joins France and England from above ground; but we can somehow feel it, and the construction of the tunnel has profoundly altered the geographical relationship between Britain and continental Europe.

These structures move us, but they are also hard working. Climate change is compelling us to rethink how to obtain the energy we need but for the time being our lifestyles depend on power stations and oil rigs. Skyscrapers, and skyscraper clusters, make it possible for large numbers of people to work in close proximity, generating the intense transaction of knowledge and information on which modern cities rely. Large halls bring people together in another way and bridges and tunnels in yet another. And often thousands of people have to work together in order to design and build them: engineers, architects, constructors and finance experts. They are triumphs of human collaboration, no less than of knowledge and imagination.

We see in most of these structures a unity of purpose and appearance. Their amazing forms are logical solutions to both their function and their constructional challenges. Sometimes the starting point was economy, which one might think of as being far removed from the achievement of beauty, let alone magnificence. But look at Maillart's Salginatobel Bridge in Switzerland: the design was selected because, using the least quantity of concrete, it was the cheapest of all the submitted options. The result is pure poetry, an elegant arc supporting a slim deck: poetic economy. That it has been so often copied only adds to glory of the original.

So many of the examples in this book, such as the Empire State Building, Sydney Opera House and the Bilbao Guggenheim Museum, have become symbols of their cities, in the long tradition of the Acropolis, Taj Mahal and Eiffel Tower. As a boy I built model bridges and cranes with Meccano kits. I was drawn to architecture because it combined art and science to improve people's lives and to expand possibilities. The structures illustrated in these pages suggest that the possibilities are endless.

SUNAND PRASAD

Opposite: Neue Nationalgalerie, Berlin, Germany

Below: Øresund Bridge, Denmark to Sweden

INTRODUCTION

The defining characteristic of human beings is their ability to reshape the world. It is within our power to change the course of mighty rivers, to create vast artificial lakes, to build towers of immense height and to cross large expanses of water without getting our feet wet. This book is a celebration of some of the man-made structures that have come to define the modern world. All of the structures featured demonstrate, in some way, the ingenuity, skill and, very often, the sheer courage of which engineers, architects and builders are capable.

But this is not an exhaustive list. There are enough staggeringly large and beautiful bridges alone to fill a book of this size. The same can be said of tall buildings and even dams. The structures in this book provide a snapshot of what engineers have achieved over the last 100 years, not only in terms of their completed works but also in terms of the techniques that have been developed to achieve their aims. The development of pre-stressed concrete and the steel frame; the invention of computers and the emergence of digital design; the advent of the global positioning system and many other similar advances have all enabled us to build higher, span further and dig deeper than ever before. We can also build increasingly fast because of technological and engineering advances and, as a result, vast structural undertakings like Taiwan's Taipei 101 tower (page 34) or the Millau Viaduct (page 106) can be delivered in the space of a few years rather than generations.

The structures within the book are split into five chapters – Height, Span, Volume, Surface and Power. The first two are relatively self-explanatory, with only the odd "curve ball" thrown in: a collection of some of the world's tallest structures and a chapter featuring bridges and tunnels. These are the engineering equivalent of "A-list" stars, the headline grabbers. However, the Volume, Surface and Power chapters contain structures that are no less ambitious, and it is here that we can begin to appreciate the scope of the engineer's work. From the sheer size of buildings such as the Millennium Dome (page 184) to the complexity of the Osaka Maritime Museum (page 172), the beauty of the Sagrada Familia (page 208) and the precision engineering of the Lovell Telescope dish (page 216) to the scale of the Hoover Dam (page 282) or ingenuity of the Falkirk Wheel (page 262), engineers have played a crucial role in every structure.

Another link between all of these structures is that they are all expressions of power in one way or another. They fulfil a social, economic or political need. Some were controversial at the time. Others, like the Three Gorges Damin China (page 290), are still provoking protest and praise in equal measure. A few of them were built as demonstrations of technological ability, others as expressions of cultural ambition. In all cases, the architects and engineers pushed the boundaries of what was considered possible in order to deliver structures that are simultaneously mesmerizing and highly functional.

A good number of the structures featured here will be familiar to readers. The Pompidou Centre (page 212), for example, the Empire State Building (page 50) and the London Eye (page 72) – each of these is instantly recognizable because the extraordinary achievement of their creation is lodged deep in the public consciousness. Other structures will be less familiar: the wind tunnels at Farnborough, the Keck Telescopes in Hawaii (page 76), or the Stanford Linear Accelerator in California (page 288), for example, but we have found a place for them in this book because they are, nonetheless, clever and often unique, ground-breaking structures.

Not every case study within this book is "iconic" – some will never be and others are yet to be completed, after which they may or may not go on to become globally recognized. However, every structure embodies a certain beauty, because of the effectiveness with which it fulfils its particular function. And there is no end to mankind's engineering ambition: before this book is more than a few years old, taller skyscrapers, longer bridges and exciting new "power structures" will be growing before our eyes.

As a species, we are driven to strive for the next step, the as yet unattainable goal. Often people attribute this fierce competitive spirit to sportsmen and women, or business leaders, but take one look at the phenomenal built achievements in the world and you'll see that some of our greatest accomplishments can often be measured in bricks and mortar, steel or concrete.

DAVID LITTLEFIELD AND WILL JONES

Right: Akashi Kaikyo Bridge, Akashi Strait, Japan

01
HEIGHT

HEIGHT is undoubtedly the defining characteristic of modern structural accomplishment. The ability to span considerable distances or construct large volumes is well established, but the ability to build high with a relatively small "footprint" is a very recent phenomenon. The possibilities of steel framing, enhanced by the advent of the elevator, generated such excitement that an entirely new architectural term was coined – "skyscraper". Indeed, the first true skyscrapers, such as the towers of 1920s and '30s Manhattan, were of such astonishing dimensions that they are still among tallest structures on the planet. New York's Empire State Building, built in 1931, still towers over anything in Europe and, although no longer the world's tallest building, it still retains its iconic position in the popular imagination.

PETRONAS TOWERS KUALA LUMPUR, MALAYSIA

Claiming the accolade "tallest building of the twentieth century", the Petronas Towers in Kuala Lumpur, Malaysia are considered among the architectural wonders of the modern world. Designed by US architect Cesar Pelli & Associates, who also designed London's One Canada Square, better known as Canary Wharf Tower, and the World Financial Center in New York, these twin towers are 452 metres (1,483 feet) tall.

The story of their rapid development and frenetic construction highlights the impassioned desire of the East to create architectural history. However, the result is not the gigantic eyesore that it could have been, rather a modern monument demonstrating man's ability to build both big and beautiful.

Pelli won the commission to design the towers in a competition in 1991, which he and other renowned skyscraper architects were invited to enter. The client, a conglomerate called Kuala Lumpur City Centre Berhad, which incorporated the Petronas corporation, had laid down instructions that the designs had to be "identifiably Malaysian and of world-class standards that the Malaysian people could be proud of". Pelli's answer was to design a scheme that envisioned two slim 88-storey towers, each with a 44-storey annex. The towers' circumference gradually decreases, giving the impression of two elegant buildings spiralling heavenwards and, cleverly, when viewed from above, the floor pattern is based on an Islamic eight-pointed star– two overlapping squares symbolizing the interlocking of heaven and earth.

Strengthening the Malaysian feel, Pelli specified local materials and designs to adorn the interior of the two towers. However, the winning feature of his competition design may well have been the Skybridge linking the two buildings; this serves to link the towers for evacuation purposes and for day-to-day access of shared facilities, such as the executive dining room and Surau (prayer room). However, according to Eastern philosophy, the enclosed space created between the bridge and the two towers can be seen as a spiritual portal or open doorway to infinity or the future.

Each of the Petronas Towers houses 88 storeys of occupiable space, plus an additional architectural point, to complete the towers' gradual structural narrowing, before finally a tall spire reaches to 452 metres (1483 feet) high. In the beginning, there were no plans to upstage the Sears Tower in Chicago (see page 38), then the world's tallest building at 442 metres (1,450 feet). The original design was 15 metres (49 feet) short of Sears, at 427 metres (1,401 feet). Detailed designs were already well underway when the potential to create the highest building in the world was realized.

Pelli redesigned the building, extending the height of the architectural point and spire. After checking the new design in a wind tunnel to verify its stability, he announced that the race was on for the world's tallest building. Even after Pelli had completed his designs, the project management team spent eight months figuring out the logistical details, right down to the position of the cranes on the site.

Construction of this mammoth project began in earnest in 1993. Built on soil substrata, the Petronas Towers are anchored to the earth via a forest of deep concrete friction piles that sink up to 120 metres (394 feet) below ground. These piles transfer the load of the buildings out through the ground by means of the cohesion between the soil and the embedded surface of the pile. On top of these is a huge reinforced-concrete pad foundation on which the towers sit.

The towers themselves are also largely concrete, of which each tower contains some 80,000 cubic metres (2.83 million cubic feet). A structure of high-strength reinforced-concrete core walls and columns was chosen because, in Malaysia, local contractors are more familiar and comfortable working with concrete than with steel. The 23-by-23-metre (75-by-75-foot) concrete cores and an outer ring of widely-spaced super columns support the towers. This allows for a slender profile and provides 1,300–2,000 square metres (13,993–21,528 square feet) of column-free space per floor; in total there are 74,322 square metres (800,000 square feet) of office space. Concrete also provides better stability to dampen the sway of the towers in winds, and minimizes vibration.

Construction was fast and furious, with the two towers racing skywards. It was quite literally a race as the construction of each tower had been contracted to separate companies, and each wanted to beat the other to the top. Eventually, Samsung Engineering and Construction, the builders of Tower 2, won the race, despite starting a month behind Tower 1, which was built by Hazama Corporation. Tower 1 had run into problems when surveyors discovered that

Left: Rising higher than any other building in Malaysia, the twin spires of the Petronas Towers dwarf even large skyscrapers nearby. The buildings are just a few metres taller than Chicago's Sears Tower.

Opposite: Illuminated with floodlights situated on the Skybridge which joins the two towers, the intricate shape of the external facade is highlighted perfectly.

the structure was 25 millimetres (1 inch) off from vertical, and construction had to slow to minutely adjust concrete formwork to realign the tower.

At the forty-first and forty-second floors of the twin towers is the Skybridge. This dramatic 58-metre (190-foot) long, 750-tonne (827-ton) addition was added to the design as the towers were developed. Some people think it is a stabilizing element, but in reality not only does it not add any stabilitybut its design had to take into account the differential movement of each tower and be able to flex between them.

The Skybridge was built on the ground and hoisted up to its 170-metre (558-foot) high location using cranes. After it was lifted into position, the legs which had been installed on the towers were swung down into place, and connected under the bridge. The Skybridge was not a requirement of the building program, but as the project developed it became an essential part of the overall function of the towers due to its integration into the fire escape evacuation plans. Its structural design is an inverted V-shaped three-pinned arch that supports the bridge in the centre; this arch accommodates all movement in the towers, while remaining equidistant from both of them.

Although completed in 1996, the towers were not officially opened until August 1999. They are now home to many multinational companies, the Petronas Corporation being the main tenant. The public are allowed inside to visit the Skybridge, with a limit of 800 free tickets available each day.

ORIENTAL TOWERS

Building taller than anyone else has always been a magnet for the proudest, richest and most egotistical of people and places. Still relatively young as a country, the USA stamped its mark on the built environment with a horde of super tall skyscrapers in the first half of the twentieth century. In the 1930s New York saw the rise of the Chrysler Building (320 metres/1,050 feet), Empire State Building (381 metres/1,250 feet) (see page 50) and other tall towers. Later, in the 1960s and 70s, Chicago joined the act, with the John Hancock Tower (344 metres/1,129 feet) and Sears Tower (442 metres/1,450 feet) (see page 38).

However, more recently, Asia has usurped the West, building towers to rival America's dominance. The Petronas Towers in Malaysia became world's tallest in 1996 (452 metres/1,483 feet). Hong Kong got in on the act with Two International Finance Center in 2003 (415 metres/1,362 feet), and Taiwan's Taipei 101 currently holds the record at 509 metres (1,670 feet) (see page 34). In the next few years, more eastern and Arabic influence will be evident as South Korea finishes the Busan Lotte Tower (494 metres/1,621 feet), Saudi Arabia the Makkah Abraj Al Bait Hotel (485 metres/1,591 feet), and the United Arab Emirates the gigantic Burj Dubai Tower (the height of which is being kept secret).

The reasons behind this shift from West to East are blurred. Has the West tired of skyscrapers or does it fear another 9/11? Or is the Eastern economy now booming sufficiently for it to allow such displays of wealth and power? Whatever the reasoning there will always be someone wanting to build the tallest tower in the world.

Left: Kuala Lumpur spreads out around the Petronas Towers. Once the tallest building in the world, its towers are built amidst the city blocks on relatively slim but very deep concrete pile foundations.

Opposite: From beneath the entrance canopy, the true majesty of the Petronas Towers can be appreciated against the night sky.

project data

- At 452 metres (1,483 feet) tall measured to the highest point, the Petronas Towers were the tallest buildings in the world at the date of their completion. However, the Sears Tower in Chicago (page 38) still has the highest occupied building floor, more than 61 metres (200 feet) higher than the highest occupied floor of the Petronas Towers.
- The Petronas Towers have 32,000 windows.
- The Skybridge weighs 750 tonnes (827 tons) and is 58 metres (190 feet) long. It spans the towers at 170 metres (558 feet) above ground level.
- The construction of the towers cost 1.8 billion Malaysian ringgit (US$1.2 billion).
- At the peak of construction, there were 7,000 operatives working on the site.
- The 120-metre (394-foot) deep pile foundations are said to be the deepest of their kind in the world.
- Each tower contains 80,000 cubic metres (2.83 million cubic feet) of concrete, 11,000 tonnes (12,125 tons) of steel reinforcing and 7,500 tonnes (8,267 tons) of structural steel beams and trusses.

Opposite: The two-storey Skybridge joins the towers at the forty-first and forty-second floors. Visitors can ride in fast lifts up to the bridge to admire views out over the city.

Right: The towers narrow in circumference as they rise. This not only aids in their structural design, reducing the weight of the building, but also produces an aesthetically pleasing profile.

GLASGOW TOWER GLASGOW, UK

The Glasgow Tower has a chequered history. It has been a source of controversy since before it even existed and to this day is either loved or despised by the people of the Scottish city. The winning entry of the European Millennium Tower competition in 1993, the tower was designed by Richard Horden Associates, a practice renowned for using yachting technology in high-tech architecture. However, in 1995, a second architectural firm, Building Design Partnership (BDP), won a different competition to design the Glasgow Science Centre on the south side of the River Clyde. The European Millennium Tower was integrated into this project and the whole package was awarded to BDP.

The Glasgow Science Centre includes three buildings in all: the Science Mall, an IMAX theatre and the European Millennium Tower, subsequently renamed as the Glasgow Tower. Each is impressive in its own right: the titanium-clad Science Mall has over 5,000 square metres (53,820 square feet) of exhibition space and also contains a planetarium, two theatres, laboratory, café, shop, offices and workshops. The IMAX theatre is the first of its kind in Scotland. And, finally, the Glasgow Tower, at 122 metres (400 feet), is Scotland's tallest free-standing structure, and has the unique ability to rotate according to the wind direction. From an exhibition area within the podium, two scenic lifts carry visitors 105 metres (344 feet) up to an observation cabin offering magnificent views of Glasgow and beyond.

Built on the former Govan dockyards, the project was the catalyst for the regeneration of the surrounding area. With an overall project cost of £75 million, it was the largest Millennium Lottery-funded building project in Scotland. Construction started on site in January 1999, and the Imax Theatre was first to be completed in September 2000, followed by the Science Mall and Tower in mid-2001.

While the Science Mall and IMAX theatre draw crowds, the tower is the most distinct landmark. Its wing-like design makes it extremely aerodynamic. Computer-controlled motors turn the entire structure into the wind no matter what the direction: it can literally spin 360 degrees on its base and is the first building in the world with this capability.

Richard Horden Architects' penchant for yachting technology was combined with modern aircraft design to conceive the tower. Its form is that of a wing pointing to the sky. A turning mechanism based on a spherical bearing in the tower's base allows the tower to shift with the wind, thus reducing wind load on the structure and enabling a lighter construction. The lifts to the viewing cabin descend slowly by their own weight rather than by using power.

The structure consists of a main shaft, which encloses the lift and a 520-step stairwell, and aerofoil-shaped outriggers that control the airflow around the shaft and steady the tower. Fabricated from triangulated tubular steel to keep the weight to a minimum, the stair shaft is clad in painted aluminium to form a precise aerodynamic shape. The outriggers are curved steel plates with internal webs. All the parts were assembled with bolted joints to form a tripod-like shape, which is essential to the tower's aerodynamic performance. The tail section, made of curved aluminium cladding, helps to balance the structure aerodynamically.

Left: The Glasgow Tower is potentially the most unusual building ever built, its small viewing cabin sitting on top of a tall revolving column.

Opposite: The tower makes for a striking vertical contrast to the ground-hugging form of the Science Mall, the structure's slender profile belying its strength.

project data

- The Glasgow Tower is the world's first tower capable of revolving through 360 degrees from the ground up.
- Standing at over 122 metres (400 feet) in height, the tower is the tallest building in Scotland. On a clear day it allows views of some 64 kilometres (40 miles) in all directions.
- The tower was designed by Richard Horden Architects, and then subsequently integrated into the Glasgow Science Centre project and completed by the Building Design Partnership.
- The lifts descend slowly by their own weight without using any power.
- 520 steps and two lifts ascend up the tower to the 105-metre (344-feet) high viewing platform.
- The tower has a 25 metre (82 foot) carbon fibre mast at its tip.

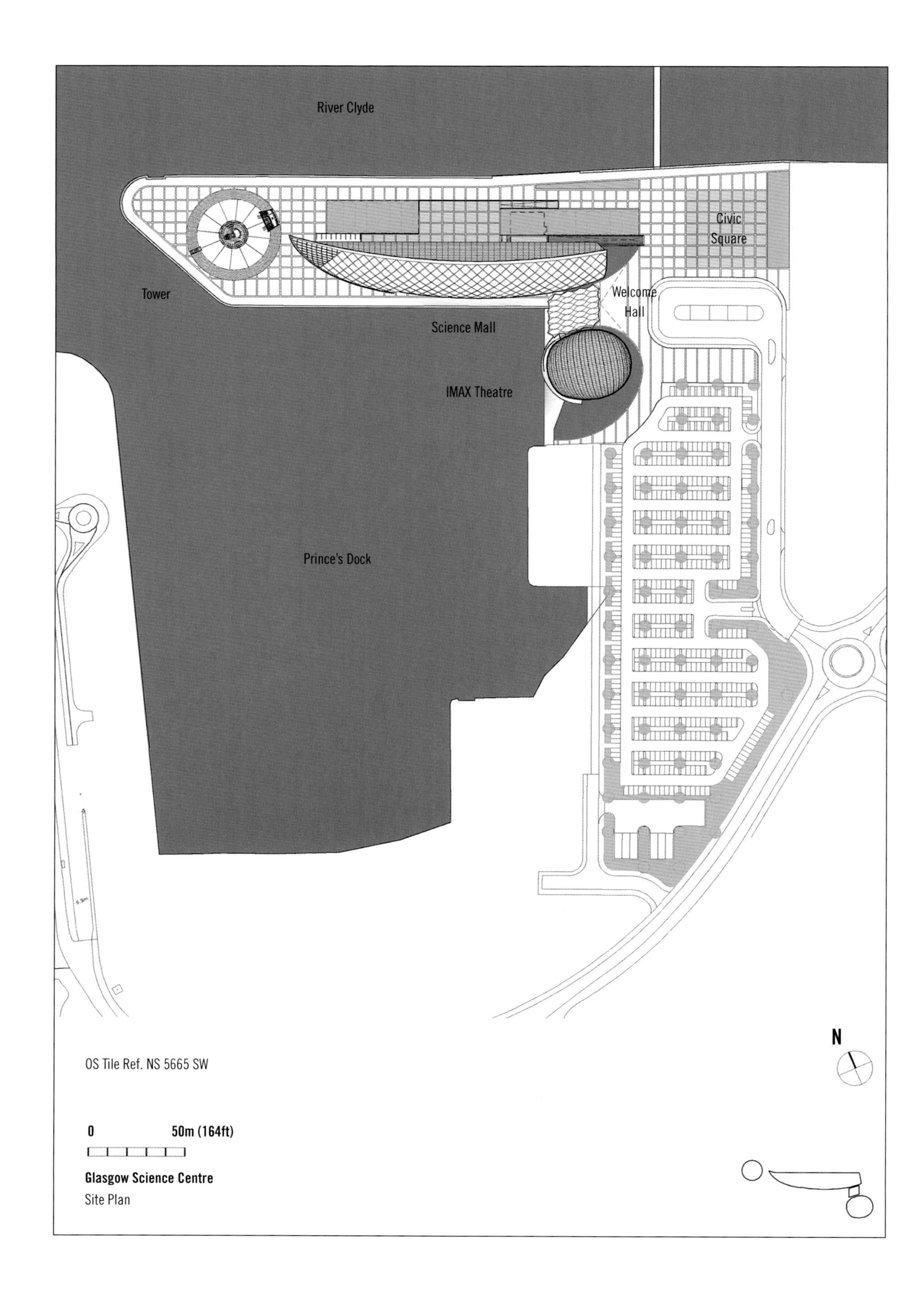

Glasgow Science Centre
Site Plan

A key part of the tower's engineering is the control of the wind flow to achieve a steady wake and lessen movement as much as possible. The aerodynamic design was achieved using computational fluid dynamics programs. The profiles of the towers' various components were developed using a two-dimensional panel-method program to design profiles with true aerodynamic qualities: the program computes the shape required to achieve a calculated allowable pressure distribution.

Scale models of the tower were tested in wind tunnels using real data from Glasgow Airport on the magnitude and frequency of occurrence of high wind speeds. And the engineers on the project based their calculations for the allowable deflection of the tower on the wobbling of a carriage-ride on the London Underground – it was deemed that people find this amount of buffeting acceptable so long as they can hold on to something – any more than this and the tower would have to be closed. Study results revealed that the tower could theoretically withstand almost everything that the Glaswegian elements could throw at it and that it would have to be closed because of high winds on only six days a year.

The viewing cabin at the top is modelled on a helicopter cabin. It is made from glass-fibre-reinforced polymer, placed on a base of foam strips that formed the shell's core. The shell was then fitted to a steel chassis, which was manipulated to fit the top of the shaft structure. A 25-metre (82-foot) tall mast at the rear of the cabin is made of carbon-fibre composite with stiff strips of carbon on each side.

At the tower's base, steel plates hide the bearings that allow it to turn around. The tower's framework comes together into one strong column as it disappears from view below ground. Underneath, the "root" is over 3 metres (10 feet) long and housed in a reinforced-concrete chamber. It is precisely machined to fit 24 bearings that are each 700 millimetres (27½ inches) in diameter and 300 metres (984 feet) deep. These turn the tower perfectly steadily to face into the wind. However, there are also secondary bearings located higher up the tower to help it maintain a constant vertical: these are located in an upper bearing ring in the roof of the entrance podium and take the strain of large lateral loads, transferring them to the root chamber via a ring of columns.

However, since its completion, the tower has been plagued by safety and engineering problems. Ten people were trapped in one of the lifts in 2005 following a malfunction, while problems with the custom-made bearings on which it rotates led to its closure between February 2002 and August 2004.

Opposite: A site plan of the Science Centre shows the Glasgow Tower (top left); the Science Mall next to it; and the Imax cinema nearby. All overlook the River Clyde and Prince's Dock.

Above: A close-up view of the tower reveals its sail-like quality. The passenger lift travels up the more solid section (to the right), while the struts project outwards, creating a type of aerofoil to direct the tower into the wind.

Right: The tower stands tall and slim in marked contract to the colossal Science Mall. While the latter teaches about the potential of science, the tower is positive proof of its application.

CN TOWER TORONTO, CANADA

The CN Tower, in Toronto, is the world's tallest structure, a record it has held since 1975. It has even been called the world's tallest building, but that depends on one's definition. Generally, telecommunications towers such as this are described as "structures" because their primary purpose is to provide a technological service, rather than a place of work or residence – observation platforms and restaurants are secondary facilities, there only by virtue of their height, and the builders of conventional skyscrapers would not consider slimline telecoms needles fair competition. However, semantics aside, the CN Tower certainly qualifies as one of the most elegant, daring and extraordinary structures on the globe.

A need for such a structure became apparent during the 1960s, when the low-rise city of Toronto began to be populated with a series of towers that blocked telecoms reception. However, the Canadian authorities took the decision to construct not only a premier broadcasting tower to circumvent the appearance of high-rise building, but also to build something as a demonstration of Canadian engineering prowess. Constructed by a team that worked 24 hours a day, five days a week, the tower was completed in just 40 months and has provided the people of Toronto with some of the best radio and television reception in North America ever since.

Building the tower's foundation was a tall order in itself. After conducting a series of soil tests, more than 56,000 tonnes (61,750 tons) of earth and shale were removed and a concrete and steel foundation 6.71 metres (22 feet) deep was installed. Once the foundation was in place, construction commenced on the tower's concrete core. This core is composed largely of three intersecting legs which taper gradually towards the peak, and was constructed by pouring concrete into an immense slip form (essentially a mould). As the concrete set, the slip form was moved upward with the help of 45 hydraulic jacks at an average of 6.5 metres (21 feet) a day, and it was gradually compressed to achieve the taper. Building materials for the seven-storey sphere were hauled up by the jacks using miles of steel cables.

By the end of 1973, the concrete tower was the tallest form in Toronto; by February 1974, it was the tallest in Canada; in August that year, work began on the seven-storey sphere, which now contains most of the tourist attractions (revolving restaurant and observation decks); by March 1975, construction work was virtually over. The tower was topped out with the help of a giant Sikorsky "Aircrane" helicopter, which delivered 44 elements of the antenna, and the entire structure was considered complete by 2 April, 1975.

Apart from proving to be a telecoms success, the tower has also become one of Canada's premier tourist attractions, and more than two million visit its observation decks every year. The tower actually contains three observation decks: the highest is the SkyPod, which sits 447 metres (1,467 feet) above the ground and can, during ideal conditions, provide views up to 120 kilometres (75 miles) away. Beneath the SkyPod, at 346 metres (1,135 feet), sits the Look Out level, which has a café large enough to seat 130 people and even contains a dance floor. Just beneath that, at 342 metres (1,122 feet), is the glass floor, installed in 1994, which underwent three months of tests before being opened to the public. Comprising five different types of glass of varying thickness, laminated into a single sheet, the 6.35-centimetre (2½-inch) thick floor is said to be stronger than the concrete slabs elsewhere in the tower. Set within a steel grid, a team of construction workers, suspended in mid-air from a system of safety ropes, installed the 20 glass elements over a period of 10 days. The floor continues to undergo regular safety tests, and a protective surface layer is changed annually to provide as clear a view of the ground as possible.

The CN Tower also contains a restaurant that revolves once every 72 minutes. At 351 metres (1,152 feet) the restaurant contains what is said to be the world's highest wine cellar, which was fitted out in 1997. The construction of the "cellar" involved installing a 2.3-tonne (2.5-ton) water-cooling system in order to maintain a storage temperature of 12.8°C (55°F) and 65 per cent relative humidity. Specialist insulation and vapour barriers also needed to be installed.

That the CN Tower should contain a wine cellar is a bizarre and slightly incongruous detail for a structure that is primarily a telecoms facility. More appropriately, broadcasting systems were upgraded in 2002, including the replacement of the 1-millimetre (0.039-inch) thick Teflon-coated, fibre-glass Radome at the top of the tower, which protects around 40 microwave, VHF, UHF and television antennas.

project data

- **The CN Tower is the world's tallest structure, standing 553.33 metres (1,815 feet 5 inches).**
- **In a wind of 120 miles (193 kilometres) per hour, the tip can sway 1.07 metres (3½ feet) from its centre; the SkyPod will move 46 centimetres (1½ feet); while the main pod will move 23 centimetres (9 inches).**
- **1,537 people working 24 hours a day, five days a week built the tower between 6 February, 1973 and 2 April, 1975. It was officially opened on 1 October, 1976 and cost Canadian $63 million.**
- **The tower weighs 117,910 tonnes (130,000 tons) and contains 40,524 cubic metres (1.43 million cubic feet) of concrete, 128.7 kilometres (80 miles) of post tensioned steel, 4,535 tonnes (5,000 tons) of reinforcing steel and 544 tonnes (600 tons) of structural steel.**
- **It contains three viewing platforms, offering views up to 120 kilometres (75 miles) away.**
- **A glass floor was added in 1994, 342 metres (1,122 feet) above the streets of Toronto. The glass is far stronger than required, containing five types of glass laminated into a single sheet; the floor can reportedly take the weight of 14 hippopotamuses.**
- **The tower was refurbished in 1998 at a cost of Canadian $26 million, adding a range of new entertainment facilities.**
- **The tower is recognized by the American Society of Civil Engineers as a "Wonder of the Modern World".**
- **Several architects were involved in the project, including John Andrews Architects, Webb Zerafa, Menkes Housden and E. R. Baldwin Architects. The main structural engineers were NCK Engineering.**

Opposite: Toronto's CN Tower. Completed in 1975, this telecommunications tower is still the tallest structure in the world. People living within its broadcasting range receive among the best transmission signals in North America.

FLATIRON BUILDING NEW YORK, USA

In 1903 the Fuller Building was completed, standing on the triangular site at the intersection of Broadway and Fifth Avenue in New York. Built as the headquarters for George A. Fuller Construction, it was soon renamed as the Flatiron Building due to its distinctive shape.

At the time of its construction, the Flatiron was the tallest building in New York. Scaling 22 storeys and 87 metres (285 feet), its steel-frame skeleton was a pioneering design that helped shape the future of all skyscraper architecture. Although Americans pioneered skyscraper design, the origins of construction with metal, especially iron and steel frames, hark from across the Atlantic, in the UK. In 1792 mill owner William Strutt used vertical iron supports to carry timber beams in his mills: soon after all mills were being built with metal frames.

This innovation revolutionized construction techniques. No longer were thick heavy masonry walls needed to support the building. Up until then, if you had wanted to build high, the sheer weight of the stone walls required a massive foundation and a huge structural base, onto which sections of diminishing size were added, like a tiered wedding cake. Metal frames now allowed architects to design buildings of a height which had only previously been dreamt about, and they could do it on restricted sites within cities.

Designed by architect Daniel Burnham, the Flatiron was still no light-weight: it contains 3,680 tonnes (4,057 tons) of structural steelwork. It is claimed that it was the first building of its kind in New York and, even if it isn't, the building's considerable height and position at a windy intersection meant that the structural design was groundbreaking for its time. The Flatiron had its doubters, however: sceptics dubbed it Burnham's Folly, believing it would be blown down by high winter winds; some even placed bets on how far the debris would disperse in the event of a collapse.

The weather played a further part in the building, gaining yet more attention upon its completion. It is said that its unique shape created freak bursts of wind

Far left: The Flatiron building amazed the residents of New York when it was constructed. These steel frames were the first to be seen in the city and the start of what would prove to be a skyscraper boom.

Opposite: Today, this classical old building – a triangular oddity in a city of square blocks – is as unique and striking as it was when first completed (**left**). Sculptural stonework cladding hides the steelwork and gives it the air of an era gone by.

MILLENNIA
COME AND GO.
ART IS FOREVER.
ONE WAY

project data

- At the time of its completion, the Flatiron was the tallest building in New York, standing at 87 metres (285 feet). Today, Taiwan's Taipei 101 (page 34) is five times that size, at 509 metres (1,670 feet).
- It is credited as being the first metal-framed skyscraper in New York.
- The Flatiron was named a National Historic Landmark in 1979.
- Metal framed buildings first originated in the UK in the eighteenth century.
- Some 3,680 tonnes (4,057 tons) of steel were used in its construction.
- The building features in the *Spiderman* films and is also the most photographed skyscraper in New York.

along 23rd Street, and groups of boys would gather to watch the wind blow up girls' skirts in the hope of catching a glimpse of a slender ankle. Remember, this was the early 1900s.

Burnham designed the Flatiron's facade in a Beaux Arts style, inspired by the buildings erected for the 1893 World Columbian Exposition in Chicago, the city of his birth. At its most narrow, on the single-windowed facade at the cross section of Broadway and Fifth Avenue, the Flatiron is just 1.98 metres (6½ feet) wide. The building's metal frame supports the limestone and glazed terracotta tile facade. It has three distinct horizontal motifs, using fleur-de-lis, gargoyles and eagles, and changes at several levels. From the top down, there is a balustrade and overhanging cornice; a band of maidens peep out from blocks between the windows; a row of two-storey round-headed windows and a large pride of lion heads scowl down from on high. And this is all on the top third of the building. Below, gently undulating bays break the sense of sheer wall. At fifth-floor level foliated ovals alternate with decorations that contain Greek masks of women, while the first four floors are clad in heavily rusticated limestone blocks to present a monumental feel.

The Flatiron's construction coincided with the introduction of the picture postcard, and manufacturers wasted no time in producing postcard images, first as renderings then as photographs of the building under construction. As it neared completion, photographers retouched their images to make the structure appear complete and fully occupied. Since then, the building has never lost its appeal, even in the wake of the many much taller skyscrapers of New York. In fact, it is still credited as being the most photographed building in the city, its size making it one of the few skyscrapers that will wholly fit within a snapper's viewfinder.

The building has also been featured in a number of films, including the *Spiderman* movies – as the headquarters for the *Daily Bugle* newspaper – and *Godzilla*. Even screen goddess Katharine Hepburn had her take on the building. In 1979, when asked in an interview what it was like to be a legend, she replied that it was like being some grand old building you pass and look up to. And, when it was put to her which one it would be, Hepburn responded without hesitation: "The Flatiron Building."

Soon after its completion, writer Edgar Saltus wrote an article entitled "New York from the Flatiron: The Most Extraordinary Panorama in the World" for *Munsey's Magazine*, whose offices were in the upper floors of the building. His prose hints at the building's exalted position in New Yorkers' collective psyche and its importance from an architectural perspective: "From the top floors of the Flatiron, on one side is Broadway, the longest commercial stretch on the planet. On the other side is Fifth Avenue, the richest thoroughfare in the world. For as you lean and gaze from the top floors on houses below they seem like huts: it may occur to you that precisely as these huts were once regarded as supreme achievements, so, one of these days, from other and higher floors, the Flatiron may seem a hut itself. Evolution may be slow; yet, however slow, it achieved an unrecognized advance when it devised buildings such as this. It is demonstrable that small rooms breed small thoughts. It will be demonstrable that as buildings ascend so do ideas. It is mental progress that skyscrapers engender."

The Flatiron Building is still used for offices today, as it was on its completion in 1903. It is now over a century old and of a design once so unique that it has since been literally copied. There are now flatiron buildings in Toronto, Atlanta and Cleveland, as well as other cities around the world. It was named a National Historic Landmark in 1979.

Opposite: Viewed side-on from a nearby park just off Broadway, the ornamentation of the Flatiron's stone cladding can be fully appreciated.

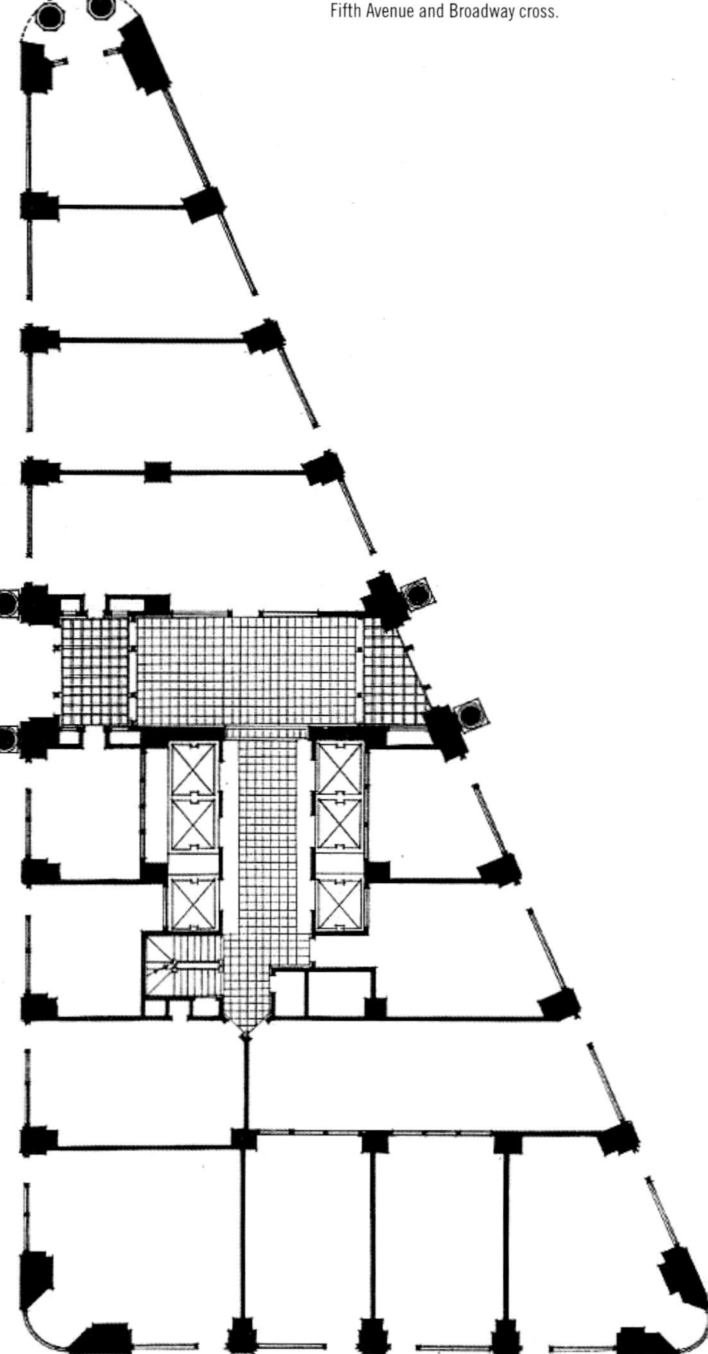

Below: A plan view of the ground floor shows the main structural columns and the circulation core including lift shafts. The building's distinct triangular shape is in response to the unusual corner site where Fifth Avenue and Broadway cross.

ORIENTAL PEARL TOWER SHANGHAI, CHINA

The Oriental Pearl Tower, located in the Pudong district of Shanghai, is one of the most distinctive pieces of Chinese design to have emerged in recent years. Built on the banks of the Huangpu River, the broadcasting tower's spheres are designed to be reflected in the water, conjuring up the image of pearls on a jade plate. It is a highly popular structure and attracts three million visitors a year; indeed, the 350-metre (1,148-foot) high observation deck was opened to the public long before the entire structure was fully completed.

More than 2,000 people worked on the construction of this tower at any one time. Beginning in 1991, the construction team excavated a foundation 18 metres (59 feet) deep, on which is built a trio of 9-metre (29½-foot) diameter concrete columns and a further trio of diagonal braces (this time 7 metres/23 feet in diameter), which converge at the level of the first major sphere. The form is reminiscent of the 55-storey Reunion Tower at the Hyatt Regency Hotel in Dallas, Texas – but where the Texan tower rises uniformly and is topped with a sphere, the Chinese incarnation is far more elaborate. Sources vary on the number of spheres within the Oriental Pearl Tower – some mention three, others eight, and others 11; it depends on what you count. The tower certainly contains three principal spheres, comprising two very large and very obvious (50-metre/164-foot and 45-metre/148-foot diameters) structures and a smaller 14-metre (46-foot) diameter module at a height of 350 metres (1,148 feet). Between the

Left: Shanghai's Oriental Pearl Tower, seen from beneath. Completed in 1995, the tower embodies a distinctly Oriental design.

Below: The tower is akin to the Reunion Tower in Texas, USA, although this Chinese version is far more ambitious.

two largest spheres there is a string of five more discreet spheres, sandwiched within the structure of the tower, which contains a 20-room hotel. Three further spheres wrap around the diagonal braces toward the base of the tower and are merely decorative.

At 468 metres (1,535 feet) in height, the Oriental Pearl Tower is the third tallest broadcasting structure in the world and is the tallest TV tower in Asia. As mentioned elsewhere in this book, opinion varies about the definition of a building and a tower, and this "tower" certainly appears to be more fully inhabited than other comparable structures (if classed as a building, the Oriental Pearl would be comfortably taller than the Petronas Towers of Kuala Lumpur (see page 12), the world's tallest buildings until 2004). Ostensibly built to enhance the television and radio reception of the 13 million people who live in and around Shanghai, the tower was also built (as was Canada's CN Tower – see page 22) as a symbol of strength and ambition. It is already a recognizable icon for the city.

In terms of construction and sheer numbers, the tower, like its rivals in Moscow and Toronto, is a spectacular feat. Using more than 13,000 tonnes (14,330 tons) of steel and 12,500 cubic metres (441,500 cubic feet) of concrete, the tower supports a 118-metre high (387-foot), 450-tonne (496-ton) antenna, which serves 19 different broadcasters. Moreover, the tower was built to survive extremely strong gales and has been designed to sway up to 2.7 metres (8¾ feet) from its centre point.

Like most other towers of its ilk, the Oriental Pearl Tower contains a revolving restaurant and a series of observation platforms. The highest viewing deck, called the Space Module, is located at 350 metres (1,148 feet) and has a conference hall with views of up to 100 kilometres (62 miles), weather permitting; the lower Sightseeing Floor is located 259–263 metres (850–863 feet) above ground level; and another observation deck, Space City, is found 90 metres (295 feet) above ground in the largest sphere. The revolving restaurant, which rotates 360 degrees every hour, is located just above the Sightseeing Floor. Access to these facilities is provided by six elevators, either of the double-decker variety, which can accommodate 50 people, or of a smaller super-fast class which can reach speeds of 7 metres (23 feet) per second.

Located opposite Shanghai's Bund, the late nineteenth- and early twentieth-century European-inspired development that put Shanghai at the financial centre of China, the Oriental Pearl Tower marks out China's more confident international ambitions for the twenty-first century. As well as referencing pearls on a jade plate, the tower's designer is also said to have derived inspiration from a Tang Dynasty poem. Whatever the truth, this structure clearly synthesizes Chinese culture with a very contemporary view of cosmopolitan living – the tower even provides facilities such as dance floors and coffee bars.

Above: Rising to 350 metres (1,148 feet), the Oriental Pearl Tower dominates the skyline of Shanghai's Pudong district.

Opposite: Built on a curve of the Huangpu River, the Oriental Pearl Tower occupies a significant position within Shanghai. At night, the tower's spheres are intended to reflect in the water "like pearls on a jade plate".

project data

- The Oriental Pearl Tower is the tallest TV tower in Asia and the third highest broadcasting structure in the world, after Toronto's CN Tower (page 22) and the Ostankino Tower in Moscow (page 32).
- The tower is 468 metres (1,535 feet) high and weighs 120,000 tonnes (132,277 tons).
- Construction began in 1991 and the tower was inaugurated on 1 May, 1995.
- Up to 2,600 people worked on the construction site at any one time.
- The tower cost US$100 million to build.
- The architect was Jia Huan Cheng of the Shanghai Modern Architectural Design Co.
- Supported on three vast columns, the structure contains 11 spheres of different sizes and is topped by a 118-metre (387-foot) antenna weighing 450 tonnes (496 tons).
- The antenna can sway up to 2.7 metres (9 feet) from the vertical.
- The tower is built on a foundation reaching 18 metres (59 feet) into the ground.
- Some of the elevators can travel at speeds of up to 7 metres (23 feet) per second.
- Walking to the top of the tower would require climbing 2,280 steps.
- Around three million people visit the tower every year.

OSTANKINO TOWER MOSCOW, RUSSIA

Ostankino Tower is the second tallest free-standing tower in the world, and the tallest in Eurasia. Constructed between 1963 and 1967, the tower is a wonder of Soviet engineering and drew on almost as much technical expertise as the space race. Standing 540 metres (1,772 feet) high and weighing 51,400 tonnes (56,600 tons), the design and construction of this telecommunications structure involved more than 40 research institutes and a huge network of construction organizations, government agencies and specialist manufacturers.

The Ostankino Tower was, therefore, a great source of Soviet pride in the Cold War era, and was completed, symbolically, on the eve of the fiftieth anniversary of the Russian Revolution. It is still regarded as a significant achievement, and its pencil-thin assembly remains an iconic form, especially in the traditionally low-rise Russian capital. The tower is a vertical cantilever structure and can deflect comfortably in a high wind; theoretically, the top of the tower is able to deviate from the vertical by 12 metres (39 feet) in a "once in 50 years" high wind.

Certainly, Ostankino's vital statistics are impressive: until the completion of the 553.33-metre (1,815-foot) high CN Tower in Toronto (see page 22), the Ostankino tower was the tallest free-standing structure in the world. Its main elevator, which can accommodate 13 people, rises at a speed of 7 metres (23 feet) per second and takes less than one minute to reach the observation deck at 337 metres (1,106 feet) and restaurant at 334 metres (1,096 feet) above Moscow; one would have to climb 1,706 steps to avoid travelling in the elevator. The tower transmits signals from 19 television stations and 15 radio stations.

The Ostankino Tower has been much modified during its 40-year life, and new broadcasting and transmission equipment was added in upgrades in 1982 and 1991. Proposals to extend the height of the structure by replacing its topmost antenna have so far come to nothing, however, due to financial constraints. The tower itself has been the subject of considerable modifications, too, since a major fire broke out 463 metres (1,519 feet) above the streets of Moscow on 27 August, 2000. The fire, reportedly caused by a short circuit in the original 1960s electrical systems, began at an extremely narrow point of an already very slender structure and firefighters struggled to bring it under control. Four people died and the fire was finally extinguished almost 24 hours later. Although there were initial fears that the tower might collapse (and police moved people to a considerable distance in case it did) the tower's survival is a credit to its engineers – although there was damage to some steel reinforcing cables and cracks were subsequently discovered in the tower's upper reaches.

The Ostankino Tower was designed by Nikolai Vasilyevich Nikitin, a highly-decorated Soviet engineer best known for his monumental structures. Assisted by architects L.I. Batalov and D.I. Burdin, Nikitin designed the tower around a 385.5-metre (1,265-foot) high core of reinforced and pre-stressed concrete (see page 151). Held in place by a 63-metre (207-foot) high conical base (to spread the load of the structure) the tower rises like a slowly-tapering needle, broadening only to accommodate the observation platform and Seventh Heaven restaurant complex (closed since the fire of 2000), which are located two-thirds of the way up. It is a daring piece of work, and one that took the authorities a considerable amount of time to approve.

The need for a mega-scale broadcasting structure was identified as early as 1956, and the Ostankino site was secured in 1959. Ground preparation work was begun in 1960 but work slowed in 1961 when doubts began to be raised about the tower's initial design; in fact, the Russian Federation Ministry of Construction virtually stopped the project in its tracks. A final solution, for an even taller tower than the one anticipated, was eventually agreed in June 1962 and construction began in earnest almost a year later. Around 350 people worked on the construction site every day for four years, and many workers were decorated for their efforts. Once in operation in 1967, all television aerials on Muscovite roofs were turned towards Ostankino. Some 350,000 people visit the tower every year.

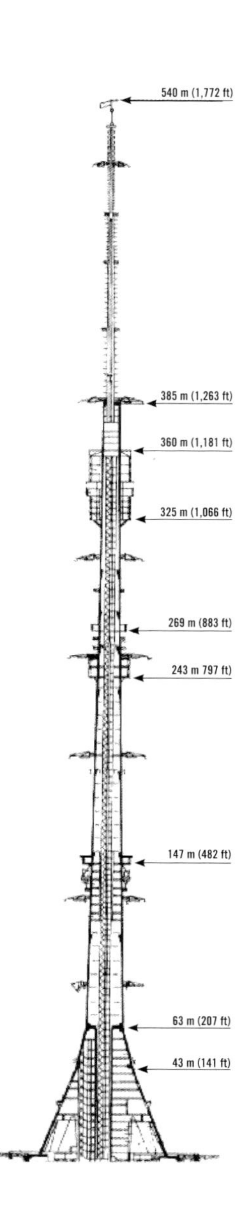

Above: An elevation of the 540-metre (1,772-foot) high Ostankino Tower, clearly illustrating its needle-like profile.

Left: A plan-section through the Ostankino Tower. The tower is 18-metre (59 feet) wide at its base, shown here.

Opposite: The Ostankino Tower, Moscow, which suffered an almost catastrophic fire in 2000 that broke out 463 metres (1,519 feet) above ground level. The tower survived, with some cracks, in spite of fears it would collapse.

project data

- Ostankino Tower is the world's second tallest free-standing tower, and is the tallest in Europe and Asia.
- The tower is 540 metres (1,772 feet) high and weighs 51,400 tonnes (56,600 tons), including 9,800 tonnes (10,800 tons) of 38-millimetre (1½-inch) steel cabling.
- The shaft of the tower is 18 metres wide (59 feet) at its widest, and 8.2 metres (27 feet) at its narrowest.
- Ostankino Tower has an observation platform at 337 metres (1,106 feet).
- The tower can broadcast a stable television signal a distance of 120 kilometres (75 miles).
- In 1994 Russian authorities planned to raise the height of the tower to 561 metres (1,841 feet) and increase its transmission capacity to 40 channels, but the plan was not realized due to a lack of funds.
- A serious fire – caused by elderly, poorly maintained electrical systems – broke out on 27 August, 2000. In spite of fears the tower might collapse, and even tentative ideas to demolish it as a precaution, the tower survived and has been both refitted and strengthened.
- The tower's first high-speed elevator was installed in 2005.
- The construction period was 54 months.

TAIPEI 101 TAIPEI, TAIWAN

Taipei 101 was, at the time of writing, the world's tallest building. Constructed between 1999 and 2004, the building rises an incredible 509 metres (1,670 feet) above the capital of Taiwan, and is so large that some geologists have wondered if it was the cause of a series of earthquakes to hit the area. The tower is 101 storeys tall and contains a six-storey shopping mall at its base as well as the Taiwan Stock Exchange, further office space, and observation and restaurant spaces on the eighty-sixth and eighty-eighth floors (which, unfortunately, are often swathed in cloud).

The tower is a highly symbolic building, not just in terms of its architectural references but in the very fact that it exists at all. Taipei is not short of office space and the tower was not constructed to fulfil any particular spatial or economic need, rather it represents the ambition of the Taiwanese people; the building has certainly put Taipei on the architectural and engineering map. In architecturally symbolic terms, however, the tower is unusual in that it is not based on a sleek Western model – instead, its form and decoration draw on Eastern references. The tower's distinctive pagoda-like composition is reminiscent of bamboo while simultaneously being configured around the number eight, which symbolizes prosperity. At the heart of the Taipei 101's composition are eight sections, each of which contains eight floors. Furthermore, large circles near the base of the tower are symbolic of coins. All the designs of the tower, internal and external, also have the approval of a Feng Shui practitioner.

Taipei 101 is massive in every respect and can be described as the world's tallest building when measured in a number of ways. At 509 metres (1,670 feet) it is the tallest building in terms of the distance between the ground and its structural top (that is, where the building is structurally meaningful, rather than decorative); at 439 metres (1,440 feet) it is the tallest in terms of the distance between the ground and the highest occupied floor. Nevertheless, the antenna atop Chicago's Sears Tower (see page 38) still reaches higher than Taipei 101.

The building is also massive structurally. Taipei 101 is constructed from both steel and concrete: indeed, 16 concrete-filled, steel-plated columns rise up to the sixty-second floor, while a series of concrete-filled "super-columns" and "sub-super-columns" are arranged towards the exterior of the building up to the twenty-sixth floor. All major steel joints are welded, rather than bolted, to increase strength and to create an almost continuous "skeleton" structure. The building is, therefore, extremely strong and heavy and is designed to withstand the impact of an earthquake or the winds of once-in-a-century

Below and opposite: Taipei 101, in Taiwan. The world's tallest building, dominating all that surrounds it, it is set in an earthquake zone. A giant mass damper, hanging like a vast pendulum, is located near the top of the building to help counterbalance any movement that may occur.

project data

- Taipei 101 was designed by C.Y. Lee and Partners and constructed by KTRT Joint Venture.
- The tower has 101 storeys above ground (hence the name) and five beneath ground level.
- 380 piles are sunk deep into the ground as the building's foundation.
- The tower is 509 metres (1,670 feet) tall and contains the world's fastest ascending elevator, which can travel at 17 metres (56 feet) per second.
- Taipei 101 contains 61 elevators.
- The building weighs 700,000 tonnes (771,600 tons) and contains what is arguably the world's largest mass damper – a 725-tonne (799-ton) sphere which hangs on the eighty-eighth floor.
- An external observation deck is located on the ninety-first floor, although the humidity of the region often leaves the upper reaches of the building wrapped in cloud.

typhoons. The building needs to be strong, as although the ground on which it sits is judged to be sound, the tower is located just 198 metres (650 feet) from a known geological fault line. In fact, during construction (31 March, 2002) an earth-quake measuring 6.8 on the Richter scale caused a construction crane to fall from the fifty-sixth floor, killing five people.

Geologist Cheng Horng Lin, from the National Taiwan Normal University, wrote a paper suggesting that the sheer weight of this 700,000-tonne (771,600-ton) tower is placing too much stress on the ground beneath it. It is not as if the load is spread out: like the heel of stiletto shoe, this weight is concentrated over just 1.5 hectares (3.7 acres). In the two years following the construction of the tower, there were two noticeable earthquakes directly beneath the building. However, other academics disagree and say that earthquake data needs to be gathered over a long period of time before any meaningful conclusions can be made. Also, they add that although the building no doubt exerts a considerable stress on the ground, this stress is unlikely to reach 10 kilometres (6 miles) below the Earth's surface, which is where the earthquakes occurred.

Taipei 101 has been designed to protect itself from earthquakes in more ways than one. As well as being big and heavy, it also contains what is arguably the world's largest "mass damper". Hanging like a vast pendulum and surrounded by hydraulic shock absorbers, this 725-tonne (799-ton) sphere is suspended from the ninety-second floor down to the eighty-eighth floor and will counterbalance any movement of the building. Engineers estimate this 5.5-metre (18-foot) diameter ball can reduce the tower's movement by up to 40 per cent.

Being as tall as it is, the tower has been equipped with some of the most advanced elevators in the world. There are 61 of them, and each is aero-dynamically formed to allow them to travel quickly and smoothly. The elevator taking visitors from the ground to the "Topview Taipei" observatory travels the 352 metres (1,155 feet) distance in just 37 seconds. The fastest elevators in the tower can travel at 17 metres (56 feet) per second. Visitors can also walk up a staircase to an external viewing gallery located on the ninety-first floor – at the time of construction this was the highest external observation deck in the world, although it will be surpassed with the completion of the Shanghai World Financial Centre in 2008.

Taipei 101 was topped out on 17 October, 2003, when the Mayor of Taipei fitted a golden bolt to part of the pinnacle assembly. The tower was officially opened in December 2004.

Opposite: Taipei 101 took the title of "World's Tallest Building" when completed in 2004. More than 500 metres (1,640 feet) high, the building is so heavy that some academics have wondered if it has been the cause of earthquakes.

Right: The form of Taipei 101 draws on Oriental references. Reminiscent of the segmented nature of bamboo, the building contains eight distinctive upper sections (eight being symbolic of prosperity).

TOWER HEIGHTS

At the time of writing, Taipei 101 was the tallest building in the world. However, there is currently such a spate of tower construction that buildings are not holding this coveted record for long.

Taipei 101 took the "world's tallest" mantel from the Petronas Towers in Kuala Lumpur (see page 12), exceeding this 452-metre (1,483-foot) twin-tower construction by 57 metres (187 feet). However, US architectural firm SOM is due to complete what is promised to be the much taller Burj Dubai in Dubai in 2008. At present, both the architects and the developer, Emaar, refuse to say exactly how tall this concrete and glass building will be, but the design team is confident that this tower will be the world's tallest building by a large margin – and they have done nothing to contradict rumours that the building will reach 700 or even 800 metres (2,297 or even 2,625 feet) in height. The Freedom Tower in New York, also designed by SOM, with architect Daniel Libeskind, will come in at 417 metres (1,368 feet) but a cable-stayed antenna will take the tip of the building to 541.3 metres (1776 feet) when completed in 2010. This antenna height will exceed that of the Sears Tower (see page 38), giving the Freedom Tower the highest building pinnacle in the Americas.

SEARS TOWER CHICAGO, USA

Chicago's Sears Tower was the skyscraper the world had been waiting for since the early 1930s. After New York's Chrysler Building (1930) and Empire State Building (1931) (see page 50), very tall buildings had been designed along the lines of International Modernism – that is, box-like structures, which were becoming predictably uniform. When the Sears Tower finally made an appearance in 1973, it proved that skyscrapers could embrace a variable composition (unlike the now destroyed Twin Towers of New York's World Trade Center, which were briefly the world's tallest buildings when completed in 1972/73).

The Sears Tower was the world's tallest building for nearly a quarter of a century, until the completion of the Petronas Towers in Kuala Lumpur (see page 12), which exceeded Sears by just 22 metres (72 feet). The Sears Tower still retains the record for a building with the highest tip, however, due to the pair of 84-metre (276-foot) antennae on top of the building. Including these antennae, the building rises to 526 metres (1,726 feet).

Designed for US retailers Sears, Roebuck and Co., the tower replaced an earlier design for a pair of towers half its height. Effectively, the 442-metre (1,450-foot) high building is nine towers bundled together into a single unit. Designed by US architectural and engineering firm Skidmore, Owings & Merrill (SOM), the Sears Tower is composed of nine separate tubes, which, individually, are not especially strong, but, when bound together, have the strength and stability to form an extremely tall and slender structure. It was this engineering tactic that enabled SOM to introduce those dramatic steps into the building's form, which also had two useful secondary advantages: the Sears company could inhabit the larger floorplates in the lower half of the building and rent out the smaller spaces at the top; the steps reduce the tower's impact on Chicago's skyline by cutting into what would otherwise have been a vast, monolithic structure. Each square "tube" measures 23 metres (75 feet) across and there are no columns between the central core and perimeter. Two tubes rise up 50 storeys, a further pair rises to 66 storeys, a trio up to 90 storeys, while a final pair rises to the full 110-storey height of the tower. Underneath this vast mass is a 160-space car park.

Located in the strategically important West Loop of downtown Chicago, the elegance of the building is enhanced through its cladding of bronze-tinted glass and black, anodized aluminium. The building is fitted with more than 16,000 windows, which are cleaned at regular intervals by a set of robotic machines that move along tracks built into the curtain walling system. During 2006/07 all of the building's windows were replaced with laminated glass containing a specially formulated plastic layer that absorbs ultra-violet light, reduces heat gain and admits more natural light; the hope is that the new windows will create a significant reduction in the building's use of energy in its cooling systems.

This is not the first makeover in the tower's history. SOM enlarged the lobby and other spaces in 1985; seven years later the lobby was treated to a US$70 million refurbishment by DeStefano & Partners, and a glass canopy was added to the building's Franklin Street entrance shortly afterwards; a set of extra television antennae were added to the roof by helicopter in 2000.

Unfortunately, in spite of its architectural and engineering prowess, the Sears Tower has not proved to be a complete success for all of its users.

Left: At 442 metres (1,450 feet) the Sears Tower dominates the Chicago skyline. The world's tallest building for a quarter of a century, the Sears Tower still retains the record for reaching higher than any other building, due to its 84-metre (276-foot) antennas.

Below: Designed and built in the early 1970s, the Sears Tower reinvented downtown Chicago. The building now acts as a focus for a number of other tall structures.

Chicago (as its nickname "the windy city" suggests) has a reputation for high winds, although it is almost certainly not the windiest place in the US, and the Sears Tower certainly moves in the wind – generally by around 15 centimetres (6 inches), although it has been designed to sway by as much as 30 centimetres (1 foot). Tall buildings like the Sears Tower have to accommodate movement – if they were stiff they would be in danger of cracking, so they are designed to move like trees. Nevertheless, people have been known to complain of motion sickness at the upper reaches of the Sears Tower, and windowpanes have apparently cracked (there are also reports that the building actually creaks). However, scale models of the building were tested in a wind tunnel during the design phase, and the tower is doing nothing that would cause an engineer any concern.

Sears, Roebuck and Co. does not now inhabit the tower – the company vacated the building in the 1990s and the building has been owned by a string of investment companies ever since. There have been periods when large parts of the building have been vacant, but latterly the tower has once again become a prestigious office address. The Sears Tower, still the tallest building in the Western hemisphere and one of the most recognizable of the world's towers, is a tribute to the engineers of the early 1970s.

Left top: US architecture and engineering firm SOM designed the Sears Tower as a cluster of nine square "tubes". Individually, these tubes are not particularly strong; bound together they make an incredibly strong and robust structure.

Left bottom: In spite of being such an advanced building, the construction of the Sears Tower still required the confidence and daring of individual construction workers.

Opposite: The Sears Tower was intended to provide a new focus for downtown Chicago. Underneath this huge edifice, is a 160-space car park.

project data

- The Sears Tower, at 442 metres (1,450 feet) was the world's tallest building between 1973 and 1996.
- Weighing 204,570 tonnes (225,500 tons), the tower is comprised of nine interlocking square "tubes", only two of which rise to the full height of the building.
- 70,800 cubic metres (2.5 million cubic feet) of concrete were used in the construction of the tower.
- The tower was designed by Bruce Graham and Fazlur R. Khan of US architectural and engineering firm Skidmore, Owings & Merrill. Khan was the principal engineer on the project and was recognized by the City of Chicago by renaming a nearby street "Fazlur R. Khan Way" in 1998.
- The tower provides 107 floors of office space plus retail, parking and mechanical/broadcasting levels.
- Building work began in August 1970 and the tower was "topped out" on 3 May, 1973; the building was officially opened in September 1973, although some construction work continued into the following year.
- A pair of cylinders, 4 metres (13 feet) in diameter and 26 metres (85 feet) high, provide the base for the antennae which top out the building.
- Double-decker elevators lift people from the first two floors to observation platforms at levels 33/34 and 66/67; the Skydeck, on the one-hundred-and-third floor, attracts 1.5 million visitors a year and is one of Chicago's premier tourist attractions.
- Climber Dan Goodwin scaled the outside of the Sears Tower on 25 May, 1981, and was arrested for trespass; Frenchman Alain Robert repeated the stunt on 20 August, 1999 – he, too, was arrested for trespass.
- It cost over US$175 million.
- Sears, Roebuck & Co., the US retail giant which commissioned the building, now occupies a low-rise complex of buildings elsewhere in Chicago.

30 ST MARY AXE LONDON, UK

Standing in the middle of the City of London, some 40 storeys high and 180 metres (590 feet) tall, the "technically, architecturally, socially and spatially radical" 30 St Mary Axe, or the Gherkin, as it is more commonly known, is the UK capital's first environmentally progressive tall building.

Designed by Foster and Partners, the building's unusual circular foot-print bulges from a ground-floor diameter of 49.3 metres (162 feet) to 56.5 metres (185 feet) on the seventeenth floor, before tapering to its apex. Its form responds directly to the demands of the small 0.57-hectare (1.4-acre) site in London's financial district, and makes the building seem less bulky than a conventional rectangular block of the equivalent floor area. The tower is slimmer at its base to allow extra daylight to penetrate at ground level and its aerodynamic form encourages wind to flow around the building, minimizing wind loads on it and reducing wind deflection and down-draughts in the public plaza at its base.

Construction work began on the Gherkin in March 2001, and Londoners looked on amazed as the bulging cylinder of the building rose out of the mass of surrounding low-rise properties. With over 500 contractors swarming over it, the external structure was completed just 20 months later in November 2002 and the tower opened for business in May 2004.

The unique structure of the Gherkin consists of a highly efficient structural steel core and a perimeter diagonal grid (diagrid) of interlocking steel elements, which together weigh over 10,000 tonnes (11,020 tons). Sitting on a foundation of 333 straight-shafted piles, this structure is inherently stiffer than most medium- and high-rise buildings. This is because, while on many tall buildings the central core provides the necessary lateral structural stability, on the Gherkin the diagrid spreads the lateral forces out to the tower's exterior, allowing the core to act purely as a load-bearing element.

The diagrid has been designed using parametric, 3-D computer modelling. Originally used by the automotive and aerospace industries to create complex curved forms, this modelling software allowed for differing design solutions to be tested while constantly regenerating the design, in much the same way as a spreadsheet recalculates numerical changes. The same technology also allows curved surfaces to be rationalized into flat panels, simplifying the fabrication and allowing components to be built more economically – out of the 5,500 glass panels on the tower, the only curved panel is the glazed dome at its peak. This final panel weighs 250 kilograms (551 pounds) and is 2.4 metres (8 feet) in diameter; it was positioned using a helicopter.

The key to the diagrid's success is a steel node, or junction. Developed by structural engineer Arup, this node, of which there are 360 in the building, consists of three steel plates that are welded together at different angles to deal with the complex geometry of the perimeter structure. Each node is up to 2 metres (6½ feet) high and between them they link some 35 kilometres (21¾ miles) of straight circular-hollow section steel to make up the diagrid.

The diagrid is an important aesthetic feature from the exterior of 30 St Mary Axe, as are the black helical lines that gracefully climb the skyscraper. These tinted elements of the fully glazed facade are the most noticeable environmentally-friendly feature of the tower. They are spirals of dark-tinted

Left: 30 St Mary Axe, or the Gherkin, as the building is commonly known, is a new and dominating feature of the City of London's skyline. It is a near neighbour of Tower 42, seen here to the left.

Opposite: When illuminated from the interior, the swooping lines of the solar-tinted glazing that follows the path of light wells within the tower are dramatically highlighted.

PIZZAEXPRESS

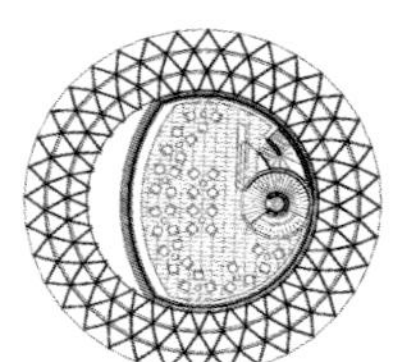
Floor plan of level 40

Floor plan of level 39

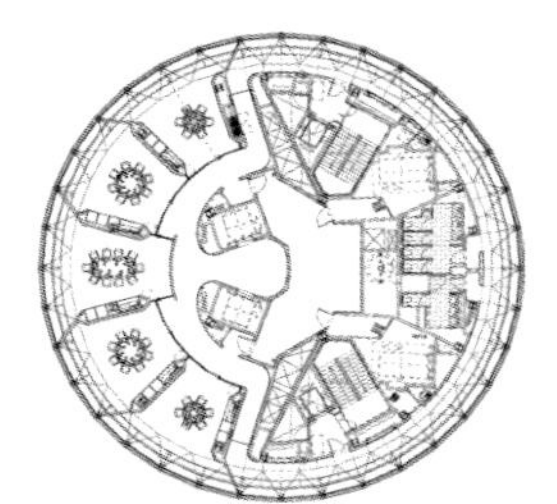
Floor plan of level 38

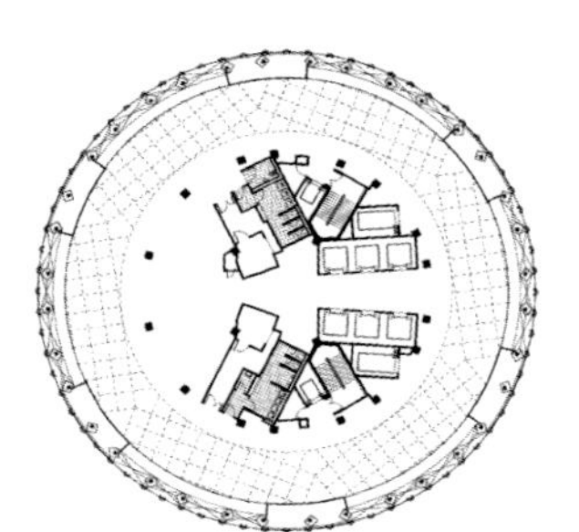
Floor plan of level 33

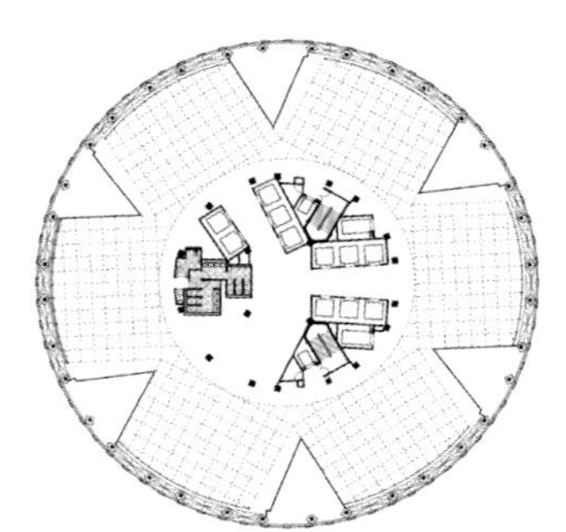
Floor plan of level 21

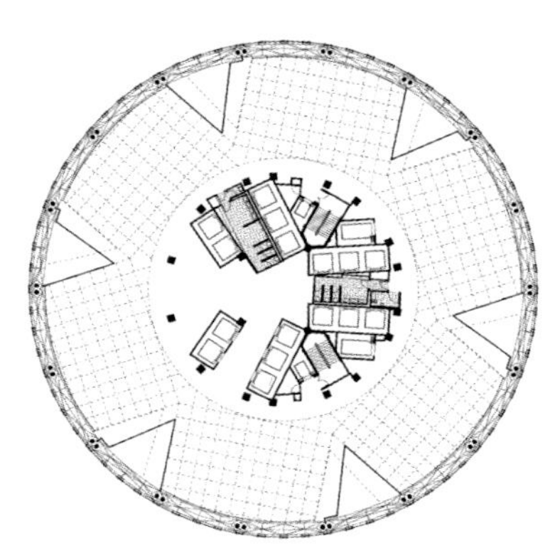
Floor plan of level 6

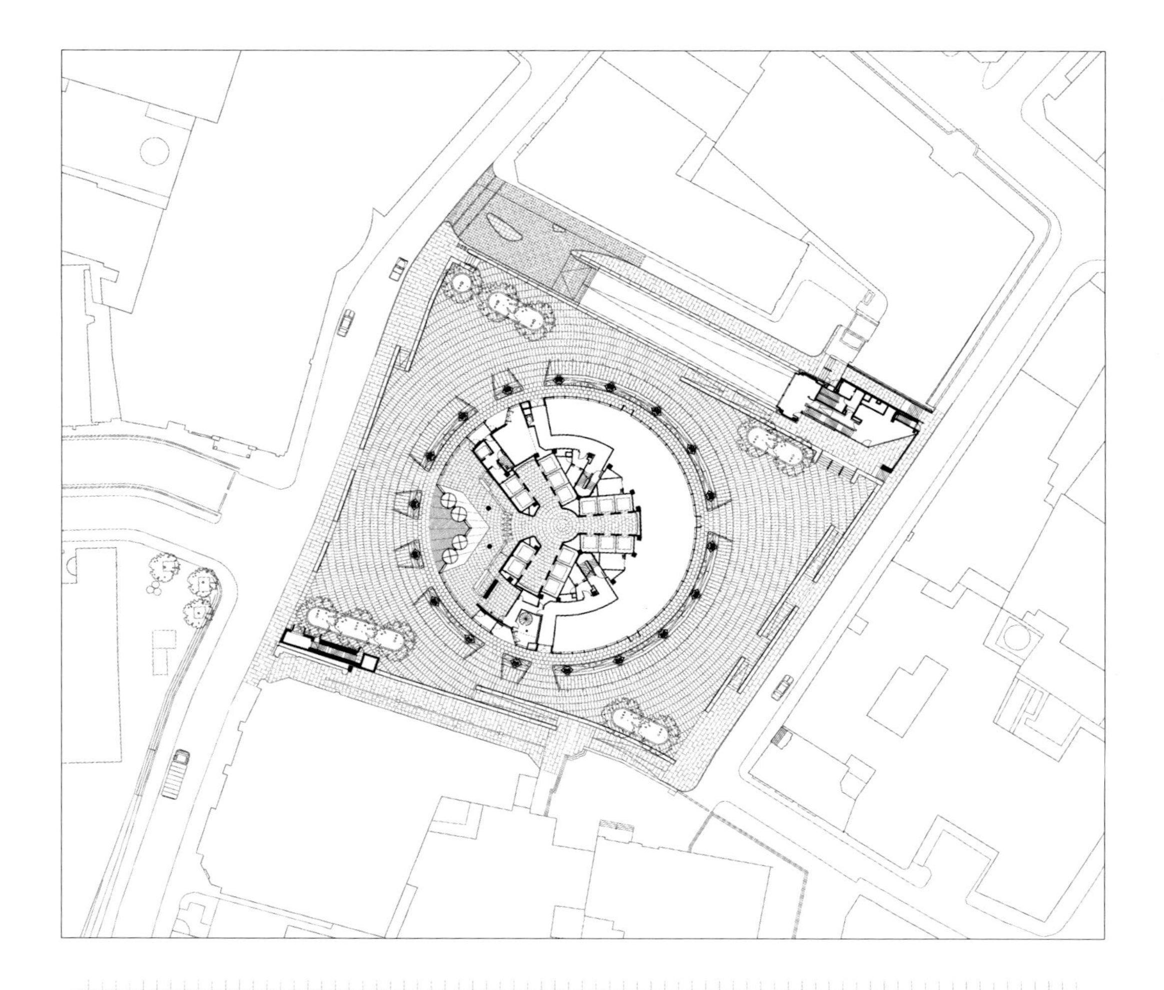

project data

- The glazed facade of the building includes 24,000 square metres (258,300 square feet) of glass, arranged in 5,500 diamond-shaped panes.
- The tower is aerodynamically designed, using parametric computer-modelling techniques developed for the automotive and aerospace industries to deal with complex curved shapes.
- The tower was commissioned by Swiss Re, and designed and built by a team comprising Foster and Partners, Arup, Skanska Construction UK and Hilson Moran Partnership.
- The building comprises 35 kilometres (21¾ miles) of steel parts, weighing over 10,000 tonnes (11,020 tons). Its foundation piles are sunk an average of 27 metres (88½ feet) into the ground and the maximum loading per diagonal column is 1,500 tonnes (1,654 tons).
- The maximum circumference of the building is 178 metres (584 feet) – just 2 metres (6½ feet) less than its height.
- The Gherkin has appeared in an episode of the BBC sci-fi series, "Doctor Who", Woody Allen's film *Match Point* and even the PlayStation game *The Getaway 2: Black Monday*.
- It is the second tallest building in The City, London's financial district, and the sixth tallest in the whole of London.
- It is London's first environmentally-friendly skyscraper and it consumes over 50 per cent less energy than a conventional office building of the same size.
- Wherever possible, the architects used recycled and recyclable materials for the tower's construction.
- It is built on the site of the historic Victorian Baltic Exchange, which was irreparably damaged by an IRA bomb in 1992.

Opposite left: Plans of floors starting at the highest observation level, including the surrounding latticework of the building's fabric; to mid-level floors, showing the spaces where light wells pass through.

Opposite right: A plan view of the entire site on which the building is situated shows that its circular shape and narrow base create much more external public space than a similarly-sized rectangular or square tower would.

Below: A computer-generated drawing of the building's structure and glazing design in plan view. Note that at the very tip, the shape changes to accommodate the "nose cone", which was positioned by helicopter.

Right: Near the top of the Gherkin, a ring of steel girders support special apparatus for cleaning and maintaining the building's external facade.

solar-control glass that protect five-storey-high light wells, which penetrate deep into the building. Rotating by five degrees as they climb, the light wells create floor plans shaped like the open petals of a flower. The light wells also maximize natural-light influx right to the core of the building and promote air to flow through it.

This natural airflow is instigated by the external air movement around the building's facade, which generates substantial pressure differences across its surface. Openings within the tinted glazing allow cool air into the interior. This passes deep into the building via the light wells and also around a perimeter cavity between the external glazed facade and internal glazing to the offices. Warm air spirals up the light wells and is passed out of the building through automatic vents in the facade. The "double glazing" also stops solar radiation before it can heat the office space.

These relatively low-tech but imaginatively designed environmental features dramatically reduce the need for artificial lighting and air conditioning. As such, the Gherkin is an environmentally-friendly skyscraper and a role model for future high-rise construction around the world.

Since its completion, 30 St Mary Axe has won multiple design awards and is one of the most recognized, if not anywhere near the tallest, skyscrapers on the planet. In December 2005 it was voted the most admired new building in the world in a global survey of architects. However, in June 2006 it was voted among the five ugliest buildings in London by *BBC London News* viewers!

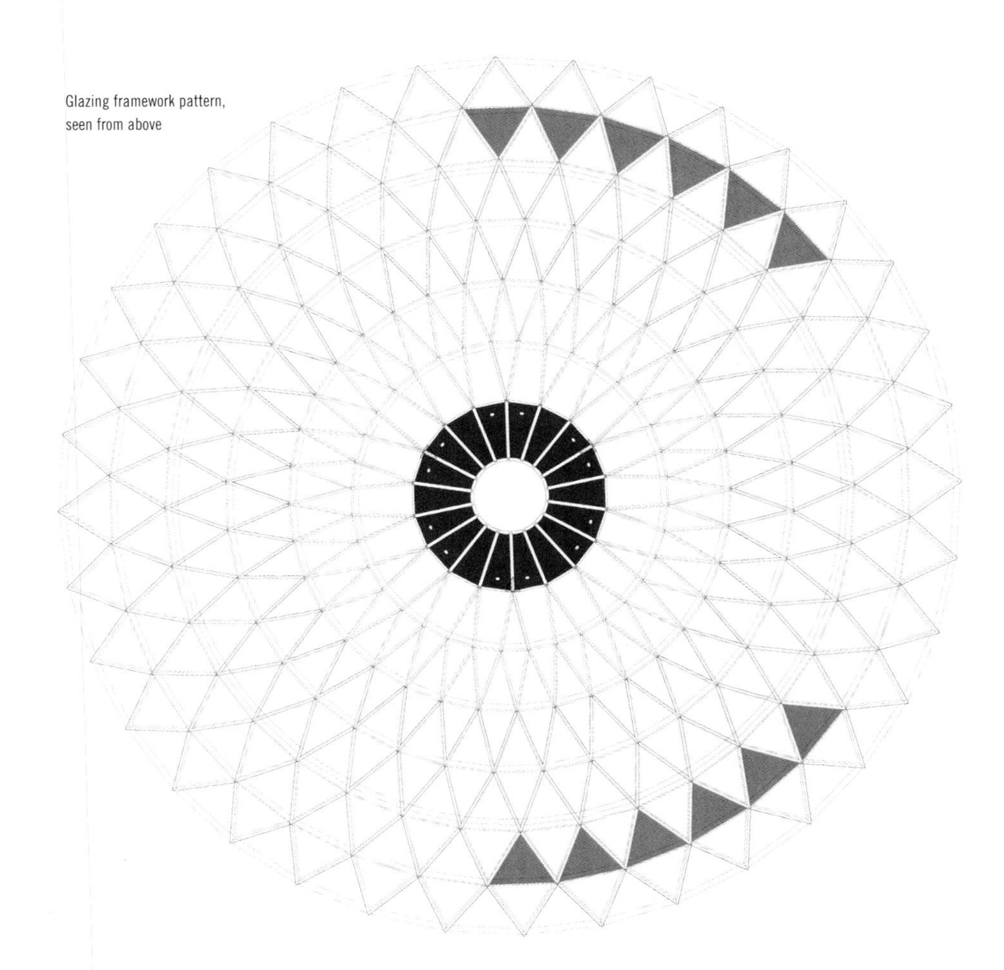

Glazing framework pattern, seen from above

BERLINER FERNSEHTURM BERLIN, GERMANY

At a height of 368 metres (1,207 feet), the Berliner Fernsehturm (television tower) was, on its completion, the second tallest concrete structure in Europe, only being beaten by Moscow's 540-metre (1,772-foot) high Ostankino Tower (see page 32). Built between 1965 and 1969, it was seen by the German Democratic Republic (GDR) as an architectural and political symbol of the might of the socialist state, and a reminder to West Berliners of the Communist block that surrounded them. Following the reunification of Germany, the tower continues to dominate the Berlin skyline and is one of the city's major tourist attractions, hosting over a million visitors each year.

In 1964, construction had already begun on a television tower in Müggelberg in south-east Berlin. However, this project had to be halted because the authorities realized that its location would have been dangerous to planes entering and leaving nearby Schönefeld Airport. And so, Walter Ulbricht, leader of the GDR's Socialist Unity Party, granted permission for the construction of the Berliner Fernsehturm on Alexanderplatz.

It was designed by architect Hermann Henselmann and engineer Gerhard Frost. Structurally, it closely resembles that of the Fernsehturm Stuttgart, which was built in 1956. Stuttgart's tower was the world's first television tower to be built from concrete, and became a prototype for many others all over the world, including the world's tallest, the CN Tower in Toronto, Canada (see page 22).

Construction began on the Berliner Fernsehturm on 4 August, 1965 and, after four years, the tower began test broadcasts on 3 October, 1969. It was officially inaugurated a few days later on the German Democratic Republic's National Day. The tower has since become one of Berlin's most popular landmarks. It has been nick-named Telespargel, due to its likeness to a spear of asparagus, and even dubbed the Death Star, of *Star Wars* fame.

The 250-metre (820-foot) high main shaft of the Berliner Fernsehturm is constructed of steel-reinforced concrete. Measuring some 32 metres (105 feet) in diameter at its base and just 8 metres (26 feet) at its slimmest

Opposite: Built within a bustling Berlin neighbourhood, the Fernsehturm, with its distinct red and white antenna, was originally planned for another site, before it was realised that the tower would interfere with flight paths.

Right: A close-up of the top of the concrete tower showing broadcasting satellite dishes and, below the sphere, the windows of the revolving restaurant. Also noticeable is the cross-like reflection caused by the sun, which locals see as religious revenge upon the once Communist state.

point, it stands on a wide but extremely shallow foundation, which sinks only 4.5 metres (14¾ feet) below ground. However, while it is shallow, the foundation radiates out for over 20 metres (66 feet) in the form of a vast circular pre-stressed concrete slab.

Pre-stressing is achieved by constructing a giant spoked "bike wheel" of steel cables which are held in tension while the concrete is poured over them. Then, when the concrete has set and cured, the cables are released, creating an incredibly strong concrete base that is only a fraction in size of the foundation required if conventional un-stressed methods were used (see page 151 for more information). This high-tech foundation transfers the load of the entire 7,900 cubic metres (279,000 cubic feet) of concrete and 3,450 tonnes (3,800 tons) of steel used in the tower's construction into the ground, distributing it evenly over a wide area.

At the top of the concrete tower shaft is a 118-metre (387-foot) long antenna, which weighs 245 tonnes (270 tons) and is constructed from 30 steel segments, each approximately 4 metres (13 feet) high. Meanwhile, at a height of 200 metres (656 feet), the spherical head of the tower dominates the vertical structure and provides its unique profile. This vast stainless-steel ball houses a restaurant and viewing platforms. The ball's individual segments were lifted into position with the help of a mounted derrick crane, fixed on top of the concrete shaft. The top of the tower has a sway of up to 60 centimetres (2 feet) from vertical when the wind is at its strongest.

The visitor platform is at a height of about 204 metres (669 feet) from the ground and offers views of over 40 kilometres (25 miles) on a clear day. The restaurant, which rotates twice an hour, is a few metres higher, at 207 metres (679 feet). Originally, the restaurant turned only once per hour but the speed was increased on the tower's renovation in the 1990s.

Inside the main shaft are two elevators for visitors and one freight car. These lifts take just 38 seconds to travel from ground level to the sphere, which is a good thing, as hot food for the restaurant is prepared at ground level and transported up. This seemingly illogical arrangement is a fire safety precaution: no naked flames, and hence no kitchens, are allowed at high level.

The tower's sphere is the subject of popular religious folklore, too. It was built at the time of Communist rule in East Germany, when religion was suppressed. However, a strange thing happens when the sun shines on the Fernsehturm's tiled stainless-steel dome: a reflection appears in the form of a giant cross. This entirely coincidental effect was not something desired by the planners and an embarrassment to the atheist doctrine of the Communist government. Berliners were entranced and immediately named the luminous cross Rache des Papstes, or "Pope's Revenge".

Former US President Ronald Reagan mentioned this phenomenon in his historical Brandenburg Gate speech on 12 June, 1987, saying, "Years ago, before the East Germans began rebuilding their churches, they erected a secular structure: the television tower at Alexanderplatz. Virtually ever since, the authorities have been working to correct what they view as the tower's one major flaw, treating the glass sphere at the top with paints and chemicals of every kind. Yet even today when the sun strikes that sphere – that sphere that towers over all Berlin – the light makes the sign of the cross. There in Berlin, like the city itself, symbols of love, symbols of worship, cannot be suppressed."

Opposite: With no other tall buildings built anywhere near it, the tower stands massive and yet almost impossibly slender, backlit by the dawn sky.

Left: The Berliner Fernsehturm's modern design is dramatic in isolation but it has most impact when viewed in the context of the city's historic architecture, and the contrast between Old Germany and its time under Communist rule.

project data

- The Berliner Fernsehturm rises 368 metres (1,207 feet) from ground level in Alexanderplatz, Berlin.
- Its three lifts travel at a speed of 22 kilometres (13½ miles) per hour, making the 200-metre (656-foot) journey from ground level to the sphere in under 40 seconds.
- The tower's restaurant revolves twice an hour.
- The weight of the concrete shaft is 26,000 tonnes (28,650 tons), while the sphere weighs 4,800 tonnes (5,300 tons) and the antenna 245 tonnes (270 tons).
- There are 986 steps on the steel emergency stairway and, if all else fails, evacuation slides can be deployed from platforms positioned at 188 metres (617 feet) and 191 metres (627 feet) above the ground.
- At 368 metres (1,207 feet), the Berliner Fernsehturm is the second tallest concrete tower in Europe, although it lags quite a way behind the world's tallest, the CN Tower (page 22), which stands at 553.33 metres (1,815 feet).
- In 2006 the entire sphere was decorated to look like a football, to celebrate Germany hosting the World Cup.
- The tower cost £21 million to build.

EMPIRE STATE BUILDING NEW YORK, USA

In the three years between 1928 and 1931 New York witnessed the greatest ever architectural race for the skies. Initially, two rivals for the title of tallest building in New York and, at that time, the world, went head to head – the Chrysler Building and the Bank of Manhattan Building. However, although its construction started a year later than the Chrysler Building, the Empire State Building soon overtook both it and the Bank of Manhattan Building to become the world's tallest, a title it retained for over 40 years.

Construction statistics for this most recognizable of tall towers are stupendous. Some 10 million bricks and 200,000 tonnes (220,500 tons) of limestone and granite went into its construction. Seventy-three lifts whisk people upwards at speeds of up to 427 metres (1,401 feet) per second via 1,886 kilometres (1,172 miles) of elevator cable. But, perhaps the most amazing feat is the speed with which the building was actually built. From the time architect Shreve, Lamb and Harmon Associates drew the first sketches, the building schedule allowed only 18 months to complete the building.

Construction on the Empire State Building raged around the clock. The 54,420 tonnes (60,000 tons) of prefabricated steel framework was raised at over a storey each day by a workforce of over 4,000 men. At the peak of construction, 14 storeys were erected in just 10 days. Lunch stands, serving hot food, sandwiches and ice cream, operated on five different levels of the rapidly growing building to save workers wasting time descending to street level. The limestone cladding is fixed directly to the steel beams of the building to save time attaching extra angles and brackets. Even the decorative chrome and nickel mullions that climb the building could be installed without scaffolding, and they doubled as covers for the joints between the windows and limestone walls.

This rush for rapid and prompt completion was perhaps the difference between the Empire State Building being the icon it is today and a dismal failure. Owner John Jakob Raskob had approached the project not with the intention of building a monument to himself, height or anything else, but as a calculated economic gamble. And, he'd undertaken it while New York was still reeling from the Stock Market Crash of 1929. The building had to be completed by 1 May, 1931, the date from which Raskob had sold commercial leases for space within the building. William Lamb, chief architect, summed up the brief he was given: "The programme was short enough! A fixed budget, no space more than 28 feet from window to corridor and as many storeys as such as possible." In reality, the task looked insurmountable to many, but the construction team brought the building in for US$9 million under its estimated US$50 million budget, and many weeks early.

With twice as much lettable office space as the Chrysler Building, the Empire State entered the office space market at a precarious time. This colossus of a building had to recoup the investment put into it, and in the harsh financial climate of 1931 there was a distinct lack of companies ready to move into New York's newest status symbol. Before long, the Empire State Building became known as the Empty State Building, as only a quarter of its floors were initially let. Raskob only stayed afloat in the early years by selling tickets to the viewing platform.

Opposite: An aerial view illustrates the massing of the Empire State Building's structure, heavy at the base and narrowing as it gets higher. It also shows the rocket-like tip, a nod towards the Art Deco style of the time.

Left: Perhaps the best known skyscraper in the World, the Empire State Building characterises the "American Dream". It is a daring engineering accomplishment achieved against the odds.

Following pages (left): The building viewed from downtown, looking up Fifth Avenue.

Following pages (right): A lightning bolt strikes the conductor on top of the building.

MACYS

Without its antenna-like spire the Empire State Building was less than 1 metre (3¼ feet) higher than the Chrysler Building, at 320 metres (1,050 feet). The 61-metre (200-foot) high spire was added, taking its height to 381 metres (1,250 feet). The Chrysler had been usurped as "world's tallest" after only 11 months, a fact particularly hard to swallow after the initial race to claim the title and the fact that the Empire State Building hadn't even been one of the main contenders. Rather, the Chrysler Building's architect William Van Alen and ex-partner and arch-rival H. Craig Severance, designer of the Bank of Manhattan Building, had battled it out to claim the tallest building. When Severance found out that the Chrysler was going to be 282 metres (925 feet) tall he added a 15-metre (49-foot) flagpole, taking the Bank of Manhattan Building to 282.5 metres (927 feet), but Van Alen had a secret weapon. In August 1930 he unveiled the "vertex", a spire made of chrome and nickel that was assembled inside the chrome-clad dome of the Chrysler and raised from within, thus elevating the building's final height to 319.5 metres (1,048 feet). The Chrysler Building's spire even surpassed the height of the Eiffel Tower, giving it the title of the world's tallest man-made structure.

The Empire State Building's own crowning spire, with its winged buttresses, was made famous by the film *King Kong* (1933), in which the giant ape battled with planes while clinging to it. The spire is now topped by a television mast; however, originally, it was designed as a mooring mast for airships. This was completely unfeasible due to high winds, but it expressed perfectly the lofty ambitions of the builders of these new super high-rise buildings.

Harold McClain wrote in his book, *Recollections of Working on the Empire State Building,* "The grandeur of the building – its height, materials and design, and the technological skill that produced it – immediately captured the minds and hearts of all Americans. To watch the tower's steel skeleton rise 102 storeys into the sky in just over eight months was even startling to the construction workers who put it up." On its completion, New York Governor, Al Smith, hailed the Empire State Building as "the world's greatest monument to man's ingenuity, skill, mind and muscle."

project data

- **The Empire State Building (381 metres/1,250 feet) was the tallest building in the world from 1931 until 1974, when the nearby 110-storey, 412-metre (1,352-foot) high World Trade Center was completed. This held the title for a matter of months before Chicago's Sears Tower (page 38), at 442 metres (1,450 feet), wrested it from New York.**
- **Over 10 million bricks were used in the building's construction, and there are 6,500 windows.**
- **In 1945, 14 people were killed when Lt-Col. William F. Smith Jr's B52 bomber crashed into the north side of the seventy-ninth storey in fog.**
- **There are 86 storeys of office space but descriptions often claim the building is 102 storeys high. This can be calculated by adding 14 storeys for the mast and two more for those in the basement.**
- **Some 3.5 million visitors look out over New York from the tower's observation deck each year.**

Left: Construction in another era: a steelworker goes about his job, precariously balancing hundreds of feet above New York's busy streets.

Below: In mid-construction. The building is only partially clad in its limestone skin; the steel frame of its upper storeys is still exposed to the elements.

Opposite: Seen soon after its completion, the Empire State Building is a giant amongst its near neighbours. Today it is surrounded by skyscrapers, but it is still taller than any other building on Manhattan Island.

MAITREYA PROJECT KUSHINAGAR, UTTAR PRADESH, INDIA

To understand the feats of architecture and engineering that will eventually culminate in the construction of the Maitreya Buddha we must first learn the story of Maitreya. According to Buddhist writing, this begins in the distant past during the time of Buddha Ratna-chattra. One of his disciples, a monk named Sthiramati, took it upon himself always to put the welfare of others before his own. He would often forsake taking food until he had established a vowed number of people on the path of pure moral discipline, concentration and wisdom. So strong was his dedication to others' happiness, and so radiant his kindness and love, that even the gods of heaven praised him. They gave him the title "Loving One", or Maitreya.

The Maitreya Project in Kushinagar, Uttar Pradesh in northern India, is an attempt to enlighten and invigorate people to think like the project's namesake. It is seen by its creators as an opportunity to provide the means for locals and others to build a thriving community that will grow and prosper both financially and spiritually now and for many years to come. As such, the project encompasses more than the gigantic bronze statue at its centre. The 304-hectare (750-acre) site will eventually include a landscaped park housing a temple, monastery, convent, guesthouse, library and food halls; meanwhile, nearby, a new public hospital is being built and free education is already provided to 500 students in the Maitreya Project Universal Education School in Bodh Gaya, Bihar.

However, the 152-metre (500-foot) tall bronze statue is in itself a remarkable structure. The Maitreya Buddha is the first statue in the world to be built as a building. Housing a 4,000-person temple, 2,000-person prayer hall within the throne base, and shrines to deities within the body of the statue, it weighs a colossal 12,000 tonnes (13,230 tons).

To put the size of the statue in context, it is nearly 60 metres (197 feet) taller than the Statue of Liberty. The appointed practice AROS Architects has taken its form from an exquisite human-sized Buddha model, which has been refined by Buddhist experts. State-of-the-art rapid prototyping technology will be used to cut moulds for the body panels directly from resin-bonded sand blocks, and some 6,000 of these panels will be cast in a specially formulated alloy.

Unlike nearly all other buildings constructed today, the statue is designed to stand for at least 1,000 years, to support the Maitreya Project's spiritual and social work for an entire millennium. With this in mind, the sustainability of the statue and throne building, both in terms of its survival and environmental impact, have been carefully considered.

While the conditions the statue will meet today can be easily measured,

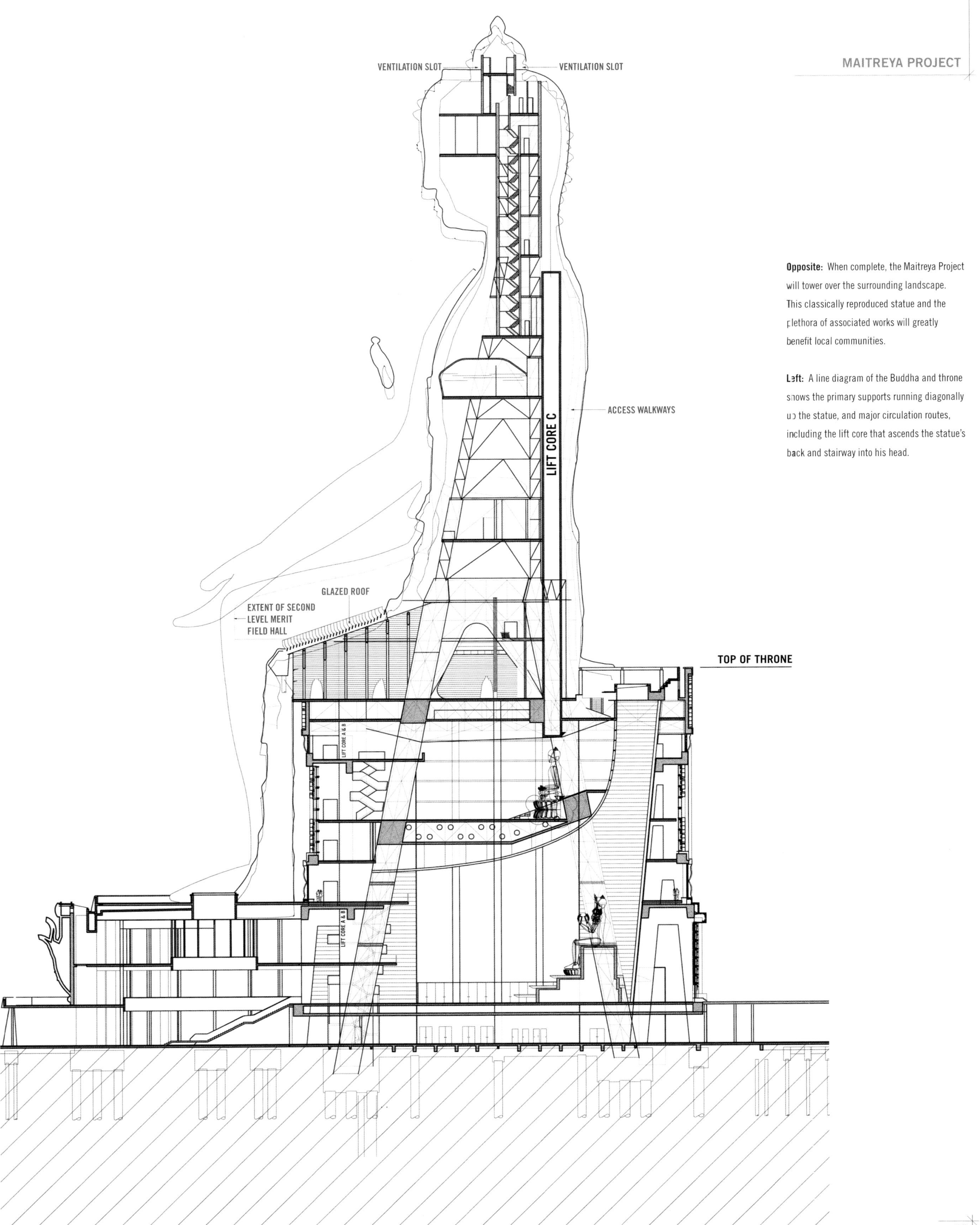

Opposite: When complete, the Maitreya Project will tower over the surrounding landscape. This classically reproduced statue and the plethora of associated works will greatly benefit local communities.

Left: A line diagram of the Buddha and throne shows the primary supports running diagonally up the statue, and major circulation routes, including the lift core that ascends the statue's back and stairway into his head.

Right: A 3-D computer graphic details the supporting structure and internal spaces set on numerous levels within the giant statue, from a giant hall in the throne to spaces for shrines in the head.

Opposite: A small statue of Buddha was used to design the Maitreya Buddha. Here, a close up of the proposed statue shows the detail which will be cast into the massive structure.

projecting data for weather patterns over its 1,000-year lifespan is much more difficult. The huge structure must withstand high winds, extreme temperature changes, seasonal rains, possible earthquakes and floods, and environmental pollution. For this reason, the statue has been "over-designed" to withstand the most challenging conditions that could conceivably arise. A computer model has been examined for wind loading, heat expansion, seismic shock and extreme-weather conditions.

Extensive research has also gone into developing the special alloy of bronze for the outer "skin" of the statue: the result is an aluminium-nickel-bronze. As this skin will expand and contract up to 100 millimetres (4 inches) each day due to temperature changes, the statue has special expansion joints. While these must be invisible to the observer, they must also be constructed in such a way as to protect the internal supports of the statue from water leakage, erosion and corrosion. The skin is attached to a giant steel skeleton. Large A-frames are to be built up through the throne and centre of the statue to give it stability. A secondary load-bearing steel structure – a 3-D skeleton – provides attachment points for the skin panels and transfers the load down to the ground.

The entire Maitreya Project will feature the latest in environmental and energy-saving techniques, including water harvesting, water recycling and management, waste management and pollution control. The statue itself will feature an innovative natural-ventilation system to keep the interior spaces cool. Air will be funnelled through a large tunnel, being cooled as it travels by stable underground temperatures; this is released into the statue through vents. As the cool air enters it will displace the warmer air pushing it upwards and out of vents at the top of the statue; the effect is called natural-stack ventilation and no mechanical air conditioning is required.

Finally, the project will also source materials and labour from locally available resources wherever possible and maximize local access to training and skills development. And, on completion, the project will provide a vibrant local economy, creating, both within and around the park, the means for continual economic stability without damaging the local, national or global environment.

For thousands of years the world's enduring monuments have provided powerful symbols, reminders of society's most treasured values – think of the Pyramids or Stonehenge, for example. However, during the twentieth century the most remarkable buildings constructed have come about due to commercial interests. From skyscrapers to airports, shopping malls to theatres and theme parks, all are a means to a financial end. The Maitreya Buddha statue is an attempt to forgo these ideals and provide the world with an enduring monument to spiritual values, a reminder of the benefits of creating peace at every level through practising kindness and generosity to each other.

Spiritual director of the project Lama Zopa Rinpoche says, "Throughout the world, the Buddha is recognised as a symbol of peace. Maitreya can be translated as 'loving-kindness'. The vision of Maitreya Project is to effect peace at every level of society through the practice of "loving-kindness": peace within the family, the community and the world, as well as inner peace for the individual.

"Construction of the statue is not the goal – it is the method for achieving the goal. Our goal is to benefit as many people as possible for as long as possible."

project data

- **The statue is estimated to cost £103 million.**
- **The complete Maitreya Project cost, including the statue, development of the 304-hectare (750-acre) site, healthcare buildings and educational programmes is estimated at a total of £132 million.**
- **The Maitreya Buddha is 152 metres (500 feet) tall, 59 metres (194 feet) taller than the Statue of Liberty when measured from the base of the foundation to the tip of her torch.**
- **The statue will weigh around 12,000 tonnes (13,230 tons) and is built to last 1,000 years.**
- **It will be covered in over 6,000 bronze alloy panels – each made using high-tech techniques in Sheffield, England.**
- **Even though the statue is in India, no air-conditioning will be used to cool the spaces within. Instead, ground-cooled air from a huge tunnel under the statue is filtered through it, displacing warm air and keeping the internal temperature down.**
- **Maitreya is translated to mean "Loving One" or "loving kindness": it was the name given by the gods to a monk named Sthiramati.**

SPACE NEEDLE SEATTLE, USA

What is now called the Space Needle was originally called the Space Cage, and was conceived as more of a "tethered balloon" form by Western International Hotels President Edward E. Carlson, who was intrigued by the idea of a "restaurant in the sky". The design, in the hands of architect John Graham and his team, who had recently completed the world's first shopping mall in Seattle, became more flying-saucer shaped. The tower was designed as the centrepiece of the 1962 World's Fair in Seattle, which had "Century 21" as its central theme; a "futuristic" structure was therefore needed to suggest the possibilities of the next century and the tower is a good expression of the science-fiction visions of the 1950s and '60s (Los Angeles International Airport's Theme Building is another). In fact, the design team even had fun with the names of the colours used to decorate the structure – the legs of the Needle were dubbed "astronaut white", the core was called "orbital olive", the halo was "re-entry red" and the roof was coloured "galaxy gold".

The construction of this immense tripod was incredibly rapid – indeed, the purchase of the land (from an obsolete Fire Department alarm centre) was not secured until just 13 months before the fair was due to open. The search for land was difficult in itself, and the lack of a suitable plot nearly ended the project before it even began. The 37-by-37-metre (120-by-120-foot) plot was almost immediately excavated to a depth of 9 metres (30 feet) and filled with concrete for the tower's foundation: so big and heavy is this foundation that it weighs more than the tower itself, and the structure's centre of gravity lies just 1.5 metres (5 feet) above ground.

Left: Seattle's Space Needle soon after completion, with its roof of "Galaxy Gold" paint. The revolving restaurant at the top rotates once an hour.

Opposite: The Space Needle was designed by John Graham & Company, and built as the centre-piece of the World's Fair of 1962.

The legs of the structure are constructed from steel "I" beams, weighing 41 tonnes (45 tons) each, which are engineered to well over the specifications required by 1962 building codes in terms of earthquake performance and wind loads. In fact, the Space Needle sways by around 2.5 centimetres (1 inch) for every 16 kilometres (10 miles) per hour of wind. When it was completed in December 1961 (after just nine months as a construction site), at 184 metres (605 feet) the tower was the tallest American structure west of the Mississippi River and 26 metres (86 feet) taller than Seattle's next tallest structure (the Smith Tower, which had been Seattle's tallest structure since 1914). The Space Needle is topped by a total of 24 lightning rods.

The tower was built with the world's second revolving restaurant (the first, now closed, was in Hawaii). Designing a revolving structure at a height of 152 metres (500 feet) involved creating a near perfectly flat and balanced deck, and this feat was so well executed that the restaurant needed the power of just a single

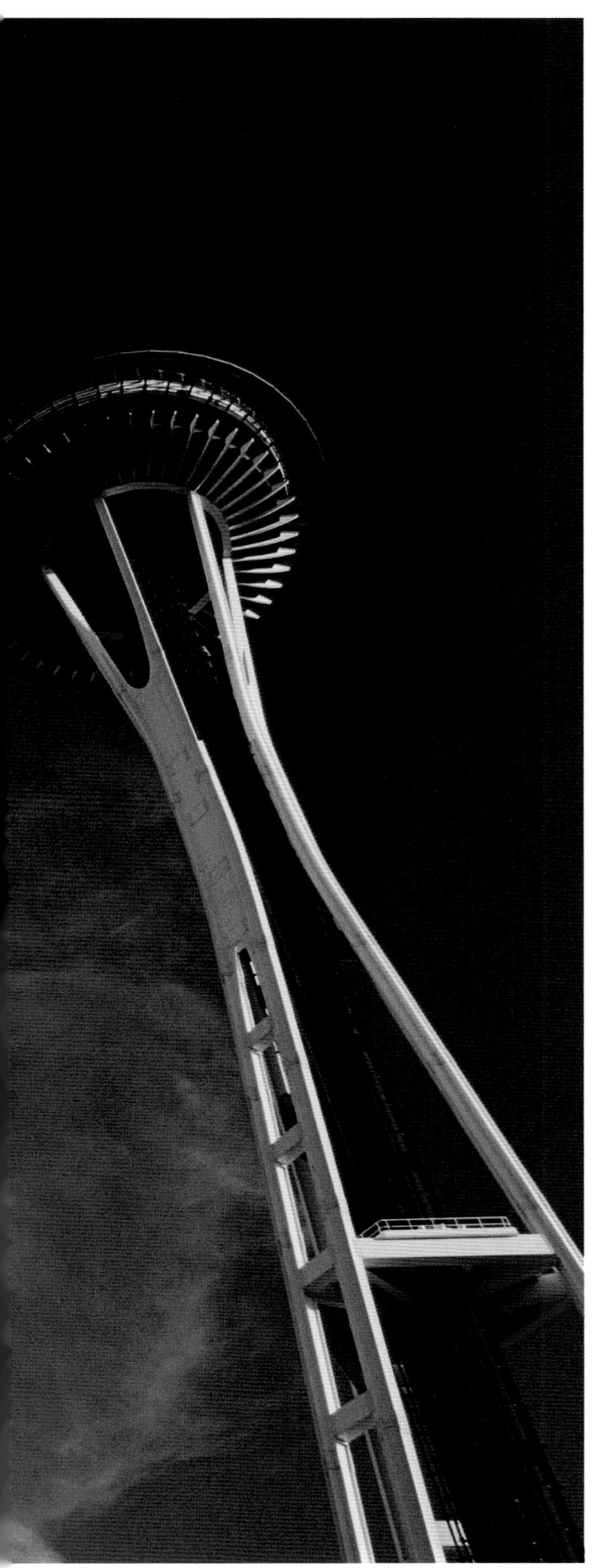

one horsepower motor to move it one revolution an hour (although a 1.5 horsepower motor is now used).

The tower was completed just in time for the opening of the World's Fair, and the last of its three elevators (one of which is used for freight) arrived only one day before the fair opened. These elevators were replaced in 1993 by faster and safer mechanisms. Each one is equipped with seven cables, although just one is sufficient to carry the entire 6,350-kilogram (14,000-pound) weight of each elevator (and the cables are changed annually). The two passenger elevators travel at 16 kilometres (10 miles) per hour, but are reduced to half that speed in high winds.

The 33-metre (100-foot) high "SkyLine" restaurant facility, a two-storey metal and glass pavilion, was added to the tower in 1982 by building on a platform that was part of the original structure. A "legacy light" was then added in 1999, which shines a beam of light from the top of the structure on major national holidays; the skyward beam was modelled on the illustration of the Space Needle on the original 1962 World's Fair posters.

The Space Needle is now one of Seattle's icons, if not the city's primary one. It attracts one million visitors a year and, on 21 April, 1999, the city's Landmarks Preservation Board gave the tower its official blessing as a "landmark". "The Space Needle marks a point in the history of the city of Seattle and represents American aspirations towards technological prowess," said the Board's report.

Three people have committed suicide by jumping from the structure, while six people have parachuted from its top (four legally, as part of a promotional stunt; the other two being arrested for trespass).

project data

- Designed by John Graham & Company, Seattle's Space Needle was conceived as the focal point for the World's Fair, held in the city in 1962.
- Built by Howard S. Wright Construction Co., the structure is constructed on a 9-metre (30-foot) deep foundation weighing 5,306 tonnes (5,850 tons) (the tower itself weighs 3,356 tonnes/3,700 tons).
- The construction of the foundation involved 467 cement trucks filling a hole 9 metres (30 feet) deep and 37 metres (120 feet) across. At the time it was the largest continuous pour of concrete in America's West.
- The tower is secured to its foundation with 72 bolts, each 9 metres (30 feet) in length.
- The tower is said to be twice as resistant to earthquakes as specified in contemporary building codes (it easily survived a 6.8 Richter quake in 2001), and it has been designed to withstand winds of up to 322 kilometres (200 miles) per hour.
- The tower is 184 metres (605 feet) high to the tip of its aircraft warning beacon. Its observation deck is located 158 metres (520 feet) above ground.
- 848 steps lead from the base of the tower to its top, although there are three elevators.
- Built for US$4.5million in 1962, the Space Needle was renovated in 2000 for US$20million.

Left: The Space Needle is configured as a huge tripod. In spite of the tower's immense height, the size of its foundation means that the Space Needle's centre of gravity lies almost at ground level.

YOKOHAMA LANDMARK TOWER YOKOHAMA, JAPAN

The Landmark Tower in Yokohama is Japan's tallest building. Completed in 1993, this steel and granite-clad building sits on a wide base and gradually tapers toward its top. Until relatively recently, tall buildings were forbidden in Japan, due to the high incidence of earthquakes (up to 1,000 a year). During the later part of the nineteenth century, many two- and three-storey buildings were constructed along European lines in brick and stone, most of which were destroyed in 1891 by a massive earthquake which measured 8.4 on the Richter scale. In 1920 new laws were passed to improve the quality of construction and limit the height of new buildings, so another major earthquake in 1923 (this time measuring 7.9 on the Richter scale) passed without becoming a catastrophe. These building codes were retained until 1965, when the pressure on land forced the authorities to reconsider the law and permit the construction of tall buildings.

The succeeding decades witnessed a boom in the construction of towers 100–200 metres (328–656 feet) tall, especially around Tokyo, Osaka and Kobe. Japan is now accustomed to large towers, many of which are residential buildings, and the Yokohama tower will undoubtedly lose its "Japan's tallest" status with the construction of newer structures in Tokyo's high-rise Nishi Shinjuku district over coming years. Although the Landmark Tower is not within the super-tall category of buildings (such as those within the 400–500-metre/1,312–1,640-foot mark), it is likely to remain in the world's top 35 buildings for a while. Indeed, it is taller than many better-known buildings, including Boston's John Hancock Tower (241 metres/791 feet), London's One Canada Square in Canary Wharf (244 metres/800 feet) and New York's Woolworth Building of 1913 (241 metres/792 feet).

Yokohama's Landmark Tower is a good example of the "hefty" appearance of many towers in earthquake zones. During an earthquake (including small shocks as well as major events) movements in the earth create sudden discharges of energy that radiate outwards, often as waves. Tall buildings can, subsequently, move backwards and forwards in much the same manner as long grass. Engineers have observed that tall buildings can vibrate at about the same frequency as these "ground waves" – the mass of the building can start to compensate this vibration by soaking up the movement, while artificial dampers (machinery which creates friction and therefore reduces the energy of the vibration) can also help prevent buildings from shaking themselves to pieces.

Structurally, the Landmark Tower is constructed as a "tube within a tube" rather than a simple latticework of steel beams. Extra mass than would ordinarily be necessary outside of an earthquake zone has been incorporated into the lower part of the building (up to the ninth storey) as a further anchor to prevent overturning. Furthermore, at the 282-metre (925-feet) level, two dampers are linked to a spring mechanism via a computerized control system to help compensate for any building movement.

When completed in 1993, the Landmark Tower was fitted with the world's fastest elevators (a boast now made by Taiwan's Taipei 101 tower – see page 34). Developed by Mitsubishi, these elevators can travel through one floor per second.

The tower is part of a much larger mixed-use complex of buildings providing shopping and parking facilities and the Grand Mall. The site is even linked by elevated moving walkways. The top two floors of the tower contain restaurants and an observation deck providing views of Mount Fuji and the Pacific Ocean.

The Landmark Tower, completed in 1993, was one of the first of the new wave of significant skyscrapers to be built in Asia. Constructed in Yokohama to attract business away from Tokyo (where land prices are astronomically high), the building clearly makes reference to local Japanese culture and iconography. The powerful horizontal banding is said to reference traditional Japanese combs, while the building has also been likened to a translucent box lantern. Indeed, the building's form and heavy corners also appear to echo the tight wooden jointing of Japanese pavilions. It is clearly not a building designed on a Western model and wears its "clothing" confidently without resorting to cliché or obvious mimicry.

Left: The Yokohama Landmark Tower is Japan's tallest building. Traditionally, Japan shied away from constructing tall buildings because of the threat of earthquakes, but the scarcity of land resulted in the revision of building codes in the 1960s.

project data

- **Yokohama Landmark Tower is the tallest building in Japan at 296 metres (971 feet) high and contains 70 storeys.**
- **Floors 49–70 are occupied by the 603-room Yokohama Royal Park Hotel – Japan's highest hotel; the rest of the structure contains a number of offices and retail developments.**
- **The tower contains the world's second fastest elevator, which can reach speeds of 45 kilometres (28 miles) per hour.**
- **Designed by The Stubbins Associates, the tower was constructed by Taisei Corporation.**
- **The building was completed in 1993.**
- **The building contains two tuned mass dampers at the top of the tower, located on opposite corners, to reduce movement during an earthquake.**

MITSUBISHI ELEVATORS

Mitsubishi supplied the fast-moving elevators for the Landmark Tower and the Japanese engineering giant is continuing to develop elevators to travel at even faster speeds to even greater heights.

It was the development of the original safety elevator by Elisha Otis in the USA in 1853 that made the construction of tall buildings a realistic proposition, and manufacturers continue to be pressed into developing more efficient, safer, more reliable and lower-vibration systems.

Mitsubishi Electric constructed a 65-metre [213-foot] high test tower at its Inazawa Works in 1965, which was used to develop new products until 2007. Now the company has built a 173-metre [568-foot] tall tower, which is the world's tallest elevator test facility. The tower is being used to develop a new generation of elevators, such as ultra-high-speed lifts that can climb up to 1,200 metres [3,937 feet] per minute. The 5-billion-Yen test tower will also be used to develop high-passenger-capacity products.

TRANSAMERICA PYRAMID SAN FRANCISCO, USA

The Transamerica Pyramid is one of the world's most distinctive towers. Highly controversial when completed in 1972, the building is now almost as symbolic of San Francisco as the Golden Gate Bridge. Indeed, the Transamerica Corporation, which no longer owns the building, still uses the shape of the tower as its logo.

The building was designed by William L. Pereira, an architect who was influenced by both the Art Deco style of the 1920s and '30s and the Futurism of science fiction. The Transamerica Pyramid arguably embodies both – with its almost playful form and quartz and aluminium cladding, the tower appears as a sort of pared-back Chrysler Building.

What makes this building interesting from a structural point of view is its attempt to respond to the danger of earthquakes. Defined by its distinctive taper, most believe the pyramidal form of the building is what makes it "earthquake proof". This is partly true. In fact, this shape was conceived to maximize the amount of daylight that reached ground level, and to reduce the visual impact of a tall building in a city that is not characterized by towers. Although the building's form spreads its load toward its base, the principal anti-earthquake measures are two-fold: firstly, its massive basement is sunk deep into the earth, like a well-secured fence-post; secondly, the trusses that form the plinth of the building are configured as a set of triangles and X-braces, enabling the base of the building to soak up both vertical and horizontal loads. In other words, these trusses can cope with the weight of the building above it and any forces that come at it laterally (such as shaking ground).

Left: The Transamerica Pyramid, completed in 1972, was intended as an "architectural sculpture". The building has since become an icon of San Francisco.

Opposite: The Transamerica Pyramid's lift cores and stairs are situated in boxes protruding from two sides of the building, freeing up floor space inside.

Instruments installed in the tower by the US Geological Survey showed that the 1989 Loma Prieta earthquake, which had a magnitude of 7.1 on the Richter scale, caused the pinnacle of the building to move by around 30 centimetres (12 inches), something it was able to do without sustaining any damage. Furthermore, structural engineers Chin & Hensolt Inc. pioneered computer modelling to predict how the building might behave in an earthquake and designed special welding sequences for the building's steelwork to minimize cracking. This was highly advanced technology for the late 1960s, an age when engineers habitually used the slide rule for calculations and the hand-held calculator was still under development.

When completed, the building was met with a storm of protest by

GREEN

Left: Occupying a city block within the crowded streets of San Francisco, the Transamerica Pyramid was not universally well received upon its completion. Some considered William Pereira's design to be more suited to Las Vegas.

Opposite: The building is set upon giant trusses which can soak up vertical and lateral movements during earthquakes. During the 7.1 Richter scale earthquake of 1989, the pinnacle of the tower shook by around 30 centimetres (12 inches).

people who thought the design unsuitable for San Francisco (it was more "Las Vegas", said the critics). The design was typical of Pereira, who had already made his name with the futuristic, spider-like Theme Building at Los Angeles International Airport. Pereira was a highly creative individual who keenly felt that architecture was both a matter of image-making and engineering. In the 1930s he moved to Los Angeles and, after practising as a solo architect, found work as an art director and film producer in Hollywood – Pereira even shared an Academy Award for special effects in 1942.

The Transamerica building embodies both a sculptural aesthetic and a functional practicality. For Pereira, architecture was about more than creating shelter: "Occupying as it does one of the most commanding sites in all of San Francisco, the building must be more than a receptacle for desks and chairs and people. We felt that it could be a statement of architectural sculpture."

The building's sculptural form did leave it open to criticism, however. Quite apart from the scale of the building in relation to its surroundings, a key objection was that floor spaces decrease the further one travels up the tower; indeed, the highly desirable upper floors are the smallest and therefore the least practical and economically efficient. Just two of the building's 18 elevators reach the upper storeys of the building. However, the two "wings" (the windowless boxes that span from the thirtieth to the forty-eighth storey) contain an elevator shaft, stairs and smoke ventilation shafts, freeing up more space within the narrow pyramid itself.

Originally, the Transamerica Corporation requested a much larger tower – one of 350.5 metres (1,150 feet), but city officials considered this too large. Even so, the construction of the building was still a major undertaking for San Francisco, and the 2.75-metre (9-foot) thick concrete foundations of the building were poured in a single day – then the largest single pour in the history of the city.

Upon completion, the Transamerica building was the tallest US skyscraper west of the Mississippi River, a position it held for just two years when it was surpassed by the more traditionally box-like Aon Center in Los Angeles, which is just 1.5 metres (5 feet) taller.

Since the 9/11 terrorist attacks, the tower's twenty-seventh storey observation deck has been closed to the public. Instead, a "virtual gallery" has been created by siting four cameras at the top of the building, each covering a cardinal point. Pictures from these cameras can be viewed on monitors in the building's lobby.

project data

- The Transamerica Pyramid was designed by architect William L. Pereira & Associates, with structural engineers Chin & Hensolt Inc. (who pioneered the computer modelling of how a building might behave under earthquake conditions).
- The tower was built between 1969 and 1972 for US$32 million.
- This 260-metre (853-foot) pyramidal building is 48 storeys high and topped by a 64.6-metre high (212-foot) aluminium-clad spire.
- The concrete foundations of the building are 2.75 metres (9 feet) thick, and were poured over a single 24-hour period.
- The foundation consists of a steel and concrete block that sits 16 metres (52 feet) underground.
- The four-storey concrete base of the building is strengthened by more than 483 kilometres (300 miles) of steel reinforcing rods.
- The building has 18 elevators, only two of which reach the top floor.
- The concrete panels of the building's cladding contain crushed quartz, which provide the tower with its distinctive whiteness.
- The largest floor is the fifth; the forty-eighth floor is the smallest and is configured as a single room with panoramic views in all directions.

GUANGZHOU TV AND SIGHTSEEING TOWER GUANGZHOU, CHINA

China's construction boom is a phenomenon like no other. The country is experiencing economic growth on a gigantic scale and structures are being built to reflect its prosperity and to impress the State's power upon the rest of the world. While Beijing puts the finishing touches to its sporting venues, hotels and shopping malls in readiness for the 2008 Olympic Games, China's third largest city Guangzhou is also busy preparing for a major sporting event, the 2010 Asian Games.

Part of this preparation is the creation of a brand-new high-rise city centre, with row upon row of residential and office towers, all of 40 storeys or more. In the midst of this is the construction site for the Guangzhou TV and Sightseeing Tower: a dramatic architectural statement, which, upon its completion in 2009, will be the highest free-standing structure in the world. The current record holder is the 553.33-metre (1,815-foot) high CN Tower in Toronto (see page 22). Guangzhou's new tower will beat that mark by over 50 metres (164 feet), measuring in from its base to the tip of its spire at 610 metres (2,001 feet). The city's nearest rival to it is the 391-metre (1,283-foot) CITIC Plaza Tower.

Dutch firm, Information Based Architecture (IBA), won an international competition in 2004 for the design of the tower, a 17.9-hectare (44¼-acre) park at its base and the master plan for the surrounding 56.6-hectare (140-acre) site, which includes an elevated plaza, pagoda-park, retail facilities, offices, television centre and hotel. Designed in collaboration with engineer Arup, the tower's spiralling lattice-like form, which narrows at "waist" level, has been derived by twisting the top and bottom of the structure and pulling to elongate it; the form is similar to that of a Chinese finger-trap toy. Mark Hemel, IBA architect and director, said, "Our aim was to design a free-form tower with a rich and human-like identity, where all views towards the tower would be different from whatever vantage point."

The structural design of the tower includes an inner central concrete core and external steel frame. The core houses lifts, an escape stairwell and vertical building services risers. The outer steel-framed structure consists of 24 steel columns with concrete in-fill, a series of 46 oval-shaped rings of different sizes and single-direction diagonal members throughout the structure.

This complex geometry has been designed using parametric associative software, which can generate geometrical and structural models based on a set of variable parameters and then link that data to architectural drafting software. Specialist technologies were also employed to check the tower's ability to cope with high winds and earthquakes: special design criteria were created to take into account both building safety and human comfort.

Because of the tower's complex structure, the team has adopted the most advanced technologies in wind engineering and wind tunnel studies based on 3-D sectional models and computer simulation. Using the wind data local to the area, a series of performance-based design options were assessed. The subsequent design explores and exploits the organization of structural materials over a complex free-form that both curves and twists simultaneously. The density of the external steel columns varies according to structural necessity – they get closer together as the tower becomes slimmer – while at the same time forming an environmental or weather screen, which filters the light and modifies views to and from the surrounding city.

Arup's design team leader, Tony Choi, says, "The complex geometry and the slim waist of the tower makes it a very challenging structural design in the process of striking [a] balance between architectural form, safety and cost. Performance-based approaches have been adopted to achieve breakthrough on the local regulations on planning, fire escape and structural design issues."

Located within the metal latticework will be a series of internal spaces, observation decks and sky gardens. Visitors will be able to access them from the base level via high speed and scenic lifts. Hidden out of site within a basement are all the functional elements for lifts, mechanical and electrical power and also direct links to the metro and bus interchange. Above this level are shops, a museum and car parking. On the first elevated floor of the Guangzhou Tower, at 95 metres (312 feet) above ground level, there will be a 4-D cinema. At around 170 metres (558 feet) an open staircase called the Skywalk begins and spirals up for another 200 metres (656 feet), all the way through the waist of the tower. The first sky garden is the second public floor, situated at 195 metres (640 feet) above ground level, and there will be a dining room at 310 metres (1,017 feet).

A temperate zone garden area and a hotel will occupy the fourth floor, 345–350 metres (1,132–1,148 feet) above ground, while the rotating dining rooms will occupy the fifth floor at 430 metres (1,411 feet). At this high level, observation boxes will cantilever out from the structure, allowing visitors to look straight down the exterior of the tower. Finally, another stairway will lead to the top viewing deck, known as the North Pole Square, some 450 metres (1,476 feet) above ground. From the roof above the square an antenna will stretch up to 610 metres (2,001 feet).

When complete, it is hoped that the Guangzhou TV Tower will attract 10,000 visitors daily. Its mix of internal space and external viewing platforms make it a unique and exciting tourist attraction to rival the many other new landmark buildings being built in China.

Left: This computer-generated view from near the base of the tower illustrates the way the structural steel columns twist as they climb, creating a narrow waist before widening towards the top of the tower.

Opposite left: When complete, the tower will be the highest free-standing structure in the world.

Opposite right: Sections through the tower detail numerous internal and external platforms for visitors to ascend to.

project data

- **At 610 metres (2,001 feet) high, the Guangzhou TV and Sightseeing Tower will be the tallest free-standing structure in the world. It will take the title from Toronto's CN Tower (page 22), which measures 553.33 metres (1,815 feet) high.**
- **The open-air viewing platform, North Pole Square, will be the highest of its kind ever, at 450 metres (1,476 feet) above ground level.**
- **Visitors will be able to ascend the tower in high-speed and scenic lifts, as well as along spiralling open-air stairways.**
- **Guangzhou is China's third largest city. It has a population of 10 million.**
- **The tower will be put into use as a television antenna soon after its completion, broadcasting the 2010 Asian games.**
- **The tower will include open-air gardens within its lattice-like structure, as well as a restaurant and 4-D cinema.**
- **A reinforced-concrete core is further strengthened by concrete-filled steel columns to ensure that the gigantic tower is stable.**

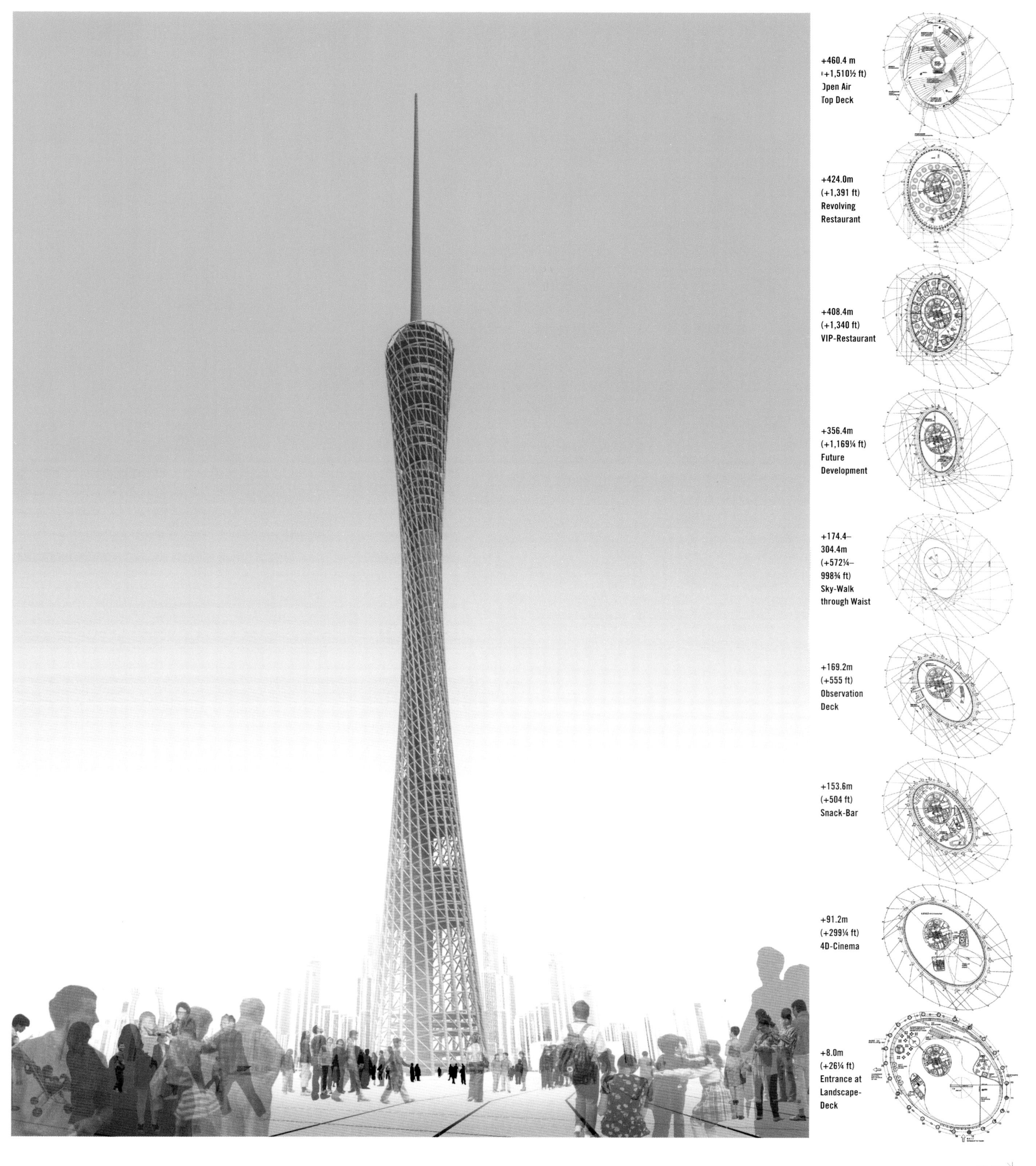
+460.4 m
+1,510½ ft)
pen Air
op Deck
+424.0m
(+1,391 ft)
Revolving
Restaurant
+408.4m
(+1,340 ft)
VIP-Restaurant
+356.4m
(+1,169¼ ft)
Future
Development
+174.4–
304.4m
(+572¼–
998¾ ft)
Sky-Walk
through Waist
+169.2m
(+555 ft)
Observation
Deck
+153.6m
(+504 ft)
Snack-Bar
+91.2m
(+299¼ ft)
4D-Cinema
+8.0m
(+26¼ ft)
Entrance at
Landscape-
Deck

LONDON EYE LONDON, UK

At 135 metres (443 feet) high and weighing 1,600 tonnes (1,750 tons), the London Eye is the world's tallest observation wheel. Located on the banks of the River Thames it offers unrivalled views over London of up to 40 kilometres (25 miles) in all directions on a clear day. It is visited by a phenomenal 3.5 million people each year – an average of 10,000 each day – and in its short life it has become the most popular paid-for tourist attraction in the UK.

Since opening in 2000, the London Eye has become an iconic landmark, with a status that can be compared to Tower Bridge, Big Ben and the Tower of London, and as such it has been used as a backdrop in countless films and TV programmes. This is much more than its financial backers originally envisaged however, as, just like the Eiffel Tower in Paris, the London Eye was originally meant to be a temporary structure, to be dismantled after only a year.

Marks Barfield Architects were relatively unknown before this monumental commission, but after entering a competition to design a London landmark, which no one won, the practice persevered with its ambitious design that had been conceived at a kitchen table in 1993.

The designs for a Ferris wheel in the UK's capital were published first in the architectural press and then in national newspapers. They immediately captured the public imagination. Commercial backer, British Airways, stepped forward and the London Eye project was born.

The giant wheel – some 424 metres (1,391 feet) in circumference – is a relatively simple design, similar to that of a bicycle wheel. Unlike earlier Ferris wheels that relied on trusses and braces for strength and stability, the Eye uses 6 kilometres (3¾ miles) of steel cables imported from Italy to achieve the same rigid shape with much less mass. In total, 64 spoke cables and 16 rim rotation cables stretch across the steel rim, creating a taut circle. The cables vary from 60–110 millimetres (2½–4½ inches) in diameter and are a type called "locked coil": this means the individual strands are "S" shaped and lock together to form the equivalent of a solid piece of steel.

The foundation required to support this massive structure, which is cantilevered out over the River Thames, was designed in two parts. The compression foundation, situated underneath the giant A-frame legs, required 2,200 tonnes (2,425 tons) of concrete and 44 concrete piles, each 33 metres (108 feet) deep. The tension foundation, set back from the river's edge and responsible for anchoring the backstay cables, used 1,200 tonnes (1,323 tons) of concrete.

The massive steel components that make up the support legs, hub and the 330-tonne (364-ton) spindle of the wheel were manufactured in Rotterdam,

project data

- The wheel is not the first in London; a much smaller Ferris wheel used to stand opposite Earls Court station during the latter part of the nineteenth century.
- Although the Eye is listed in *The Guinness Book of Records* as the tallest observation wheel in the world, it is unlikely to keep that title for long. A 185-metre (607-foot) wheel dubbed "Giant Wheel" is due to open in 2008 in Berlin; and a 200-metre (656-foot) wheel is planned for Shanghai.
- The Eye has won over 40 awards for tourism, architecture and engineering.
- The A-frame legs that support the wheel weigh a colossal 450 tonnes (496 tons).
- Just 18 months after its opening, over six million visitors had "flown" on the Eye, and in July 2005 the 20-millionth customer was welcomed on board.
- The Eye has been invaded by protesters on three occasions. In October 1999 two Spanish environmental protesters climbed up the structure and spent two nights in its girders; in August 2000 a man scaled it to protect against UN sanctions against Iraq; and in December 2000 protesters took to the wheel and doused themselves in petrol, protesting about riots in Turkey.
- The cast steel spindle around which the wheel revolves is 23 metres (75 feet) long, 2.1 metres (7 feet) in diameter, has walls 300 millimetres (1 foot) thick and weighs 330 tonnes (364 tons).

Left: A view from below of the London Eye's huge supporting arms towards its central axle, illustrates the monumentality of the structure along with its reliance on relatively thin cables to hold the wheel in place.

Opposite: Drama on the bank of the River Thames, the London Eye looms over festively-lit trees on a Winter's evening. The Eye itself is illuminated for special events and is a focal point for London's New Year's Eve firework displays.

The Netherlands. These were delivered by sea and brought straight up the River Thames on barges, in sections up to 100 metres (328 feet) long. Delivery was timed to coordinate with low tides on the river, so that large parts could be safely negotiated under London's bridges; clearance under Southwark Bridge was a mere 40 centimetres (1⅓ feet) at times.

The huge wheel parts were fixed together while lying flat across the river, resting on large pontoons anchored to the river bed, and then lifted into place using one of the world's largest floating cranes. On 10 October, 1999, the project team started to hoist the assembled London Eye into its vertical position. This method of erection had never been attempted before and the engineers went ahead cautiously, initially lifting it at a rate of about two degrees per hour. Six giant backstay cables now anchor the wheel to the tension foundation.

The wheel carries 32 sealed and air-conditioned passenger capsules attached to its external circumference. The capsules were assembled in France, using glass that was double-curved and laminated in Italy. They were designed to be just within the maximum width allowed on the French roads over which they would make their way to the English Channel and up the Thames.

The London Eye rotates at a rate of 0.26 metres (10¼ inches) per second (about 0.9 kilometres/½ mile per hour) so that one revolution takes about 30 minutes to complete. The capsules are maintained in a horizontal position by computers using specially designed software: these monitor the angle of the capsules, activating tilt switches to level them once an angle of one-and-a-half degrees is reached. The wheel does not usually stop to take on passengers; the rotation rate is so slow that passengers can easily walk on and off the moving capsules at ground level. It is, however, stopped on occasion to allow disabled or elderly passengers time to disembark safely.

The Eye was opened by the British Prime Minister, Tony Blair, on 31 December, 1999, although it was not opened to the public until March 2000. In all, over 1,700 people in five countries would be involved in building the London Eye, including the population of an entire alpine village, who tested the embarkation procedures. Almost every component and construction technique was invented from scratch. Transportation of the components took on a scale reminiscent of pyramid construction at times but, from start to finish, the London Eye was built in a total of just 16 months.

Opposite: In total, 32 passenger pods are installed on the London Eye. Up to 25 passengers can travel in each one, on a one-revolution ride that takes about 30 minutes.

Left top: The London Eye's pods are attached to the outside of the main wheel via computer-controlled sleeves that slowly rotate them, keeping their floors horizontal at all times.

Left: Seen from across the River Thames, the London Eye is a dramatic recent addition to the city's skyline and already one of its most visited attractions.

KECK TELESCOPES W. M. KECK OBSERVATORY, HAWAII

The Keck telescopes at the W. M. Keck Observatory are the world's largest optical instruments of their kind. Designed to look deep into space, and powerful enough to distinguish a car's headlamps as two distinct light sources from a distance of 805 kilometres (500 miles), these telescopes are perched on top of the dormant volcano of Mauna Kea in Hawaii. The Keck telescopes (named after their principal sponsor, the W. M. Keck Foundation) are not tall structures as such, but they are located 4,205 metres (13,796 feet) above sea level and their geographical location is a crucial element of their operation.

Being located so high – Mauna Kea is above 40 per cent of the Earth's atmosphere – these two telescopes have less air to peer through, while the absence of nearby mountain ranges and the thermal stability of the Pacific Ocean creates a relatively dust-free, dark and stable atmospheric environment from which to observe deep space. Designed to try and answer questions about the origins of galaxies and planetary systems, the Keck telescopes have also proved to be useful in locating distant objects through the technique of "gravitational lensing" – a way of identifying objects by determining how their light is distorted by the gravity of nearer massive objects, such as stars. These telescopes, Keck I and Keck II, therefore, needed to be highly engineered, and weight reduction was crucial to minimize the impact of Earth's own gravity, which could distort the telescopes' all-important mirrors. Each telescope is the equivalent height of an eight-storey building and weighs 272 tonnes (300 tons). Furthermore, both installations can serve as an "inter-ferometer", combining their data and acting as a single, super-large telescope.

At the heart of the Kecks (the first of which began operating in May 1993, the second in October 1996) is a highly advanced and daring design for the light-collecting mirrors. Until these telescopes came along, the world's largest telescope was the 5-metre (16-foot) Hale instrument at the Palomar Observatory on Palomar Mountain, California, dating from 1948. Researchers wanted a telescope double this size; however, doubling the area of the reflecting mirror would increase its thickness so much that

Left: Located nearly 4,206 metres (13,800 feet) above sea level, a height which reduces the interference caused by Earth's atmosphere, the Keck telescopes share the top of Mauna Kea with a host of other astronomical instruments. The reflecting mirrors of the Kecks are each composed of 36 computer-controlled, hexagonal mirrors.

Below: A diagram showing the composition of the Keck telescopes' reflecting mirrors. This design was considerably more structurally efficient than building a single massive mirror.

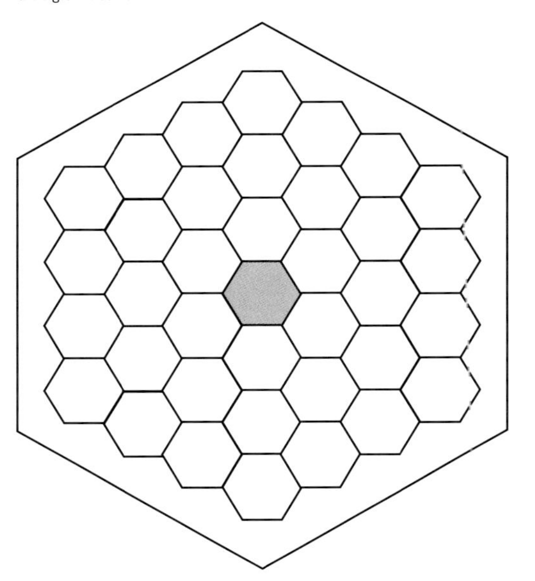

project data

- The Keck telescopes have their origins in a study group formed in 1977, but it was not until 1990 that the initiative bore fruit and the first pictures were taken of distant galaxies.
- Each 10-metre (33-foot) mirror in the telescopes are formed from an assembly of 36 hexagonal mirrors, each 7.5 centimetres (3 inches) thick. When perfectly aligned, these separate parts combine to form a single parabolic (dish-like) surface.
- These telescopes also carry infrared equipment, allowing them to "see" a different part of the light spectrum.
- Both telescopes can act together, combining the light gathered by their giant mirrors into a single image, greatly improving the resolution of what they see.
- The two Keck telescopes were made possible through donations totalling US$140 million from the W. M. Keck Foundation.
- The telescopes sit atop Mauna Kea, a dormant volcano on Hawaii's Big Island. The volcano rises approximately 9 kilometres (5.6 miles) from the seabed; it began erupting on the sea floor around 800,000 years ago, but experts believe the volcano has not erupted within the last 3,500 years.

Above: The Keck telescopes are engaged in the search for answers to cosmological questions, such as how the galaxies were formed.

Opposite: Located at such a height that they are above 40 per cent of the Earth's atmosphere, the Keck telescopes can be coordinated and their data combined to form a "super-telescope".

a complex, unwieldy and heavy structure would be needed to prevent the mirror from collapsing. Also, a telescope with a mirror of this size could cost more than US$1 billion.

Astrophysicist Jerry Nelson, however, proposed a radical new design. Instead of fashioning a giant mirror from a single piece of glass, Nelson proposed combining a honeycomb of separate hexagonal mirrors and positioning them under computer control to act in concert. The idea was developed throughout the late 1970s and early 1980s and ended up as a 36-piece mirror supported and controlled by 168 electronic sensors and 108 tiny motors called "position actuators" which constantly recalibrate each mirror in relation to all the others. First demonstrated in 1984, this complex instrument was finally assembled in 1991. Computer monitoring can detect if any mirror is out of alignment by 4 nanometers, (25,000 times thinner than the width of a human hair), and immediately correct the anomaly. Monitoring is a constant process and corrections are made approximately twice every second.

Construction began on Mauna Kea in September 1985. The foundations for the first telescope had been prepared by summer 1987, and work then began on the tube and dome that would protect the telescope. This building envelope had to be highly insulated and fitted with air conditioning to ensure the internal temperature not only remained cool (heat can distort a telescope's mirror) but matched external temperatures to prevent the formation of condensation. If necessary, all 19,800 cubic metres (700,000 cubic feet) of air inside each of the Kecks can be replaced every five minutes.

By 1989 this container had been completed – with a dome 30 metres (98 feet) high and 36 metres (118 feet) wide (much smaller than the dome at Palomar Observatory, in spite of the mirror's increased size). The 1,100-piece frame that holds the mirror was installed next, and the first of the 36 hexagonal mirror elements was installed on October 12, 1990. Soon afterwards, with just nine mirror elements installed, the telescope captured precise images of the NGC 1232 galaxy 65 million light years from our own solar system. By April 1992 the telescope's mirror was completed and an identical telescope, the Keck II, followed soon after.

Each telescope, as well as using computer monitoring and control to regulate the shape of its mirror, is directed remotely. Astronomers located elsewhere can control which part of the sky the telescopes scan. Now operated by the California Association for Research in Astronomy, and used principally by astronomers from the University of California and the California Institute of Technology (Caltech), the Keck telescopes are used principally to study quasars and to search for planets orbiting distant stars.

02

S P A N

FOR as long as man has existed we have travelled and, in doing so, come up against obstacles. What we have built to surmount them is often incredible. The bridge is probably the one structure for which engineers have been celebrated above all others. Unlike a building, in which architects play the leading role, a bridge has but one function and its structure – always on show – is the supreme embodiment of that function, finely tuned to counter any forces or stresses that may be put upon it. In contrast, the construction of a tunnel could be seen as an unglamorous exercise in digging a hole. However, to simplify it in those terms is to completely disregard the plethora of skills required here. As with bridges, engineers were and still are the principal designers of tunnels: the detailed calculations, analysis and planning required to bore a hole beneath the sea or through the base of a mountain, without that tunnel collapsing in on itself, cannot be underestimated.

AKASHI KAIKYO BRIDGE AKASHI STRAIT, JAPAN

This, the longest cable-stay (suspension) bridge in the world, is an engineering feat of extraordinary proportions and one that – amazingly – actually withstood the ravages of the 1995 Kobe earthquake while it was still under construction. The Akashi Kaikyo Bridge spans the Akashi Straits, connecting the Japanese islands of Honshu and Awaji. It is one part of the Kobe–Naruto highway route, which links Honshu and the southern island of Shikoku. The Ohnaruto Bridge, a similar but smaller suspension bridge, connects the southern end of Awaji with the island of Shikoku, completing the waterway crossings along the 81-kilometre (50-mile) highway.

The bridge was completed in 1998, at nearly 4 kilometres (2½ miles) long. Its central span stretches 1,991 metres (6,532 feet) and the two bridge towers are the tallest in the world, standing at almost 283 metres (928 feet). It was designed by the Honshu Shikoku Bridge Authority and built by Matsuo Bridge Co. Also known as the Pearl Bridge in Japan, it is 2,856 metres (9,370 feet) longer than New York's famous Brooklyn Bridge and 366 metres (1,201 feet) longer than its nearest rival, the StoreBaelt (East Bridge) in Denmark.

Construction began in 1988 and involved more than 100 contractors. However, the Kobe Earthquake of January 17, 1995 nearly destroyed the Akashi Kaikyo Bridge before it was even completed. The earthquake's epicentre was right between the two towers of the bridge: measuring 7.2 on the Richter scale and lasting just 20 seconds, it decimated large swathes of heavily populated land around the bridge. Over 5,500 people were killed and 300,000 made homeless, and the Hanshin elevated highway collapsed.

The bridge towers survived where much else was destroyed because the engineered design had taken into account the harsh environment in which it was to be built: however, the earthquake had moved the ground beneath them and they were now approximately 1 metre (3 feet) further apart. Thankfully, because the construction of the deck had not started, engineers were able to recalculate its design to accommodate the phenomenon and make the central clear span 1,991 metres (6,532 feet) instead of 1,990 metres (6,529 feet).

The engineered design had to take into account numerous potentially damaging phenomena. The bridge is built in up to 110-metre (360-feet) deep water with tidal currents of 4.5 metres (15 feet) per second; it is exposed to wind speeds of 80 metres (262 feet) per second; and there is always the threat of an 8.5 Richter magnitude earthquake to be considered.

With these parameters in mind, the Japanese engineers came up with a truss design to support the roadway, or deck. Operating as a network, open triangular braces make the bridge very rigid, but also allow the wind to blow through the structure, reducing wind-loading, sideways forces. This aerodynamic stability is a challenge faced by all bridge and building designers, but in the case of long suspension bridges it becomes more complex, because if the structure begins to move, it can wobble, causing a ripple effect along its length. The Akashi Kaikyo Bridge was no different and, in order to verify the design of the world's longest suspension bridge, the world's largest wind-tunnel facility was built to test full-section models in laminar and turbulent wind flow.

Erection of the bridge towers and cables was a mammoth task. The bridge has two side spans of 960 metres (3,150 feet) each, in addition to the main

Left: Illuminated at night, the Akashi Kaikyo Bridge is an awe-inspiring sight. Its two towers are 297.3 metres (975½ feet) high, including the saddles in which the massive cables rest, making the bridge the tallest of its kind in the world.

central span. All are supported from cables attached to two steel towers, which sit on massive concrete piers. The towers were built using 10-metre (33-foot) high prefabricated steel segments, 30 of which were stacked upon one another. These towers transmit the massive bridge load down, through the foundation piles, which are 63 metres (207 feet) wide by 84 metres (276 feet) long, to bedrock 60 metres (197 feet) beneath the Akashi Straits.

Prior to installing the cables, a pilot hauler rope was attached to each anchorage point and then hung over the tower tops by helicopter. The pilot rope was used to pull strands of the giant cables into position. A catwalk was also suspended at high level, from which operatives worked on the main cable erection.

The main cables were so heavy that they had to be erected in prefabricated strands. Each strand comprised 127 high-strength galvanized wires, each 5.23 millimetres (0.2 inches) in diameter. Fabricated off-site in 4,085-metre (13,402-foot) lengths, the strands were hauled from an initial anchorage point, over the top of each tower and then fastened to the opposite anchorage frame. This procedure was repeated 289 times to fabricate each main cable.

When all of the strands were in place, a cable-squeezing machine, specifically designed for the project, was used to compress the 290 parallel wire strands into the final 1.12-metre (3½-foot) diameter cable. Cable bands then compressed the cable into its circular shape. Finally, slimmer suspender cables were hung from the main cable to support the bridge's huge stiffening truss.

Steel stiffening truss girder panels were also fabricated off-site and transported by barge to the bridge's tower piers. A 145-tonne (160-ton) crane then lifted them to roadway elevation and transported them to their locations for connection to the suspender ropes.

To counteract any abnormal movement in the bridge's structure, 20 tuned mass dampers were installed in each of the towers: these are huge suspended weights that swing in the opposite direction of the wind sway. So, when the wind or an earthquake moves the bridge in one direction, the tuned mass dampers swing the opposite way, effectively "balancing" the bridge and cancelling out the sway.

The bridge roadway is built on top of the 14-metre (46-feet) deep by 35.5-metre (116½-feet) wide truss girder system that is suspended from main cables; a 65-metre (213-foot) clearance is maintained over the shipping lane. Approximately 181,400 tonnes (199,959 tons) of steel were used in the superstructure, and 1.42 million cubic metres (50.15 million cubic feet) of concrete were used in the foundation piles.

The bridge was completed in 1998, 10 years after work started on site. The earthquake caused a one-month delay in the construction schedule, during which time the bridge was carefully inspected for damage, but this lost time was made up during the remaining three-year construction period, and the bridge was opened to traffic on schedule.

project data

- At 3,910 metres (12,828 feet) in length, the Akashi Kaikyo Bridge is 366 metres (1,201 feet) longer than the next largest cable-stay bridge in the world, the StoreBaelt (East Bridge) in Denmark.
- The length of the cables used in the bridge totals 300,000 kilometres (186,410 miles) – that's enough cable to circle the earth seven and a half times.
- The bridge holds three records: it is the longest, tallest and most expensive suspension bridge ever built.
- In 1995 the partially completed bridge survived the Kobe earthquake, which measured 7.2 on the Richter scale and made 300,000 people homeless.
- The bridge cost an estimated 500 billion Yen (US$4.3 billion) to build.
- Approximately 181,400 tonnes (200,000 tons) of steel were used in the superstructure, and 1.42 million cubic metres (50.15 million cubic feet) of concrete were used in the foundation piles.
- Each main cable is over 4 kilometres (2.5 miles) long, 1.12 metres (3½ feet) in diameter and made up of 290 high-strength steel strands.

Opposite: The underside of the bridge looming out of the fog. The steel framework of the truss girders seen here stabilizes the roadway above.

Right top: The view from the top of one of the bridge's two towers provides a good indication of the structure's awesome size.

Right middle and bottom: The bridge rises at its mid-point not only to create a greater clearance height for the tallest of ships but also as a consequence of the tensile forces put upon it by the suspension cables.

LAKE PONTCHARTRAIN CAUSEWAY LOUISIANA, USA

At 38.4 kilometres (23.9 miles) long, Lake Pontchartrain Causeway is by far the longest over-water bridge in the world. It actually consists of two parallel roadway bridges – one of which is 16.1 metres (53 feet) longer than the other – which are supported by over 9,500 hollow concrete piles. The southern terminus of the causeway is in Metairie, a suburb of New Orleans, and the northern terminus is in Mandeville, Louisiana.

Each parallel span has a road width of 8.5 metres (28 feet) and over 30,000 cars cross the causeway each day. The spans are 24.5 metres (80 feet) apart, but at seven points they are connected by "crossovers", which are used as pull-over areas for auto emergencies.

Lake Pontchartrain is the largest inland estuary in the United States. At 1,580 square kilometres (610 square miles), it connects to the Mississippi Sound at its seaward end. Regular "commuter" travel across it dates back to the early nineteenth century, when Bernard de Marigny de Mandeville, founder of the town of Mandeville started a ferry service. However, in the 1920s, the first proposal was put forward to create a "dry" crossing: this involved the creation of artificial islands that would be linked by a series of bridges. The idea was never acted upon but the modern causeway started to take form in 1948, when the Louisiana Legislature created what is now the Causeway Commission.

The first Lake Pontchartrain Causeway opened in 1956. It was a two-lane span costing US$30.7 million. A second two-lane span running parallel to the first, opened on May 10, 1969 at a cost of US$26 million. The causeway reduced the time it took to drive into New Orleans by up to an hour, enabling travellers to traverse the lake, rather than driving all the way around it.

The original design for the causeway was by Palmer and Baker Inc. It was constructed by the Louisiana Bridge Company and is one of the oldest pre-stressed concrete bridges in the United States. Workers manufactured reinforced concrete bridge sections off-site, loaded them on barges and towed them to construction points on the lake. Each 17-metre (56-foot) by 10-metre (33-foot) section of the first crossing is supported on hollow concrete piles of approximately 1.4 metres (4½ feet) in diameter. These were the largest piles ever driven at the time of the first span's construction. The causeway was opened on August 30, 1956.

The connection was welcomed by all, so much so that the convenience of the route and the mileage it saved travellers eventually overwhelmed the highway. Within a few years the causeway was being used by over 3,000 cars per day, and a second lake crossing had to be built to cater for the demand.

Construction methods had evolved enormously during the causeway's first decade of existence and the new crossing was designed and built using different techniques and standards. The bridge's engineers opted for three piles per support instead of two. This increased strength allowed for an increased load support: and so, much larger 25.6-metre (84-foot) road slabs were manufactured and installed – some 8 metres (26 feet) longer than the original ones. Faster construction methods facilitated the production of 20 272–tonne (300–ton) slabs each week at off-site manufacturing plants, while on site fabrication was also much swifter: the construction teams raced to build up to 85 metres (279 feet) of bridge per day.

The causeway, as it stands today, is approximately 4.8 metres (15¾ feet) above the water for much of its 37-kilometre (23-mile) length. However, to enable water-going craft to pass by, there are three main "ship passes" where the bridges elevate to a height of 7.6 metres (25 feet): two marine spans with a 15.25-metre (50-foot) clearance, and a drawbridge catering for larger vessels.

For land lovers the causeway holds relatively few dangers, although fog, cross winds and thunderstorms can present particular hazards for drivers. Special rules apply in bad weather and motorists must drive slowly in convoy when visibility is particularly poor, to ensure that no one vehicle is stranded alone on the causeway. Boats also have to beware: there have been 16 collisions with the causeway since it was built, but today a radar system is in use to alert officials when any boat draws to within a mile of the roadways.

Even with these precautions there can be the occasional accident and at various locations along either side of the causeway there are spots where the roadway decks are extended: these are used as stock-pile areas for spare sections of causeway. In 2005 these stock-piles came to good use when Hurricane Katrina swept through the area and damaged parts of the causeway. After the storm an inspection showed that most of the damage was largely cosmetic; a few road sections were replaced but the structural foundations remained completely intact. And, with the nearby I-10 twin-span bridge severely damaged, the causeway was used as a major route for recovery teams to get into New Orleans.

The causeway has always been a toll bridge. Until 1999, tolls were collected from traffic going in each direction. However, to alleviate congestion on the south shore, toll collections were eliminated on the northbound span. The standard tolls for cars changed from US$1.50 in each direction to a US$3.00 toll collected on the north shore for southbound traffic only.

project data

- Lake Pontchartrain Causeway is 38.4 kilometres (23.9 miles) long – the world's longest over-water crossing.
- In 2005 Hurricane Katrina devastated the surrounding region but the bridge remained intact and served as the primary transport artery for the emergency services.
- The causeway sits only 4.8 metres (15¾ feet) above the water for the majority of its length. It rises to 15.25 metres (50 feet) in two places to allow tall boats to pass beneath.
- Over 9,500 hollow concrete piles support large pre-stressed concrete road slabs to form the causeway.
- A radar system is in use to alert officials when a boat draws to within 1.6 kilometres (1 mile) of the spans.
- Following previous ferry navigation, the lake was first crossed by car in 1956. A second roadway was built 13 years later due to traffic demand.
- The causeway is a toll bridge. It costs $3.00 to cross but only if you travel from the south.

Opposite left top: Vehicles pass through a toll station at one end of the 38.42-kilometre (23.87-mile) long Lake Pontchartrain Causeway, then it's a 20-minute drive across the world's longest bridge, before reaching the other side.

Opposite left bottom: In close up, the causeway's construction can be seen: cylindrical reinforced concrete piles support concrete cross members, on which large pre-stressed concrete road sections sit.

Opposite right: The causeway stretches away to the horizon: its dual traffic roadways each have two lanes. In the distance a maintenance pier can be seen protruding from the main traffic lanes.

GATESHEAD MILLENNIUM BRIDGE GATESHEAD, UK

The Gateshead Millennium Bridge spans the River Tyne, which runs between the cities of Gateshead and Newcastle, in north-eastern England. It is the newest in a tradition of remarkable steel bridges, each a triumph of its time, two of the most famous being the Tyne Bridge, which is actually a smaller version of Sydney Harbour Bridge, and Robert Stephenson's High Level Bridge, which is a double-decked structure with trains on top and a road underneath. Both of these engineering marvels can be seen from the latest addition, the award-winning Gateshead Millennium Bridge.

However, designed by Wilkinson Eyre Architects and Engineers, and linking new developments on both sides of the river, the Millennium is the first opening bridge to be built across the River Tyne for more than a 100 years. It is also the world's first pivoting, or tilting, bridge.

This tilting mechanism, which throws the bridge's deck upwards and out of the horizontal plane to allow river craft beneath, is quite unique. The bridge's curved cable-stayed, double-arched structure pivots to an angle of 40 degrees to give a 25-metre (82-foot) high navigational clearance. The result is a phenomenon that many think looks like an eye opening and closing – hence the nickname, "Blinking Eye Bridge".

This manoeuvre sounds complicated but it is based on a simple principle. At each end of the bridge, the deck, which curves at a similar rate to the arch, meets with it on large support hinge assemblies. These cylindrical shafts are supported at either end by bearings. A bank of hydraulic rams operate when the bridge opens, exerting pressure against a steel paddle attached to the cylindrical shaft; this pushes the whole of the structure pivoting on the bearings, and tilts the bridge.

In its open position, the bridge's suspension cables lie horizontal but remain in tension, pulling against the now vertical deck arch and holding the pair of arches together. Huge 15-tonne (16½-ton) castings on either side withstand the outward and radial thrust loads. The opening manoeuvre takes 4½ minutes.

Unlike many of its neighbours, which fuelled vehicular traffic flow to and from Newcastle and Gateshead at their extremities, the Millennium Bridge is specifically designed for pedestrians and cyclists. It harks back to a more sedate time before mass transport and the earliest days of steel bridges; the form is extremely modern however. It has two lanes, one for walkers and one for cyclists: pedestrians use the inner walkway and cyclists the outer deck.

A stainless steel fence separates the two lanes, and there are built-in benches on the pedestrian side providing views upriver. The footway is manufactured from solid steel, while the cycle path is perforated aluminium, with gaps in it, offering a view of the water below. The central barrier also has gaps in it, although they are rather larger, allowing cyclists to stop and walk onto the footway to take in the views, rather than speeding past them.

The bridge itself is quite a spectacle but its delivery was a sight that drew crowds of up to 36,000. The bridge was delivered to site, rather than built over the river. At 850 tonnes (937 tons) it was floated 10 kilometres (6 miles) up the River Tyne and lifted into place by a crane named Asian Hercules II.

The crane is quite remarkable in its own right. Knowing that the project would require a crane of this magnitude, the construction team ordered it well in advance. It arrived from Singapore (where it was built), after a wandering trip that saw it travel across the Mediterranean, where it lifted a 1,200-tonne (1,323-ton) deck into position on an offshore Egyptian oil field and installed two bridges in Spain, before going on to Newfoundland, Canada to work on the Terra Nova oil field. The crane's deck is 76 metres (249 feet) long and 30 metres (98½ feet) wide, and its lifting legs are over 107 metres (351 feet) tall. It is installed on a 10,560-tonne (11,640-ton) barge that is navigated in a similar way to any water-going craft. The crane has enough power to lift a weight equal to over 4,000 cars.

Before this colossal piece of equipment or the bridge were moved, the whole scenario – from lifting the bridge on to the crane to its final delivery and placement – was analysed using sophisticated 3-D computer techniques. Similarly, the feasibility of the bridge's operation was also analysed, long before any blow was struck against steel.

project data

- **The Gateshead Millennium Bridge cost £22 million to build and weighs 850 tonnes (937 tons).**
- **The height at the tip of the arch is 50 metres (164 feet) and its foundations go down some 30 metres (98½ feet).**
- **The bridge was lifted into place in one piece by Asian Hercules II – a crane taller than Big Ben – on November 20, 2000.**
- **It was opened to the public on September 17, 2001.**
- **It has a total span of 126 metres (413 feet) and will open in just 4½ minutes.**
- **The design is so efficient that it only costs £3.60 in electricity each time it opens.**
- **Huge hydraulic rams tilt the bridge back on special pivots to allow boats to pass underneath. Its appearance during this manoeuvre has led to it being nicknamed the "Blinking Eye Bridge".**
- **It sits on 19,000 tonnes (20,950 tons) of concrete – enough to make 600,000 paving stones that would stretch 290 kilometres (180 miles) if laid end to end.**
- **It has the same 25-metre (82-foot) clearance above the river as the Tyne Bridge.**
- **The pivoting systems demanded that the bridge was manufactured precisely to a tolerance of just 3 millimetres (0.12 inches).**
- **The bridge even tidies up after litter louts: rubbish dropped on the bridge will automatically roll into traps each at end every time the bridge opens.**

Opposite: The Gateshead Millennium Bridge is dramatically lit at night. Resting in its closed position, the bridge frames The Sage, Gateshead's new music venue.

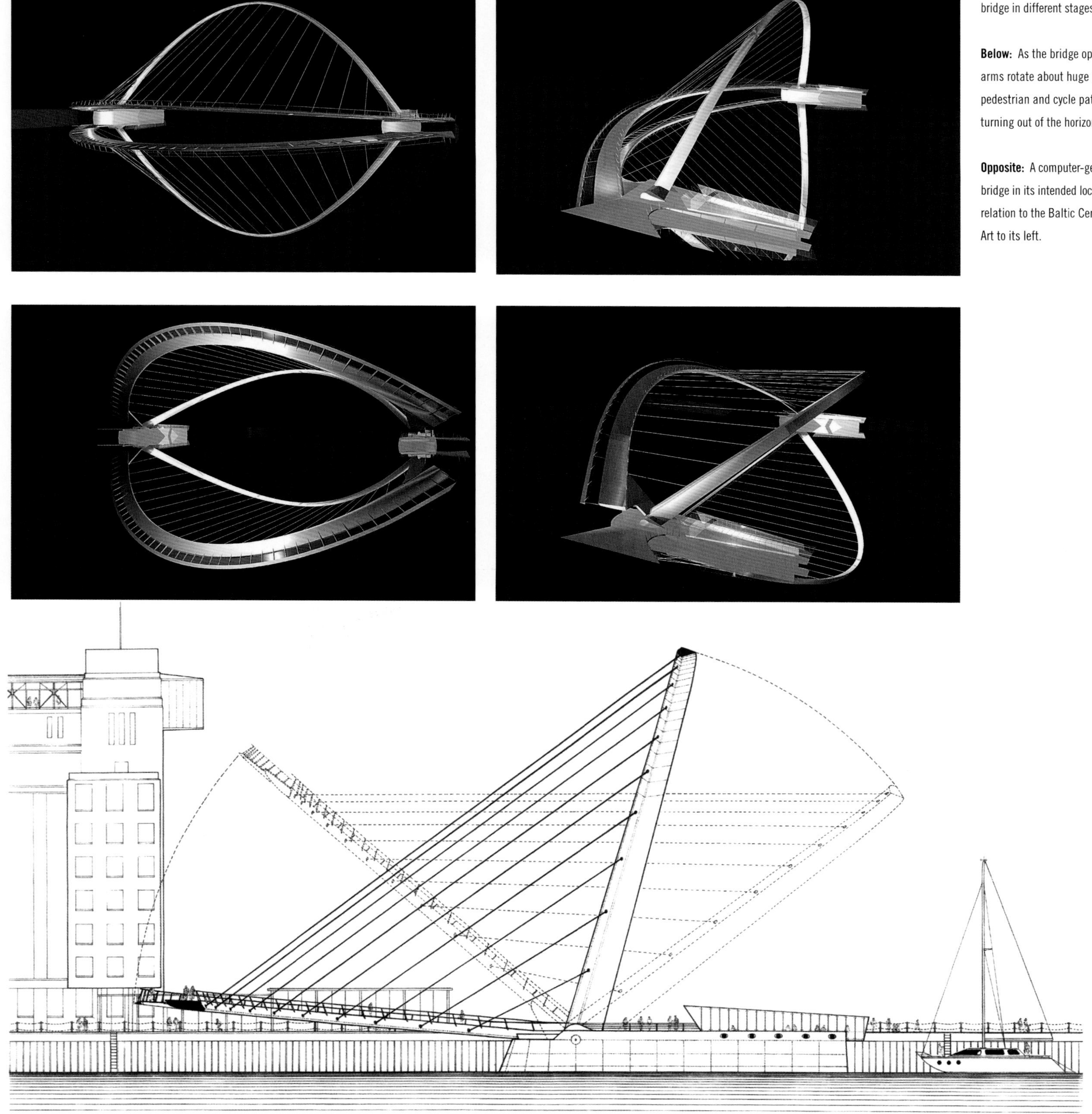

Left: Four computer-generated models detail the bridge in different stages of opening and closing.

Below: As the bridge opens, its two curving arms rotate about huge hinges and the pedestrian and cycle paths can be seen turning out of the horizontal plane.

Opposite: A computer-generated model of the bridge in its intended location. Note its size in relation to the Baltic Centre for Contemporary Art to its left.

The operation to transport the bridge up the river from its construction site took three days in all. The lifting of the bridge, from its construction site in Wallsend, onto the crane's transport deck took one whole day. Including all the necessary stabilizing chains and bars, the bridge weighed more than 1,210 tonnes (1,334 tons). And, because the bridge is longer than some parts of the river are wide, it had to be turned around 90 degrees to point upriver, before Asian Hercules II could set sail.

The second day saw crowds line the banks of the Tyne as the bridge was floated upriver to the Gateshead Quays. The crane is the largest vessel ever to float this far up the Tyne. It had just 2.5 metres (8 feet) of clearance either side of the riverbanks, and, on arrival, the crane raised and then lowered the bridge gently into place. Finally, on day three of this mammoth operation, all checks were completed and the crane removed the main 165-tonne (182-ton) support strut and withdrew from the site. The Gateshead Millennium Bridge was complete, taking its place alongside a collection of bridges over the Tyne that date back to the Roman Empire.

THE FIRST IRON BRIDGE

Built in 1779, at Coalbrookdale, Shropshire, in the UK, the first ever iron bridge still spans the River Severn today. It was designed by architect Thomas Farnolls Pritchard and built by local ironmaster Abraham Darby III.

Farnolls designed the bridge in cast iron with a high single-span arch, rising to 18.3 metres (60 feet) so that river traffic would not be impeded. His choice of building material was prompted by the abundance of iron ore in the Severn Gorge, across which the bridge would cross. The bridge's arch spans 30 metres (98½ feet) over what was once one of Europe's busiest rivers. It has five arch ribs, each cast in two halves. These are each 21.3 metres (70 feet) long and weigh 4.76 tonnes (5¼ tons). The bridge has more than 800 castings in all. They were cast separately and fastened together using methods familiar in woodworking, such as mortise and tenon, and blind dovetail joints. Bolts were used to fasten the half-ribs together at the crown of the arch.

All the major parts were erected in three months without a single accident. However, the cost of the bridge had nearly doubled the original estimates of £3,200, and Darby, who had agreed to fund any overspend, remained in debt for the rest of his life.

Farnolls died before the bridge was completed. It opened to traffic in 1781, and in 1934 the bridge was closed to vehicles and listed as a monument of national importance. Today, it is used by pedestrians, features as the main attraction at the Iron Bridge Gorge Museum and is part of a World Heritage Site.

SIMPLON TUNNEL SWITZERLAND TO ITALY

Although often overshadowed by the St Gotthard Tunnel, built a century earlier, the Simplon Tunnel is important to the history of modern engineering in the fact that it is reputed to be the first partly machine-made tunnel. At 19.8 kilometres (12.3 miles) long, it held the record as the world's longest tunnel from 1906, when the first of its two bores was completed, right up until 1982.

The tunnel is built under the Simplon Pass, an Alpine route which links Italy and Switzerland, and it completed a rail link between Paris and Istanbul. As a result it lent its name to the most glamorous train ever to cross Europe – the Venice Simplon Orient Express.

Tunnel boring through mountainous areas is notoriously expensive – even today – and so, when it was mooted that the Simplon was to be built, many engineers shunned the proposals for a tunnel that would forge a path straight through the Alps between Brig in Valais, Switzerland and Domodossola in Piedmont, Italy. Most thought that a tunnel wasn't feasible and suggested funiculars (vertical railways) to scale the Alpine peaks, while those in favour of tunneling suggested a shorter version at a much higher altitude.

However, the JuraSimplon Railway company was not to be defeated and created a consortium specially to design and construct the long tunnel at the base of the mountains. The company was headed by German engineers Alfred Brandt of Hamburg and Karl Brandau of Kassel and included the firms Locher and Company in Zurich, Sulzer Brothers of Winterthur and the Bank of Winterthur.

Brandt, the chief engineer on the northern section, was to become a leading light on the project. His idea of two single-track bores, instead of the traditional one-bore tunnel for two lines was taken on, and a hydraulic drillthat he invented especially for the project greatly increased the speed of construction while reducing danger and dust.

The tunnel's parallel bores were planned at 17 metres (56 feet) apart and connected by lateral galleries every 200 metres (656 feet). This was the first time that a tunnel featured two bores connected at intervals along its length; it has since been used many times since on major projects including the Channel Tunnel (see page 102).

Constructing the tunnel, however, was anything but easy. Even Brandt's drill estimations of completing the first bore in five years and nine months were wildly optimistic: it actually took seven and a half years, though what the tunnel diggers achieved was remarkable. Sixty-seven men were killed

Left: The first locomotive to travel through the Simplon Tunnel is met with banners and flags commemorating the time it took to construct the former "longest tunnel in the world" beneath the Alps.

Opposite: One of the heavy stone entrances to the Simplon Tunnel heralds the start of the 19.8-kilometre (12.3-mile) passageway beneath the Alps. Each end of the tunnel has two entrances, one for each bore.

project data

- Chief engineer Alfred Brandt never lived to see the tunnel completed. In November 1899, two years after the start of construction, he died while inside the tunnel. He was 54.
- The Simplon Tunnel served as a test bed for the engineers building the Channel Tunnel between Britain and France.
- The Simplon Tunnel has been refurbished in recent years at a cost of about SFr60 million (£25.25 million or US$49.75 million).
- In 2007 the opening of the new 34.6-kilometre (21.5-mile) long Lötschberg Tunnel in Switzerland will generate increased passenger and goods traffic through the Simplon.
- The tunnel connects Brig in Switzerland with Domodossola in Italy, the same locations that the historic Simplon Pass runs between at over 2,000 metres (6,562 feet) above sea level in the Lepontine Alps.
- At 19.8 kilometres (12.3 miles) long, the Simplon Tunnel was the longest in the world for 76 years. Today, the Seikan Tunnel in Japan holds the record, at 53.85 kilometres (33.46 miles).
- Two visitors to the tunnel, who had travelled 10 kilometres (6 miles) in the dark to witness the moment that the Swiss and Italian excavations met, were killed by the sudden rush of hot water from the Swiss side.

during the construction of the tunnel, though, at the start of the century, this was a small number on a large engineering project, and pales almost into insignificance when compared with the 800 lives lost while building the St Gotthard Tunnel.

At the time, the conditions in which the men worked were thought of as cutting edge. Hydro-electric power from dams in nearby valleys was used to provide a crude form of mechanical ventilation and light, while the tunnel walls, which at times reached temperatures of 50°C (122°F) due to internal hot springs, were sprayed with cold water to cool them down.

All did not go as planned, however. In September 1901, two miles in from the Italian side, miners struck what is now known as the Great Spring, an underground river which burst into the tunnel, filling it at a rate of 37,854 litres (10,000 gallons) per minute. The flooding stopped work initially and over the next six months only 46 metres (151 feet) of tunnel were dug. To continue digging workers shored up the gallery with close-timbers, using heavy baulks of square pitch pine packed close together and each 0.5 metres (19¾ inches)

thick. The water broke through again, filling the tunnel gallery with more wreckage. Steel girders were tried but these became distorted and were bent out of shape. Finally, steel girders were placed side by side to form a square, and the square structure was then filled with concrete: this structure resisted the water pressure and work could begin again in earnest.

On the Swiss side of the excavations, engineers hit volcanic springs, which released scalding water into the tunnel at 6,057 litres (1,600 gallons) per minute. Men frequently had to stand in hot water when working at the tunnel's face. Costs also spiralled whenever poor ground conditions were encountered: soft patches were nearly as debilitating to progress as springs and rivers. Each time one was encountered it required reinforcing with granite masonry 2.6 metres (8½ feet) thick, slowing down work and costing £1000 per metre (£305 per foot).

Nevertheless, at 7 a.m. on February 24, 1905, an explosive charge was set off in the roof of the Italian tunnel to blow through into the Swiss excavation. It blasted the last rock away and linked the two tunnels 2,100 metres (6,890 feet) below the Alpine peaks.

The tunnel was officially inaugurated on May 19, 1906. What had originally excited investors in the tunnel was its potential to speed up travel between northern Europe and Italy, even as far as Istanbul. The Orient Express had run for more than 20 years by 1905, but it had had to snake its way east from Paris around the Alps via Strasbourg, Vienna, Budapest and Bucharest. The ability to enter Italy via the Simplon Tunnel shaved half a day off the journey time to Venice, and by 1921 the company was running an extended Simplon Orient Express route right into Turkey.

Above: The Swiss entrance to the tunnel, in Brig, is a heavy stone building with one bore entrance stepped back from the other.

Opposite: Four images of the tunnel during and after construction. **(Top left)** Workers shore up the walls with timber scaffold. **(Top right)** A party to open the tunnel. **(Lower left)** Access tunnels with ventilation pipes fixed to the ceiling. **(Lower right)** The drilling machine designed by tunnel engineer Alfred Brandt.

MAESLANTKERING STORM SURGE BARRIER THE NETHERLANDS

The North Sea Flood of 1953 killed 1,835 people in the Netherlands and forced the evacuation of 70,000 more. Dykes and seawalls were breached, some 10,000 animals drowned and 4,500 buildings were completely destroyed. In order to prevent such a tragedy from happening again the Dutch government embarked upon an ambitious flood-defence system called Deltaworks.

It is claimed that the Deltaworks project is the world's largest flood-protection project. With over 16,496 kilometres (10,250 miles) of levees and 300 structures, the project is one of the most extensive engineering projects in the world. It isolates 13 estuaries from the ocean and has reclaimed approximately 1,650 square kilometres (637 square miles) of land from the sea.

Since more than one third of the Netherlands lies below sea level, its protection is no simple or new task. Large numbers of earth mounds can be found in the south and west of the country: called *vliedbergen*, meaning "refuge mountains", these were built in the Middle Ages to provide refuge from rising waters. They were not intended for permanent habitation, rather they provided temporary places of safety for local people and their animals. More recently, dunes along the entire Dutch coast were raised by as much as 5 metres (16½ feet), while islands in the Zeeland province have been joined together by dams and other large scale constructions to shorten the coastline.

One of the most impressive of these constructions is the Maeslantkering Storm Surge Barrier at the entrance to the Port of Rotterdam. The fact that it protects one of the world's busiest harbours means that obstructive measures, such as were employed in the Thames Barrier in London (see page 114) could not be used, as they would be too intrusive across this major shipping lane.

The Maeslantkering Barrier actually swings across from either bank to seal the New Waterway channel when tidal surges are forecast.

Designed by Bouwcombinatie Maeslant Kering (BMK), the barrier's two hollow semicircular gates are attached by means of steel arms to pivot points on both banks. Chosen from six entries in a design competition in the late 1980s, one of the advantages of the BMK design, in relation to the others submitted, is that of ease of maintenance, as the giant gates are positioned in dry docks on either bank of the 360-metre (1,181-foot) wide channel.

In the event of a storm tide, the docks housing the hollow gates are filled with water, causing the gates to float. This enables them to be easily swung out into the New Waterway. Once the gates meet, the buoyant compartments within them are filled with water and they sink to the bottom, sealing off the harbour entrance. After the high water has passed, the gates are pumped out and the structure begins to float again. When the harbour masters can be sure that the next high water will not be another abnormally high one, the two gates are returned to their docks.

Construction of the barrier began in 1991. First, the dry docks were built and a concrete foundation was laid on the bed of the New Waterway. The two gates are 22 metres (72 feet) high and 210 metres (689 feet) long. These were constructed and welded to the 237-metre (778-foot) long steel trusses, which anchor them to their pivot joints.

The trusses transmit the immense forces exerted on the gates by high tides to joints at the rear of each gate. During the opening and closing process, these ball-shaped joints allow the gate to move freely side to side, and up and down, to counteract the influence of water, wind and waves. It is, in

project data

- **Standing upright, the steel trusses of the gates would be as high as the Eiffel Tower, but each one of them weighs four times more than the tower does.**
- **Queen Beatrix opened the Maeslantkering Storm Surge Barrier on May 10, 1997, after a six-year construction project.**
- **The storm surge barrier is closed once a year to test its operation – usually in September or October, just prior to the November storms.**
- **The Netherlands has a history of flood defence dating back to the Middle Ages, when *vliedbergen*, or "refuge mountains", were built to provide refuge from rising waters.**
- **From the time the dry docks are first flooded, the barriers take just 30 minutes to close the 360-metre (1,181-foot) wide waterway.**
- **Maeslantkering Storm Surge Barrier is part of Deltaworks, the largest flood-defence system in the world.**
- **The construction of the barrier cost 450 million Euros.**
- **The ball-shaped joints on which the gates swing are the largest in the world, with a diameter of 10 metres (33 feet) and a weight of 680,000 kilograms (1.5 million pounds).**

Left: The view looking down an arm from the barrier.

Opposite top: The Maeslantkering storm surge barrier in its closed position. The giant triangular steel trusses swing the barrier from its position in dry dock to the centre of the channel.

Opposite bottom: Sunrise through the barrier's steel truss arms.

effect, like the ball-shaped joint between your arm and shoulder.

The barrier is connected to a self-operating computer system that is linked to weather and sea-level data. When a storm surge of 3 metres (10 feet) above normal sea level is anticipated, the barrier will close automatically. Ships in the vicinity are warned four hours before the closing procedure begins; two hours before closing all traffic in the New Waterway is halted. Thirty minutes before closing the dry docks in which the gates are housed are flooded; when the gap between the gates has closed to about 1.5 metres (5 feet) wide, they are submerged to the bottom of the waterway.

The barrier was opened officially by the Netherlands' Queen Beatrix on Saturday May 10, 1997. The giant storm-surging doors were sailed equally from the shores onto the New Waterway for the first time in an operation that took about two hours.

The storm-surge barrier will only be closed in extremely bad weather – in probability once every 10 years. A test closure is conducted once a year in order to check the equipment. However, with the rise in sea levels due to global warming, it is anticipated that the storm-surge barrier will need to close more frequently in the future.

The Maeslantkering Storm Surge Barrier is a dramatic piece of engineering on a grand scale. However, it and the rest of the massive Deltaworks will eventually have to be reinforced, as the mainland is subsiding and, due to climate changes, sea levels are continuing to rise. Future works are already being discussed, although some people argue that relocation of population centres and giving up land to the sea would be a longer-lasting solution than constantly fighting the sea. Only time will tell if low-lying land can be retained, or if the Dutch will have to revert to a modern form of *vliedbergen*.

Below: The Maeslantkering Storm Surge Barrier in dry dock, enabling easy maintenance

CAMPO VOLANTIN BRIDGE BILBAO, SPAIN

Known locally as the Zubizuri – Basque for "white bridge" – Campo Volantin Bridge in Bilbao, Spain is one of architect and engineer Santiago Calatrava's best-known structures. Spanning the River Nervión, and linking Campo Volantin on the right bank and Uribitarte on the left, the arched steel suspension bridge offers pedestrians a convenient route from hotels in the centre of Bilbao to the nearby Guggenheim Museum that was designed by Frank O. Gehry.

Calatrava's design was a replacement for a design that had hit trouble under its initial sponsors. The original Uribitarte Bridge was designed as a steel inclined tied-arch bridge with a pre-cast concrete deck. The local authorities commissioned Calatrava to design a bridge that remained true to the original idea of "a statement symbolizing the trade of land between the connecting municipalities". What he produced is a much-refined version of the original, and a structure with a far lighter air to it.

The design is a steel inclined parabolic arch. Its main span is 75 metres (246 feet) and the tubular steel arch rises 15.2 metres (50 feet) above the bridge deck. However, neither of these facts is of great consequence – more important is the aesthetic beauty of the structure as a whole.

Designed and built between 1994 and 1997, the Campo Volantin Bridge features a main arch constructed from a 45-centimetre (18-inch) diameter pipe with walls that are 5 centimetres (2 inches) thick. It curves upward and leans over in the opposite direction to the curve of the pedestrian deck. Steel cables pass through the tubular arch and descend, connecting to similar tubular pipes that project on fins either side of the walkway. In doing this they span over the

Left: The Campo Volantin Bridge is an intricate structural design that includes a web-like array of suspension cables and a spine of steel girders over which the glass walkway runs.

Below: The bridge in context with its urban surroundings, as it spans the River Nervión in Bilbao, northern Spain.

heads of pedestrians on the bridge, twisting with the curvature of the walkway, and looking more like delicate threads than load-bearing cables.

The actual deck on which people walk is raised some 8.5 metres (28 feet) above the river and has a width of between 6.5 and 7.5 metres (21 and 25 feet). The deck is composed of 41 steel ribs, which project from a structural tubular spine located centrally underneath the deck. The glass decking is arranged in planks 180 centimetres (6 feet) long by 28 centimetres (1 foot) wide, running lengthways along the bridge. The glass planks are held in place by stainless-steel runners and a 70-centimetre (2-foot-4-inch) galvanized-steel edge plate at either side of the walkway. Stainless-steel and cable handrails complete the intricate design, each leaning in accordance with the direction of the suspension cables nearest to it. The startling effect is that of movement: the bridge seems to be forging down river, its shape streamlined against the flow.

The bridge supports are a classic example of Calatrava's other love – sculpted concrete. Like inclining bridges themselves they include arching spans before a cantilever at the uppermost point, onto which the main steel-bodied bridge span is connected. The spectacle is made more dramatic by the positioning of the supports at right angles to the bridge. In reality this is due to the lack of space in which to create a long, gradual ascent to the bridge in line with it. However, the fact that the supports are offset to one side only serves to make the finished bridge look more precarious and light – how can something so heavy be supported on the end of such slender structures?

Calatrava is unusual in the fact that, after completing his years of architecture training, he decided that he needed to know more about how things were constructed and took a PhD. in civil engineering at the Federal Institute of Technology in Zurich. The methods and otherworldly designs that Calatrava produces are a subtle combination of architecture and engineering, melding aesthetics and structural dynamics to create some of the most distinctive buildings and structures in the world. However, this grounding in engineering has been both a blessing and a curse to Calatrava. While he has built many structures, for much of his early working life the majority of his commissions were bridges: a staple structure of the engineer. He has since gone on to build some of the most striking buildings in the world, including the City of Arts and Sciences in Valencia, the Olympic Sports Complex in Athens and the Milwaukee Art Museum in the United States. But, throughout his career, bridges have been a mainstay, and Calatrava has designed and built over 50 so far in countries as far afield as Denmark, Canada, Spain and Israel.

The design of the Campo Volantin Bridge and all others by Calatrava is an exercise in the realization of the beauty of structural members, cables, arches, spires and decks. The architect has elevated bridge design beyond that of an engineered solution into the realms of artistry, and, in so doing, he has challenged the assumption that bridges are meant merely as a point of crossing or a means to travel. This view is now propagating throughout the world of architecture and more practitioners are taking up the challenge of designing unusual and stunning bridges – take Norman Foster's Millau Viaduct (see page 106) or Wilkinson Eyre's Gateshead Millennium Bridge (see page 88), for instance.

Calatrava states that bridges, as design objects, can combine technological intelligence with poetry to enhance the sense of identity and cultural significance of a particular place; they bring people together across a divide and are a symbol of community.

Below: The curving walkway of the bridge meets the banks of the river and turns through 90 degrees onto the riverside paths. This is due to limited space at the sides of the river.

Opposite: Pedestrians walk underneath the web of suspension cables attached to the top arch. Below their feet the illuminated glass panels of the walkway have an ethereal glow in the evening light.

project data

- Completed in 1997, Campo Volantin Bridge is known locally as the Zubizuri; this translates as "white bridge" in Basque, the language of the region.
- The bridge spans 75 metres (246 feet) over the River Nervión in Bilbao, Spain. Its deck is 8.5 metres (28 feet) above the water and the arch reaches another 15.2 metres (50 feet) higher.
- The bridge offers pedestrians passage over the river to the famous Guggenheim Bilbao Museum designed by Frank O. Gehry.
- The bridge's designer, Santiago Calatrava, is trained both as an architect and an engineer.
- Calatrava has built over 50 bridges all over the world, including 16 in his native country of Spain.
- The deck of the bridge is made from glass planks set between stainless-steel runners.

Left: The British entrance to the Channel Tunnel near Folkestone, Kent. The main rail track, on the left, is bordered by a large area of sidings. The tunnel entrance is at the lower end of this picture.

CHANNEL TUNNEL UK TO FRANCE

A tunnel link between Great Britain and France had been proposed many times before it was actually achieved in 1994. As early as 1802, French engineer Albert Mathieu-Favier proposed a tunnel under the English Channel in which horse-drawn coaches would travel, via a road lit with oil lamps. Between 1864 and 1883 preparatory work started on a different design, only for it to be halted due to British military concerns of invasion.

In 1922, the British government got as far as boring 120 metres (394 feet) of tunnel into the chalk cliffs between Folkestone and Dover before this was halted due to political objections. And, as recently as 1974, another attempt was made to construct a tunnel by the British and French governments and trial borings were made on both sides. However, a fuel crisis meant that the British Prime Minister Harold Wilson cancelled the project.

The current Channel Tunnel is the second longest tunnel in the world: only the Seikan Tunnel in Japan beats it. However, at 49.94 kilometres (31.03 miles) long, it is the longest tunnel ever constructed under the sea and actually consists of three parallel tunnels. There are two rail tunnels, situated 30 metres (98 feet) apart and measuring 7.6 metres (25 feet) in diameter. In between, a smaller service tunnel runs, measuring 4.8 metres ($15^2/_3$ feet) in diameter. This is connected by cross-passages to the main tunnels at intervals around once every 375 metres (1,230 feet), to provide workers both access to the rail tunnels and also safe escape route in emergencies.

The two main tunnels are linked every 250 metres (820 feet) by pressure relief ducts that pass over the top of the service tunnel. These ducts allow the air, which is forced along in front of the high-speed trains, to pass into the opposite tunnel, dispelling the "piston effect" that the trains cause. There are also enormous caverns near each end of the tunnel, allowing for a rail crossover between the main tunnels, should a section of tunnel need to be closed. At 156 by 18 by 10 metres (512 by 59 by 33 feet), the British cross-over cavern is the largest ever under-sea excavation.

In December 1987 construction started on the service tunnel and for the next seven years a total of 15,000 workers bored under the English Channel from France and Great Britain simultaneously. The prime contractor for the construction was the Anglo–French TransManche Link (TML), a consortium of 10 construction companies and five banks.

Engineers used 11 gigantic tunnel boring machines (TBMs) to cut through the varied strata under the English Channel. These huge pieces of apparatus are mobile excavation factories, which drill and remove spoil, shoring up the tunnel walls with a concrete lining as they progress slowly on a laser-guided course. As the TBM excavates and the rock is removed, two drills just behind the cutters bore into the rock walls of the tunnel; grout is pumped into these holes and bolts hold curved steel shoring panels in place until the permanent lining can be installed. The TBM also has a massive erector arm that raises segments of the tunnel lining into place, ready for workers to complete installation.

In France, a circular access shaft, 70 metres (230 feet) deep and 55 metres (180 feet) in diameter was excavated and lined with concrete. Into this, all materials, workers and equipment were lowered, and the TBMs were assembled in position to begin drilling.

project data

- **When the two ends of the under-sea service tunnel met on December 1, 1990, it became possible to walk on dry land from Great Britain to France for the first time since the end of the last Ice Age 8,500 years ago.**
- **At 49.94 kilometres (31.03 miles) long, the Channel Tunnel is the second longest in the World. The record is held by Japan's Seikan Tunnel, at 53.85 metres (33.46 miles).**
- **In 2005, 7.45 million passengers travelled through the tunnel on Eurostar while in the same year Eurotunnel carried 3.43 million vehicles on its shuttle trains.**
- **When construction began in 1987, British and French tunnel workers raced to reach the middle of the tunnel first; the British won.**
- **The tunnel was officially opened by Queen Elizabeth II and French President François Mitterand in a ceremony that was held in Calais on May 6, 1994.**

As the TBMs burrowed into the underground rock, construction trains transported the linings, the spoil and the workers to and from the workface. Spoil from the TBMs was deposited at a treatment plant at the base of the shaft, where it was mixed with water and pumped up and out to a disposal site 500 metres (1,640 feet) away.

The British tunnelling team did things differently, using earlier tunnel workings at a platform at the foot of Shakespeare Cliff near Folkestone, as one of two access shafts. A small railway ferried equipment and materials to the main marshalling area underground. The six TBMs were each assembled in a large cavern area over 20 metres (66 feet) high that was equipped with overhead cranes for lifting the TBM sections.

At their quickest rate the TBMs excavated a distance of 75.5 metres (248 feet) per day. The three French TBMs bored from Sangatte to meet three British TBMs digging from Shakespeare Cliff. Two more machines were used on associated French tunnels, while three more British machines dug from the south coast to Folkestone in Kent, the official tunnel entrance in the United Kingdom.

On December 1, 1990, the French and English service tunnels broke through at the halfway point, with tunnellers Phillipe Cozette and Graham Fagg meeting each other 40 metres (131 feet) below the English Channel. The main rail tunnels met on May 22, 1991. Guided by laser-surveying methods, the difference in the centre lines of the two ends of the tunnel was surveyed as just 358 millimetres (14 inches) horizontally and 58 millimetres (2¼ inches) vertically.

Almost 4 million cubic metres (141.3 million cubic feet) of chalk were excavated on the British side, much of which was dumped below Shakespeare Cliff to reclaim 36 hectares (89 acres) of land from the sea. In all, 8 million cubic metres (282.5 million cubic feet) of spoil, most of it chalk-based, were removed, at an average rate of 2,400 tonnes (2,646 tons) per hour.

TUNNEL BORING MACHINES

Tunnel boring machines (TBMs) have been around for over a century and a half. They were first used in 1853 and are now the most common way of excavating underground transportation passageways. They bore through any substrata and the more advanced versions automatically shore up and finish off the tunnel lining as they progress.

A TBM's armoury is its rotating cutting wheel, which is positioned at the front of the shield. This spins at a relatively slow speed of 1–10 revolutions per minute as the TBM advances, pushing multiple hard-tipped teeth into the wall rock before it. Behind the cutting wheel and the shield, depending on the type of TBM, the excavated soil is either mixed with slurry to be pumped away or left as dry aggregate to be transported to trucks on conveyors.

On today's TBMs a set of hydraulic jacks are the power source, driving the machine forward. These clamp tight to the finished part of the tunnel and slowly push the TBM along.

The first boring machine built was used in the 1870s during the construction of the Hoosac Tunnel in Massachusetts, USA. Wilson's Patented Stone-Cutting Machine, as it was known (after its inventor Charles Wilson), managed to drill only 3 metres (10 feet) before breaking down. Conversely, the two biggest TBMs to date were built in 2005 to dig two tunnels in Madrid, Spain: named Dulcinea and Tizona, they were 15 metres (49 feet) in diameter, and both have since been dismantled following completion of their work.

A passenger journey through the tunnel lasts about 20 minutes, while a shuttle train journey takes about 35 minutes, including travelling a large loop to turn the train around. In 2005, some 7.45 million foot passengers and 3.43 million vehicles crossed between Britain and France via the Channel Tunnel.

Above: A tunnel engineer works within one of the main train tunnel bores during the construction project. The tunnel actually has three bores: two for trains and a central escape tunnel.

Opposite: The tunnel exit into France. All electrical and emergency services are secured to the reinforced concrete tunnel walls. Beyond the tunnel, a mass of power cables lead off into the French countryside.

MILLAU VIADUCT RIVER TARN, NEAR MILLAU, FRANCE

The Millau Viaduct, in southwest France, is the first great civil engineering structure of the twenty-first century, and arguably one of the most impressive construction feats of all time. Built to span a deep gorge created by the River Tarn and to link the highway systems of France and Spain, the Millau Viaduct is the world's highest road bridge – at 300 metres (984 feet) high, the bridge is 23 metres (75 feet) taller than the Eiffel Tower.

The need for a new road bridge was identified in 1988. Officials from the French National Highway Department then spent five years examining different routes and conducting geological surveys. By 1993 the decision had been taken to build a slender, high-level bridge, rather than a series of low-level structures and tunnels; a team proposing a cable-stayed bridge won a design competition in 1996. With this option, much of the weight of the road surface is suspended from slender cables, which reduces the need for massive structural elements and provides a more lightweight appearance. Construction work began in October 2001.

Despite the care taken with selecting the site, the design and construction team was still faced with tremendous difficulties. The structure provides a link between two plateaux, one of which is 74 metres (243 feet) higher than the other; also, the 2,460-metre (8,071-foot) long bridge crosses undulating terrain, so each of its seven "piers" is of a different height. Finally, because of the height of this structure, new building techniques had to be developed.

The steel reinforced concrete piers, which range from 77–245 metres (253–804 feet) in height, sit on foundations up to 16 metres (52 feet) deep; laid across these piers is the road surface – a steel box girder construction 35 metres (115 feet) wide that can accommodate two double lanes of traffic. Above this there are seven 97-metre (318-foot) high pylons, which provide the support for 154 steel cables. Moreover, because the bridge was conceived as a "slender ribbon", the piers taper both to express the degree of structural work they are doing and to reduce their impact on the landscape. Each pier, or column, also splits in two, which further reduces their visual presence and provides room for the concrete desk of the roadway to expand and contract according to the air temperature. Foster and Partners, the London-based architects that worked closely with the French engineers and contractors, says the

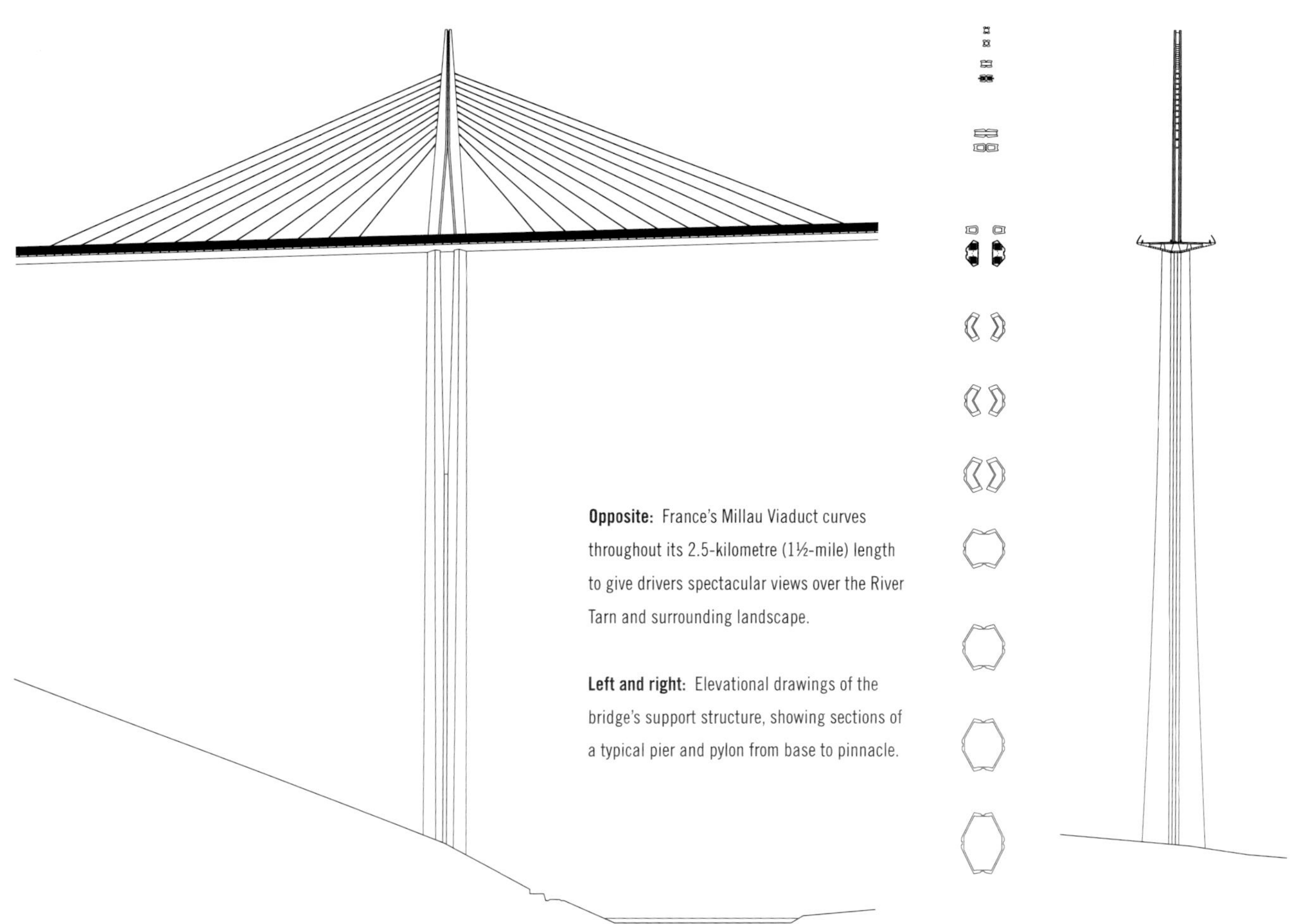

Opposite: France's Millau Viaduct curves throughout its 2.5-kilometre (1½-mile) length to give drivers spectacular views over the River Tarn and surrounding landscape.

Left and right: Elevational drawings of the bridge's support structure, showing sections of a typical pier and pylon from base to pinnacle.

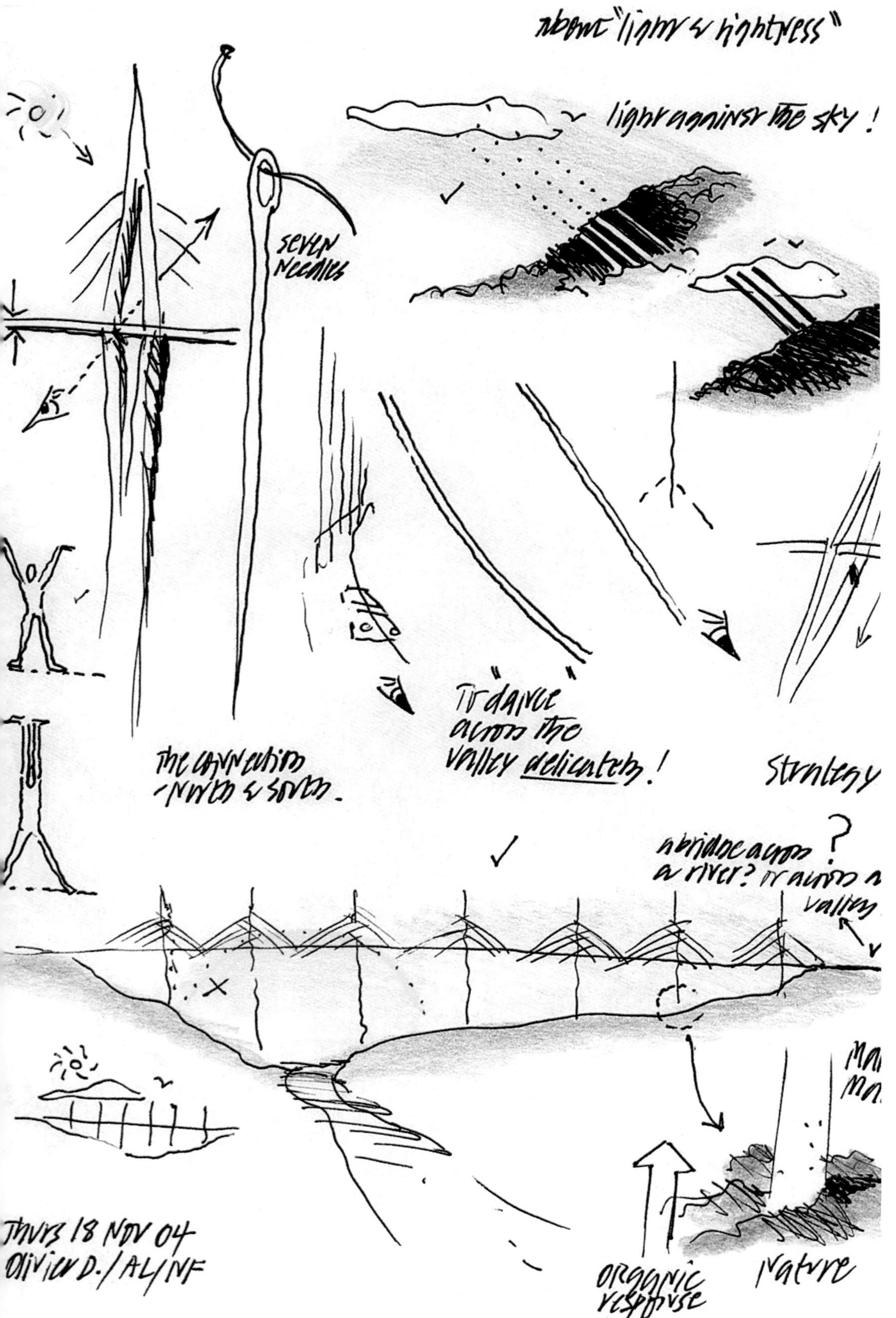

Millau Viaduct expresses “a fascination with the relationships between function, technology and aesthetics in a graceful structural form”. As a diagram, the bridge is relatively simple to understand, but it proved difficult to put into practice.

Ordinarily, the road sections of a cable-stayed bridge would be lifted into place by crane, but due to the height of the Millau Viaduct, this was not an option. Instead, the road was constructed in two sections, one on each plateau, and gradually pushed across to meet at the bridge’s most vertiginous point – directly over the River Tarn. To reduce the amount of distance the road had to travel between piers (and minimize deflection), a series of temporary piers were installed – the road deck therefore had to travel 171 metres (561 feet) in mid-air before meeting a supporting surface. Crucially, the “launch ends” of the two road elements were equipped with their pylons and cables to prevent deflection when they met in the middle.

Powered by satellite-guided hydraulic rams, moving the road elements was a slow and exacting process – the 36,000-tonne (39,683-ton) road surface generally moved in 600-millimetre (24-inch) sections every four minutes. Launch speeds often varied according to weather conditions, and road movements were suspended if average wind speeds rose above 37 kilometres per hour (23 miles per hour). Each launching operation, spanning a distance of 171 metres (561 feet), took five days.

The two road elements met on 18 May, 2004, and the remaining five concrete pylons were then put in place – an anxious process as the bridge (without the support of the pylons and the cable-stays) was operating at its structural limits. Once complete, the bridge opened on 14 December 2004, to acclaim by French President Jacques Chirac: “The Millau Viaduct is a magnificent example, in the long and great French tradition, of audacious works of art, a tradition begun at the turn of the nineteenth and twentieth centuries by the great Gustave Eiffel.”

Left: Conceptual drawings by British architect Norman Foster, who imagined the bridge as a slender structure threading its way through sharply profiled concrete piers – like cotton through the eye of a needle.

Opposite top: The bridge during construction. The red temporary piers are clearly visible.

Opposite bottom: Elevation and topological drawings of the bridge, showing how this magnificent structure links two plateaux of unequal height, which curve along its length.

project data

- The Millau Viaduct was designed and built by a team comprising three French engineering consulting firms, British architectural practice Foster and Partners, and building company Eiffage (the same company which built the Eiffel Tower).
- The bridge, which gently curves along its 2.5-kilometre (1½-mile) length, rises 343 metres (1,125 feet) above the River Tarn; the roadway is 270 metres (886 feet) above the river. The bridge consists of eight spans, resting on seven piers; the two side spans measure 204 metres (669 feet), while the six intermediate spans extend 342 metres (1,122 feet).
- Each of the 16 sections of road deck weighs 60 tonnes (66 tons), and measures 4 x 17 metres (13 x 56 feet). These sections were built in two factories elsewhere in France.
- The road was laid with 6 centimetres (2.4 inches) of flexible bitumen, while a further 4,000 tonnes (4 409 tons) of standard bitumen was laid for the emergency strips on either side of the roadway.
- The road deck was constructed from 36,000 tonnes (39,683 tons) of steel (five times that used in the Eiffel Tower); 19,000 tonnes (20,944 tons) of steel were used to reinforce the concrete piers, and a further 1,500 tonnes (1,654 tons) of steel were used in the cables.
- The road deck cross-section is a "streamlined orthotropic steel box-girder" (the principal supporting elements were made of steel plates welded together to form box beams – the top of the box is an integral part of the driving deck); it carries two lanes of traffic in each direction.
- Traffic is set back 3 metres (10 feet) from the edges of the bridge, to reduce vertigo. Also, wind barriers were installed on edge of the structure to add to its aerodynamic image and reduce "wind shocks" to traffic arriving on the bridge.

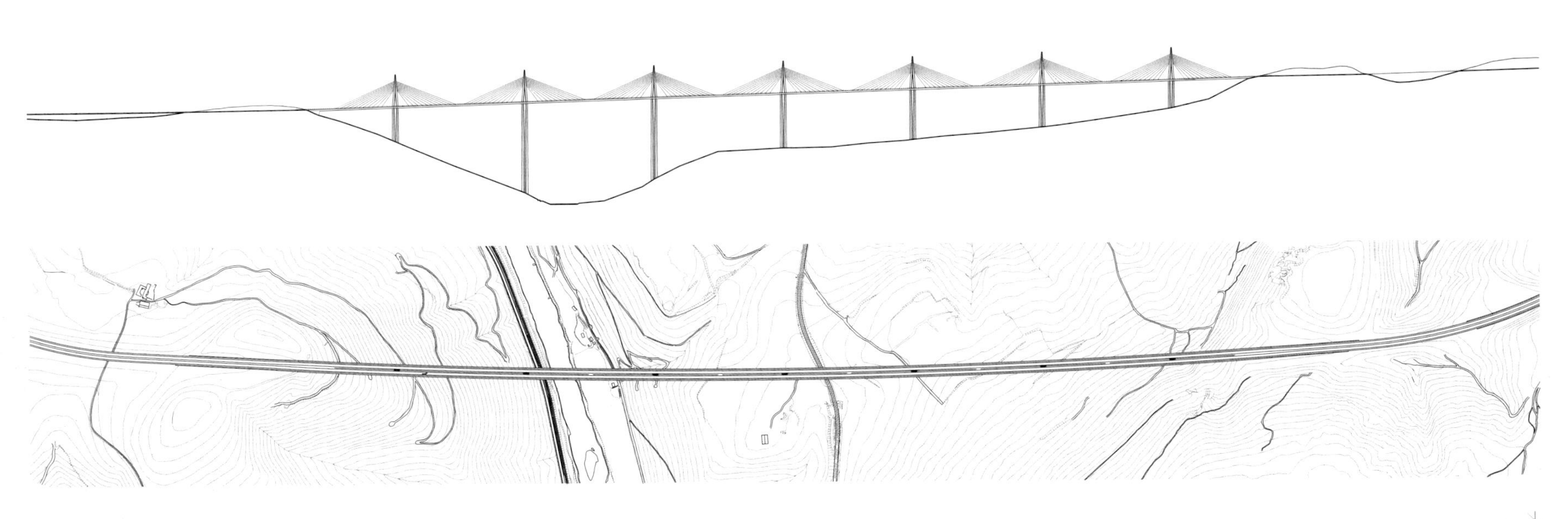

SYDNEY HARBOUR BRIDGE SYDNEY, AUSTRALIA

Sitting alongside the Sydney Opera House (see page 226), Sydney Harbour Bridge is one of Australia's best-known landmarks. At the turn of the twentieth century there were several smaller bridges located farther westward in the harbour, but ferries were the more common form of transport and the harbour had become crowded with them, and so plans were made to build a huge new bridge.

However, the First World War put a stop to that and it was not until 1922 that civil, structural and transport engineer J.J.C. Bradfield and the New South Wales Department of Public Works devised plans for a new steel-arch bridge. The New South Wales Government invited worldwide tenders for the construction of the bridge and the contract was won by the English firm Dorman Long & Co. of Middlesbrough.

Dorman Long's Consulting Engineer, Ralph Freeman, carried out the detailed design of the bridge, which coincided with the building of Sydney's underground railway network, known today as the City Circle. The bridge was constructed to carry eight lanes of road traffic (including two tram lanes), flanked by two railway tracks and a footpath on each side.

Over 800 families living in the bridge's path were relocated and their homes demolished before work on the new structure could start. Then, in 1924, work began. In all, it would take 1,400 men eight years to build, using six million hand-driven rivets and 52,800 tonnes (58,200 tons) of steel. Sixteen workers lost their lives during construction of the bridge.

Following the construction of factories to manufacture bridge parts, in January 1925 the excavations to accommodate the abutments and approach

Below: The monumental stone abutments were built in stages, with the steel arch of the bridge being completed before the stone towers were topped off.

Opposite: Today, Sydney Harbour Bridge stands as a monument to the engineers and workers who struggled to build it between 1924 and 1932, including the 16 men who lost their lives on the project.

spans began; in October the building of the abutments and approach spans themselves were started. These were completed in September 1928 and construction of the actual bridge began in early 1929.

Two separate teams built up the arch on each side of the harbour using creeper cranes. The first panel was erected on the southern side in March 1929. Work on the southern end of the bridge was scheduled a month ahead of the northern end, in order to detect any errors in the design and allow for corresponding adjustments on the northern end.

During their construction, the two halves of the arch were held up by large support cables. Once complete, the cables were slowly released to bring the two halves together. This was finalized on the afternoon of August 19, 1930. Following a planned settlement, or parting, that occurred, due to the contracting of metal in the cool evening, the ends were rejoined at 10 p.m., and have remained so ever since.

Safety measures during construction were poor by today's standards. The workers who died during construction were mainly killed by falling from the bridge. Several more were injured from unsafe working practices undertaken while heating and constructing the rivets, and deafness experienced by many of the workers in later years was also blamed on the project.

The road and the two sets of tram and railway tracks were completed in 1931. Power and telephone lines, and water, gas and drainage pipes were also added to the bridge in that year. On January 19, 1932, the first test train – a steam locomotive – safely crossed the bridge.

The road across the bridge is 2.4 kilometres (1.5 miles) long, making it one of the shortest highways in Australia. The bridge deck, which measures 1.15 kilometres (0.7 miles) long, is concrete and lays on beams that run along the length of the bridge; these beams rest on steel beams that run the width of the bridge and which are visible to boats passing underneath.

The arch is composed of two 28-panel arch trusses. The heights of the trusses vary from 18 metres (59 feet) to 57 metres (187 feet). The arch span is 503 metres (1,650 feet) and the weight of the steel arch is 39,000 tonnes (42,999 tons). The arch's summit is 134 metres (440 feet) above mean sea level, though this measurement can increase by as much as 180 millimetres (7 inches) on hot days, as the result of the steel expanding in heat. Two large metal hinges at the base of the bridge accommodate these expansions and contractions. The pairs of granite-faced pylons at each end are 89 metres (292 feet) high. In their bases are abutments that support the ends of the bridge.

The bridge was formally opened on March 19, 1932, at a cost of over £10 million – twice the original quote. The Premier of New South Wales, Jack Lang, was to open the bridge by cutting a ribbon at its southern end. However, just as he was about to do so, a man in military uniform charged forward on horseback and slashed the ribbon with a sword, declaring the bridge to be open "in the name of the decent and respectable citizens of New South Wales". He was promptly arrested. The ribbon was hurriedly re-tied and Lang performed the official opening ceremony. The intruder was identified as Francis de Groot, a member of a right-wing paramilitary group opposed to Lang's leftist policies.

Traffic, the reason for which the bridge was originally built, remains a problem in the modern metropolis that is Sydney. In 1992 the Sydney Harbour Tunnel was opened to cope with ever increasing harbour-traffic problems. Built in four years, it is 2.3 kilometres (1.4 miles) long and cost AU$554 million to construct. The tunnel carries around 75,000 vehicles a day, in addition to the 160,000 that travel over the bridge.

Above: Sydney Harbour is recognisable worldwide thanks to its two great landmarks, the Harbour Bridge and, seen here beneath it, the Sydney Opera House.

Opposite: The massive steel arch structure takes the weight of the roadway beneath it via massive steel straps. A maintenance vehicle sits on top of the arch.

project data

- **Sydney Harbour Bridge is the world's largest (but not the longest) steel-arch bridge: its highest point stands 134 metres (440 feet) above the harbour.**
- **The total financial cost of the Sydney Harbour Bridge was £10,057,170.7s.9d (double the original quote). This was not paid off in full until 1988.**
- **Fondly known by the locals as the "Coat Hanger", the bridge celebrates its seventy-fifth birthday in 2007.**
- **The top of the arch actually rises and falls about 180 millimetres (7 inches) due to expansion and contraction brought on by changes in the temperature.**
- **When the bridge opened it cost a horse and rider three pence and a car six pence to cross. Now horses and riders cannot cross, bicycles and pedestrians go for free, while cars pay around AU$3.00 for a southbound trip and it is free to go northbound.**
- **In 1932 the average annual daily traffic flow across the bridge was around 11,000; now it is around 160,000 vehicles per day.**
- **The Tyne Bridge in Newcastle-upon-Tyne, England is a much smaller version of the Sydney Harbour Bridge, with a length of 397 metres (1,302 feet) and a main span of 161 metres (528 feet).**

THAMES BARRIER LONDON, UK

The Thames Barrier, completed in 1982, is one of the most significant infrastructure projects completed in the United Kingdom in recent decades. Measuring 520 metres (1,706 feet) long, the barrier is designed to protect London from high tides – a danger which is becoming more of a regular threat, due to a combination of global warming and the geology of the south-east of England. London is gradually settling on its bed of clay, while this part of the country is slowly sinking anyway; add to that a higher incidence of storms, tidal surges and higher sea levels, and it is easy to see why London requires a flood-defence mechanism of some magnitude. Tide levels in the Thames Estuary are rising by approximately 60 centimetres (2 feet) per century.

The barrier has its origins in the 1950s, after the catastrophic flood of 1953 that caused the deaths of more than 300 people. This flood did not reach central London but even then thought was given to a movable flood barrier that could effectively wall the capital off from incoming tides. The size of shipping at the time made this an unrealistic proposition, but by the mid-1960s, when the advent of container shipping led to the decline of London's docks, and freighters began docking much farther downstream, the idea began to make sense. The Thames Barrier and Flood Protection Act was passed in 1972 and construction started later that year. The barrier was completed in 1982 and was first used a year later, but was not officially opened by Queen Elizabeth II until 1984.

The barrier stretches right across the River Thames at Woolwich Reach, a site chosen for its straight riverbanks and the fact that the chalk beneath the river bed was strong enough to act as a foundation for the vast concrete and steel assembly that was required. In fact, a good deal of chalk was removed and replaced with rock and concrete.

Although London's docklands are now home to office towers rather than ships, the Thames is still navigable and it was important that the barrier be permeable to shipping rather than become a dead end. Moreover, the barrier, when open, does not interfere with the flow of water in the river. Hence, the largest four gates are immense – 61 metres (200 feet) wide, 20 metres (66 feet) high and weighing 3,700 tonnes (4,079 tons); these central gates can each withstand a water load of more than 9,000 tonnes (9,921 tons).

The barrier, designed by the GLC Department of Public Health Engineering with consultant engineers Rendel Palmer & Tritton, is composed of nine concrete piers and 10 gates. The piers contain the hydraulic mechanisms, shielded by stainless-steel canopies,

Left: The Thames Barrier was built to last until 2030. London authorities are now considering an even larger barrier downstream to cope with the increased sea levels associated with global warming.

Opposite: The Thames Barrier in the closed position. Immense steel gates swing upwards from cradles in the bed of the river, presenting a solid wall to the advancing tide.

E
D
C
7
B
8
9

which control the gates. Apart from the four central gates described above, there are a further two gates, each 31 metres (102 feet) wide, creating a total of six openings out of the 10 that are navigable to shipping. These navigable gates sit in concrete grooves (or "sills") in the river bed and can be swept upward through 90 degrees when flood warnings are sounded. A further four gates, closest to the riverbanks, are suspended above water level and are lowered into place – these form unnavigable passages.

All the gates are radial in form, appearing as half cylinders that rotate on pivots. The six navigable gates are known as the "rising radials" because they sit on the river bed and swing upward; the remaining four are called the "falling radials" because they sit free of the water and swing downward. However, even the rising gates have the capacity to swing right out of the water for maintenance purposes.

The barrier, which was dogged by industrial disputes in the 1970s, is an engineering marvel – before the age of global positioning satellites, the vast concrete sills were prefabricated and positioned to an accuracy of just a few millimetres between the piers.

The barrier has already proved its worth. It was raised 80 times in its first two decades and the barrier's activation appears to be increasingly common. The principle objective is to shield London from surge tides, a mound of water that is created when low-pressure systems move across the Atlantic Ocean; if such an event were to occur at the same time as a high spring tide (which occurs twice a month) then the relatively shallow North Sea could inundate the Thames Estuary, putting London at risk. Dangerous tidal systems can be identified 36 hours in advance by the Storm Tide Forecasting Service, which monitors sea levels via satellite, land-based centres and data sent from North Sea oil rigs.

The Thames Barrier was built to last until 2030 and the authorities are now considering how to extend the life of this impressive structure. There are even suggestions that a much larger barrier – one that would dwarf the scale of the Thames Barrier – could be built in a location much farther downstream.

project data

- The Thames Barrier stretches 520 metres (1,706 feet) across the River Thames and contains 10 gates – six of which are navigable. When closed, the barrier presents a continuous steel wall to incoming tides.
- The barrier cost nearly £500 million to build.
- Each of the barrier's 10 gates was constructed as a hollow steel structure.
- Construction of the barrier went hand-in-hand with further flood-prevention measures, including raising the heights of river embankments along a 23.5-kilometre (14.6-mile) stretch of the Thames – 18.5 kilometres (11.5 miles) downstream of the barrier, and 5 kilometres (3.1 miles) upstream.
- The Thames Barrier is the world's second largest movable flood barrier. The largest movable barrier, the 9-kilometre (5.6-mile) long Oosterschelkering Barrier, is located in the Netherlands and was opened in 1986.

Left top: The Thames Barrier was designed to admit shipping: of the 10 gates in the barrier, six are navigable.

Left: Located on a straight stretch of the Thames, the flood barrier was built to protect London from sudden surges from the North Sea.

Opposite: Clad in canopies of stainless steel, the hydraulic mechanisms of London's Thames Barrier present a convincing vision of the engineer's attempt to control the forces of nature.

4
5
6
7

ØRESUND BRIDGE/TUNNEL DENMARK TO SWEDEN

The Øresund bridge/tunnel provides a 16.4-kilometre (10.2-mile) link between Denmark and Sweden, representing the first time the countries have been connected since the latter days of the last Ice Age. Having agreed to this audacious project in 1991, the two governments secured a mutually agreed design by the end of 1994 and finally opened the new link in 2000.

The link consists of three principal elements: a 7.8-kilometre (4.8-mile) bridge, a 4-kilometre (2½-mile) access tunnel on the Danish side and a 4-kilometre (2½-mile) long artificial island that connects the tunnel with the bridge. The link is, in fact, the world's longest double-deck road–rail bridge.

It was an incredibly complex venture: crossing the open seas as it does, designers and engineers had to ensure that the link did not interfere with fish migration and bird feeding grounds. Also, the form of the new Peberholm island, created from sand dredged from the seabed to accommodate the tunnel element of the structure, was the subject of considerable refinements to minimize its impact on sea currents. Today, the bridge even contains four nesting boxes for Peregrine falcons.

Work on the project began in September 1993, when ground preparation was started for the road and rail links that would eventually run through the link. Dredging began in October 1995, principally for the tunnel element, which consists of 20 immense concrete tubes laid in a trench cut into the seabed. These prefabricated concrete tubes, each weighing 55,000 tonnes (60,627 tons) and measuring 176 metres (577 feet) in length, were floated out to sea on barges, lowered into place and joined together. During this process one unit actually sprang a leak and filled with water. In spite of this mishap, the Øresund link is a tribute to the advantages of off-site prefabrication: construction elements need not be made on the construction site and quality control is usually better when work is completed under controlled conditions in specialist facilities. Elements for the bridge were even made in Cadiz, Spain. "This being a Scandinavian project, it was built according to the principles of Danish Lego and Swedish Ikea – from a sort of flat-pack, prefabricated tunnel-and-bridge kit," said a BBC report when the link opened.

The tunnel surfaces on the artificial island of Peberholm and the road/rail link rises as a bridge, which continues the rest of the way into Sweden's Malmo. The bridge is formed from three parts – two approach sections and a higher, central,

Opposite: The Øresund link, completed in 2000, forms the first bridge between Sweden and Denmark since the last Ice Age. The pylons at the centre of the bridge are the tallest structures in Sweden.

Below: Drawings of the road/rail bridge, illustrating the composition of the structure – vehicles above, trains below.

project data

- The Øresund bridge/tunnel link was opened on July 1, 2000, and by September 18, 2000 one million cars had already traversed it. Two years after it opened, 10 million cars had passed through the link.
- The tunnel accommodates two lanes of traffic in each direction – a double-track railway and a service tunnel.
- The artificial island of Peberholm is made of material that was dredged from the seabed; a total of 1.6 million cubic metres (56.5 million cubic feet) of stone and 7.5 million cubic metres (264.9 million cubic feet) of sand went into its construction.
- The original design of Peberholm would have slowed down the rate of water flow by 2.3 per cent – a refinement of the design, however, reduced this impact to just 0.5 per cent.
- The link provides the first connection between Denmark and Sweden for 7,000 years, when the Ice Age linked the two countries. The idea of an artificial link was first suggested, however, in the late nineteenth century.

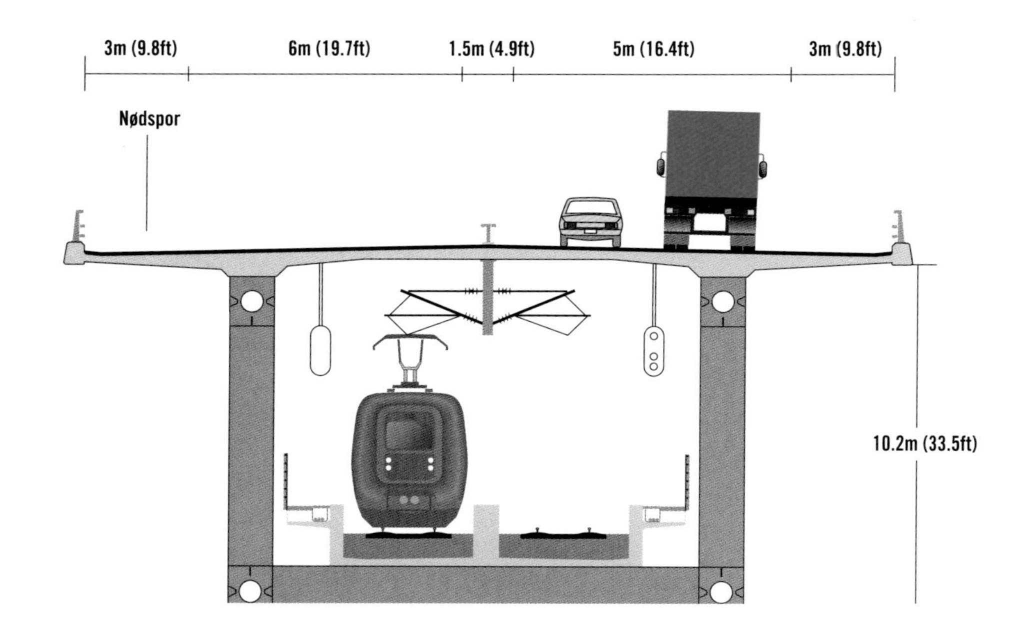

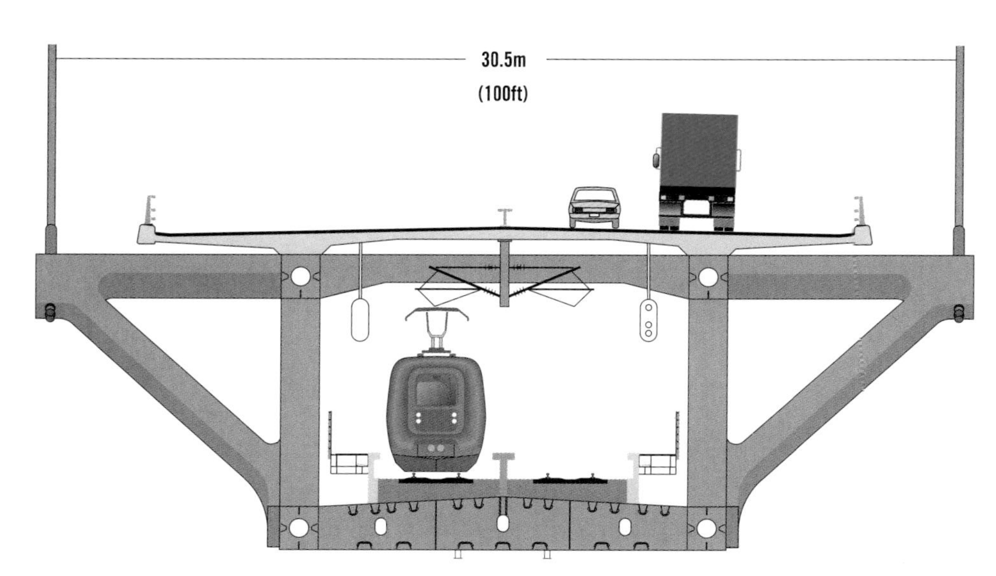

THE BRIDGE ACROSS ØRESUND

The elevated bridge across Øresund has a span of 490m (1,607ft) across the Flinte Channel. Its concrete pylons reach a height of 204m (670ft) above sea level.

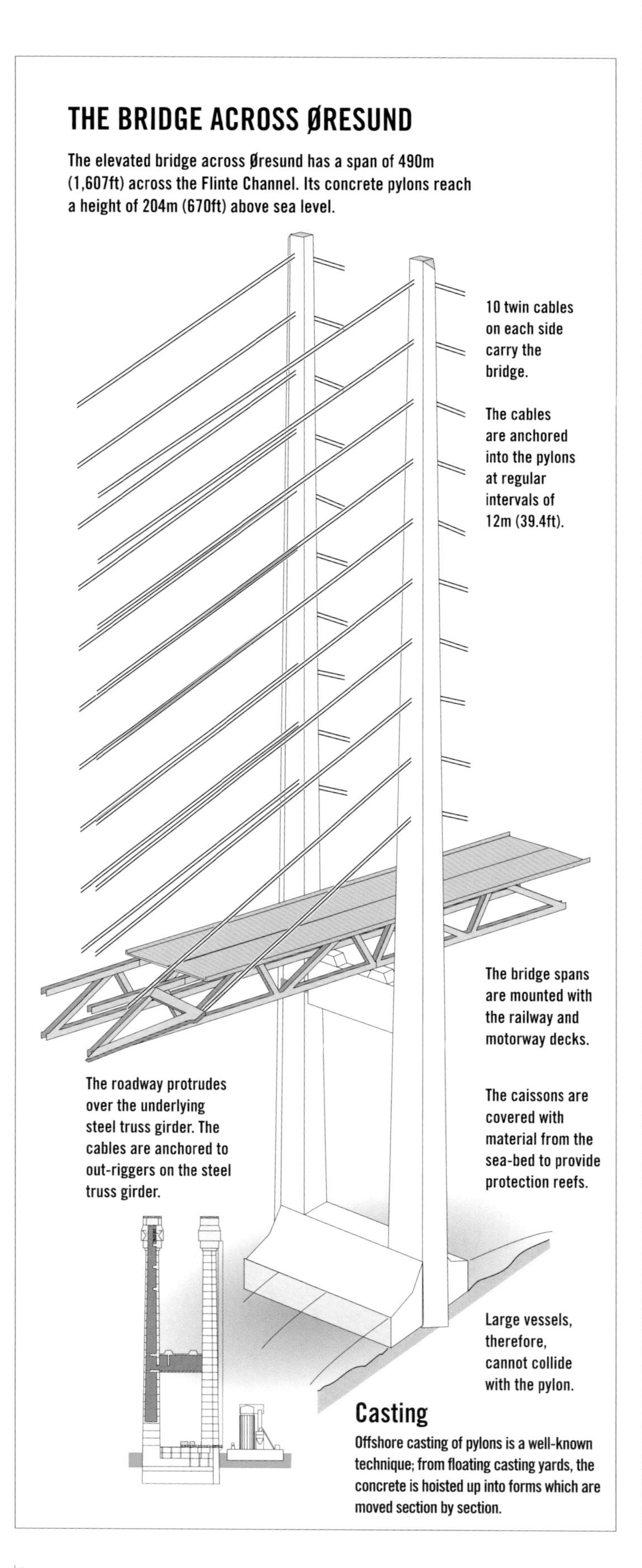

Casting

Offshore casting of pylons is a well-known technique; from floating casting yards, the concrete is hoisted up into forms which are moved section by section.

cable-stayed section that is suspended from a pair of pylons, whose foundations reach 17 metres (56 feet) into the seabed. These pylons, 204 metres (669 feet) in height, are the tallest structures in Sweden and support a 490-metre (1,608-foot) length of the bridge. The rest of the bridge assembly sits on 51 columns (or piers), manoeuvred into place by a giant floating crane, the Svanen.

Given that it was such a vast undertaking, the link was completed in just four years. The road tunnel was actually completed first, and the first car drove from Denmark to the new island in March 1999; the final bridge section was slotted into place in August that year, allowing the railway track to be completed a month later.

The design of the link is intended to minimize its impact both visually and environmentally. As with the Millau Viaduct in France (see page 106) it gently curves, allowing travellers to keep it in view as they cross it. Its slender lines, low approach bridges, black cables and the fact that the railway line is slung beneath the flat road deck, make it a thing of elegance, rather than a crude imposition on the seascape. However, the economics of the scheme are designed to have a far greater impact. A US$2.4 billion construction project, the Øresund link is intended to provide a spur to economic development in the Copenhagen–Malmo region, effectively turning it into a new, single metropolis. The transport systems of both cities are becoming integrated and it has become common for people to live in one country and work in another. Jointly, the region accounts for 20 per cent of the wealth of the two countries, and Malmo is now providing serious competition for the Swedish capital Stockholm. The fact that Copenhagen's international airport lies close to the link is also an important factor in the economic success of the bridge.

Opposite left: Axonometric drawings of the Øresund link's bridge, illustrating the two-deck arrangement – cars run along the top of the bridge, while trains are carried below.

Opposite right: The bridge element of the Øresund link between Denmark and Sweden.

The higher, wider spans of the bridge are supported by steel cables.

Left: This sequence of construction photos shows the erection of the Øresund bridge. The bridge was composed of pre-cast elements that were manufactured off-site and shipped in for assembly.

ØRESUNDSKONSORTIET

The construction of the Øresund link required tremendous cooperation between the governments of Sweden and Denmark. Both countries made environmental sensitivity a strict condition of the project, and the subsequent series of environmental impact assessments proved to be the biggest in Sweden's history. The politicians of both parliaments agreed to the link in principle in August 1991 and a dedicated consortium – Øresundskonsortiet – was formed giving each government a 50 per cent stake in the venture. Øresundskonsortiet was responsible for issuing construction contracts, which went to two other principal consortia: Øresund Tunnel Contractors and Øresund Marine Joint Venture for the bridge. Both contracting groups handed the link over to Øresundskonsortiet in the spring of 2000 and the link was inaugurated on July 1 of that year.

SALGINATOBEL BRIDGE SCHIERS, SWITZERLAND

The Salginatobel Bridge is an icon of twentieth-century engineering and is regarded as a masterpiece by bridge designers. Designed by Swiss engineer Robert Maillart, who was responsible for a number of bridges throughout Switzerland, this sleek and elegant structure crosses the Salgina Gorge at a height of 90 metres (295 feet). It is set in a landscape of outstanding beauty, and one that is hardly conducive to large-scale constructions; the bridge is a testament to the skill and determination of the people who built it.

The bridge was commissioned in 1928 and was selected from 19 competition entries simply because it was the cheapest option. The key to its price was in using reinforced concrete (a new and expensive material) very sparingly. This minimal use of concrete was possible because of Maillart's development of the "hollow-box girder, three hinged arch" structure. A hollow box is literally that – a structural element comprising thin vertical and horizontal walls, leaving a hollow space within, that is strong enough to carry loads. The three-hinged arch is an arch that is pinned at three places – at either end and at the top (the arch's "crown"). At the Salginatobel Bridge, the road deck forms the top element of the hollow-box girder and the crown hinge.

The bridge would not have been possible, however, if it were not for the scaffolding/formwork expertise of Richard Coray, which added 45,000 Swiss Francs (CHF) to the 135,000 CHF cost of the bridge. The scaffold was erected by just six construction workers using 700 cubic metres (24,720 cubic feet) of timber; this temporary structure had its own elegance and was perfectly balanced and symmetrical, allowing the application of concrete to be made quickly and accurately. In fact, the pouring of the concrete (which was mixed by hand and transported by wheelbarrow) took just three months. The most exacting job was the casting of the plate for the thin arch, which was completed in 40 hours. The scaffolding was dismantled in August 1930.

The bridge came quickly to international attention – ironically so, as the client had not been that impressed with the spindly image of the structure and had voted for Maillart's design on price alone. In 1991 the American Society of Civil Engineers (the ASCE) declared the Salginatobel Bridge a World Monument. More recently, the British magazine *Bridge – Design and Engineering* voted this structure the most beautiful bridge of the twentieth century.

Robert Maillart had a chequered career. Eminently successful in the early twentieth century, the engineer set up his own design and construction company in 1902 and built structures in Spain, Finland, Egypt and Russia, until the Russian Revolution in 1917 created a serious reversal of fortune. Maillart also entered bridge competitions which he didn't win – at the time concrete was generally used to replicate the heavy form of masonry bridges and Maillart's refined and graceful designs, although beautiful, did not always look convincing. Interestingly, the ASCE believes that these sleek and daring forms were not the product of numerical calculation but were, instead, derived from an engineer's intuition: "Rather than growing out of rigorous mathematical analysis, Maillart's stunning designs emerged from his intuitive understanding of concrete's structural possibilities and of the efficient use of materials. It was Maillart's astute perception of cost, not the ingenuity displayed in his designs, that convinced often sceptical officials to implement his plans."

The Salginatobel Bridge is Maillart's best-known structure. Other notable Swiss bridges by him include the Stauffacher Bridge (1899), The Zuoz Bridge (1901) and the Tavanasa Bridge (1906).

CONCRETE

Concrete is not a new building material. A form was used by the Romans (most impressively in the roof of Rome's Pantheon), yet it was not until the early twentieth century that it began to be used widely in construction.

Made principally of three elements (cement, water and aggregate – such as sand and stones) concrete becomes solid due to the process of hydration, a chemical reaction between the cement and water which causes hardening. Strangely, the principles behind concrete are still not fully understood, and nature has made some concretes (such as Hertfordshire Pudding Stone in England) that are far more durable than anything made artificially. Research is ongoing, however, and concrete is being made available with different additives to give it particular properties.

The biggest problem with concrete is its porosity, and particular effort has been put into reducing this. Porosity mean that water can creep into the fabric of the concrete and expand when frozen, causing cracking. For reinforced concrete (which contains iron or steel rods) this is particularly problematic, as the water can rust the very items that are meant to strengthen it. Chemicals are now being added to reduce this problem.

Water can also be trapped within concrete after it hardens. In a fire, this water can turn into steam, making the concrete explode. Researchers have experimented with including microscopic plastic threads in the mix; these melt under heat and create channels for the steam to escape without causing structural damage.

project data

- **The Salginatobel Bridge is a hollow-box girder construction configured as a "three-hinged arch".**
- **Designed by Swiss engineer Robert Maillart, the bridge was made possible by the scaffolding ingenuity of Richard Coray. The scaffolding is considered to have been an artwork in its own right.**
- **The bridge has a total length of 132.3 metres (434 feet), while the arch spans 90 metres (295 feet).**
- **The roadway is 3.5 metres (11.5 feet) wide, and slopes by 3 degrees (which is a drop of nearly 4 metres/13 feet).**
- **Made from reinforced concrete, the bridge was constructed in 1929/30 and restored in 1997/98.**
- **"Maillart's most elegant structures are simply engineering structures par excellence," wrote David P. Billington, of Princeton University's Department of Civil Engineering.**

Opposite: The concrete structure of Switzerland's Salginatobel Bridge actually enhances its rugged setting. Completed in 1930, the bridge has been a source of inspiration for engineers ever since.

PANAMA CANAL ISTHMUS OF PANAMA, CENTRAL AMERICA

In October 2006 Panamanians voted in a national referendum to expand the Panama Canal. Expansion will build a new lane for shipping traffic along the canal by creating an extra set of locks at each end, so doubling capacity and allowing today's wider ships to use the continent-splitting waterway.

In light of today's environmentally sensitive society, new water-saving basins are to be constructed next to the locks to reuse 60 per cent of the water that pours through them during each opening for a ship's passage. This eliminates the need to build dams to hold water "stores" and flood large areas along the canal's watershed. The work is estimated to cost US$5.25 billion.

These plans are the latest chapter in a story that dates back to the sixteenth century. Charles V of Spain was one of the first to consider the potential of a canal across Panama, following reports from explorers of the riches to be found in Peru, Ecuador and Asia. Charles' advisors suggested that by creating a shipping channel, trips would be made much shorter. A survey of the isthmus was ordered in 1534 and a working plan for a canal was duly drawn up, but the project was shelved as Charles V fought wars in Europe.

Next it was the turn of the Spanish. In 1819 the government formally authorized the construction of a canal similar to that planned by Charles V nearly 300 years before. Again, surveys were made and an international company was formed, but this attempt also foundered and it wasn't until 1880, when Ferdinand Marie de Lesseps, the builder of the Suez Canal, put forward new proposals that a canal really looked possible.

Below: The Miraflores Locks, in the foreground, are the first set of locks to be encountered by ships travelling from the Pacific to the Atlantic oceans.

Right: A ship sails through one of the channels within the lakes that are connected by the man-made waterways and locks of the Panama Canal.

Above: Ships seem diminished in size by the lock, but look to the left bank (middle of picture) to see a workers' cabin for a sense of scale.

Left: A major new suspension bridge, the Puente Centenario (Centennial Bridge), spans the Panama Canal providing a new six-lane route. The only other bridge is the famous Puente de las Americas (Bridge of the Americans), built in 1962.

Opposite: Construction of the massive metal lock gates and reinforced concrete lock basins early in the twentieth century.

As de Lesseps touted his flat sea-level canal plan, the US Congress created the Isthmian Canal Commission to explore the potential of a shipping route through Central America. De Lesseps beat them to it, however, and work began on the mammoth task of excavating the millions of tonnes of earth required to forge a sea-level canal across Panama.

The length of the canal that was actually built is approximately 82 kilometres (51 miles). Travelling from the Atlantic, ships sail through a 11-kilometre (7-mile) dredged channel in Limón Bay, then travel 18.5 kilometres (11½ miles) to the Gatun Locks. This series of three locks raise ships 26 metres (85 feet) to Gatun Lake, before they sail carefully south for 51.5 kilometres (32 miles) through a channel dredged into the bottom of Gatun Lake to Gamboa, where the Culebra Cut begins. This channel through the cut is 13 kilometres (8 miles) long and 241 kilometres (150 metres) wide. At its end are a second set of locks – the Pedro Miguel Locks: these lower ships some 9.4 metres (31 feet) to an expansive lake, where they sail to the final Miraflores Locks and drop the final 16 metres

project data

- It is estimated that over 80,000 people took part in the construction and that over 25,000 lives were lost in total in both French and American efforts.
- Until Lake Mead was formed by the building of the Hoover Dam, Gatun Lake was the largest artificial body of water in the world.
- A ship travelling from New York to San Francisco can save 12,689 kilometres (7,885 miles) by using the Panama Canal instead of going around South America.
- 4,535 tonnes (5,000 tons) of dynamite were used in each year of construction to blast rock.
- The Gatun Locks alone used 1.53 million cubic metres (54.03 million cubic feet) of concrete in their construction.
- It has a total span of 126 metres (413 feet) and will open in just four and a half minutes.
- It takes around nine hours to travel the length of the 82-kilometre (51-mile) canal. However, the Hydrofoil Pegasus of the United States Navy made the fastest transit, completing it in 2 hours and 41 minutes.
- 196.85 million litres (52 million gallons) of water are used during every ship's passage through the canal.
- The cargo ship Ancon was the first vessel to transit the canal on August 15, 1914.

(52½ feet) to sea level, at the canal's Pacific terminus in the bay of Panama. The journey takes around nine hours.

These sets of locks are what make the canal a workable proposition, but initially de Lesseps went ahead with his sea-level plan. Between 1881 and 1888, de Lesseps' company toiled and then from 1904 to 1914 the Americans took over and attempted to complete the flat canal design. However, unforeseen tidal differences between the Pacific and Atlantic and the vast amount of spoil that needed to be moved made work virtually impossible.

When, in 1899, the French attempt was deemed a failure, operatives had excavated 59.75 million cubic metres (2.11 billion cubic feet) of spoil, including 14.26 million cubic metres (503.58 million cubic feet) from the Culebra Cut. The Americans moved into what looked a promising proposition, with a lot of work already done. Steam shovels set to excavating the Culebra Cut on November 11, 1904, and by December 1905 there were 2,600 men at work on that stretch of the canal alone. During this time engineers made the decision that the sea-level canal was not going to work and in June 1906 they announced plans to build a stepped canal with locks along its route.

Excavations continued along all sections of the canal. Work in the Culebra Cut produced 512,500 cubic metres (18.1 million cubic feet) of spoil in one three-month period at the start of 1907, with the help of 100 Bucyrus steam shovels, each capable of excavating approximately 920 cubic metres (32,490 cubic feet) in an eight-hour day and a workforce that now totalled 39,000. Spoil was taken away in over 4,000 wagons pulled by 160 steam locomotives.

As in many epic engineering projects of the time, construction didn't always go to plan, however. The first major mud slide occurred in 1907 at Cucaracha. Without warning, approximately 382,000 cubic metres (13.49 million cubic feet) of clay slid en masse more than 4 metres (13 feet) in 24 hours, seriously setting back work efforts. Many more slides were to follow, and deaths were a common occurrence, too. It is estimated that as many as 30,000 lives were lost during the 34 years it took to build the canal.

In the completed and working Panama Canal, there are now two parallel sets of locks at Gatun, each consisting of three flights. Built using a total of 1.53 million cubic metres (54.03 million cubic feet) of concrete, each lock is 33 metres (108 feet) wide and 300 metres (984 feet) long, with the walls ranging in thickness from 15 metres (49 feet) at the base to 3 metres (10 feet) at the top. The steel lock gates are 2 metres (6½ feet) thick, 19 5 metres (64 feet) in length and stand 20 metres (66 feet) high. The smallest set of locks is at Pedro Miguel: it has one flight, while the Miraflores Locks have two flights.

Spoil from the canal excavation was reused for the building of the Gatun Dam. This dam holds back the flow of the Chagres River, creating the Gatun Lake. The dam itself is 2.5 kilometres (1.6 miles) in length and is nearly 800 metres (½ mile) wide at its base. It contains almost one tenth of the entire excavation spoil from the canal project – some 16.9 million cubic metres (596.82 million cubic feet) of rock and clay. The dam was constructed by building two walls along its length from Culebra Cut stone, which were then filled out and built up with clay. (Clay is a good damn building material as it is relatively impervious and gradually dries and hardens into a solid mass almost equal to concrete in its water-resistant properties.)

The dams at Pedro Miguel and Miraflores are small in comparison to Gatun. Their foundations are on solid rock and are subjected to a head of water of only 12 metres (39 feet), whereas the Gatun Dam holds back a 24-metre (79-foot) head. Pedro Miguel Dam is an earth construction approximately 300 metres (984 feet) in length with a concrete core wall. At Miraflores there are two dams – one earth and one concrete – forming a small lake with an area of about 5 square kilometres (2 square miles). One of the dams is constructed of earth and is 210 metres (689 feet) long.

In a bid to be more sustainable, the dam at Gatun generates electricity to run all of the motors that operate on the canal locks, as well as the trains that tow the ships through sections of it. No mechanical force is required to adjust the water level between the locks. However, as the lock operates, water flows into the locks from the lakes or out to the sea-level channels. This isn't very environmentally economical and the canal currently relies on the plentiful rainfall of the area to compensate for the loss of the 196.85 million litres (52 million gallons) of fresh water that are consumed during each crossing.

MILLENNIUM BRIDGE LONDON, UK

When it opened in June 2000, London's Millennium Bridge quickly proved to be an engineering marvel and a public relations disaster. The bridge, conceived as a "blade of light", is a slender and very low-profile suspension bridge that reaches 325 metres (1,066 feet) over the River Thames. Linking the tourist sites of St Paul's Cathedral on the north side of the Thames with the Tate Modern art gallery to the south, the bridge is a crucial part of the redevelopment of London's riverside and was designed to maximize views while minimizing its impact on the cityscape.

The bridge is carried by eight cables (two sets of four), which run from anchor points on the riverbanks via two Y-shaped piers (conceived as "tapering ellipses" in plan) set into the water. Steel sections, on which the 4-metre (13-foot) wide aluminium deck is set, run between the sets of cables every 8 metres (26 feet). It is an elegant and daring structure, and attracted between 80,000 and 100,000 people on its opening day – crowds large enough to cause the bridge to behave in unexpected ways.

Ordinarily, suspension bridges are characterized by tall towers and gracefully drooping cables (such as the Golden Gate Bridge on page 132). The Millennium Bridge, however, has a much shallower profile than most suspension bridges, and its cables are in greater tension than is usual. In fact, the eight cables never rise more than 2.3 metres (7.5 feet) above the deck of the bridge; this rise is around six times shallower than would normally be expected for a bridge of this type and span. Designed by a team comprising architects Foster and Partners, engineers Arup and sculptor Sir Anthony Caro, this concept pushed bridge engineering to a new level. Unfortunately, the design team paid a heavy price for their innovation.

Once opened, the heavy crowds caused the bridge to sway uncomfortably and the decision was taken to close it until a solution could be found. Unfortunately, although the symptom was plain to see (a highly noticeable wobble), the cure was far from obvious. The engineers quickly concluded that the movement was caused by a phenomenon known as "synchronous lateral excitation", which meant that the natural lateral movement of the bridge was emphasized by large numbers of people falling into step to compensate for this movement. Historically, soldiers have been told to break step (i.e. not march in time) when crossing bridges to even out the impact of their presence. Pedestrians on the Millennium Bridge, however, were unconsciously falling into step and turning a slight movement into one that was both visible and even frightening.

"The movement at the Millennium Bridge was caused by a substantial lateral loading effect which appears to rise in the following way," said a report compiled by Arup for the Royal Academy of Engineering. "Chance footfall correlation, combined with the synchronisation that occurs naturally within a crowd, may cause the bridge to start to sway horizontally. If the sway is perceptible, a further effect can start to take hold. It becomes more comfortable for the pedestrians to walk in synchronisation with the swaying of the bridge. The pedestrians find this makes their interaction with the movement of the bridge more predictable and helps them maintain their lateral balance. This instinctive behaviour ensures that the footfall forces are applied at the resonant frequency of the bridge and with a phase such as to increase the motion of the bridge. As the amplitude of the motion increases, the lateral force imparted by individuals increases, as does the degree of correlation between individuals."

The phenomenon was not new – just unexpected. Essentially, the engineers had to find a way of stopping the bridge from moving, therefore removing the need for pedestrians to react to the motion. The answer lay in the retrospective

Below: A plan and elevation of London's Millennium Bridge, which stretches over the Thames between Tate Modern and St Paul's Cathedral, illustrating the structure's ultra-low suspension design.

Opposite: Now a popular London landmark, the bridge made headlines when it wobbled dangerously after opening in 2000. It was closed just two days after opening and reopened in 2002.

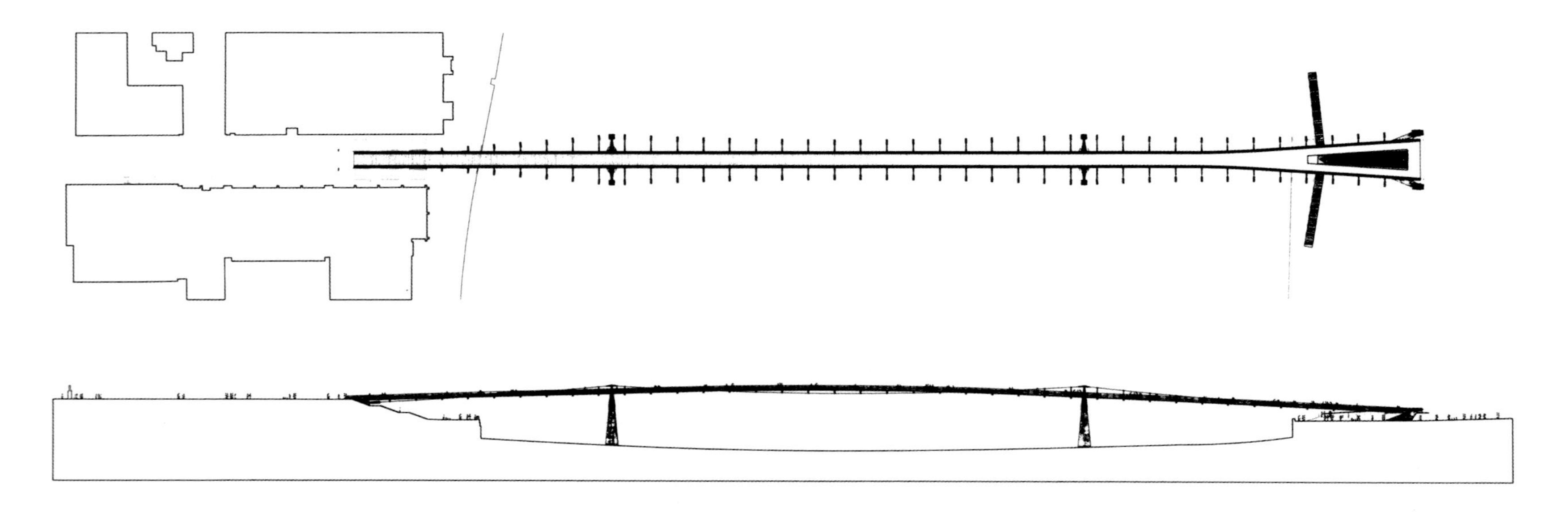

Opposite: The southern end of the bridge splits before forcing pedestrians to double back on themselves to reach ground level. The northern end of the bridge finishes more conventionally.

Below: Conceived as a "blade of light", the Millennium Bridge adds a distinctive element of contemporary swagger to a historic stretch of the River Thames.

Below right: An elevation of one of the bridge's concrete pylons, which appear as mammoth structures compared with the delicate, metal-clad deck. The pylons can survive the impact of a Thames barge.

project data

- Construction on the Millennium Bridge began in late 1998 and it opened on June 10, 2000, only to close on June 12, after it swayed too much when being crossed by large numbers of people.
- The pedestrian bridge reopened in February 2002, after dampers were fitted to reduce the bridge's movement. Questions have often been asked as to who bore the cost of these multimillion pound changes (the design team or the London taxpayer) but this remains a closely guarded secret.
- The bridge is configured in three stages, an 81-metre (266-foot) north span, the 144-metre (472-foot) central span and the 108-metre 354-foot) southern span.
- The abutments to which the eight cables are attached consist of reinforced-concrete masses tied into the ground by 2.1-metre (7-foot) diameter concrete piles (12 on the north bank, 16 on the south bank).

fitting of dampers – mechanisms that respond to, and compensate for, movement. The design issue, however, was fitting a large number of dampers without reducing the sleek lines of the bridge. Most of the dampers (designed to soak up both lateral and vertical movement) were eventually installed beneath the deck of the bridge and are, in effect, invisible to the casual observer. The bridge was reopened in February 2002, after first being tested by 800 Arup staff and then by 2,000 people drawn from local schools and businesses. The 95 dampers worked and the bridge had lost its wobble.

The point of this tale is that cutting-edge engineering is not always risk free. The bridge was designed to remain aerodynamically stable in freak winds and its concrete piers were built to withstand the impact of a large river barge (many of which still ply the Thames), but the effect of "synchronous lateral excitation" was never anticipated. Indeed, during the furore that accompanied the closure, Arup declared that it was "embarrassed but not ashamed" and the research published by the firm eventually won it an award from the Institution of Structural Engineers. In fact, the Millennium Bridge is now a much-loved London landmark and the circumstances of its closure will no doubt become a historical footnote over time.

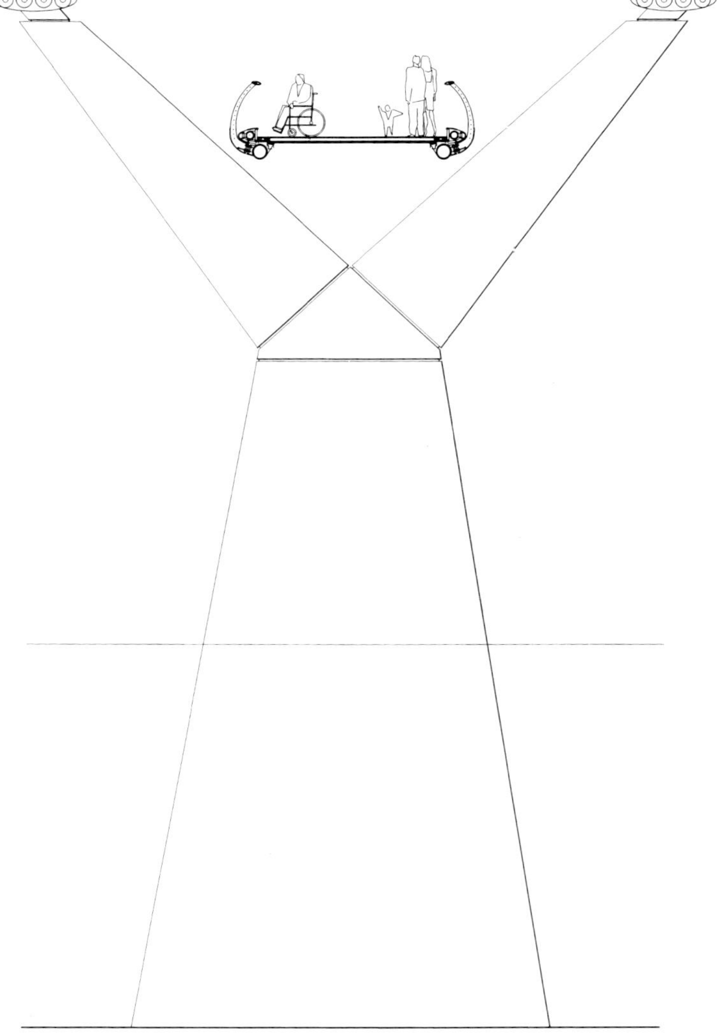

GOLDEN GATE BRIDGE SAN FRANCISCO, USA

project data

- The Golden Gate Bridge is 2.7 kilometres (1.7 miles) long and 27 metres (89 feet) wide.
- The bridge clears high water by 67 metres (220 feet).
- The summits of the towers are 152 metres (499 feet) above the roadway, and 227 metres (909 feet) above the water.
- The cables, which support the deck of the bridge, put a load of 56,000 tonnes (61,500 tons) on each tower.
- The main towers are constructed from 40,200 tonnes (44,000 tons) of steel; the suspended structure embodies 21,772 tonnes (24,000 tons) of steel.
- The bridge cost US$35 million to build and was completed in May 1937.

Left: One of the most famous and iconic bridges in the world, the Golden Gate Bridge needed the approval of the US War Department, who needed to be convinced that warships could pass beneath.

The Golden Gate Bridge spans the Golden Gate Strait, which separates the city of San Francisco from the county of Marin. It s a suspension-bridge structure measuring 2.7 kilometres (1.7 miles) in length and was constructed between January 1933 and May 1937, although the idea of spanning the strait began as early as 1872. Then, during the First World War, a local newspaper editor began to campaign seriously on the issue, gaining the support of San Francisco engineer Michael O'Shaughnessy, who made his own enquiries into the possibility of such a venture. O'Shaughnessy identified Joseph Baermann Strauss, a seasoned bridge engineer, and got him to submit sketches and a cost estimate of US$17 million in 1921.

The issue soon became hugely political and many years were spent raising funds, seeking Federal approval and setting up a new city district to administer the project. Crucially, the United States War Department needed to be convinced that the bridge would not interfere with naval shipping. By 1930, in spite of the Depression, local finance was raised (Federal funds being unavailable) and construction contracts were issued towards the end of 1932. The design was for a suspension of immense proportions for its day: a pair of towers, each weighing 40,200 tonnes (44,000 tons) and standing 227 metres (745 feet) above the water level, would support a pair of cables 91 centimetres (3 feet) in diameter.

To the credit of Strauss, who had eventually been appointed Chief Engineer, safety standards at the construction site were the most rigorous ever put in place for a project of its type. For the first time, protective head-gear was made mandatory and workers were issued with glare-free goggles and cream to help protect their skin against the harsh wind. A safety net was also strung beneath the emerging bridge, which saved the lives of 19 men (they became known as the "Half-Way-to-Hell Club"), who would otherwise have fallen to their deaths. Ordinarily, one worker would be killed for every US$1million spent on a construction project of this nature, but just one man had died by February 1937, and then, tragically, 10 men, whose scaffolding assembly collapsed, actually tore right through the net to their deaths.

The bridge depends on its two massive towers, from which it is suspended, for its structural integrity and strength. These towers sit on "legs" that are 10 by 16 metres (33 by 54 feet) in area and are topped by cables, which pass over them to be anchored at either end of the strait. The construction of the cables was a feat in itself: taking just over six months to "spin", each cable consists of 61 strands, each of which is composed of hundreds of individual wires. In each cable there are more than 27,000 individual galvanized wires. Suspended from these gigantic cables are a series of vertical suspension cables, which carry the weight of the bridge's deck. Today, the deck of the bridge weighs 139,791 tonnes (154,093 tons), which is 11,158 tonnes (12,300 tons) less than the original deck: this is because it was resurfaced in 1986 with stronger, lighter materials (largely replacing concrete with steel).

One of the features of a suspension bridge is that it can move and flex according to the loads it carries and the strength of the wind. The Golden

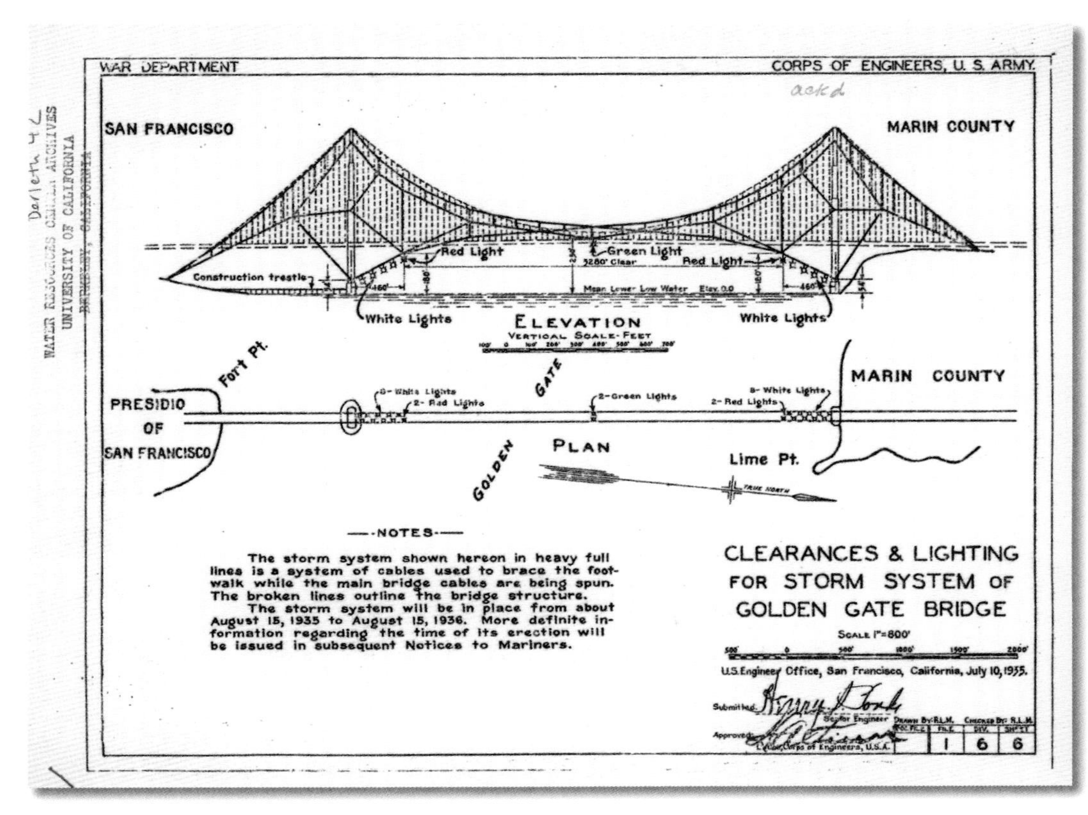

Opposite: The Art Deco lines of the bridge were added by architects Irving and Gertrude Morrow, giving the structure a degree of elegance and refinement that is unexpected in a construction of such magnitude.

Above: An elevation and plan of the Golden Gate Bridge showing the proposed details of its storm system.

Right top: Completed in the 1930s, the Golden Gate Bridge is one of a number of US mega-projects which define the era. The Hoover Dam (see page 282) is another prime example.

Right bottom: The use of "international orange" paint on the Golden Gate Bridge seems to suggest that the structure's size and beautiful proportions are not sufficient to draw attention to it!

Gate Bridge, built in an area of high winds that are often channelled between the banks of the strait, can deflect upward, downward and laterally, depending on loading and temperature. If loads such as traffic are concentrated in the middle of the bridge, the central span can deflect downwards by as much as 3.3 metres (10.8 feet); if, on the other hand, loads are concentrated on the edges of the bridge leaving the central span empty, it can deflect upwards by 1.77 metres (5.8 feet). Sustained and strong wind loads could even cause the bridge to sway sideways by up to 8.4 metres (27.6 feet).

Part of the achievement with this bridge is also architectural. The commissioning of architects Irving and Gertrude Morrow refined the aesthetics of the bridge to make it a sleeker, sharper, more refined endeavour. It was the Morrows' Art Deco approach that caused the towers to taper slightly toward their summits, exaggerating their already immense height. They also simplified the pedestrian railings, designed the lighting scheme and added subtle steel "ribbing" to catch the sunlight and enhance the sharpness of the entire structure. A crucial element of the lighting scheme was to vary its intensity, reducing the power of the lights as the towers recede from view, emphasizing their height by creating the illusion that they simply disappear into the night sky. Budget constraints caused the scheme to be put on ice, but a US$1.2 million lighting project enabled it to be installed 50 years later.

The bridge is painted in "International Orange", a colour that is deemed to be highly visible in foggy conditions but also one that the architects considered would best emphasize the qualities of the structure (as opposed to the more usual steel grey). International Orange is a colour that can easily be replicated by following the CMYK colour system: cyan 0 per cent; magenta 69 per cent; yellow 100 per cent; black 6 per cent. Whatever the colour, the bridge needs a good coat of paint to protect it from the salty conditions of the air, which is highly corrosive. After being painted in 1937, it needed to be touched up on an occasional basis, but the original paint was not replaced until 1968, and then again in the 1990s.

In 1993 the Society of American Registered Architects gave the bridge its "Distinguished Building Award", the first time the award had gone to a structure rather than a building. And in 1994 the bridge was named as one of the "Seven Wonders of the Modern World" by the American Society of Civil Engineers.

03
VOL
UME

SIZE isn't everything but in this chapter it is the defining factor. The ability to encompass large volumes of space is not new: ancient cathedrals and temples are testament to our past achievements. However, as the twentieth century progressed, engineers came to the fore with new techniques and material advances that allowed them to stretch the realms of possibility, creating gigantic new buildings with structural designs never seen before. Advances including the invention of pre-stressed concrete (1916–18) and the geodesic dome (1922) presented new opportunities for building large, enclosed spaces without the need for a forest of supporting columns. More recent buildings such as London's Millennium Dome and Cornwall's Eden Project show that engineers still strive to push boundaries further. And there are no signs of them stopping.

FIAT FACTORY TURIN, ITALY

Located in the Lingotto district of Turin, Italy, the most famous of Fiat's car-manufacturing factories was built between 1915 and 1921, although the car production plant was installed later. The first cars rolled off the production line and up to the factory's rooftop test track in 1923. They had been built on what was the most advanced factory in the world, on an assembly line that boasted to being Europe's longest. Today, the building has been reinvented as a mixed-use venue that includes an exhibition and conference centre, a concert hall, shops, commercial work outlets and a hotel.

The factory was designed by naval architect and engineer Giacomo Mattè-Trucco. Although he did not go on to design any other buildings of note, in the Fiat factory Mattè-Trucco created a building that is widely recognized as a pioneering work in reinforced-concrete architecture and a structure that changed the way architects thought about and approached industrial design and concrete-construction techniques.

The original factory building consisted of a pair of parallel five-storey reinforced concrete facades, joined by reinforced-concrete beams and columns. Service towers, containing stairwells, toilets and the like, thrust up like squat columns between the outer walls, and four courtyards allowed light to flow into the building's interior. At each end, over 500 metres (1,640 feet) apart were the automobile ramps: these enabled vehicles to be driven up and down from the roof.

In addition to the main factory, there was also an administration block and, beyond the southern-most of the ramps, a vast single-storied press shop, where steel panels for all of Fiat's family of vehicles were formed in huge shaped presses.

The main factory was longer than an ocean liner. Over 6,000 workers were employed on its five floors that equated to 400,000 square metres (4.3 million square feet) of floor space. The production line was arranged over these floors in such a way that vehicles were built and tested, finished and painted as they moved upwards through the building. Maintenance and motor testing happened on the ground floor; engine machining and body assembly took place on the first floor; the second floor housed a gear box and differential steering shop; whilst spraying, upholstering, suspension and differential steering checks took place on the third floor level; lorry production on the fourth; and outdoor vehicle testing on the external rooftop test track.

The factory was of an unprecedented size for its time. It was planned large enough for executives to be able to actually drive around the building

Right: An aerial view of the gigantic Fiat factory in Turin. The massive rectangular building featured a test track on its roof and Europe's largest production line within its walls.

Opposite top, middle top and middle bottom: Three views of vehicles driving around the rooftop test track, including a view of the inclined corners that enabled high-speed testing.

Opposite bottom: The engine construction production line housed within the Fiat factory was one of the most advanced of its time.

Left: A view from one end of the rooftop test track. Light was allowed down into the centre of the building via the atrium at its centre. This was interspersed with lift and stair cores, which spanned the gap between the track.

Opposite: The intricate design of the reinforced concrete ramps within the building. These allowed vehicles to be driven from top to bottom and created a dramatic architectural statement within the factory.

and view all of the production processes without ever stepping out of their cars. Not even McDonald's has taken the drive-in principle further! From an engineering standpoint, however, the most remarkable innovation of Mattè-Trucco's design was the inclusion of the helicoidal car ramps at either end of the factory block. No factory had ever included this type of grandiose yet functional element and none have done so since. Braced by reinforced concrete ribs, the ramps led upwards to the rooftop test track, with off-shoots onto each of the factory floors. The test track was a reinforced-concrete speedway some 2.4 kilometres (1.5 miles) long and 24.4 metres (80 feet) wide. It was the building's crowning glory, situated at over 21 metres (69 feet) above ground, with banked corners that rose 4.5 metres in 16.8 metres (15 feet in 55 feet) to create a steep and fast test circuit.

Like any machine, Mattè-Trucco's functionalist factory, so tailored to a particular mode of manufacture, had a limited life. Car assembly changed during the 1970s: robots replaced manpower. Linear assembly lines, such as this one, were replaced by out-of-house manufacture; components began to be made independently, rather than under one roof. The Turin factory, with its long narrow floors and constant 6-by-6-metre (20-by-20-foot) concrete column grid, didn't work well with the new methods and its design was not flexible enough to allow it to be adapted: thus it became obsolete.

However, such an iconic building was not demolished or left to crumble. Fiat resolved to convert it into a multi-functional resource for Turin and its region. Architectural practice Renzo Piano Building Workshop (RPBW) was chosen to redevelop the factory into a centre of technological innovation, entrepreneurial initiative and cultural creativity.

Today, the first floor is the main public level, reached by escalators and lifts set in openings carved in the old factory's concrete frame. This level is a shopping centre, complete with arcades and cafés, the like of which Italy is renowned for. Located below, on the ground floor, are exhibition facilities, auditoria, reception facilities and business units, while the upper levels have been redesigned as a business centre, a four-star hotel and Turin University's science faculty.

A major concert and congress hall some 48 metres (157 feet) long by 24 metres (79 feet) wide and 20 metres (66 feet) high has been excavated below ground, and, a jewel-like conference room, quite unlike any other, crowns the highest point at roof level. This glazed bubble is held aloft on huge beams that cantilever over a court from the top of an old service tower, and is counterbalanced by a cantilevered helipad.

This new incarnation has breathed new life into the old factory. However, even though it was designed to be purely functional, the factory has always attracted attention. Its striking design took early twentieth-century architecture by storm. On the factory's completion, the Futurist school of architects claimed that it was the first built example of a new school of design called, rather predictably, "Futurism".

Although Mattè-Trucco was flattered by the attention, he didn't see himself as a Futurist, more as a level-headed, if slightly adventurous, structural engineer. The factory design had been influenced by Mattè-Trucco's admiration of architect Albert Kahn's designs and, most importantly, by the words of his client Giovanni Agnelli, whose strict instructions were: "You must have no aesthetic concerns. That's how you must work for industry." Mattè-Trucco did not question his Fiat boss. The result, however, was a masterpiece, a building that was all but mythical before it was completed.

Famous Modernist architect, Le Corbusier, took inspiration from the rooftop test track for his Unité d'Habitation apartment block built in Marseilles in 1952, which features a running track around the perimeter of the apartment block. Italian architects considered Turin's Fiat Factory one of the few industrial buildings in Italy possessing architectural value. And, although Mattè-Trucco was never personally involved in the Rationalist movement, the Fiat building figured prominently in the first Esposizione dell'Architettura Razionale (Exhibition of Rationalist Architecture) in Rome in 1928.

project data

- **The Turin Fiat Factory had a 2.4-kilometre (1.5-mile) racetrack on its roof, which was used to test new vehicle models before they left the factory.**
- **The factory was huge in scale and boasted the longest production line in Europe, which stretched over five floors and culminated in the rooftop test track.**
- **It had 400,000 square metres (4.3 million square feet) of floor space on which 6,000 employees toiled.**
- **The newly converted factory has multiple facilities, including a shopping mall, hotel, conference centre, start-up business units and a concert hall.**
- **At roof level, an onion-shaped, blue-glass conference room teeters next to a landing pad for helicopters.**
- **The Fiat name is an acronym for Fabbrica Italiana Automobili Torino (Italian Car Factory of Turin).**

EDEN PROJECT CORNWALL, UK

The Eden Project is the culmination of an idea by entrepreneur Tim Smit, who, having established a reputation for large-scale garden management with his Lost Gardens of Heligan project in Cornwall, fought for a centre to preserve, study and showcase the plant life of different world regions. Having identified a near-exhausted china clay pit as the site for the venture, Smit and his assembled team of botanists and businessmen identified Nicholas Grimshaw and Partners as the project architects.

Grimshaw is a high-tech designer like other British architects Richard Rogers and Norman Foster – known for creating architecture where structure is ostentatiously on show and a virtue is made of the technical brilliance that makes complex buildings function. Having made his name with the sinuous curves of the Waterloo International railway station in London, Grimshaw was appointed by the Eden Project team to develop a design for a series of vast "biomes" which could recreate tropical and Mediterranean conditions.

The biomes are, in fact, Phase Two of the project. Phase One involved the building of a visitors' centre at the top of the site, constructed from "rammed earth" protected by a large overhanging roof. The design and construction of the two biomes (each composed of four interlinked domes) was more difficult. Part of the difficulty was caused by the fact that mining was still continuing when designs began to evolve, so the topography of the site was subject to considerable alterations. Also, the brief for the project required large, uninterrupted spans to accommodate large trees and to create the best impression of a single climatic environment for visitors. The domes, as built, range in size from 18–65 metres (59–213 feet) in radius; they took two and a half years to build and opened in March 2001 as one of Britain's millennium projects.

The design – which evolved by swapping a three-dimensional digital model between architects, engineers and contractors – employs the principles developed by American architect Buckminster Fuller for enclosing spaces within geodesic domes (see page 182). "It represents the perfect fulfilment of Buckminster Fuller's vision of the maximum enclosed volume within the minimal surface area," said the architects.

project data

- The Eden Project, which opened on March 17, 2001, is located near St Austell in Cornwall, England.
- Built on a 15-hectare (37-acre) site, the two "biomes" cover a total of 2.2 hectares (5.4 acres).
- Composed of two pairs of four inter-linked domes, the two biomes are connected by a central entrance building.
- The domes are enclosed with Ethylene TetrafluoroEthylene (ETFE) cushions, a substance which has all the performance characteristics of glass but which is 99 per cent lighter. ETFE is also strong, anti-static and recyclable.
- The humidity within the domes is created by reusing rainwater.

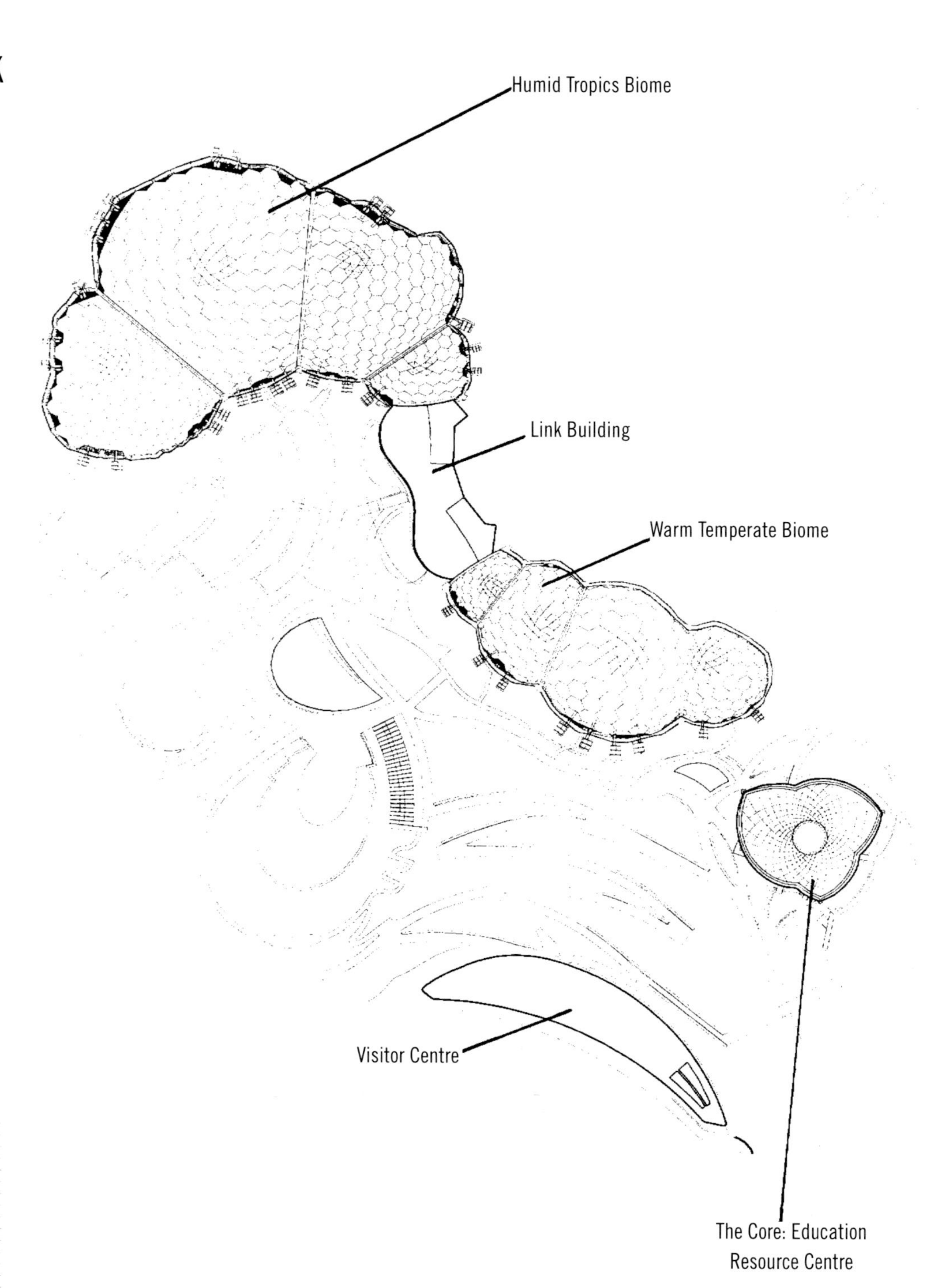

Above: A plan of the Eden Project site, showing the two biomes, and linking entrance unit, snaking their way around the perimeter of the former china clay pit. The visitor centre, perched above the site, can be seen at the bottom of the drawing.

Opposite: The interior of one of Eden's biomes, illustrating the enormity of the project. The domes are composed of identically-sized steel hexagons, filled with lightweight "cushions" of ETFE – a substance which is 99 per cent lighter than glass.

Each dome is constructed from a series of identically-sized steel hexagons (5 metres (16 feet) in diameter for the smaller domes, 11 metres (36 feet) for the larger ones), each of which was assembled on the ground, hoisted into position and bolted to its neighbour. There is also a smaller number of triangles and pentagons in the mix. Once complete, the domes were provided with a secondary structure of steel elements that run as a lattice across the node points of the hexagons. In all, 667 tonnes (735 tons) of steelwork were used in the creation of the domes. The entire assembly is anchored into the ground and hillsides on concrete foundations.

The canopy is enclosed by filling the honeycomb structure with Ethylene TetrafluoroEthylene (ETFE) (see page 155) air-filled cushions which are long lasting and admit a wide spectrum of light. These insulating cushions allow the biomes to act as greenhouses, warming up to temperatures suitable for the plant life within. Covering 30,000 square metres (322,917 square feet), the ETFE panels fill 625 hexagons, 190 triangles and 16 pentagons and enclose 536 tonnes (591 tons) of air; 230 panels are computer controlled and can open to regulate temperature and humidity. There is also a heating system within the biomes, but this is a secondary facility, used merely to supplement natural solar gain (i.e. the heat of the sun) as necessary.

The Eden Project has been an astonishing success. Visitor numbers were forecast at 750,000 per year, but the site attracted 1.9 million people in its first 12 months. In fact, this success has enabled the project to pursue other building schemes, including The Core, an education centre, whose roof structure is based on the mathematics that control the way plants grow. Called phyllotaxis, this number-based system explains the structure of a pine cone or the pollen of a daisy and is a patterning system consisting of two sets of spirals – one set going clockwise, the other counter-clockwise.

Originally, the Grimshaw team (now the architects of choice at the Eden Project) planned out the building with equal numbers of spirals moving in each direction, but they just couldn't get it all to hang together. When the architects began working with artist Peter Randall-Page, a sculptor of natural forms, they realized they had made a false assumption. The patterning of forms like pine cones is not composed of equal numbers of spirals. Phyllotaxis is slightly more complex than that – a pine cone, for example, might have 13 spirals moving in one direction, and eight in the other. Eventually the designers settled on a form composed of 21 and 34 spirals moving across each other. Note, all these numbers are part of the Fibonacci sequence, a system where the sum of two numbers creates the next number, and so on (1+2=3; 2+3=5; 3+5=8, 5+8=13…). By sticking to such a structural form, the architects have managed to magnify the principles of flower formation in the roof of The Core.

The Eden Project, now inhabiting the most iconic structures in Cornwall (indeed, in the west of England), is currently considering adding a third biome, dedicated to the Dry Tropics, to its site.

Below top left: Openings in the ETFE cladding of Eden's biomes allow these artificial environments to "breathe".

Below top middle: If it was not for the structure encompassing this treescape, Eden's vegetation and mist could easily be mistaken for the tropics.

Below top right: The form and ethereal glow of the Eden Project's domes give them an almost otherworldly presence.

Below bottom: A section drawing through the Eden Project's biomes. The circles illustrate how the form of the domes are derived from a series of overlapping, imaginary arcs.

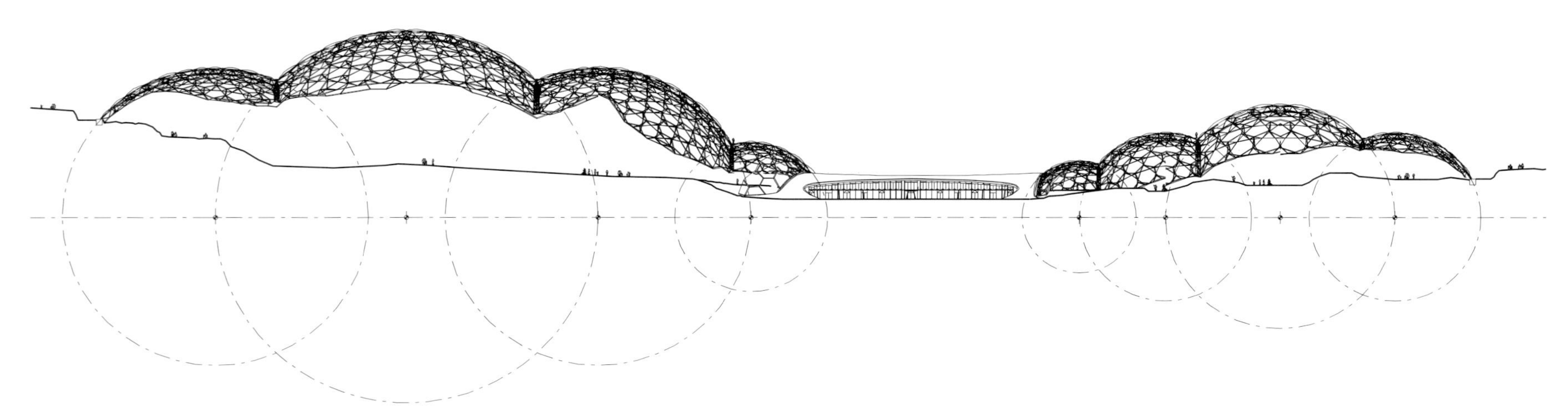

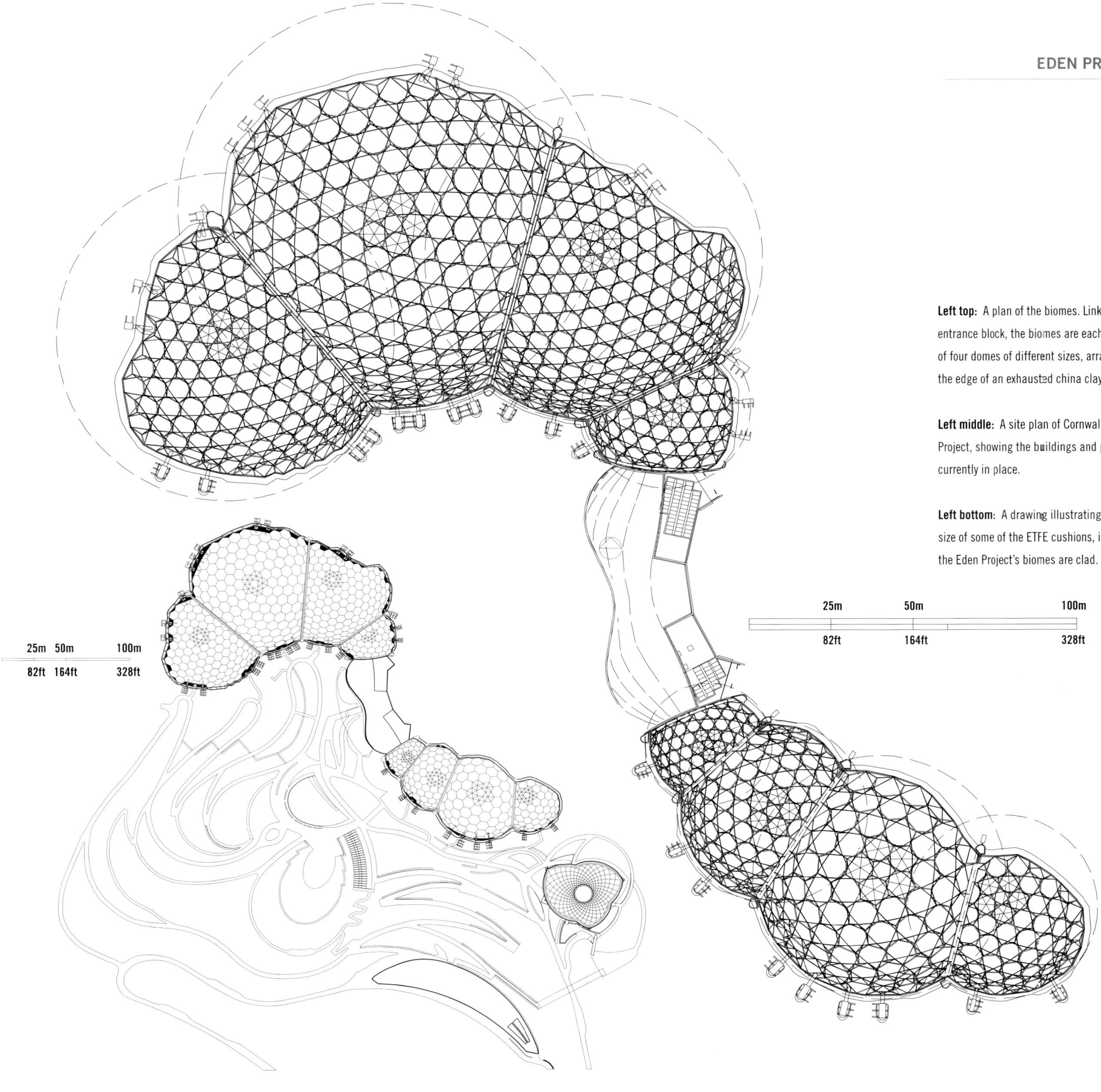

Left top: A plan of the biomes. Linked by an entrance block, the biomes are each composed of four domes of different sizes, arranged along the edge of an exhausted china clay pit.

Left middle: A site plan of Cornwall's Eden Project, showing the buildings and pathways currently in place.

Left bottom: A drawing illustrating the vast size of some of the ETFE cushions, in which the Eden Project's biomes are clad.

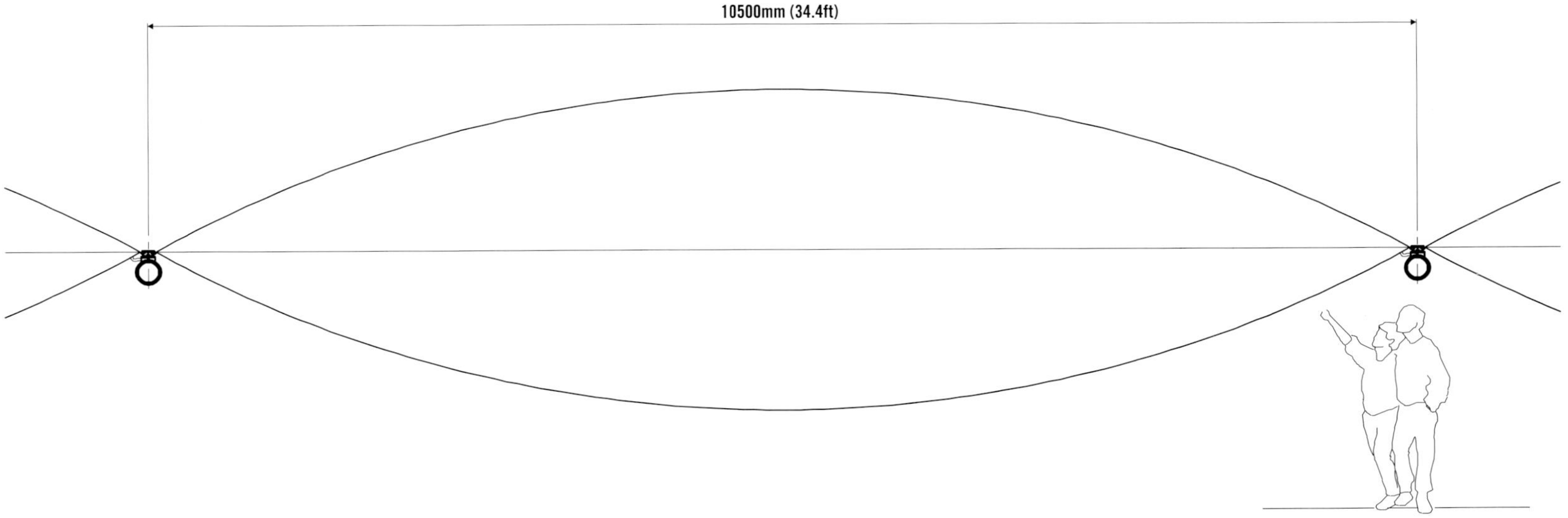

25m 50m 100m
82ft 164ft 328ft

25m 50m 100m
82ft 164ft 328ft

10500mm (34.4ft)

NEUE NATIONALGALERIE BERLIN, GERMANY

Completed in late 1967 and opened to the public in 1968, Berlin's New National Gallery (Neue Nationalgalerie) has over 5,000 square metres (53,820 square feet) of exhibition space and boasts 800 metres (2,625 feet) of walls on which paintings can be hung: not that you would think this on first seeing the building.

The museum, dedicated to twentieth-century painting and sculpture, is mostly hidden, lying below an 11,550-square-metre (124,320-square-foot) raised granite terrace. This vast paved area is dominated by the famous minimalist glass-and-steel pavilion, which was designed for temporary exhibitions. A single storey in height, with walls of sheer glass and an almost overbearing roof constructed using a huge steel panel, the pavilion is devoid of any decoration.

The New National Gallery is a marked contrast to the other buildings of Berlin's Kulturforum and is the only building not designed by architect Hans Scharoun. Scharoun designed the exciting expressionistic Philharmonie, Kammermusiksaal (Philharmonic and Chamber Music halls) and Staatsbibliothek (State Library), which are made up of unusual forms and colourful facades. The New National Gallery is an exercise in rationalization, created by possibly the most influential Modernist architect of the era, Ludwig Mies van der Rohe.

Mies, as he is often known, along with Le Corbusier and the lesser-known Walter Gropius, is widely regarded as one of the pioneering masters of the Modernist movement in architecture. He sought to create a new architectural style that would represent modernity in its style and use of materials, just as the classical and Gothic architects did in their own eras. Mies and his contemporaries believed that the age of the machine would revolutionize the way buildings were constructed, removing many of the handcrafted elements and replacing them with factory-made "parts". However, while many architects of the time sought to rationalize in order to reduce construction costs, Mies made use of modern materials, such as industrial steel and plate glass, to define austere, elegant spaces. He stated that, "while their usage may change, our buildings will last for a few hundred years", and his buildings were often unusually expensive, considering the products used, because so much time was spent perfecting the details, such as joints and intersections between materials.

With this guiding principle, Mies designed the New National Gallery, the building that would be his last, just as he had done all of his others – as an object, independent of its surroundings and neutral to its intended use.

Much of the museum's exhibition space and all of its administrative offices and exhibit stores are located underground. There are no windows in three of the elevations built under the 110-metre by 105-metre (361-foot by 344-foot) terrace. However, the rear, or west side, of this cavernous space opens up with a fully glazed facade onto a sculpture garden. Above, the pavilion is a precise steel framework with a glass enclosure – a simple architectural statement but a powerful expression of Mies' ideas about flexible interior space, open and unencumbered by the external structural order.

The pavilion's steel frame and roof includes 1,200 tonnes (1,323 tons) of steel and featured the largest free-spanning steel panel in the world at the time of construction. The roof structure is supported along its perimeter on just eight columns, two on each side set in from the corners. Once completed, the pavilion measured 2,508 square metres (26,996 square feet); it is 8.5 metres (28 feet) high, with walls of sheer glass running some 50 metres (164 feet) in length.

This steel and glass box represents more than a rationalization of the building into its simplest form. Its design is much cleverer than first perceived. For example, the roof, at 65 by 65 metres (213 by 213 feet), is constructed in the form of an orthogonal grid of web girders 1.8 metres (6 feet) deep, separated at 3.6-metre (12-foot) intervals; it curves gradually upward by 10 centimetres (4 inches) to the centre to avoid the visual illusion of it sagging, and the columns are slightly tapered, to ensure that they do not look wider at the top than their bases.

This dramatic ground floor now serves principally as a lobby and ticket sales area. Nevertheless, it is the space with the most impact of the entire museum. The glass walls, interrupted only by slim metal structural supports, allow natural light to flood in and reflect off the dark, highly polished floor. The ceiling, exposed as a grid of dark metal beams, is decorated with long lines of LED displays, which continuously scroll abstract patterns down their length.

The unusual upward natural illumination and the continuous suggestion of motion in the ceiling combine to excite the senses. Yet, at the same time, the simple and rigorous geometry of the building makes the design seem tranquil, natural and unimposing.

The austerity of Mies' composition is commonly seen as an appropriate interpretation of a classical system of columns and beams. In fact, the gallery has been described as a Greek temple of modern architecture or a temple to art on a man-made acropolis. The similarities between it and the Parthenon, perched on the Acropolis in Athens, are understandable in an architectural appreciation of form. And, while both buildings are of relatively simple construction, both stand the test of time.

project data

- Ludwig Mies van der Rohe was born in Germany on March 27, 1886. He died on August 17, 1969, just one year after the opening of the New National Gallery.
- Mies called his buildings "skin and bones" architecture, for their minimal use of materials and reliance on simple steel frames and glass facades.
- The steel panel roof is 4,225 square metres (45,478 square feet) in size, while the granite terrace on which the museum sits measures 11,550 square metres (124,320 square feet).
- Mies' most famous other buildings are the Barcelona Pavilion (1929), which has been demolished and rebuilt; the Farnsworth House in Illinois (1951); and the Seagram Building in New York (1957).

Opposite top: The colossal roof structure of the New National Gallery in Berlin is heavy in terms of both weight and form. It seems almost impossible that it is supported by little more than thin walls of glass.

Opposite bottom: A view through the gallery's glazed facade illustrates the building's transparency and also the almost oppressive "weight" of the 65-by-65-metre (213¼-by-213¼-foot) steel girder roof.

Above top: The gallery roof is itself an art exhibit, illuminated along its structural girders by multi-coloured light-emitting diodes (LEDs).

Above bottom: The paved podium on which the glass box of the gallery sits is itself used to exhibit sculpture. It also hides another storey of gallery space and offices below it.

Right: The supporting structure of the massive 1,200-tonne (1,323-ton) roof consists of eight steel columns, such as the one in the foreground here: two are placed along each side of the structure.

AIRSHIP HANGARS ORLY, FRANCE

Eugene Freyssinet was a French engineer and pioneer of concrete construction. His prowess led him to be commissioned to design and build two massive airship hangars at a small airport at Orly in France between 1916 and 1924.

Freyssinet's instructions were to create buildings to house giant airships with a diameter of 50 metres (164 feet). The resulting hangars were 175 metres (574 feet) long, 91 metres (299 feet) wide and 60 metres (197 feet) high. They were dramatic in form, made up of a series of pre-stressed concrete parabolic arches, joined together to create snug shelters for the airships.

Pre-stressed concrete is now a commonly used technique, often employed for bridges. However, when Freyssinet set about designing the hangars it was unheard of. The engineer realized that, due to the size of the buildings, he was going to have to invent a construction method that would give his concrete arches strength in tension as well as in compression so that they could withstand the sideways forces of the wind on the exposed airfield, as well as the downward forces of their own weight. His solution was to cast tensioned steel bars into the arches, so that when the concrete set it took on the properties of the steel and became strong in tension.

While designing this new technique, Freyssinet also hit upon the idea of using movable formwork – moulds – to cast his concrete sections. This, too, was a first in concrete construction. However, as with all buildings, construction had to start from the bottom and work upward.

Wide horizontal foundation pads of concrete were poured into the ground at a depth where it was compact enough to withstand the massive weight that the new building would exert upon it. Onto these pads, springing elements were formed.

The springing point of an arch is the first instance when a vertical member starts to bend toward the centre – this can be seen in arched church windows, for example. In the case of the hangars at Orly, there were to be no vertical walls, the arches started to curve from just below ground level and continued to curve towards their apex 60 metres (197 feet) in the air.

These springing elements, the base section of the arches, were constructed from heavy concrete sections 7.5 metres (24½ feet) wide and 4.4 metres (14½ feet) deep, which rose some 16 metres (52½ feet) into the air. Above this, each arch became progressively slimmer. At the crown of the arch the curved concrete beam was 3.4 metres (11 feet) deep at its edges, but hollowed out towards its centre in order to cut down its weight and reduce pressure on the lower parts of the arch.

Freyssinet's design called for multiple arches to be cast in situ: the arches were formed using wooden moulds made from pine planks. First, the springing element moulds were constructed with the steel running through them; the concrete was then poured and allowed to set. As each element became hard, the wooden moulds were stripped from it and set up again, ready for the next section to be poured. Then, when the springing elements were hardened, or cured, the tapering arch sections above were constructed using the same repetitive technique with slimmer moulds and tensioned steel rods, held up using a mobile timber framework. The engineer filled the narrow gaps left by

the moulds between the arches with windows within the arches, such was his confidence in this new pre-stressed concrete technique.

Freyssinet's new techniques for concrete construction depended upon a number of factors. Firstly, the concrete itself had to be easily compactable so that it would fill the slim moulds easily without leaving any gaps or air bubbles. This was achieved by making the concrete fluid, enabling it to be poured easily into the moulds. However, fluidity didn't bode well for the rapid hardening required in order to strip the moulds quickly, move on and construct the next arch section. Freyssinet's answer was to use a combination of 350 kilograms (772 pounds) of cement and 1 tonne (1.1 tons) of a natural mixture of sand and gravel. This is a high percentage of cement to aggregate compared to conventional mixes, but it makes the concrete set much quicker.

The arched building presented a relatively small profile when viewed from the end, and the arches needed only minimal secondary bracing between them. However, the very broad side elevation of 60 by 175 metres (197 by 574 feet) meant that the buildings were at the mercy of strong winds in their exposed position. They had to withstand these unusually high lateral forces, and here Freyssinet's pre-stressed technique, along with his corrugated design paid dividends. The pre-tensioned steel rods within the arches gave each arch a good degree of tensile strength, while the corrugated design made the arched wall much stiffer as a whole – and far better at resisting sideways wind forces than a flat wall of the same size would be.

However, despite Freyssinet's mastery of concrete construction and the innovations he showcased on the hangars at Orly, they only stood for 20 years – they were bombed and destroyed by American planes in the Second World War.

project data

- **Eugene Freyssinet carried out many commissions for hangars, but those at Orly were the largest and most technologically advanced.**
- **Today's materials enable much lighter structures to be built on the same scale but the Orly hangars were revolutionary for their time.**
- **Freyssinet invented pre-stressed concrete and the use of movable formwork while designing the Orly hangars, two innovations that have gone on to transform concrete construction..**
- **The hangars were 175 metres (574 feet) long, 91 metres (299 feet) wide and 60 metres (197 feet) high.**
- **The concept of pre-stressed concrete was patented by Freyssinet in 1928.**
- **Freyssinet planned and built eight concrete hangars at Avord airport in France before 1924 and a further 31 were commissioned around France in the succeeding years.**

Opposite: Seen from afar, the two gigantic airship hangars dominate the landscape of the airport in Orly, their multiple ribbed sections rising much higher than the warehouse building next to them.

Above: The detail of Freyssinet's pre-stressed arch design can be appreciated from close to the hangars. He was so confident of their strength that he designed in glazed apertures between the thick ribbed sections to allow light into the vast buildings

THE INVENTION OF PRE-STRESSED CONCRETE

Pre-stressed concrete is now used for all manner of things, from floor beams in blocks of flats to gigantic bridge spans over rivers. It was invented by Eugene Freyssinet, a French engineer, who was born in 1879 and died in 1962. Pre-stressed concrete is vital in buildings using horizontal concrete members, because while concrete is very strong in compression – in a column with weight pressing down on it, for example – it is not strong in tension. Therefore, a non-stressed concrete beam will not hold much weight.

Freyssinet's invention uses pre-tensioned "tendons" of steel rod or cable. These are stretched to load them and then the concrete is poured around them. When the concrete has set, the tendons are released from tension, but instead of simply springing back to a relaxed state, their tension is transferred to the concrete as compressive stress: this gives the concrete the ability to resist greater imposed tensile stresses and creates a much stronger member.

A newer method is bonded post-tensioned concrete, where the compressive stress is applied after the concrete has set. The concrete is cast around a curved plastic or metal duct that follows the area where tension would occur. A set of tendons is fed through the duct and the concrete is poured. Once the concrete has hardened, the tendons are tensioned using jacks wedged against the end of the concrete member. When the tendons have been stretched sufficiently they are fixed in position and maintain tension after the jacks are removed, transferring pressure to the concrete. The duct is then filled with grout to complete the job.

ALLIANZ ARENA MUNICH, GERMANY

The Allianz Arena, in Munich, Germany, is one of the world's newest and most impressive stadiums. Completed in May 2005, this 69,901-seat structure was built for two different football teams, and the facade can change colour to reflect the strip of the team that happens to be playing.

Designed by Swiss architects Herzog & de Meuron, the Allianz stadium is home to both Bayern München, which plays in red, and TSV München 1860, which plays in blue. The facade of this giant marshmallow-like structure accommodates digitally-controlled colour filters and neon tubes that can illuminate the building in any number of ways – the stadium can glow in a single colour, it can divide into parallel strips or fragment into diamonds; it can also pulse, or send points of light racing across its surface, and the whole thing can even appear to revolve.

Beyond all that, the facade of this stadium wraps over the top to become a transparent canopy that keeps the rain off spectators and admits enough light to allow the grass on the pitch to grow. It sounds simple, but the construction of this stadium was an enormous undertaking. Its Ethylene TetrafluoroEthylene (ETFE – see page 155) surface is currently the biggest in the world and, at 64,000 square metres (689,900 square feet), covers an area more than twice that of Nicholas Grimshaw's Eden Project in England (see page 142). And if that isn't already complex enough, the stadium itself is not a symmetrical structure. The statistics concerning this facade are awesome: made up of 2,760 rhomboid-shaped cushions, just two of which are the same, these ETFE units (which are connected to a permanent air supply) range from 2–4.5 metres (6⅔–14¾ feet) in length and can bear a snow load of 1.6 metres (5¼ feet) depth. These air-filled rhomboid cushions are configured as a series of spirals that run diagonally from the bottom of the facade to the inner edge of the over-hanging roof.

The biggest headache for the design team was caused by the need to allow each cushion to expand or contract by up to 13 millimetres (½ inch). Ordinarily, ETFE cushions are held in place by a rigid aluminium profile system, but this would have been too inflexible for the Allianz Arena – the sheer scale of the building would have made this kind of structure prohibitively complex. Instead, the cushions are held in place via a watertight, rubber-clamping system, freeing the builders from having to install an aluminium frame that followed the geometry of the ETFE cushions exactly.

The design team, including German contractor Covertex, also had to consider how to print each ETFE cushion to ensure an even spread of light, and prevent the ETFE facade being illuminated unevenly. Each cushion is printed with white dots at its outer edges, in order to reduce its opacity, while the centre is left clear. That way, the light becomes more of a homogenous glow.

The building of the stadium dates back to 1997, when Munich's two football clubs decided their facilities needed upgrading. In 2001 the clubs identified the Fröttmaning district of Munich as the site of a new stadium, and a local referendum held in October passed the plans by

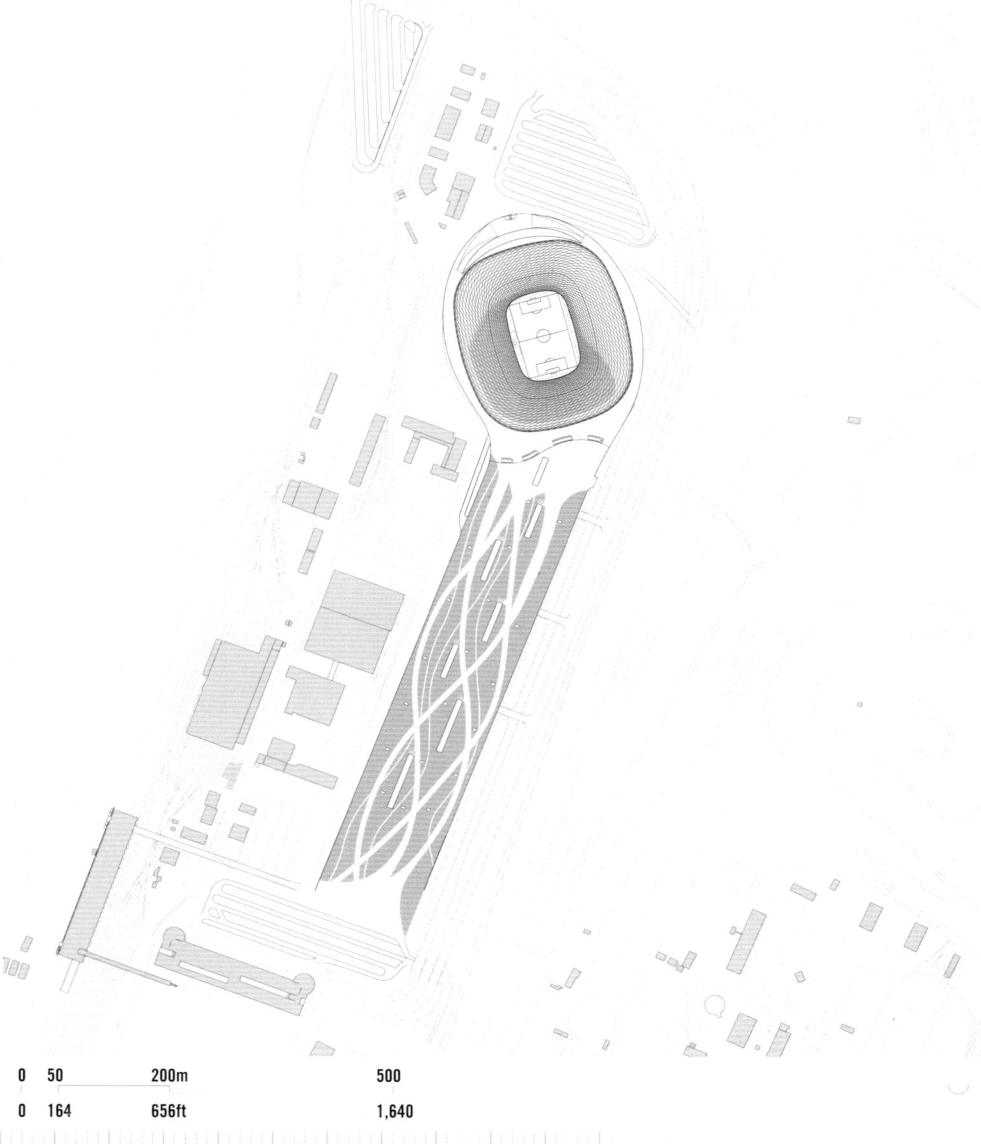

Above: A site plan of Munich's Allianz Arena, set within a vast road system and car park.

Opposite: The arena is partially clad in transparent cushions, allowing sunlight to reach the grass of the pitch, while protecting spectators from the elements.

project data

- The Allianz Arena measures 258 metres (846 feet) by 227 metres (745 feet) by 50 metres (164 feet) and cost 340 million Euros.
- The stadium was designed by Swiss architects Herzog & de Meuron with sporting and structural advice from British engineers Arup.
- 24,000 square metres (258,300 square feet) of the stadium's 64,000-square-metre (689,900-square-foot), facade can be lit up by computer-controlled lights in three colours.
- 120,000 cubic metres (4.24 million cubic feet) of concrete and 22,000 tonnes (24,250 tons) of steel were used in the construction of the stadium.
- The roof is made up of a steel cantilever that spans up to 60 metres (197 feet) and covers the entire seating area; other solutions were available, but the contractor argued that the cantilever system better suited the building programme.
- Stadium seating is provided in three tiers, each with different rakes: the lower tier is set at 24 degrees, the middle tier at 30 degrees and the upper tier at 34 degrees.
- The stadium provides nearly 11,000 car-parking spaces, 1,200 on two levels in the stadium, 9,800 in esplanade car-parks (mostly underground).

Allianz Arena

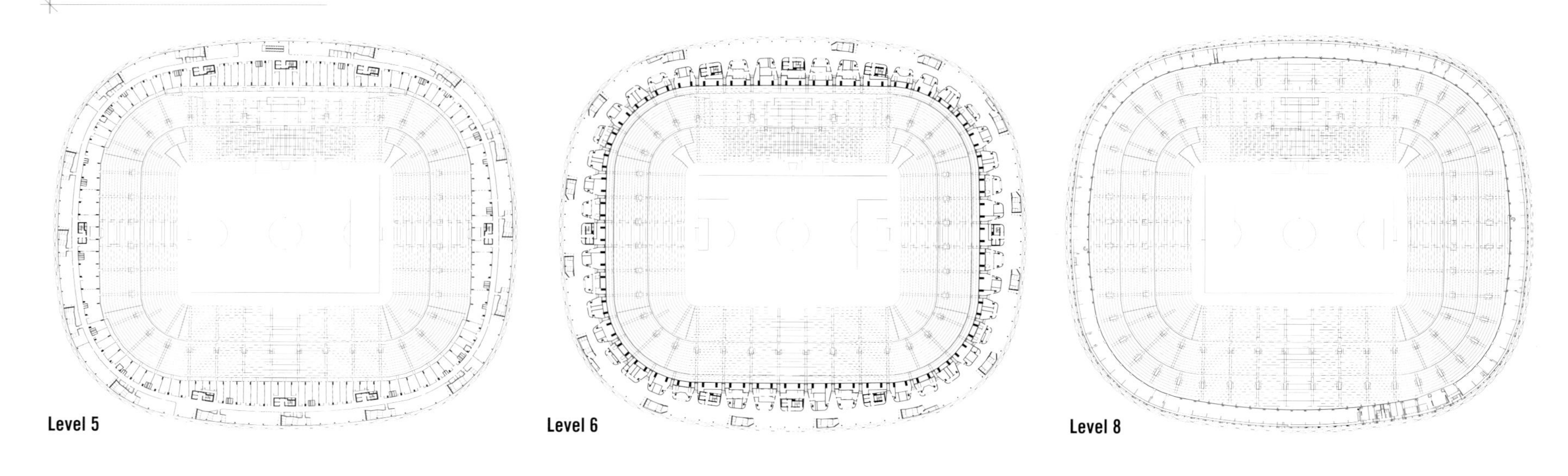

Level 5

Level 6

Level 8

Opposite top: Plans of the stadium, sliced through at varying levels, clearly showing the lozenge-shaped form of the structure.

Opposite: One of the approaches to the stadium, which (unilluminated) looms above visitors like a giant marshmallow.

Above: A close-up of the Allianz Arena's skin, emphasizing the precision and craftsmanship of the enterprise.

Below: A sectional drawing through the entire site of the arena, illustrating the rake of the stadium's seating and the volume of space between the inner bowl and the skin of the building.

an overwhelming majority (65.8 per cent of voters were in favour). An architectural competition ended in a shortlist of just two firms: Herzog & de Meuron and German practice von Gerkan, Marg + Partners. The Swiss firm was declared the winner on February 8, 2002. Design work, assisted by engineering company Arup, proceeded using advanced computer-aided "parametric" design of the sort usually used by the aerospace industry: this enabled different configurations to be generated quickly and 33 subtly different forms for the bowl were modelled before a final decision was taken.

The foundation stone was laid on October 21, 2002, and the structural work was completed on March 26, 2004. The first ETFE cushion was installed on May 26, 2004, and the entire facade system was in place just six months later. The inaugural football match took place on May 30, 2005.

ETFE

Ethylene TetrafluoroEthylene (ETFE) is one of the newest and most exciting building products to emerge in recent years. Weighing about one per cent of the equivalent area of glass, ETFE is a cheaper, lighter and arguably more energy-efficient way of roofing a space. Developed by DuPont for the space industry in the 1960s, ETFE does not degrade or discolour under ultraviolet light and its anti-static properties means it almost cleans itself (dust particles don't like sticking to it).

ETFE tends to be used as "pillows" or "cushions" – air-filled units that are secured in place by rubber or aluminium clamps. Often, these cushions have an inner layer (like at the Eden Project – see page 142) and the pumps that keep them inflated can be controlled to regulate the amount of air inside (more air means more insulation on colder days). Some cushions contain as many as five layers of ETFE.

The beauty of multi-layered cushions is that they can alter their appearance and adjust to changing levels of sunlight. The system works by printing patterns on internal and external layers; the inner layer can be moved up and down pneumatically, and light penetration can be controlled by adjusting the overlap between the graphics.

The developers of ETFE systems are excited by their potential. Some dream of filling the cushions with helium and floating roofing systems into place.

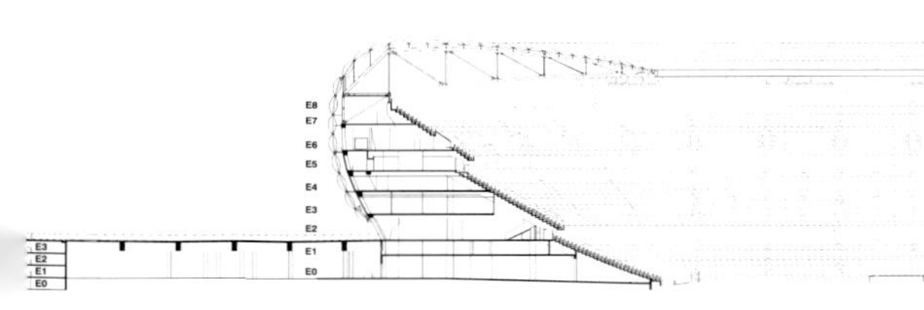

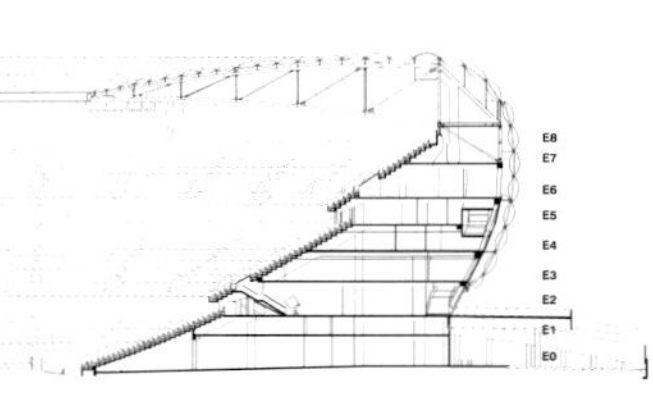

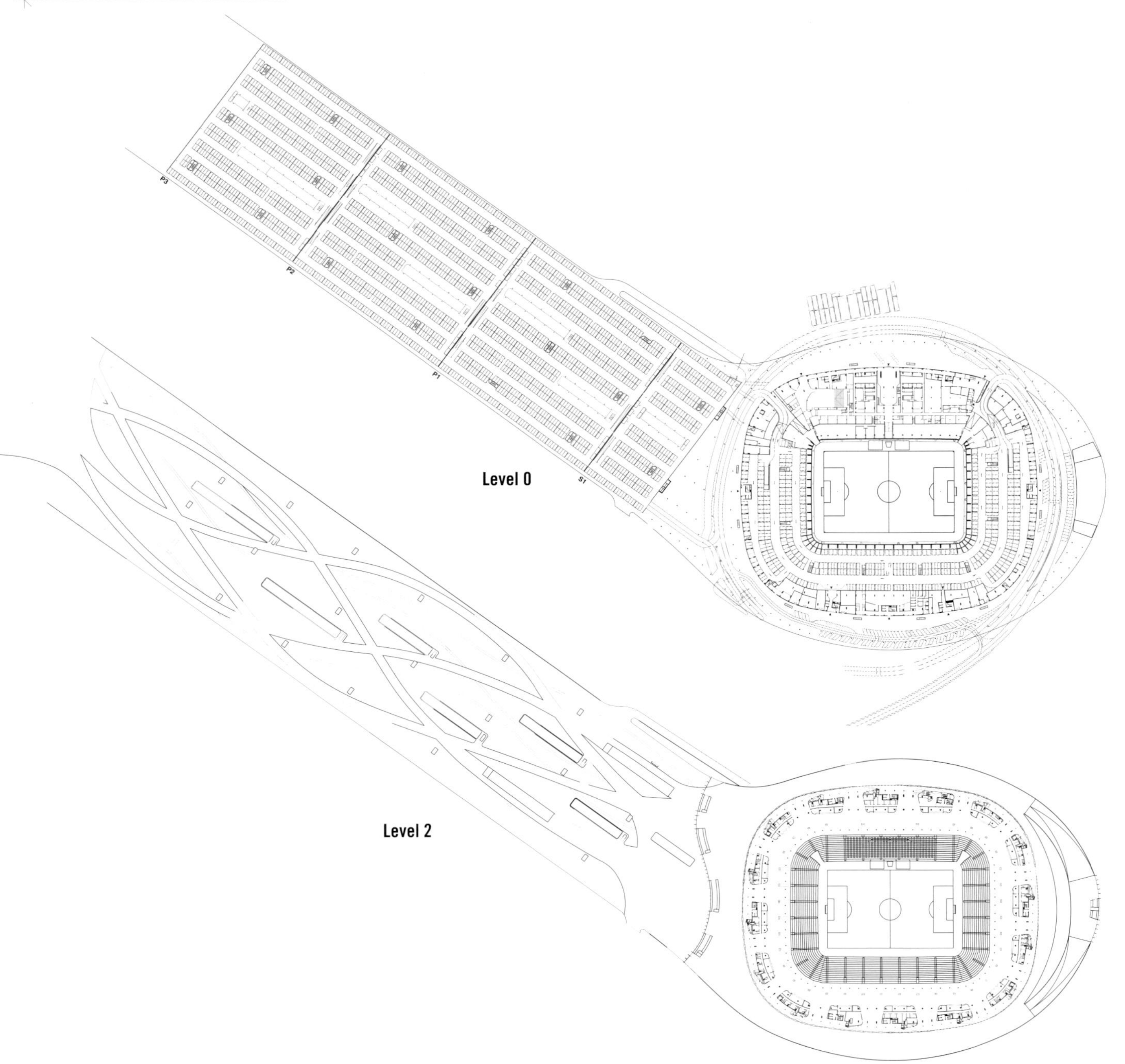

Left: Plan drawings of the Allianz Arena, showing both the stadium and the main approach route. Stadium designers are now very careful to design adequate circulation spaces for sports fans – this structure can accommodate almost 70,000 people.

Below: Designed by Swiss architects Herzog & de Meuron, the Arena has an almost science-fiction air about it: the structure is reminiscent of a space craft or a microscopic life-form.

Opposite left, right top and middle: The Allianz Arena, in Germany, is one of the largest ETFE-covered structures in the world. Computer controlled LEDs buried within the cladding can change the stadium's colour – and even make the structure appear to revolve.

Opposite right bottom: Plan drawing of the arena, illustrating how the cladding cushions spiral into the centre of the structure, leaving the football pitch exposed.

Allianz
Arena

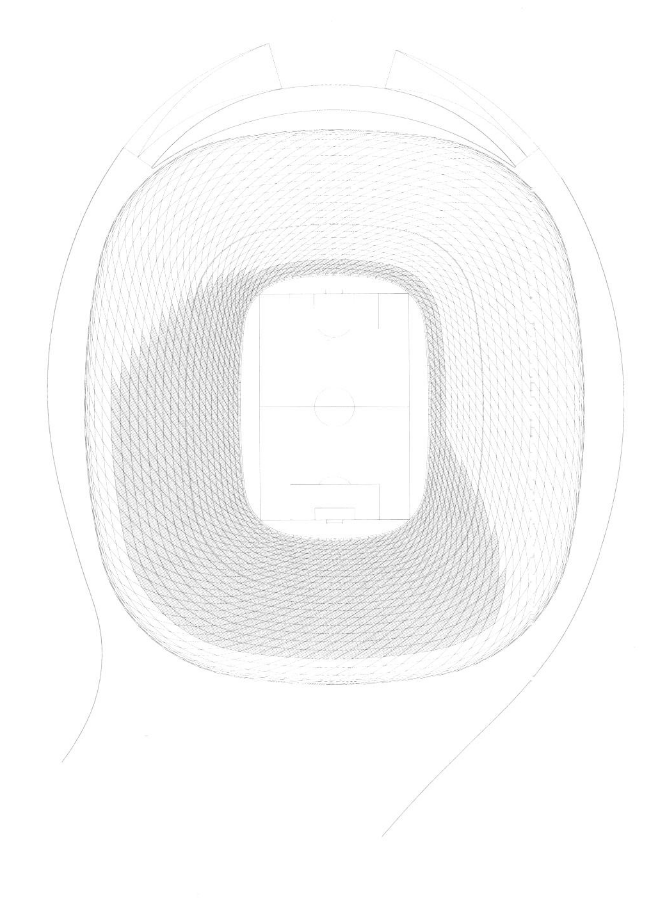

NATIONAL ASSEMBLY BUILDING DHAKA, BANGLADESH

Architect Louis Kahn didn't design many buildings, but those that were completed were a testament to his vision of "modern monuments". Kahn was inspired by the Egyptian pyramids, Angkor Wat and other structures that have stood for thousands of years, and he wanted to create buildings that would last as long, leaving an almost indelible mark on civilization.

The National Assembly, or Jatiyo Sangshad Bhaban, in Dhaka, Bangladesh, was Kahn's final building and it is probably the finest example of his monumental architecture. Taking over 12 years to build, from 1962 to 1974, it is one of the largest legislative complexes in the world, housing all the parliamentary activities of Bangladesh.

The assembly complex stands alone on a hill: its design is like nothing else in the city or in Bangladesh. The building is impressive both for its sheer scale and for the drama of the design. The Bhaban (main building) consists of nine individual blocks: eight peripheral blocks, which rise to a height of 33.5 metres (110 feet), and a central octagonal block that is 47.3 metres (155 feet) tall. All nine blocks are constructed from reinforced concrete and decorated with marble strips. They include different groups of functional spaces and have numerous levels, interlinked horizontally and vertically by corridors, lifts, stairs, light courts and circular meeting spaces. However, the entire structure is designed to be seen as a single huge building.

While construction work on this main building was completed in 1974, the year of Kahn's death, work continued on the wider 81-hectare (200-acre) complex, which he also designed, until 1982. It was only in 1982 that the building was inaugurated and began operating as the seat of government for Bangladesh. The surrounding buildings, which include the MPs' hostels and buildings for emergency facilities, with external spaces in between, filled with an intricately designed lake and lawns, are called the Jatiyo Sangshad complex.

Kahn's design philosophy for the whole complex involved providing the best use of space for meeting and circulation, while integrating an architectural style that represented Bangladeshi heritage and culture. The buildings evolved initially from the basic requirement of protection from the glare and heat of the sun. The orientation of the buildings within the complex creates areas of shade and encourages air movement throughout. External concrete facades have huge openings in them in the form of triangles, rectangles, full and segmented circles and flat arches to reveal covered walkways, similar to cloisters in monasteries. The openings are very dramatic architecturally and they also allow breezes to blow through the shaded passages.

The most important part of the Bhaban is the Parliament Chamber, which can house 354 members during sessions. The octagonal chamber's parabolic shell roof reaches a maximum height of 35.66 metres (117 feet). It was designed with a gap around it – of a single storey in height – to let in daylight; the light reflects from the surrounding walls and filters into the Parliament Chamber. Upper levels of the

Left: The monumentality of Bangladesh's National Assembly Building can be truly appreciated due to its position, standing alone surrounded by water. Its form is like no other building, creating uniqueness akin to the great historic structures that influenced architect, Louis Khan.

Opposite: At four storeys high, the entrance to the Bhaban is marked by dramatic reinforced concrete walls, cut through by concentric shapes with large cross sectional braces. The structure is very strong, while the spaces also allow good air flow through the building.

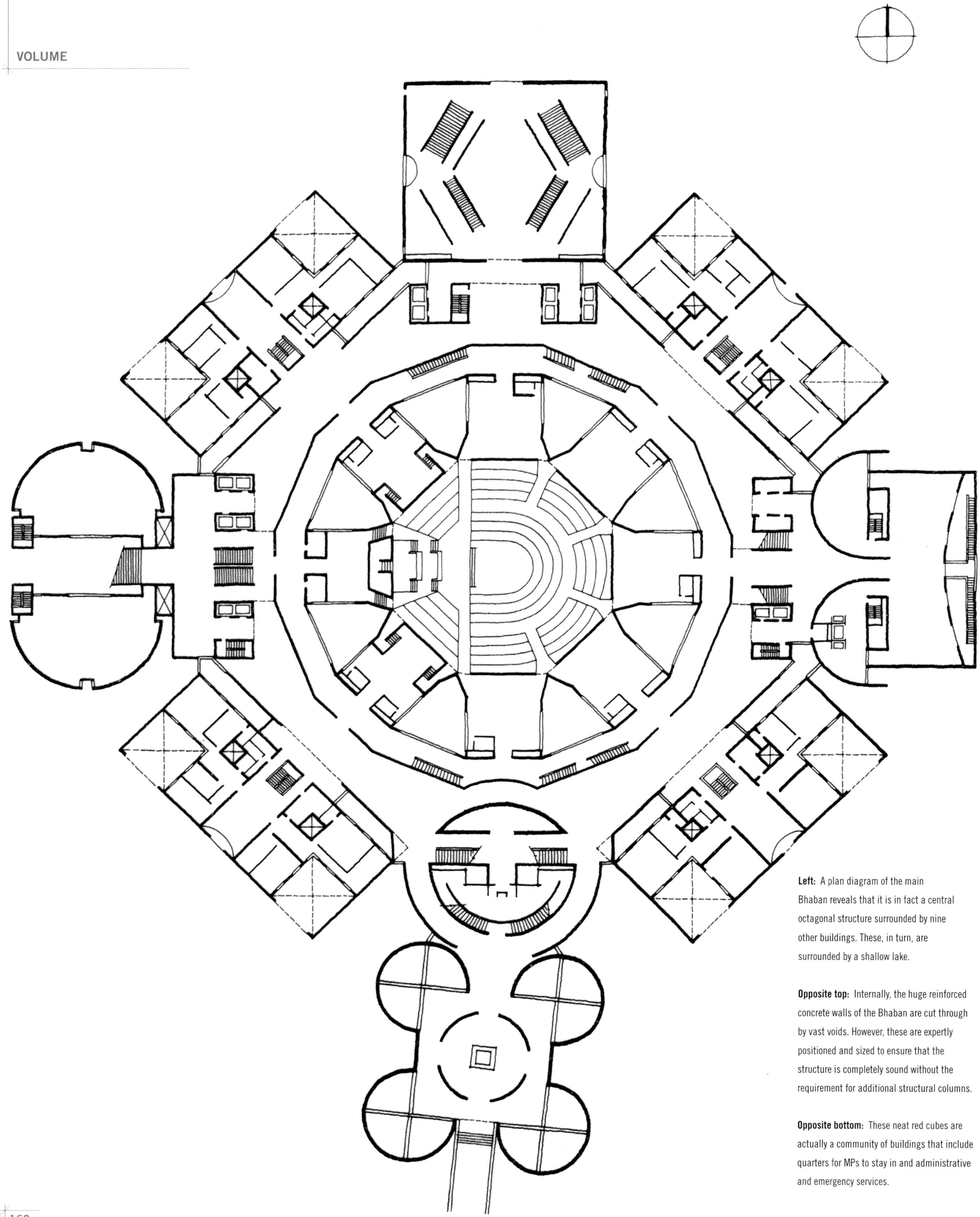

Left: A plan diagram of the main Bhaban reveals that it is in fact a central octagonal structure surrounded by nine other buildings. These, in turn, are surrounded by a shallow lake.

Opposite top: Internally, the huge reinforced concrete walls of the Bhaban are cut through by vast voids. However, these are expertly positioned and sized to ensure that the structure is completely sound without the requirement for additional structural columns.

Opposite bottom: These neat red cubes are actually a community of buildings that include quarters for MPs to stay in and administrative and emergency services.

block contain the visitors' and press galleries, as well as communication booths, all of which overlook the Parliament Chamber. Also within this central element of the complex are a library on level one, MPs' lounges on level three, and, on the uppermost floor, Party rooms. There are no columns within the building. Instead, the clever design incorporates load-bearing elements within the walls. It is as if the entire building has been carved from a solid block of concrete.

Externally, the Bhaban is almost entirely surrounded by a lake. Visitors arrive via either the north or south plazas. The south plaza is a major thoroughfare, rising 6 metres (20 feet) to the main entrance, while the north plaza includes presidential gardens and an outdoor amphitheatre where state functions are held. In total, the Bhaban covers 76,000 square metres (818,057 square feet); the south plaza is 21,000 square metres (226,042 square feet) in size and the north, or presidential, plaza is 6,000 square metres (64,583 square feet).

Kahn said of his design: "The architectural image of the assembly building grows out of the need to hold a strong essential form to give shape to the varying interior needs, expressing them on the exterior. The image is that of a many-faceted precious stone, constructed in concrete and marble. It was not belief, not design, not pattern, but the essence from which an institution could emerge."

While this analogy is fitting, the cost of the construction project caused controversy. The total cost of the complex, including the Parliament building, North and South plazas, residential buildings, hostels, gardens, roads and lakes was 1,280 million Taka (£9,415,756) – a monumental fee for such a deprived country. Annual maintenance and operational expenses of the building also add up considerably, to approximately 55 million Taka (£404,700).

However, the building was awarded the Aga Khan Award for Architecture in 1989. A citation by the Awards committee reads: "Faced with an imposing architectural work of extraordinary power, clarity of form and beauty, the jury could not help but question the compatibility of the National Assembly with the needs and aspirations of a poor country. Yet review of the building's design reveals that over time it has come to enjoy overwhelming approval, it stands as a symbol of democracy in Bangladesh and has influenced the country in a variety of beneficial ways."

project data

- The National Assembly complex cost over £9,325,177 (1,280 million Taka) to build; a phenomenal price for as poor a nation as Bangladesh to pay. However, it is loved by the entire nation.
- There are 50 staircases, 340 toilets, 1,635 doors, 335 windows in the National Assembly complex.
- The Parliament Building covers 1.39 hectares (3.43 acres), the North Plaza covers 0.59 hectares (1.46 acres) and the South Plaza covers 2.02 hectares (4.99 acres); the entire complex covers a total of 81 hectares (200 acres).
- The main buildings took just over 12 years to build but the entire complex was not completed until 20 years after the start of the project.
- The Parliament Chamber is central to the main building; it holds up to 354 members during sessions and is 35.66 metres (117 feet) high.

DOWNLAND GRIDSHELL

WEALD AND DOWNLAND OPEN AIR MUSEUM, SUSSEX, UK

The "Gridshell" building at the Weald & Downland Open Air Museum in southern England is a hybrid building – it is both traditional and cutting edge, carefully crafted out of timber and the product of current architectural thinking. Shortlisted for the prestigious Stirling Prize in 2002, awarded to what is judged the best building of the year by a British architect, the Gridshell didn't win but *The Sunday Times* thought it was by far the best entry of the year.

"If this year's Stirling Prize judges had been just and true, unswayed by famous names, political correctness, fashion-consciousness and urban bias, then this was the building that should have won British architecture's top award," wrote critic Hugh Pearman. "Why? Because it advances the art and science of architecture and engineering. Because it lifts the spirits. Because it does its job well. Because it is alive. Because it is not self-consciously, navel-gazingly architectural ... I think we need more buildings like this."

Designed by Edward Cullinan Architects with engineers Buro Happold, the building is a lightweight structure of oak strips, and serves as a research centre and a workshop for the conservation and re-assembly of historic buildings – it forms the heart of this "open air" museum. A gridshell is a structure with the form and robustness of a double-curved shell (the principles of an egg, in fact) composed of a grid of separate elements. A gridshell can be made of almost anything (Japanese architect Shigeru Ban has created them from cardboard tubes), but oak was deemed to be most appropriate for this rural building intended for the conservation of historic structures.

The oak was felled in October 2000 and sawn and machined to a standard profile of 50 by 35 millimetres (2 by 1.4 inches). Once defective pieces had been removed, these oak laths were "finger jointed" into lengths of 6 metres (20 feet) using a special polyurethane glue that can resist the acidity of oak; six laths were then joined to form lengths of 36 metres (118 feet). In the end, 600 timber laths with a combined length of 12,000 metres (39,370 feet) were used to form the gridshell.

These timber lengths were actually laid out flat at first, on a scaffold. The grid, composed of four layers of laths (two layers running in each direction), was connected with rotating joints to form a "grid-mat" of 30 by 52 metres (98 by 171 feet). Constructed on a scaffold 7.5 metres (25 feet) above ground level, the mat was ready to be distorted into a three-dimensional form by March 2001. The distortion was possible because of the inherent flexibility of the timber and the rotating joints, while gravity was used to do most of the warping – as the scaffolding was lowered bit by bit, the mat dropped down and gradually assumed its shell-like form, which gives it its innate strength. It took two weeks to drop the edges of the grid-mat just 3 metres (10 feet). When the shell was ready, it was fixed to its frame of Siberian Larch (a slow-growing and highly durable timber) and a fifth layer of laths was added to "triangulate" the grid and add stiffness.

The finished product, the form of which has been described as a "triple-bulb hour glass", is 12–15 metres (39–49 feet) wide and contains large openings at either end. By the summer of 2001 the gridshell was ready for its roof, which runs as a highly insulated ribbon along the top of the structure. Once in place, large arches of "glulam" timber (laminated strips of green oak glued together) were added to each end of the building to support the overhanging roof, and the wall cladding of locally-grown Western Red Cedar was fixed in place.

When viewed from outside the finished building appears as a single-storey structure, but it actually contains two levels – the upper level, in the gridshell itself, contains workshops and classrooms, while the lower level, set into the chalk of the site and benefiting from the more regulated temperature regime of being semi-buried, is where the storage and archival facilities are found.

What makes this project remarkable is that it is a synthesis of traditional and contemporary techniques – computer analysis was employed to determine the form of the structure and special glues, new jointing techniques and energy-reduction tactics take their place alongside age-old carpentry processes and the skill of the scaffolders. This is a building made of both glulam beams and oak-pegged mortise and tenon joints such as those found in the medieval buildings the museum was set up to preserve.

"The design process for the building has also been unusual in that from an early stage, the carpenters sat around the table with the architects and engineers to design the detail of the building. Putting all this together we have a building that is unique and innovative, both in its conception, engineering and its carpentry. It is our belief that the results speak for themselves," said the museum upon the building's completion in 2002.

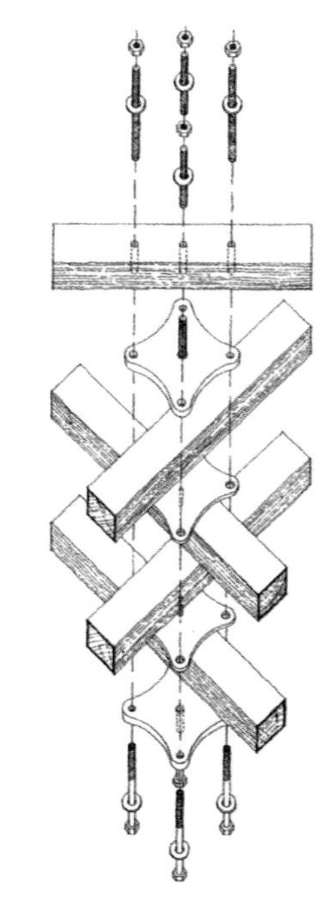

Above: A detail drawing of the gridshell's node points, illustrating the multi-layered construction of the building.

Below: A section drawing of the Downland Gridshell, showing the undulating roof form, ground-level-space and basement.

Opposite: The upper level of this beautiful and imaginative structure comprises workshops and teaching facilities. The timber structure is an apt construction for the open-air museum of medieval houses in southern England.

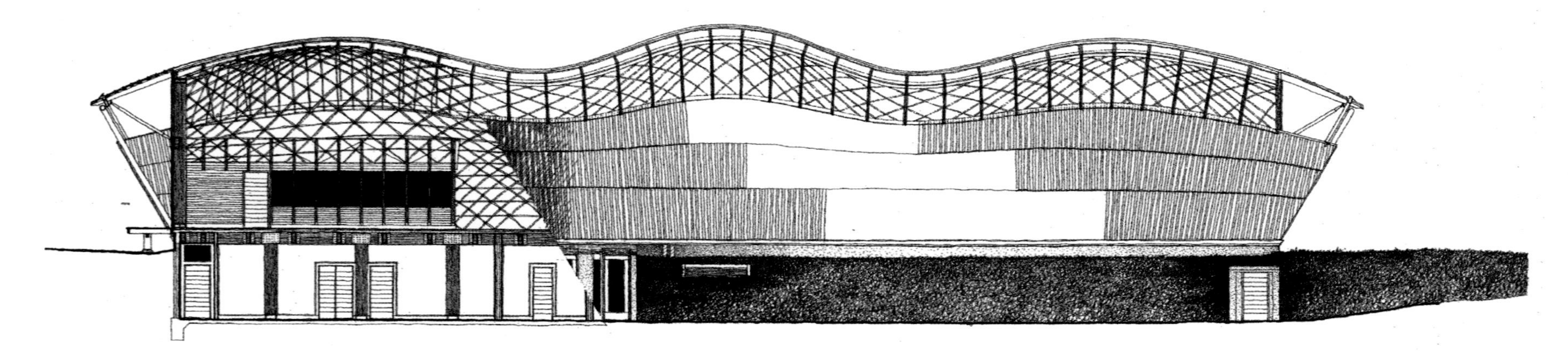

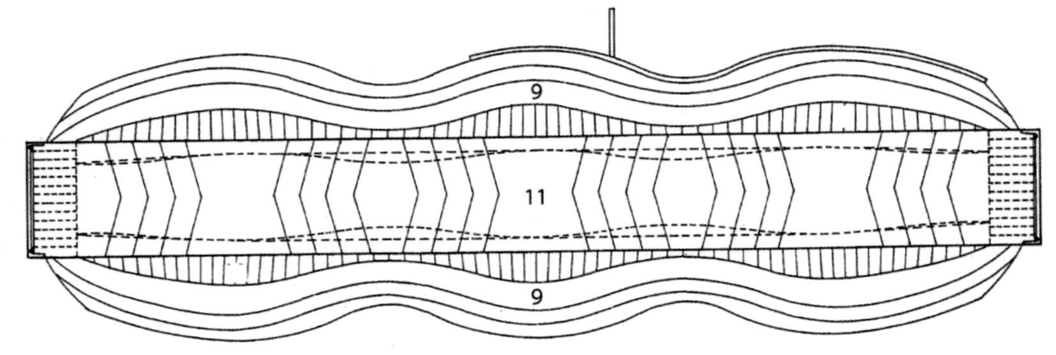

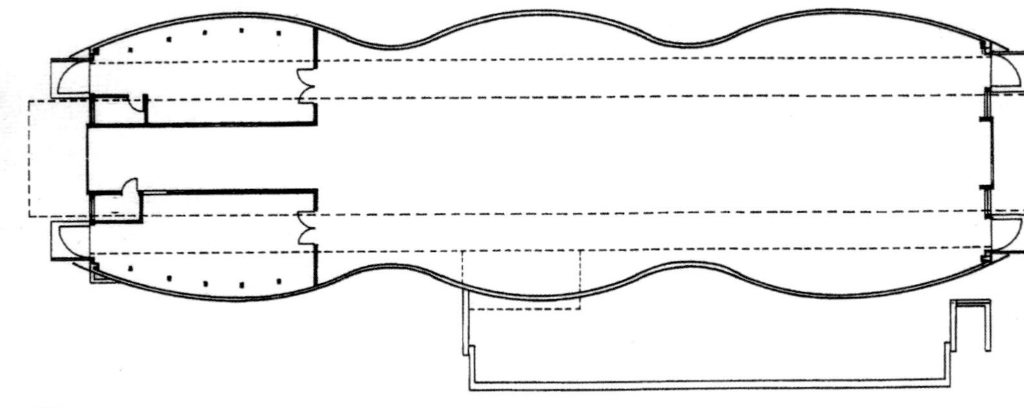

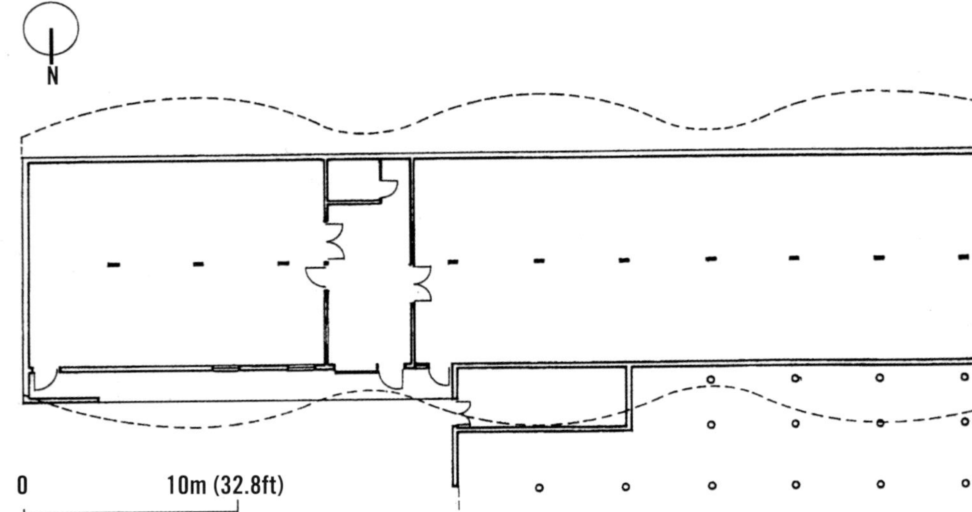

project data

- The Downland Gridshell was built for the Weald & Downland Open Air Museum in West Sussex, England.
- The Gridshell, designed by Edward Cullinan Architects, has won a string of awards, including a regional award from the Royal Institute of British Architects and an Excellence in Design Award from the American Institute of Architects.
- Organically shaped like a triple-pod peanut shell, the building is suggestive of the forms of nearby hills and is meant to sit politely in the landscape.
- Completed in 2002, the roof contains 12 tonnes (13 tons) of timber; conventional roofing would have required 10 times more material.
- This 1,800-square-metre (19,375-square-foot) building takes its inspiration from boat-building techniques, where strips of timber have been formed into complex curves for centuries.
- The strength of the building comes from its curved shape rather than the mass of its construction materials (unlike traditional "post and beam" construction where materials have to have a certain substance to prevent buildings becoming too flimsy).

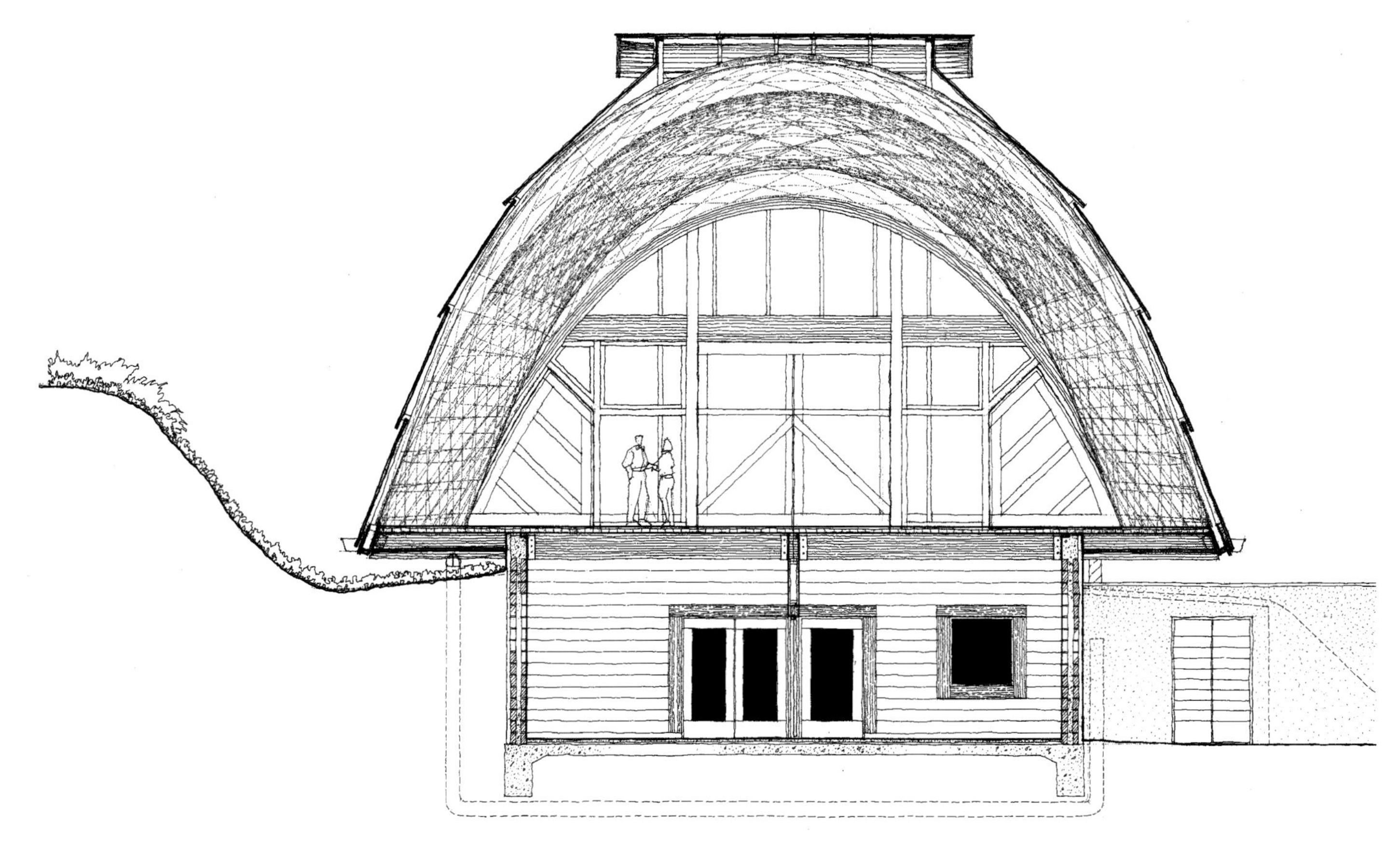

Opposite left: The gridshell in construction, showing the grid of timbers suspended on a platform of scaffolding, the gradual removal of the scaffold and the emerging structure, the roof being added, and the completed building.

Opposite right Plans of the Downland Gridshell, showing roof, ground floor and basement.

Left: A detail drawing of the gridshell's node points, illustrating the multi-layered construction of the building.

Below: The gridshell structure was designed and assembled after an unusually close relationship was established between architects, engineers and carpenters.

BEIJING NATIONAL STADIUM BEIJING, CHINA

The Beijing National Stadium, built specifically to host the 2008 Olympic Games, demonstrates both the power of contemporary design and the desire of the Chinese government to impress the world. Designed by Swiss architects Herzog & de Meuron, engineers Arup and The China Architectural Design and Research Group this structure was conceived as a "bird's nest" – a highly complex, even confusing, set of intersections that obscures an underlying logic.

"The stadium's appearance is pure structure. Facade and structure are identical. The structural elements mutually support each other and converge into a grid-like formation – almost like a bird's nest with its interwoven twigs," said the design team in its competition entry statement in 2002. "The stadium is conceived as a large collective vessel, which makes a distinctive and unmistakable impression both when it is seen from a distance and from close up. It meets all the functional and technical requirements of an Olympic National Stadium, but without communicating the insistent sameness of technocratic architecture dominated by large spans and digital screens."

Later, the engineers were to add the following: "The interwoven structural elements of the facade produce a single surface, upon which further elements are arranged in a chaotic manner to blur the distinction between the primary structure and the secondary structure." If one looks carefully at the stadium, the difference between the primary and secondary structures becomes clear – a sequence of long, diagonal elements spiral upward at an acute angle, punctuated by clusters of more vertical elements, creating a rhythm that is broken down by further members that appear almost extraneous.

The stadium will provide the focus for the track and field events of the 2008 Games and will contain 91,000 seats for the tournament – though this number will be scaled back to 80,000 once the event is over. Originally, the stadium was to have had a sliding roof that could be deployed to convert it into an enclosed arena, but this feature was removed from the design work largely for cost reasons.

Measuring 330 metres (1,083 feet) long, 220 metres (722 feet) wide, and 69 metres (226 feet) high, this immense structure is built from 36 kilometres (22 miles) of steel weighing 45,000 tonnes (49,604 tons). Most of the complex steelwork, comprising awkward angles that required extremely precise fabrication, was manufactured off-site in shipbuilding yards and transported to the construction site piece by piece.

In order to help shore up the roof of the stadium during construction, 78 temporary supporting structures, removed in a painstaking and carefully choreographed operation during September 2006, were installed at points of particular stress. Once these structures were removed, the giant steel assembly sagged by approximately 30 centimetres (1 foot), as predicted. In profile, the roof of the stadium is saddle-shaped, a form that was generated from an ellipse 313 metres (1,027 feet) long and 266 metres (873 feet) wide.

Like a bird's nest, in which the gaps between the twigs are often filled with softer material, the irregular spaces formed by the lattice-work of Beijing National Stadium's steelwork will be clad with panels of single-stressed ETFE foil (see page 155 for more information on ETFE). An "acoustics ceiling" (composed of PTFE-coated fibreglass) is suspended 50 centimetres (20 inches) below the lower chord of the roof girder. Designed to absorb sound, it helps to maintain the desired atmosphere within the building.

Built in the centre of Beijing's Olympic Park, the 258,000-square-metre (2.78-million-square-foot) stadium contains an ambulatory (a walkway that runs full circle underneath the spectator stands). The ambulatory is the main circulation space within the stadium, containing the staircases that provide access to the three tiers of seating, as well as restaurants and other amenities.

The stadium is located a short distance from the "Water Cube", the popular name for the National Aquatics Centre, which forms the other highly iconic building for the 2008 Olympic Games. While the main stadium was conceived as a bird's nest, the aquatics centre was imagined as a formation of bubbles within a square (the square being a highly symbolic form in Chinese culture). The design team, which comprised Australian architects PTW Architects, engineers Arup and China State Construction Engineering Corporation, even employed physicists from Trinity College, Dublin, to model how bubbles could be arranged in a random, organic manner in order to form a stable structure. This US$100 million, 70,000-square-metre (753,500-square-foot) centre will accommodate 17,000 people during the Games (but will shrink to just 6,000 seats afterward). The spaces within the steel structure of this building will be filled with ETFE cushions.

Left: An element of the colossal steel frame that forms Beijing's new stadium – the centrepiece of the 2008 Olympic Games. Fabricated off-site, the elements were transported piece-by-piece to the construction site.

Opposite top: Designed using the latest in parametric, computer-aided design, Beijing's stadium would have been impossible to build just a few years ago.

Opposite bottom: Known as the "Birds' Nest", Beijing's new stadium appears to have been assembled as a random collection of intersecting elements. But look closely, and a rhythm begins to appear. This naked structure will eventually be clad with panels of single-stressed ETFE foil.

project data

- The Beijing National Stadium, designed and built to host the 2008 Olympiad, occupies 204,278 square metres (2.2 million square feet) of the Olympic estate.
- The total floor area inside the stadium is 258,000 square metres (2.78-million-square-feet).
- Comprising 45,000 tonnes (49,604 tons) of steel, the structure and aesthetic of the stadium have been integrated; here the structure is exposed and celebrated, unlike other complex structures, such as the Bilbao Guggenheim Museum (page 194), where cladding materials disguise what goes on beneath.
- The outer surface of the stadium is inclined at approximately 13 degrees from the vertical.
- Architects Herzog & de Meuron and engineers Arup worked with local practice China Architectural Design and Research Group on the design of the stadium. The principal contractor on this iconic project was Beijing Urban Construction Group. The team won an international competition to design the stadium, polling eight out of the selection panel's 13 votes
- During construction the steelwork was held in place by 78 temporary supporting structures, which were dismantled in seven key stages.

CENTENNIAL HALL WROCLAW, POLAND

The Centennial Hall in Wroclaw, Poland, is a seminal work of architectural and engineering prowess, and an early example of what has come to be known as "modern" design. Built in reinforced concrete, the hall was once the largest concrete dome structure in the world. Now listed as a World Heritage Site for its "outstanding universal value" by international heritage body UNESCO, the Centennial Hall is an astonishing reminder of the capabilities of engineers a century ago.

"The Centennial Hall ... is distinguished as an outstanding example of early modern architecture and in its innovative use of reinforced concrete structures in the construction of a large hall. It was the largest dome in reinforced concrete built until its time, a modern interpretation of the amphitheatre. It was significant in creating a new technological solution of great aesthetic value, which became a major reference in the further evolution of such technology in the design of public spaces," said a UNESCO report before listing the building in 2006. "While having traces of historic evolution in its architectural forms, it was a pioneering work integrating a dynamic architectural solution to respond to emerging social needs ... The architecture of the Centennial Hall is considered of outstanding universal value from the point of view of art and science as well as presenting a significant watershed in the history of modern architecture."

When the hall was built, Wroclaw (then called Breslau) was part of Germany. Although a major German centre, the city did not have the exhibition facilities of other large cities, such as Berlin, Leipzig or Dresden, and the decision was taken in 1910 to give Breslau a boost with its own iconic structure. Called the Centennial Hall in celebration of the defeat

Left: An internal view of Poland's Centennial Hall, a stupendous achievement in concrete and a World Heritage Site.

Below: An aerial view of the hall, completed in 1913 and the centrepiece of a new park and exhibition ground.

of Napoleon at the Battle of Leipzig in 1813, the building was designed by Breslau's chief city architect Max Berg.

Berg was heavily influenced by large structures from the past, and the hall (Jahrhunderthalle in German; Hala Ludowa, "People's Hall", in Polish) bears some similarities with the sixth-century Hagia Sophia basilica in Istanbul. In plan, the building is configured as a huge "quatrefoil", or Greek Cross, with four principal entrances. Structurally, the building is set on an immense "ring beam" pierced by four large arches (41 metres/135 feet wide, 16.7 metres/55 feet high). This concrete ring supports the tiers that rise above it (like a vast wedding cake) and a series of concrete ribs that carry the domed roof. Inside the ring, visitors find themselves within a large ambulatory – a circular corridor running around the perimeter of the building – that provides access to the central exhibition hall and the upper levels.

The hall was designed to accommodate large exhibitions and public assemblies, and Berg imagined it as a wide, open space, freed from the clutter of supporting columns. The relatively new material of reinforced concrete (concrete containing steel rods, which allows it to act well in tension as well as compression) allowed Berg to realize this vision while putting the structure of the building on show. This is a building that integrates architecture and structure, which flaunts its materiality and hides nothing. When completed, the building reflected the ideas of avant-garde designers and must have been an extraordinary sight to people more used to architecture as the art of decoration. The hall is almost devoid of decoration and the texture of the concrete surfaces deliberately carries the imprint of the timber boards that provided the formwork for the structure during construction. Timber also makes an appearance in more unexpected ways: not only are the window frames made from hardwood, but timber and cork were mixed into the concrete skim for the interior spaces to provide a softer, more absorbent acoustic surface.

The building represented advanced thinking structurally, as well as aesthetically. The cement used in the production of the concrete was specially selected and the reinforcement rods were of high-grade rolled steel rather than typical structural steel. Also, in areas considered to be under high stress, a concrete aggregate containing high-quality granite was mixed, and municipal tests showed that the final product was six times harder than had been predicted. To further test the structure, a scale model was made in hardwood and subjected to a load of 6,000 kilograms (13,228 pounds).

When completed, the central, circular space could accommodate more than 6,000 people. Measuring 65 metres (213 feet) in diameter and 42 metres (138 feet) high, this space also contained the world's largest organ, which has since been removed. The building was, in fact, part of a larger building programme, which included a large park and other pavilions designed by Hans Poelzig. The Centennial Hall stood in the centre of this scheme, with the four key pathways leading to its four public entrances.

Fortunately, the hall survived both world wars intact. During the First World War the building was used as a food warehouse; Hitler used the hall for a mass gathering in 1930; and the building made it through the Second World War with little damage, while other parts of the city were devastated. By 1948 the hall, renamed the Hala Ludowa, was ready to resume exhibition work. The building has continued to operate as a well-attended performance venue and meeting place ever since. Between 1995 and 2001 the building was thoroughly overhauled to provide up-to-date and flexible facilities.

Below: The Centennial Hall was, when completed, the largest concrete dome in existence. It still gives the impression of great strength, like a vast coiled spring.

Opposite top: The Centennial Hall was designed by German architect Max Berg when the city of Breslau was part of Germany. The city later passed to Poland and was renamed Wroclaw.

Opposite bottom: A contemporary postcard of the Centennial Hall, built to celebrate a Prussian defeat of Napoleon in 1813 at the Battle of Leipzig.

project data

- The Centennial Hall was designed in 1910/11 by architect Max Berg. The City Council approved the design on June 28, 1911. By the following November the foundations had been completed and the construction of the four monumental arches began in April 1912.
- The Centennial Exhibition opened in May 1913, attracting more than 100,000 people.
- In 1924–25 the exhibition grounds and infrastructure were expanded to designs by Berg, but Second World War damage has caused these additions to be lost.
- In 1929 the hall hosted a "Living and Work-space" exhibition organized by the German "Werkbund", an important movement in the history of modern design.
- The main hall, which is 126,000 cubic metres (4.45 million cubic feet) in volume, can now accommodate a maximum of 7,200 people.

OSAKA MARITIME MUSEUM OSAKA, JAPAN

The Osaka Maritime Museum appears as a glass bubble floating on the sea. Accessed via a 60-metre (197-foot) long underwater tunnel from an entrance building constructed on reclaimed land, this striking testament to inventiveness has been designed to survive earthquakes and raging seas. Perhaps even more impressive than that, the 780-metre (2,559- foot) diameter steel and glass hemisphere was built 33 kilometres (20.5 miles) away and lowered into place as a single piece by a gigantic floating crane.

In 1993 authorities from Osaka asked Paris-based Paul Andreu Architects to draw up a scheme for a maritime museum. Once the concept of a hemispherical building was agreed, engineering companies including Arup and Japan's Tohata were brought on board to consider the complexities of building such an unusual structure in such volatile conditions. To make matters even more challenging, the building wraps around a reconstructed *higaki kaisen*, a timber trading vessel from the country's Edo period (1603–1867); rather than build the boat inside the museum, the museum was built around the boat.

The completed museum is built of four principal components: the semi-circular entrance building on land; a "land-side" tunnel; a "dome-side" tunnel buried in the seabed; and the dome itself. Each element is connected with watertight movement joints.

The dome was conceived as a simple hemisphere, built as a gridshell (a double-curved shell composed of a grid of structural elements) and fixed to a concrete wall at its "equator" point. A steel "ring beam" sits on top of the dome, supporting a 21-metre (69-foot) diameter glass cap. The glazing posed a number of issues – the design team was conscious that an all-glass structure could quickly overheat in summer but they did not want to compromise the "bubble" concept with shading devices. One idea was to install a single shading element that followed the path of the sun, blocking direct sunlight by rotating around the dome. This proved too expensive and an entirely different solution was settled upon – "lami-metal" glazing. This solution involved creating a sandwich of two sheets of glass and a central sheet of perforated metal.

Below: The dome of the Osaka Maritime Museum, set upon seawater, glows like a phosphorescent bubble during the night.

Opposite top: Designed by French architect Paul Andreu, the Osaka Maritime Museum emerged from a series of sketches. The museum was conceived as a hemisphere, floating on Osaka Bay.

Opposite bottom: The interior of the museum, showing the large spaces within the glass dome. The dome was, in fact, the last major construction episode in the building of the museum – once the interior spaces were built, the dome was literally lifted up and dropped over the off-shore site.

Computer studies showed which areas of the dome were the most susceptible to sunlight penetration at different times of the year, and the perforations in the metal were narrowed or widened accordingly. In some areas, the glazing is almost opaque, while other areas are transparent. The glazing becomes thicker toward the bottom of the dome to provide extra protection against rough seas.

The entire bubble and its three-storey contents sit on a concrete slab, which is pinned to the seabed in piles that penetrate 40 metres (131 feet) into alluvial clay (although the "dome-side" tunnel does not need piled foundations as the tunnel's weight and its buoyancy cancel each other out). Moreover, three large steel and concrete cylinders within the dome, 7.4 metres (24¼ feet) in diameter and containing escape staircases, provide extra stiffness in the event of an earthquake.

The manufacture of the dome and its installation, which took place on November 7, 1999, was an exercise in perfect timing, coordination and precision. Because the dome is so close to dry land it always made sense to prefabricate large elements and transport them to the construction site. Fortunately, just 33 kilometres (20½ miles) across Osaka Bay, Kawasaki Heavy Industry has a large manufacturing plant, which meant that the dome could be constructed, painted and glazed under controlled conditions. The hemisphere

project data

- The Osaka Maritime Museum was completed in May 2000 and officially opened two months later on 14 July.
- The museum cost 12.8 billion Yen (£80 million).
- The project was a truly international effort, being designed in Paris, engineered in the UK and Japan, and manufactured in Japan.
- The dome of the museum, 70 metres (230 feet) in diameter, is accessed via a 60-metre (197-foot) long tunnel running beneath the waters of Osaka Bay.
- The structure of the dome is composed of a diagrid of tubular steel elements 190.7 millimetres (7.5 inches) in diameter; these elements are reinforced by pre-stressed steel rods 25–36 millimetres (1–1.4 inches) in diameter.
- A series of tests were conducted on physical and computer models of the structure to test the design against earthquake shocks and heavy seas. The tests demonstrated that even under the most severe conditions (including waves 4.4 metres (14½ feet) high at 6.6 second intervals) the dome would remain watertight and stable. The stiffness of the dome and a heavy foundation assists it in surviving earthquakes (the site is near the epicentre of the 1995 Kobe earthquake).

Opposite top and bottom: The glass dome of the museum, designed as a gridshell and assembled in a local shipyard, was moved by floating crane in a carefully coordinated operation on 5 November, 1999.

Right: Inside the museum's dome, which is clad in varying types of glass positioned to restrict overheating from the sun. The centrepiece of the museum is a traditional Japanese timber ship, around which the museum was assembled.

of the dome was constructed in 12 large chunks, which were then joined together along with the upper ring beam and a network of supporting rods. Once complete, preparations began to move the 1,200-tonne (1,323-ton) structure across Osaka Bay and lift it onto its concrete base. It was an operation that had little room for error – there was clearance of just 1.5 metres (5 feet) between the internal structure of the museum and the dome itself, and the lifting manoeuvre could be carried out only in wind speeds of 7 metres (23 feet) per second or less. Sandbags were placed on the concrete internal structure to minimize damage in the event of an impact.

A floating crane transported the dome across the bay on 5 November 1999, lifting it into place two days later. The *Arup Journal* reported: "Thanks to wonderful weather, with almost no breeze, the whole operation ran smoothly to programme. The dome was in place and anchored to the substructure by lunchtime." Arup was later to win a special award from the UK Institution of Structural Engineers. On receiving the award, the company's Pat Dallard said, "Technically challenging, the steel structure, all of which can be seen, had to be elegant but able to resist severe loads whilst allowing panoramic views of Osaka Bay. Achieving this with a fully glazed dome has produced a spectacular structure."

CARGOLIFTER HANGAR BRAND, GERMANY

The CargoLifter Hangar in Brand, Germany, is claimed to be the world's largest self-supporting enclosure. At 225 metres (738 feet) wide, 363 metres (1,191 feet) long and 107 metres (351 feet) high the building could comfortably accommodate a couple of Sydney Opera Houses (see page 226).

Built on the site of a former Soviet airfield 50 kilometres (31 miles) south of Berlin, the hangar was designed for a rejuvenated airship industry using helium-filled giants capable of transporting 160 tonnes (176 tons) of goods over long distances. Unfortunately, due to financial difficulties, the building never fulfilled its role and it is now home to a covered "tropical islands" resort.

Designed by German architects SIAT Architektur + Technik, with structural input from engineers Arup, this building was conceived as more than just an industrial building. The design team deliberately wanted to reference the airship hangars of the past, and the age of the Zeppelins in particular. The building's underlying skeleton and fabric cladding provide obvious visual and structural references to the Zeppelins of the 1930s, while the gently curving form of the hangar makes it the natural home of the modern-day "blimps". The designers were also conscious of creating a building of some beauty because of the impact the immense structure would have on the surrounding flat landscape.

This structure, which can easily house two CL160 airships side by side, is the first airship hangar to be built in Germany since the late 1930s. It easily surpasses the Goodyear Airdock hangar in Akron, USA, which was previously the world's largest airship hangar (the CargoLifter structure is more than twice as wide and slightly longer) and encloses a volume of 5.2 million cubic metres (183.64 million cubic feet). In plan the hangar consists of three elements: a rectilinear central section with semicircular door units at either end (three-dimensionally, these doors form one quarter of a sphere). These doors, composed of different segments that slide

project data

- **The CargoLifter Hangar covers a total of 66,000 square metres (710,418 square feet) and is the world's largest self-supporting enclosure, enclosing 5.2 million cubic metres (183.64 million cubic feet) of space.**
- **Each of the doors at either end comprise two fixed and six moving elements that slide beneath each other. These doors are so massive that they had a major impact on the design of the entire building – steel reduction was an important part of the design brief to reduce their weight.**
- **The hangar won the Institution of Structural Engineers Structural Achievement Award in 2001 and, also in 2001, the European Steel Award for outstanding steel structure.**

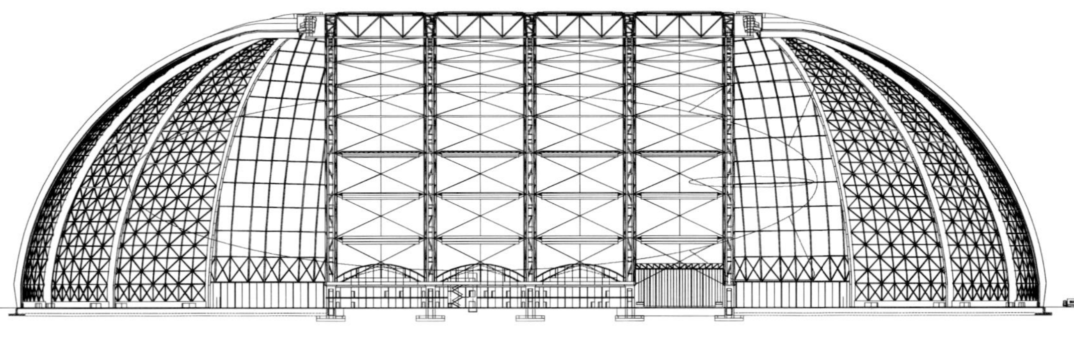

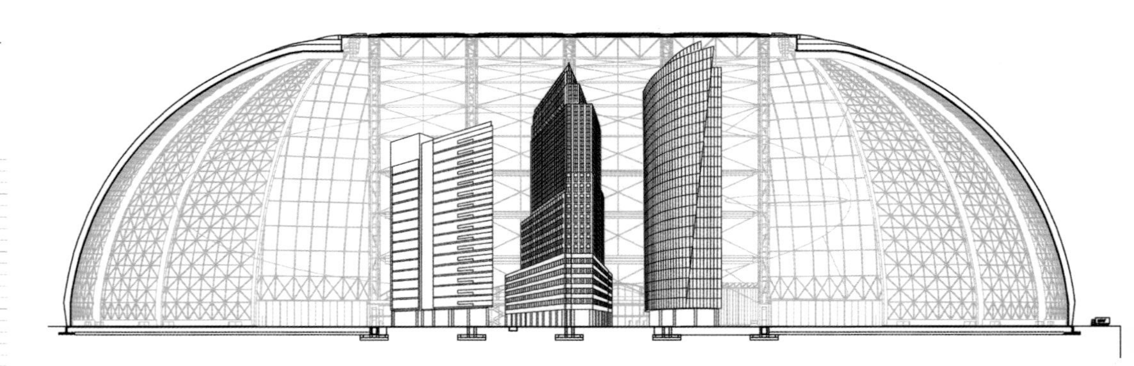

Above: A sequence of drawings of the CargoLifter Hangar, showing its short and long sections, and illustrating how this enormous structure could accommodate a series of tower blocks.

Opposite top: Three drawings illustrate the closing sequence of the overlapping door system.

Opposite bottom: Built on the site of a former Soviet airfield, this immense structure is, it is claimed, the largest enclosure in the world. Being so large, the structural engineers had to consider very carefully the effect of wind and snow loading on the building.

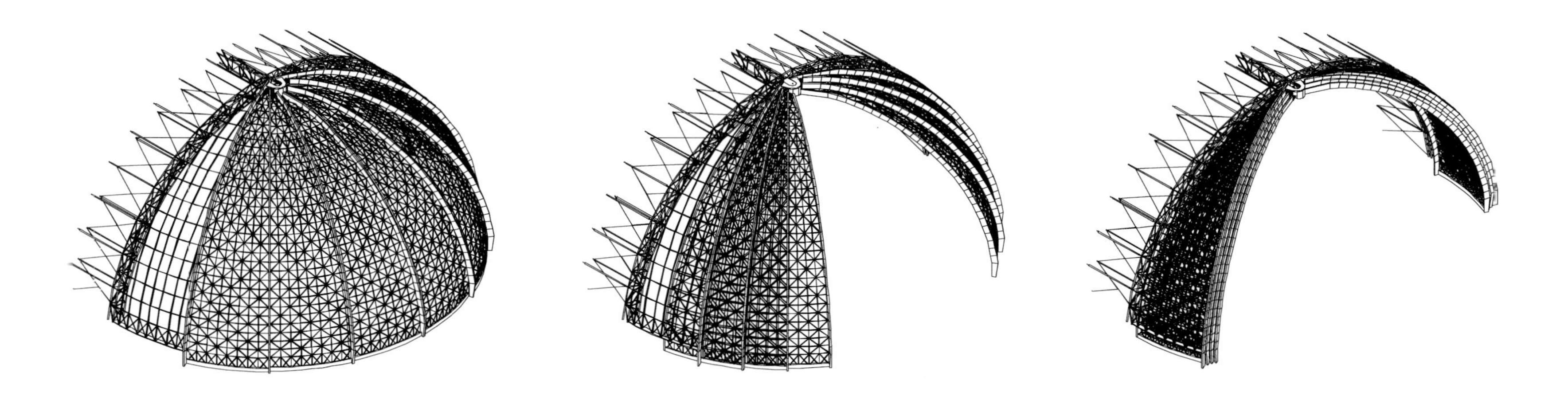

underneath each other on rails when opening, pivot on hefty steel pins at the top of the structure.

The hangar is built on a foundation and floor slab, which used 20,000 cubic metres (706,293 cubic feet) of concrete. On this foundation five enormous "arches" are set at 35-metre (115-foot) centres, each assembled from 17 steel elements that are 18 metres (59 feet) in length (these elements are actually straight, therefore these arches are not really curved, but polygonal). Glass is set above the arches, allowing daylight into the building. A ridge beam 8 metres (26 feet) deep runs along the top of these arches providing rigidity and soaking up the impact of opening and closing the large doors. The central section is covered in a translucent, PVC-coated membrane, while the doors are clad in corrugated metal sheets.

Part of the challenge of designing this immense structure was forecasting how it would perform in high winds and under loads of snow. In fact, the concrete plinths that support the steel frames are also configured as protective doorways, sheltering workers from avalanches that could run down the side of this steeply sloping building. Wind-tunnel and computer-based tests were conducted on models of the structure to test for wind loading, temperature variation and snow and ice loading. The form of the building, the size of its foundation and the type of structural steel employed (tubular hollow sections, which provide good buckling performance) means the building will perform as intended under 30 centimetres (12 inches) of ice. The aerodynamic form of the hangar minimizes the wind load on the structure (wind is not a problem in a "closed door" scenario – the doors will open only when wind velocities are below 10 metres (33 feet) per second).

Designed in 1997/98, the hangar was completed in January 2001. The building was intended to accommodate a pair of CL160 airships, a new generation of helium-filled "lighter than air" vehicles. But the airships only got as far as prototypes and the company encountered financial problems in 2002. The hangar was fitted out as a tropical theme park in 2004.

JEAN-LUC LAGARDÈRE AIRBUS ASSEMBLY HALL

The Jean-Luc Lagardère Airbus Assembly Hall in Toulouse, France, is another voluminous European giant. At 490 metres (1,608 feet) long and 250 metres (820 feet) wide, the building occupies more land than the CargoLifter Hangar, but at 46 metres (151 feet) high it is less than half the height of the German structure. The assembly hall is where the pieces for the Airbus A380 "super-jumbo" are put together, having been assembled in plants all over Europe and flown to Toulouse on the gigantic Beluga transport plane (itself one of the world's most voluminous cargo planes). This £240 million building, inaugurated in May 2004 and named after one of the founders of European aerospace company EADS, is one of Europe's largest covered spaces.

The assembly hall is the largest of the new buildings on the Airbus site near Toulouse's Blagnac airport. Together, the Airbus buildings on this site incorporate more than 32,000 tonnes (35,274 tons) of steel (the equivalent of four Eiffel Towers) and 250,000 cubic metres (8.83 million cubic feet) of concrete.

The Airbus A380 was formally unveiled on 18 January 2005. The double-decker airliner will be able, when tests are finally complete, to carry up to 800 passengers – it is so large that airports are having to spend considerable sums of money to accommodate it (especially in creating structures capable of allowing passengers to embark and disembark over two levels, as well as adapting runways and lighting). Munich airport in Germany was Europe's first airport to receive official clearance to handle the A380.

Left: The pivot point, around which the building's vast curving doors swing open. This represents one of the greatest moments of stress on the structure.

Opposite: Conceived as a hangar for a revitalized airship industry, the building is now a tropical leisure resort. The enormous helium-filled airships, which were supposed to be based in the hangar, were never built.

ENVIRONMENT CANADA BIOSPHÈRE MONTREAL, CANADA

Built originally as the United States Pavilion for the Montreal World's Fair of 1967, the pavilion, now known as the Bisophère, was a hit, welcoming more than 11 million visitors during the six months of the fair. It was meant as a temporary exhibit, to be dismantled at the end of the fair. However, such was its success that today, it remains one of the biggest tourist attractions in Montreal.

The structure itself is a geodesic dome – a dome whose framework is constructed of multiple identical triangular elements. Although light and seemingly fragile, these construction types are immensely strong and stable: they enable large hemispherical structures to be designed that feature no internal support. The creator of this pavilion was Richard Buckminster Fuller, a man renowned as the father of the geodesic dome in the twentieth century. With his earnest belief that these domes could change the way we approached the construction of all types of building, he built other similar structures, but none is as memorable or as large as the pavilion for the 1967 World Fair.

The structure has a three-dimensional steel frame, which is just over 1 metre (3 feet) wide at the base. It consists of two spheres, one inside the other which get closer together towards the top of the structure. The outer sphere is made up of triangles with 2.4-metre (8-foot) sides, while the inner sphere consists of hexagons with 1.5-metre (5-foot) sides. The two frames are connected to, and held apart from, each other by the steel tubes, welded at their joints. The entire structure is a multitude of tetrahedrons with each component attaining maximum efficiency. The dome is supported on steel bases that are embedded within the 60-centimetre (2-foot) thick foundation made of reinforced concrete.

The US Information Agency commissioned Fuller to design the pavilion in 1963. His original plans for the project were a stupendous sphere almost twice the size of the actual built pavilion: even so, a three-quarter sphere at 20 storeys high is pretty dramatic.

Built in five months, the delicate steel structure was constructed according to precise calculations, which had to take into account material-bearing loads and loading from wind and snow, as well as openings for entrances and passages for the monorail, which drove right through the middle of the dome. The resulting enormous steel-framed ball is 62.8 metres (206 feet) in height, 76.2 metres (250 feet) in diameter and has a volume of 189,725 cubic metres (6.7 million cubic feet); its total weight is 600 tonnes (661 tons).

The pavilion was built on an island in the middle of the St Lawrence River, which runs through Montreal. Fuller covered it in a transparent skin of 1,900 acrylic panels to allow light to flood in. This meant that the pavilion would be susceptible to internal heat gain and so Fuller designed a system of mobile triangular panels that would travel across the inner surface of the dome following the path of the sun and shading the interior from direct sunlight. Unfortunately, this element of his design was never fully achieved and, while it was good in theory, the technology of the day was not capable of making it work properly. Instead, valves were installed in the centre of the acrylic panels, to enable hot air to escape from the top of the pavilion as it warmed up.

While the design of the outer shell of the 1967 pavilion was awarded to Buckminster Fuller, the internal content of the pavilion was passed to Cambridge Seven Associates Inc., a group of Harvard University architecture and design professors. They devised four large platforms on which to display exhibits, which were divided into seven levels and connected by escalators, bridges and elevators, including one 37.5-metre (123-foot) escalator that was eight floors high.

The American government donated the pavilion to Montreal after the World's Fair on January 31, 1968. For several years it became an aviary filled with birds and tropical plants. Then, in 1976, while maintenance was being carried out, a fire broke out and completely destroyed the dome's acrylic skin. Only the tubular frame remained intact.

Today, the Biosphere is still in public use, as home to Environment Canada and a museum dedicated to eco-action: showcasing Canada's Great Lakes–St Lawrence River ecosystem. Montreal architect Eric Gauthier was commissioned to create a new interior in 1992. His design takes reference from the internal layout of the 1967 pavilion, using offset floor spaces and multiple levels that are roofless within the sphere. The space has been organized to maximize the amount of natural light and living contact with the Biosphère. A water garden is one of the major features within the dome, while outside, the Biosphère is reflected in a lake.

Opposite: The biosphere as it is today – devoid of its outer covering but with structure still intact. Internally, a new set of buildings has been constructed to house the environmental museum.

project data

- **The steel tubes of the structure had to be connected to a total of 5,900 nodes, of which there were 82 different types.**
- **1,900 arched transparent acrylic panels were fitted into the hexagonal inner framework of the original sphere. Today, only the steelwork skeleton remains.**
- **While the Biosphère was the largest geodesic dome at the time of its construction, that accolade is now held by the Humid Tropics Biome at the Eden Project in Cornwall, England (page 142).**
- **An ice storm that struck Quebec in January 1998 seriously damaged the Biosphère, closing it for over five months.**
- **Geodesic domes actually become stronger the larger they get.**
- **Although only built to last six months, Fuller's geodesic dome is now 40 years old.**

BUCKY FULLER AND THE GEODESIC DOME

"Geodesic" is defined in the dictionary as "an artificial structure, especially a dome, composed of a large number of identical triangles". Geodesic designs can be extended to any curved, enclosed space, although very oddly shaped designs require a high degree of calculation and so most are simple dome shapes.

The first true geodesic dome was designed and built in 1922 by Walter Bauersfeld, chief engineer of the Carl Zeiss Optical Company, for a planetarium on the roof of the Zeiss plant in Germany. However, Richard Buckminster Fuller arrived at a similar idea independently and named the dome "geodesic". He realized that this kind of dome was extremely strong for its weight and that it provided an inherently stable structure. With this in mind, he set about creating domes for numerous uses, including a new dwelling type, the Dymaxion House, to help with the housing crisis in Russia after the Second World War.

The Dymaxion House, originally conceived in the late 1920s, was well designed and used successfully for a period in Russia. However, in America it was too radical for its time and Fuller never saw his prototypes built en masse in the United States. Fuller himself lived in a geodesic dome in Carbondale, Illinois. His dome home still exists and a group called Richard Buckminster Fuller Dome Not For Profit (RBF Dome NFP for short) is attempting to restore the dome and have it registered as a National Historic Landmark.

Today, geodesic domes are used on many kinds of buildings, the largest of which is found at the Eden Project in Cornwall, United Kingdom (see page 142); the Humid Tropics Biome is 200 metres (656 feet) long, 55 metres (180 feet) high and 100 metres (328 feet) wide, with an overall area of 1.55 hectares (3.8 acres). There is even a 50-metre (164-foot) wide by 16-metre (52½-foot) high geodesic dome at the Amundsen-Scott South Pole Station, in Antarctica.

Right: Originally, the geodesic dome was clad with 1900 acrylic panels. Here we can see the monorail that ran right through it during the 1967 World Fair, for which it was built.

Far right: The sun rises over one of the largest domes in the world, during the reconstruction of the internal structure: a fitting image for an environmental biosphere.

MILLENNIUM DOME LONDON, UK

The Millennium Dome, in Greenwich, London is the largest single-roofed structure in the world. At 320 metres (1,050 feet) in diameter and a circumference of 1 kilometre (0.6 miles), the structure has an internal floor area of 100,000 square metres (1.08 million square feet). It is taller than the Royal Albert Hall, reaching 50 metres (164 feet) in height, and the 12 bright yellow masts that support the roof shoot 100 metres (328 feet) into the sky.

Had the government not changed from Conservative to Labour in 1997, the Dome project may have been a somewhat smaller affair. Under the Conservatives the celebration of the third millennium was planned as a festival of the proportions of historic World's Fairs. The Labour Party and incoming Prime Minister Tony Blair won the election, however, and seized the chance to greatly expand the project in size, scope and funding.

The rest, as they say, is history. The Dome attracted intense media coverage and generated more political and public debate than any other British building of the last century. There has been much criticism of the exhibits built within the vast structure, and although six million people visited it, this figure was four million less than predicted.

A year after the millennium celebrations were completed the internal exhibits were broken down and sold off, and the dome stood somewhat forlorn on its corner of the Greenwich Peninsula. However, the structure itself has always attracted praise. The architect, Richard Rogers Partnership (RRP), and consulting engineer, Buro Happold, have both won awards for its design.

RRP director, Mike Davies, devised the initial concept for the building, which sits at zero degrees Meridian according to Greenwich Mean Time, on the basis of the passage of time. Its 12 structural masts signify 12 months of the year, 12 hours on a clock face or 12 constellations. Buro Happold had the more "down to earth" job of transforming this design into reality. The design's key objectives were lightness, economy and speed of construction.

Spatially simple, the dome is not actually a "dome" in the structural sense. Domes are compression structures – where the structural materials rest together, pressing down to form the familiar hemispherical shape. Instead, the Millennium Dome is a lightweight tension structure built to a spherical profile. In size it has an internal enclosed space of 2.2 million cubic metres (77.7 million cubic feet). It is covered by two layers of long-life Teflon-coated fabric, which is dirt resistant and will not discolour. The 100,000-square-metre (1.08 million-square-foot) double skin reduces the possibility of condensation and traps in warm air, while still allowing through a good amount of natural light.

This layered fabric roof with a 30-metre (98-foot) diameter ring at the centre is held together by a radial tensioned cable system, which controls deflection and also provides locations from which the fabric is connected to the 12 tubular steel masts both at the top and bottom. The masts are 90 metres (295 feet) long, sit on 10-metre (33-foot) high steel bases and are hinged to allow any movement which might be caused by wind loads.

From the tips of these masts hang tensioned steel cables, arranged to connect with the series of radial cables set at 25-metre (82-foot) intervals from the centre and running around the dome: these define the spherical shape of the roof covering. On the underside there are tie-down cables connecting to the masts' base. Together, these tensioned connections hold the fabric roof in the correct position, while at the outer edge of the roof covering a series of concrete anchor points that surround the perimeter of the dome, pulling the fabric taut. On completion, the entire roof structure weighed less than the air that is contained within the dome.

The interior space was subdivided into 14 zones for the millennium exhibition – Body, Work, Learning, Money, Play, Journey, Self Portrait, Living Island, Talk, Faith, Home Planet, Rest, Mind, and Shared Ground. There was much wrangling about the content of these zones and, as a consequence, most failed to impress. Now, the Dome has been purchased and redeveloped as an entertainments complex that includes a 23,000-seat arena for sports and music events; an 11-screen cinema complex, a theatre, exhibition centre, nightclub, shops, restaurants and eventually even a beach with surfable waves.

This new use shows that structurally and architecturally, the project was a resounding success: the building has a long life ahead. And, considering the furore over the £700 million spent on the millennium celebrations, the construction was remarkably inexpensive, costing £43 million for foundation works, perimeter wall, masts, cable-net structure and the roof fabric.

Below: Situated on land in a vast bow of the River Thames, the scale of the Millennium Dome is difficult to truly appreciate. However, the tower block and regular pattern of the white-clad housing estate in the foreground provide some idea of its size.

Opposite: The dome's 12 yellow tubular steel masts provide anchorage for a plethora of cables, which hold up the Teflon-coated roof covering. The giant hole, seen here, allows an exhaust chimney from the road tunnel beneath the Dome to vent into the atmosphere.

project data

- **In the west side of the roof there is a 50-metre (164-foot) diameter opening to allow the air vents from the Blackwall road tunnel, which lies underneath, to pass through.**
- **All electrical and mechanical machinery required to power and ventilate the Dome is situated in 12 cylindrical towers that surround the structure; this kept the interior free for visitors and entertainment activities.**
- **The Dome is suspended from a series of 12 steel masts 100 metres (328 feet) in length, held in place by more than 70 kilometres (43½ miles) of high-strength steel cable which in turn support the fabric roof.**
- **It is 320 metres (1,050 feet) in diameter – large enough for over three football pitches to be laid end to end inside it.**
- **The Dome isn't a dome strictly speaking because its structure is tensioned, rather than being in compression.**
- **The Dome featured in the title sequence of the 1999 James Bond film *The World is not Enough.***

AMSTERDAM ARENA AMSTERDAM, THE NETHERLANDS

The Amsterdam ArenA (officially written "ArenA"), which opened in August 1996, was Europe's first stadium to incorporate a retractable roof in its design, allowing a large open-air space to be fully enclosed and weatherproofed. Costing 140 million Euros, the 51,628-plus-seater stadium provides a home for Ajax Football Club but also functions as a venue for the city's American football team (the Amsterdam Admirals), concerts and other large events, for which capacity can rise to 68,000. Extraordinarily, a public road and a 2,000-space car park, called the "Transferium", is sited beneath the stadium; the roof of the car park acts as a huge concrete tray and provides the foundation on which the grass pitch is laid above.

The arena was originally conceived as an Olympic stadium for Amsterdam's bid to host the 1992 Olympic Games. These Games eventually went to Barcelona, however, but a variation of the project went ahead because Ajax FC was outgrowing the De Meer stadium, which had been its home ground since 1934.

Designed by architects Rob Schuurman and Sjoerd Soeters, the stadium stands 78 metres (256 feet) high, 235 metres (771 feet) long and 180 metres (591 feet) wide, and is an imposing structure. Indeed, everything about this structure is large. The arena contains the Netherlands' press facility, containing spaces for 230 journalists and commentators, a 40-seat Royal Box and 15 banqueting rooms. In fact, the area covered by the structure, at 35,000 square metres (376,737 square feet), would cover the space of four football pitches. The arena is even equipped with two vast video units with screens measuring 50 square metres (538 square feet) and weighing 13 tonnes (14.3 tons) each, slung from the roof structure.

The structure is defined by a pair of enormous portal frames, or "goal-post frames", which support the roof structure (large goal-post frames can also be seen at Liverpool Football Club's Anfield stadium and the San Siro stadium in Milan). These frames, with their curved profile, are linked by trusses that run along the length of the stadium, and provide a table-like form from which the roof assembly is supported. The curves of the giant frames support the track that allows the central portion of the roof to slide open and closed.

The variable-speed, retractable roof, which can generally close within 18 minutes, is composed of two 118-metre (387-foot) by 40-metre (131-foot) elements: these elements overlap in the middle to provide an air gap which allows air to continue to circulate. The sliding roof weighs 400 tonnes (441 tons) and is powered by eight engines. Importantly, the roof is transparent, allowing sunlight to reach the grass of the pitch, even when the roof is in the closed position. The turf is, in fact, watered from underneath.

The health of the pitch is obviously vital to a sports facility, and a number of tactics have been employed to help ensure the health of the grass, although the turf has had to be replaced on a number of occasions. A "dry moat" which separates fans from the pitch helps prevent "pitch invasions" while avoiding the need for intrusive fencing. Also, when the pitch is covered over for other events, such as concerts, special transparent tiles are used which allow air to continue to reach the grass beneath. The arena's operators believe that these protective tiles can be left in place for up to five days without having an adverse effect on the grass.

In spite of being a multi-purpose venue, the arena is best known as the home of Ajax FC. The move to the new ground in 1996 was a necessary but difficult one for the football club and its fans, who had come to love the smaller De Meer Stadium constructed in 1934. Originally built for 22,000 spectators, and later expanded to accommodate 39,500, the De Meer ground came to be insufficient to meet the needs of the modern game and its fanbase. The new structure also provides a venue suitable for large rock concerts: performers including Tina Turner, Céline Dion and The Rolling Stones have played here.

Since the Amsterdam ArenA's completion, the Millennium Stadium in Cardiff, Wales, has also been built with a retractable roof. Completed in 1999 to a design by international architecture firm HOK, this stadium has a seating capacity of 74,500.

Opposite top: The Amsterdam ArenA, a multi-purpose venue which provides a home for the city's Ajax football club, was Europe's first stadium with a fully-retractable roof.

Opposite bottom: The arena's vast portal frames, along with the lateral beams joining them together, can be seen clearly in this image. The primary structure is almost like a giant table, under which everything else fits neatly.

project data

- **Amsterdam ArenA was officially opened by The Netherlands' Queen Beatrix on August 14, 1996.**
- **When operating as a football stadium, the arena provides 51,628 seats, although this number can be increased when using the pitch for other events.**
- **The structure weighs about 150,000 tonnes (165,347 tons) and is supported on 1,650 piles driven deep into the ground.**
- **The sliding roof can close in five minutes in an emergency; to conserve power, the roof may also take as long as half an hour to close.**
- **Beneath the surface of the pitch is a layer of sand that covers a network of drainage pipes and heating elements. There is then a further layer of sand, followed by the concrete roof of the underground car park.**
- **The arena's lawnmower covers 14 kilometres (8.7 miles) each time it trims the grass of the pitch.**
- **During its first decade of operation, 18 million people visited the arena.**

Right and below: Images of the Amsterdam ArenA showing the roof in the open and closed positions. Even when closed, enough sunlight reaches the pitch to allow the grass to grow.

MULTIHALLE MANNHEIM, GERMANY

The Multihalle, which was designed for the 1975 Federal Garden Exhibition (Bundesgartenschau) held in Germany's Mannheim, is arguably the world's first "gridshell" building. Built as a temporary structure but now a listed building, the Multihalle (multi-purpose hall and café) was one of the pioneering structures of German architect Frei Otto.

Otto is the father of lightweight buildings – tented structures, cable-nets and gridshells. These are structures that enclose the maximum amount of space by using the smallest amount of mass, often by employing natural forms that are designed to mimic the tension and equilibrium found in structures such as string bags, soap bubbles and hanging chains. Otto had begun to investigate such structures at the tail end of the Second World War as a prisoner-of-war. Otto was made responsible for maintaining the buildings at his POW camp, and as such made as much use of scarce materials as possible. He developed his ideas throughout the 1950s and 1960s and founded the Institute for Lightweight Structures at the University of Stuttgart in 1964.

In terms of his approach, Otto has something in common with Spanish architect Antonio Gaudí, who used physical models to examine the effect of gravity and to map out the geometries of complex forms. Neither architect took a sculptural approach to their work (in the sense of creating forms which then had to be rationalized; instead, their forms were rational to begin with). In the pre-computer age, physical models of weighted strings (often hanging upside down to let gravity create the arches and sinuous lines of distortion) were remarkably accurate in predicting the behaviour of actual structures.

Otto was employed as a consultant to a local firm of architects, Mutschler und Langner, to help resolve the issues surrounding the construction of an organic, undulating form for Mannheim's Multihalle. Otto had already carved out an international reputation for himself by designing the German Pavilion for the 1967 World's Fair in Montreal, as well as the high-tensile roof structure for Munich's Olympic Arena in 1972. The Multihalle ended up as a double-layer gridshell (much like the Weald & Downland Museum structure described on page 162). In other words, it is composed of four layers of timber elements (two lying in one direction, two in the other) to form a structure of

Below: An aerial view of Mannheim's Multihalle, built in 1972 as a highly experimental form for the city's garden exhibition. Conceived by architect Frei Otto, the building pushed design and construction technologies to the limit.

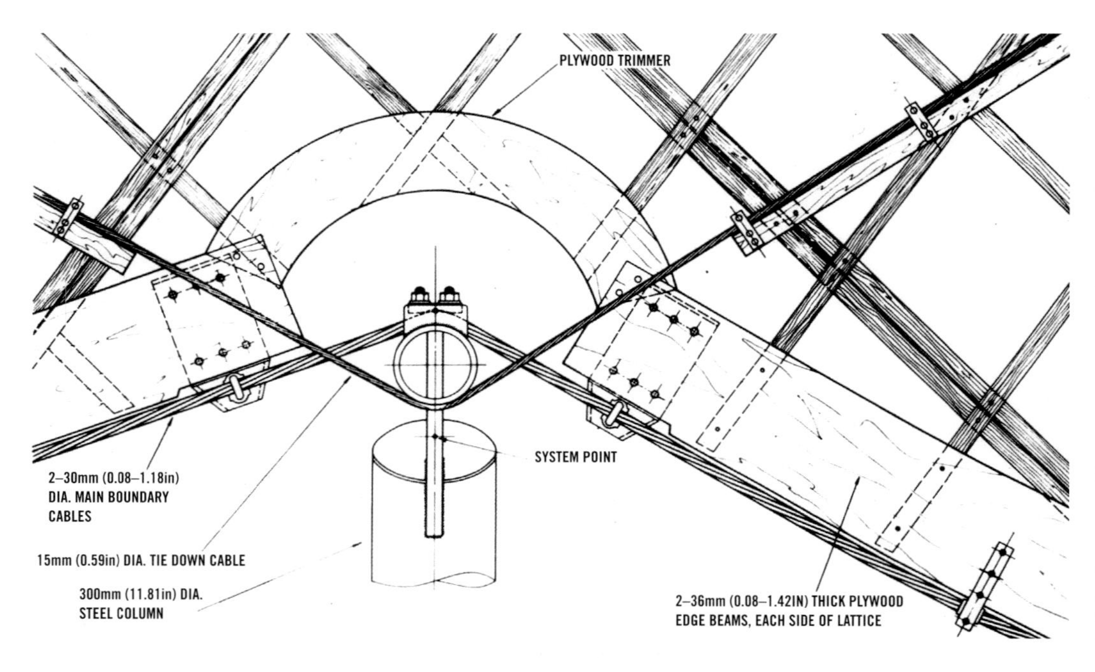
PLYWOOD TRIMMER
SYSTEM POINT
2–30mm (0.08–1.18in)
DIA. MAIN BOUNDARY
CABLES
15mm (0.59in) DIA. TIE DOWN CABLE
300mm (11.81in) DIA.
STEEL COLUMN
2–36mm (0.08–1.42IN) THICK PLYWOOD
EDGE BEAMS, EACH SIDE OF LATTICE

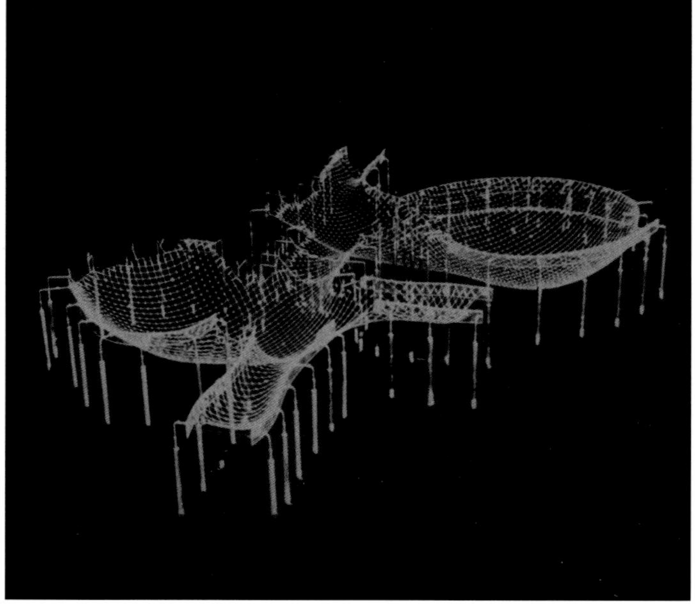

Opposite top left: A detail drawing of a connection node of the timber construction.

Opposite top right: Frei Otto created the form of the Multihalle with an upside-down string model, allowing gravity to determine its shape. The physical model became the reference for one of the world's first computerised building models.

Opposite bottom: The Multihalle occupies its site in Mannheim like an undulating jellyfish. Technically difficult to construct, its gentle and sinuous lines make it appear to be a natural and rather simple undertaking.

Below: An Image of the Multihalle before being fully clad, allowing a view of the pure structure of the building, formed from hundreds of pieces of timber and assembled as a gridshell.

two latticeworks. The principle behind this technique is that smaller pieces of timber are easier to bend and distort than more massive elements. At Mannheim, 50-by-50-millimetre (2-by-2-inch) laths of hemlock pine were positioned on a grid at 500-millimetre (20-inch) centres. However, when bending this grid of flat timbers into shape, the failure rate was high – as many as 60 per cent of the timbers broke. Now that engineers have a greater understanding of the performance of timber in gridshell structures such as this, this failure rate can be slashed – breakage rates on the Downland Gridshell were reportedly in single percentage figures.

The Mannheim structure is a more complex form than that attempted more recently at the Weald & Downland Museum, however, and it tested the ingenuity of its architects and of structural engineering firm Ove Arup & Partners. In fact, the structure was developed in two ways: as a physical model by Otto, who laboriously created a model made of individual threads (assembled as a net and hung upside down); and as a mathematical model created by Arup. The engineers, by developing a piece of mathematics called the "dynamic relaxation algorithm" (DR), were beginning to be able to mimic the physical models with early computer analysis. The problem with the models was that, although they established the form and geometries accurately enough, they could not be measured with the precision needed to calculate the exact angles and lengths of the construction assembly.

"A major constraint on the production of large-scale surface structures at that time was the accurate definition of their spatial geometry. This was necessary for analysis and justification purposes, as well as for detailed drawings and cutting patterns for construction. In these respects physical models were labour intensive and prone to measurement errors," says a paper written by Arup on the development of membrane structures. "Rather than start from an approximation to the final form by taking measurements from models, the imaginative step was to see that a precise statement of the net's topology (i.e. which element is joined to which and the lengths of each) would be sufficient input data for DR to compute the large displacements involved with all the elements starting from within the same plane as the support points. In doing this we were exactly replicating the physical behaviour of the net model as it falls and takes up its shape."

Covered in a PVC-fabric, Mannheim's timber gridshell opened on April 1, 1975, and closed the following October. It has since become a German icon – 160 metres (525 feet) long and 20 metres (66 feet) high, this sinuous, groundbreaking structure spans up to 60 metres (197 feet) without the help of columns. It is a playful, slightly beguiling structure. But that is the point. Otto's Institute for Lightweight Structures declares that architecture should be considered more like clothing, which is flexible, rapidly changed and highly reflective of contemporary culture: "Monolithic and monotonous buildings destroy not only nature itself, but also the unique individuality of humankind. To preserve the essence of humankind and its environment, Frei Otto dreamt of, and searched for, forms in natural landscapes that were as adaptable and versatile as possible. The rediscovery of lightness in architecture is a Modernist reaction to new aesthetic and economic aspects of life. Lightweight structures meet the challenges of the times in the field of architecture: with little material and effort, multi-purpose buildings can be designed that are highly stable, light and rapidly constructed."

project data

- The Multihalle at Mannheim was built in 1973–75, having first been modelled in thread at a scale of 1:500.
- The structure is covered in 9,500 square metres (102,257 square feet) of fabric.
- Frei Otto's designs are examples of what he has called the "economic" principle – "the less mass a structure needs to transfer forces, the better its form is".
- Otto received the Royal Gold Medal from the Royal Institute of British Architects (RIBA) in 2005. When presenting the medal, the RIBA President said that Otto had "a genuine claim to be one of the real greats of the twentieth century".

SUR
FACE

THE surface of a building or structure is so often much more than its outer covering. Before the development of steel-framed buildings, the surface was always the load-bearing structure of a building. The bricks and mortar, stone or timber walls were what held it up.

This still rings true for many designs but nowadays the choice of materials available to architects and engineers means that, whether structural or not, the surface of our buildings is often their defining characteristic. From the rippling titanium shell of the Guggenheim Museum, in Bilbao, to the structural gymnastics of the 2003 Serpentine Pavilion or the 1958 Philips Pavilion, the "engineered" surface plays a significant role: it may be a structural frame from which all else hangs; it is often a weatherproof skin; and more often than not, it can also bring its inert structural skeleton to life.

BILBAO GUGGENHEIM MUSEUM BILBAO, SPAIN

Along with the Empire State Building (see page 50), the Golden Gate Bridge (see page 132) and the Sydney Opera House (see page 226), the Bilbao Guggenheim Museum is, without doubt, one of the most iconic structures of the twentieth century. Designed by Canadian-born, Los Angeles-based architect Frank O. Gehry, this titanium-clad building single-handedly put the declining industrial port of Bilbao on the cultural map.

Conceived in early 1991 when city officials invited the Solomon R. Guggenheim Foundation to consider setting up a gallery in Bilbao, the building was completed in October 1997. The gallery is an exuberant, free-flowing structure that almost defies architectural definition – one description of it is "Expressionist Modern".

The most eye-catching element of the building is, of course, the highly reflective, titanium-clad galleries that appear to swoop and dance above the River Nervión. These forms, although by no means the totality of the building (there are also regular, stone-clad elements), provided both the aesthetic impetus to the project and the engineering challenge. Since the late 1980s Frank O. Gehry had been developing rolling, organic forms (in the International Headquarters of furniture company Vitra, for example, and in the curving, almost sexy lines of the Nationale-Nederlanden building in Prague), but in Bilbao the architect pushed this approach much further. Gehry's sketches and free-form models had to be deconstructed in such a way that they could be costed, project managed and actually built.

This is where 3-D computer-modelling tool Catia, a program for designing and assembling complex three-dimensional shapes such as aircraft, came in useful. The design team "digitized" the physical model by scanning it in three dimensions, producing a set of precise points within Catia; these points were then joined to create the outline of the model; the primary and secondary steel structures could then be plotted; then "scales" of the cladding were added. With this computer model, where every single building element is given a precise location and dimension, it was possible to establish the curvature required of individual panels, to establish costs and send cutting templates to manufacturers. Furthermore,

Below: The Guggenheim in Bilbao, Spain, is arguably the building that set the tone for sculptural pieces of architecture ever since, and single-handedly put Bilbao on the cultural world map.

Opposite: The titanium-clad curves of this astonishing building, although mildly discoloured, are still an epic sight. Sheets of very thin titanium were applied to the structure to give the building a shimmering appearance.

technology like this allowed the construction crew to set about building the Guggenheim with a fair degree of certainty – very often, especially on large complex projects like this, contractors find themselves solving problems that have not been anticipated in the design offices. "We use all the technology available to us to quantify in a most precise way the elements of the building. This fact alone allows us to demystify for the construction people the elements of the building so there's not a lot of guessing," Gehry told *Harvard Design* Magazine in 2005.

As well as pioneering new computer technology, Gehry also made an unusual choice in selecting titanium for the cladding of this building. The architects actually assessed the properties of 29 different cladding materials, including copper and aluminium, but titanium was chosen for its lightness and reflective qualities. Each panel is around 0.5 millimetres (0.02 inches) thick, giving the building a shimmering, almost panel-beaten look. These panels (all entirely unique in shape) do require regular cleaning, however, to avoid discoloration and staining, although the application of silicone sealants also help preserve the gleaming quality of the metal. It is estimated that this titanium "skin" will last 100 years.

The foundation stone of the gallery was laid in October 1993, beginning a construction programme lasting four years. The finished building contains 11,000 square metres (118,403 square feet) of exhibition space in 19 galleries (nine of which are housed within the titanium-clad forms). Larger artworks are accommodated by a massive, column-free 130-by-30-metre (427-by-98-foot) gallery.

The gallery has proved an astonishing success, not only by attracting 1.3 million visitors in its first year but in providing the impetus for further regeneration. The gallery is built on a former industrial site and new investment in Bilbao is helping to provide new infrastructure and a new city image. This project is a testament to the power of arts-led regeneration and the role of architecture in establishing a sense of identity in the modern world.

SOLOMON R. GUGGENHEIM FOUNDATION

The Solomon R. Guggenheim Foundation, a not-for-profit corporation, has become a significant patron of architecture since it was founded in 1937. The foundation's first major project was the building of the New York Guggenheim Museum, designed by Frank Lloyd Wright and completed in 1959. This circular whirlpool of a building has always been the defining icon of the Guggenheim brand, and the building is as significant a cultural attraction as the artwork inside.

The Guggenheim Foundation has since established outposts in Las Vegas, Berlin and Venice, but it also has ambitions to establish a presence in Asia, Latin America and the Middle East. In 2006 the foundation unveiled plans for a 30,000-square-metre (322,917-square-foot) museum, designed by Frank O. Gehry, to be built in Abu Dhabi, capital of the United Arab Emirates. The building is likely to be complete by 2011.

Opposite: As well as being clad in titanium, the Guggenheim features limestone, glass and marble. This structure was conceived and built to be an uplifting, inspirational place – much like a medieval cathedral.

Above: The design and construction of this mass of swooping, curving forms (almost like a Baroque decoration) would not have been possible without modern computing and "parametric" modelling techniques.

Right: A plan drawing of the museum in relation to its waterside site. Seen from above, it is clear that the Guggenheim is composed of both curving and rectilinear volumes.

SOUTH ELEVATION

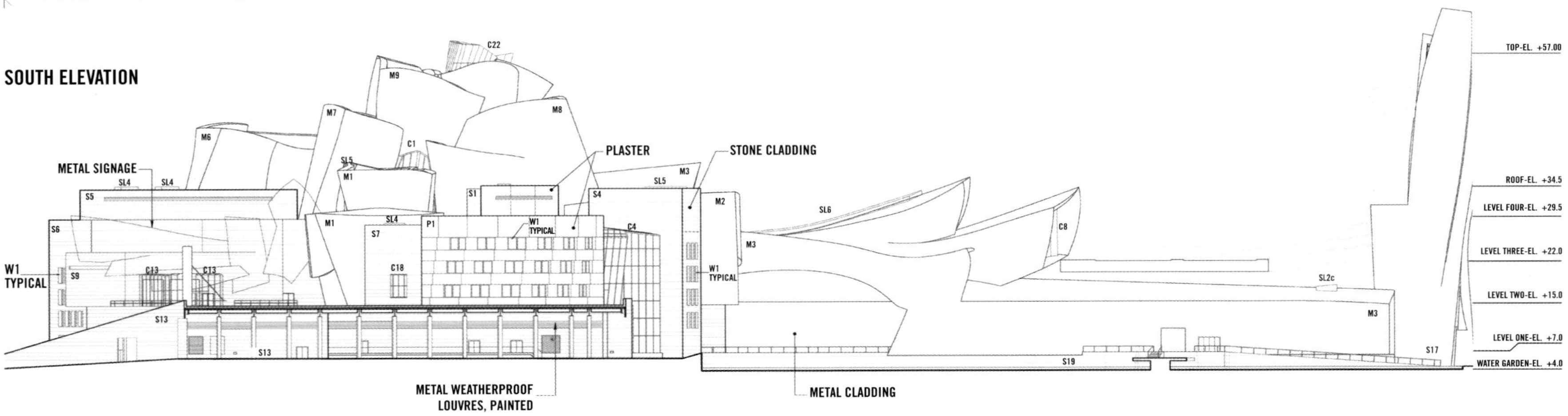

METAL SIGNAGE

W1 TYPICAL

PLASTER

STONE CLADDING

METAL WEATHERPROOF LOUVRES, PAINTED

METAL CLADDING

NORTH ELEVATION

METAL CLADDING

STONE CLADDING

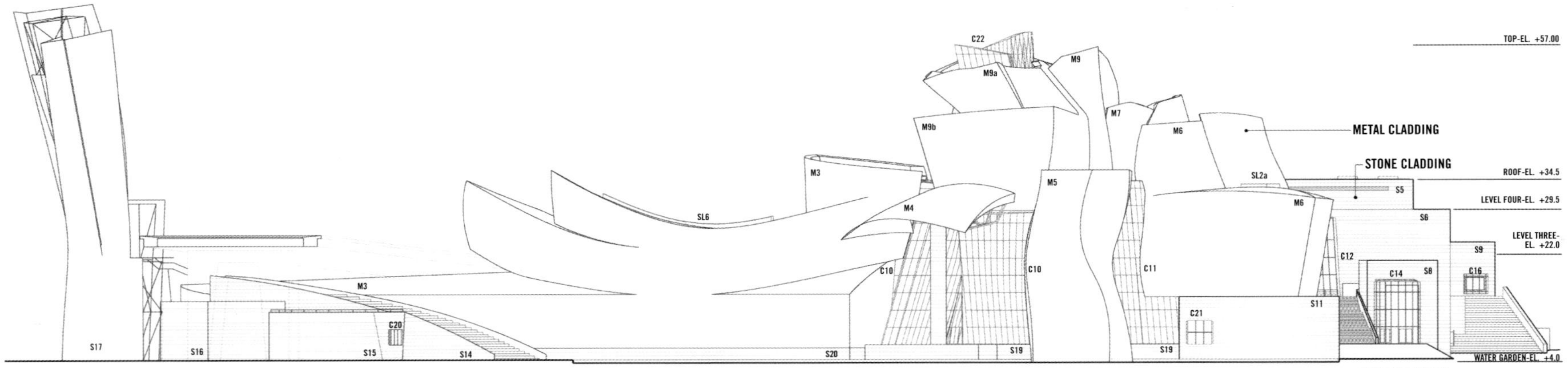

NUMBERS SL1–SL6 DESIGNATE SKYLIGHTS

NUMBERS W1–W3 DESIGNATE WINDOW TYPES

NUMBERS S1–S20 DESIGNATE STONE FORMS

NUMBERS M1–M11 DESIGNATE METAL FORMS

NUMBERS C1–C23 DESIGNATE GLASS ELEMENTS

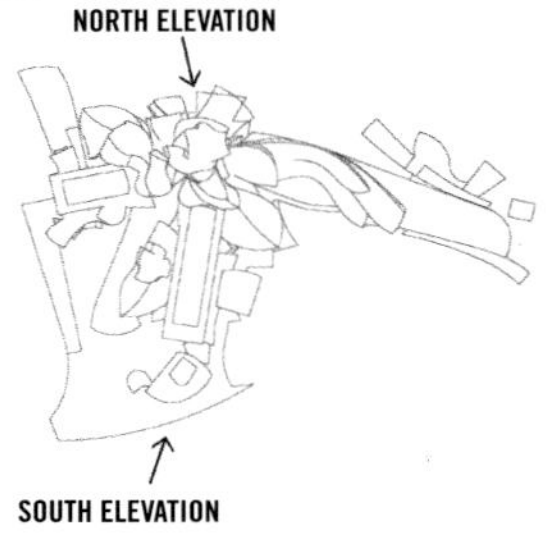

NORTH ELEVATION

SOUTH ELEVATION

BUILDING SECTION CC

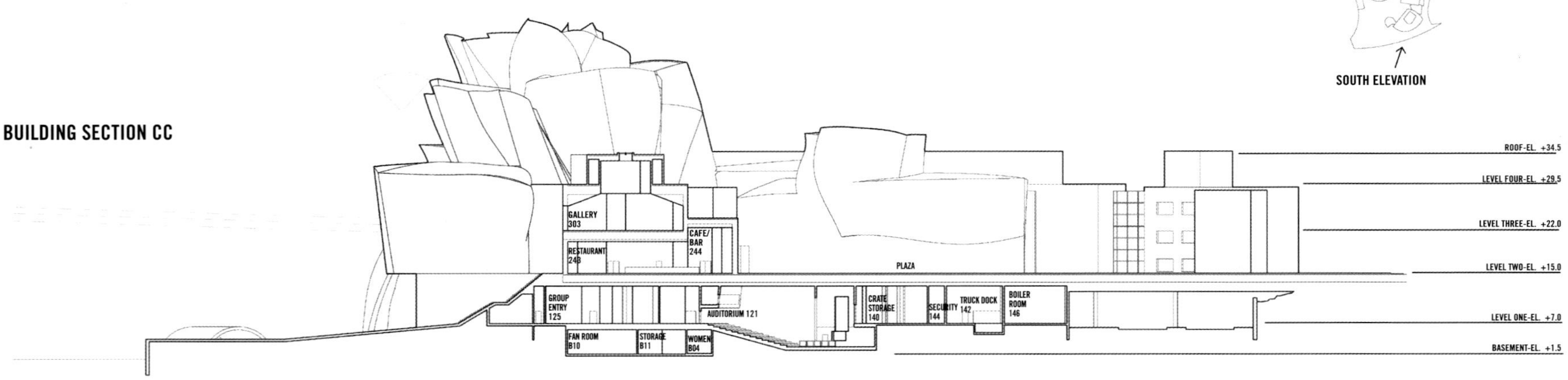

BUILDING SECTION DD

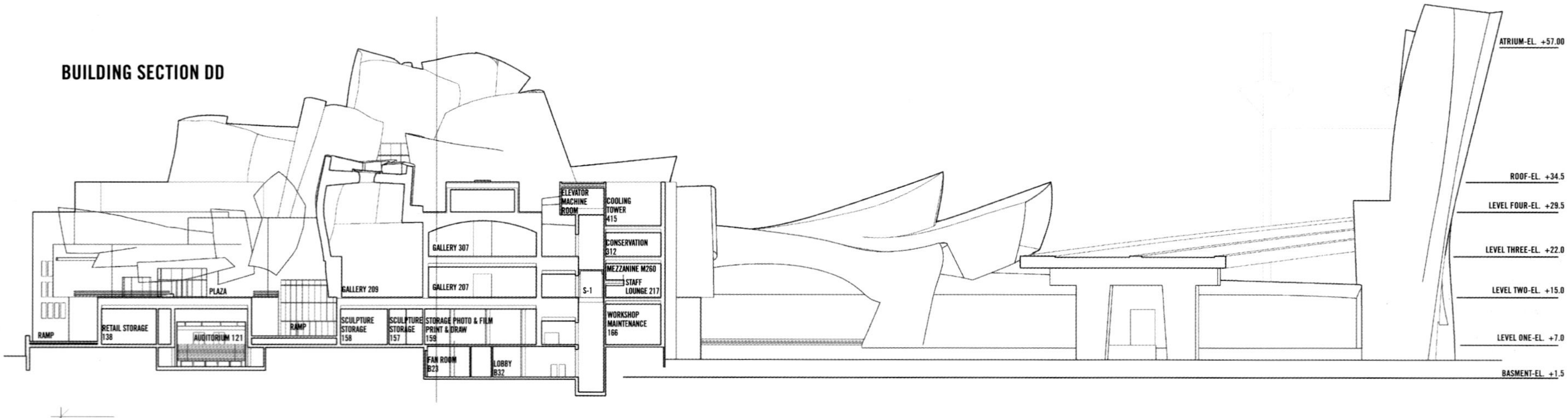

Opposite: Elevational and sectional drawings of Bilbao's Guggenheim, showing how orthogonal (box-like) spaces have been assimiliated into the curving mass of the building.

Above: The titanium panels which clad this building are all unique in size and shape. Fully assembled, they give the Guggenheim a "panel-beaten" look.

project data

- The Guggenheim building in Bilbao, Spain, began life as an idea in 1991. Frank O. Gehry was selected as architect in 1992 and he presented his first model in 1993.
- The building was completed on October 3, 1997 and opened to the public on October 19.
- Standing 57 metres (187 feet) high, the building sits within a 32,500-square-metre (349,827-square-foot) site.
- It is not completely clad in titanium panels – the less baroque, more orthogonal elements are clad in limestone and marble.
- The building contains 10 regular-shaped gallery spaces and nine irregular ones.
- The thin "fish-scale" titanium sheathing is designed to last for 100 years.

QUEEN ELIZABETH II AD 2000 THIS GREAT
Cleopatra
Great Court

GREAT COURT BRITISH MUSEUM, LONDON, UK

The Great Court at London's British Museum was created by reinventing what was originally a central courtyard, hidden since 1857, and installing a roof of mesmerizing complexity in 2000. This undulating structure, comprising more than 3,000 entirely unique triangles of glass, is a tribute to contemporary engineering and the imagination of the client.

The British Museum was conceived in the 1820s and built in the middle of the nineteenth century to the designs of Sir Robert Smirke, who drew up a quadrangle along classical lines. However, the central courtyard quickly became the site for the new British Library, and a circular reading room, designed by Smirke's brother Sydney, was placed off-centre in the quadrangle and surrounded by a warren of corridors and book stacks. The dome to the reading room was an inventive and bold structure, using cast iron and filled in with a form of papier mâché made of pulped paper, chalk and setting plaster. The completion of a new, dedicated building for the British Library in the 1990s allowed the museum to clear out the central courtyard and give this rambling courtyard a new heart.

Having raised £100 million, the museum commissioned architects Foster and Partners (who brought in engineers Buro Happold) to undertake the project. The drum of the reading room was retained and faced in limestone, while the rest of the courtyard was roofed over with a structure weighing 793 tonnes (874 tons), becoming one of the largest covered courtyards in Europe. Creating the geometry for this glazed roof was extremely complex as the circular reading room is off-centre, the heights of the four buildings which make up the courtyard are different and local conservation groups did not want the exterior of the building to be marked too much by the new structure. The roof therefore swoops and curves its way around this 73-by-92-metre (240-by-302-foot) space, wrapping around the 43-metre (141-foot) diameter reading room and appearing to rest as lightly on the existing structure as possible. More than 3,000 lines of computer code were written for this project, largely for the definition of the geometry, but also for structural analysis.

The mathematics behind the form and grid of the roof is extraordinarily complex, but it allowed the design team to test out a variety of refinements in order to arrive at a form that was regular, aesthetically pleasing and structurally sound. In early versions, the roof pattern met the boundary in an unsatisfactory manner or even necessitated the introduction of quadrilateral, as opposed to triangular, elements. The final form, comprising a series of overlapping arcs, is reminiscent of spiralling patterns found in nature (patterns that are often mathematically ordained). This solution meant installing 3,312 glass triangles, each one unique, into a steel structure of precisely welded nodes. Importantly, the roof rests on a set of hidden supports, 20 of which are hidden within the newly clad walls of the reading room. The outside edges of the roof rest on sliding bearings (allowing the roof to expand and contract through temperature changes) hidden by the parapets of the original buildings.

The erection of the roof was preceded by setting up a forest of scaffolding. Then, the steel roofing elements, made from high-purity steel by Waagner-Biro in Austria and assembled in England, were lifted into place. This construction process involved welding 5,200 steel members to 1,826 nodes, each of which

Left: The Great Court at the British Museum, London. This remarkable roof created a popular public plaza out of what was once a hidden and cluttered space.

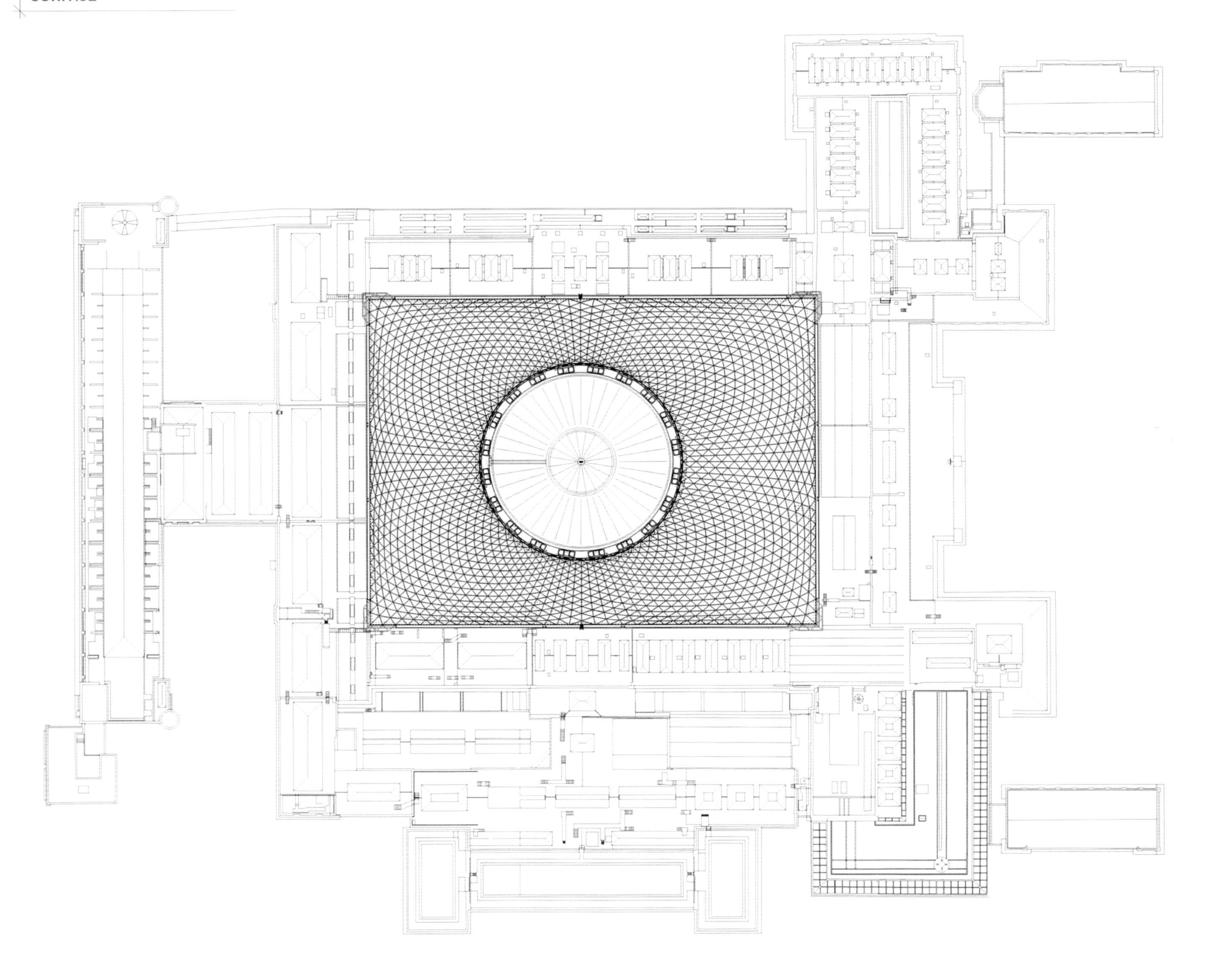

Above: A plan view of the museum's new roof, illustrating the spiralling lines of the structure which encircle the drum of the Reading Room.

project data

- The reinvention of the British Museum's central courtyard began with an architectural competition in 1993. Three practices were shortlisted: Arup Associates, Rick Mather Associates and Foster and Partners. Foster was declared the winner in July 1994.
- Building work began on March 2, 1998, and continued until December 2000.
- The reinvention of the British Museum's courtyard involved the excavation and removal of 20,000 cubic metres (706,300 cubic feet) of material. Because the museum continued to operate during the building process, much of the building material was moved by a crane that reached over the building. By November 1998 the demolition phase of the project, involving excavating to a depth of 10 metres (33 feet), was complete.
- The outer surface of the stadium is inclined at approximately 13 degrees from the vertical.
- The roof weighs 793 tonnes (874 tons), comprising 478 tonnes (527 tons) of steel and 315 tonnes (347 tons) of glass.
- The opening of the Great Court was accompanied by a furore over the quality of limestone used in the building of the new south portico, which differs from the colour of the existing stonework. Threats that planning authorities were considering ordering the portico to be demolished subsequently evaporated.

Above: Viewed from the outside, the roof of the museum appears light, bulging out like an air-filled pillow. It is, in fact, a curving assembly of steel and glass.

Below: A section through the middle of the museum, showing how the new roof wraps around the dome of the nineteenth-century Reading Room, covering the spaces below.

was configured to take an individual glass triangle. Incidentally, the pieces of glass have been "fritted" (that is, given a surface treatment of white ceramic dots) to reflect much of the sunlight and cut down on the heat admitted by the roof. Although it is not visible at ground level, 56 per cent of the surface of the glass has been fritted, cutting out 75 per cent of the heat gain.

Once the glass had been fitted to the steelwork, the scaffolding and supporting structures were removed. This was the critical stage of the project – the engineers had calculated that the roof would "relax" a little, dropping and spreading into its natural position. Fortunately, the roof did exactly as was forecast, and dropped 150 millimetres (6 inches) and spread by 90 millimetres (3½ inches). Once done, the French limestone floor could be installed in the courtyard.

The completed roof has become much admired by critics and museum visitors alike, and it shelters a courtyard that acts as a popular public space rather than merely as an element of the museum. In spite of the complexity involved in making the roof a reality, its success lies in the simplicity of the original idea – what the British Museum has called "the marriage of functionality and form".

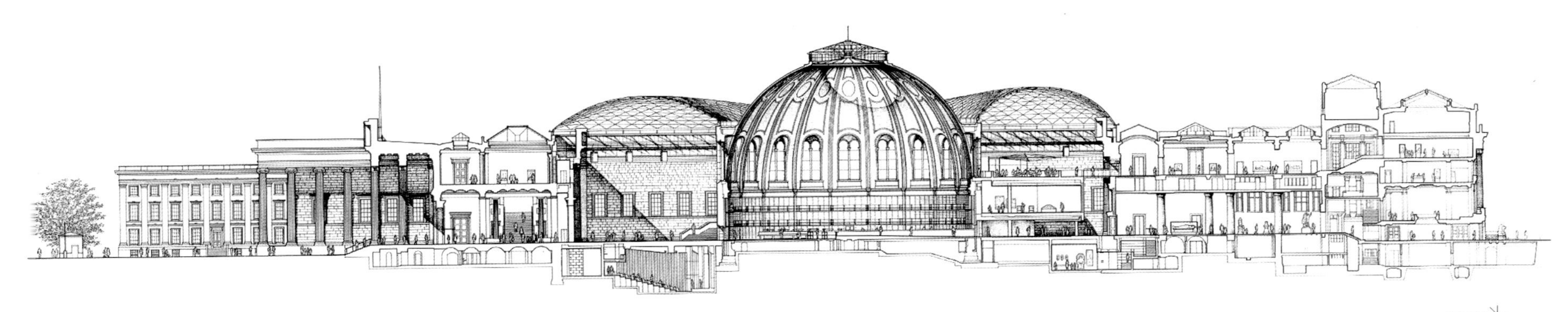

TWA FLIGHT CENTER JOHN F. KENNEDY INTERNATIONAL AIRPORT, NEW YORK, USA

Since the late 1970s airports have become vast production lines processing huge numbers of passengers as efficiently as possible. There is no drama or romance to the airport experience, probably because we now simply expect to fly, rather than dream of doing it.

This was not the case in the 1950s. Then, on the cusp of the "jet age", most people didn't ever envisage jumping on an aeroplane to go on holiday. Flying was an exciting, adventurous and expensive luxury that only a relative few could afford. And the glamour associated with it was reflected in the airports of that period – especially in the United States.

Finnish architect Eero Saarinen designed the TWA Flight Center at Idlewild Airport in New York – now the John F. Kennedy International Airport – and Washington Dulles International Airport. He created two startlingly different terminals, both of which were constructed from pre-stressed concrete.

The TWA Flight Center was perhaps the most dramatic. Opened in 1962, its swooping concrete wings have been often likened to a bird taking flight. Saarinen, however, did not use this metaphor as a design inspiration; instead he considered it, "an abstract symbol of flight", that was designed to express movement and transition. The structure consists of four vaulted concrete domes, which meet and bisect one another to form the combined roof canopy and walls in one curvaceous form. They are supported on four huge Y-shaped concrete columns to create a vast, umbrella-like shell some 15.2 metres (50 feet) high and 96 metres (315 feet) long, which curves over the passenger areas.

In spite of being made of concrete, the construction has an amazing sense of lightness. This is due to Saarinen's appreciation of the aesthetics of structural design. The upwards "movement" or inclination of the curves in the structure make them soar above visitors' heads, rather than pressing down in the way a flat concrete ceiling would. Additionally, light floods in through bands of skylights at a high level, which separate and lift the concrete structures, so that they appear to be floating.

Saarinen, his team of architects and engineering firm Amman & Whitney designed the building first in a series of scale models. The architect's previous training as a sculptor had encouraged him to work in this way, and he took the skill to particular lengths with this project. Some models were of particular details, others were entire building mock-ups. While most were small scale, Saarinen insisted on important elements being built as large models, some full size, in his office.

Both externally and internally, the building has the appearance of having been hewn out of concrete. The curved forms of the "Y" columns and the roof domes, and even the staircases and departures board, all look as though they have been constructed from the same "block". The structure was built on site but its dramatic form was only made possible by the use of lightweight pre-stressed concrete. Saarinen had taken reference from French engineer Eugene Freyssinet's patented techniques (see page 151) and braced the entire structure with a latticework of reinforcing steel.

Essentially, the concrete roof domes are thin-shell structures: curved elements that usually transmit loads equally down from their highest point so that they radiate out and dissipate the forces applied to them. The loads applied to dome, or shell, surfaces are carried to the ground by a combination of compressive, tensile, and shear stresses acting in the direction of the shell's surface. This makes these shapes particularly suited to carrying widely distributed loads on applications such as large-spanning roof structures.

This thin-shell technique allowed the domes to span over the main interior space without the support of intermediate columns, enabling Saarinen to achieve his desired grand glazed facades looking out onto the runway.

The building and all its spaces and elements, were designed to work together. This may sound like common sense but Saarinen went much further than most architects to design everything, in order to create a family of forms. This was his philosophical ideal – the necessity of extending architecture to all the physical surroundings and to design every object taking into account the way it relates to its neighbouring objects. Saarinen described his flight centre thus: "All the curves, all the spaces and elements right down to the shape of the signs, display boards, railings and check-in desks were to be of a matching nature. We wanted passengers passing through the building to experience a fully-designed environment, in which each part arises from another and everything belongs to the same formal world."

It is still considered one of the most architecturally distinguished airport-terminal designs in the world. However, built before the age of terrorism and hijackings, the flight gates in the terminal were close to the street, making it difficult to create centralized ticketing and security checkpoints. And so, following American Airlines' buyout of TWA in 2001, the flight centre went out of service. The Port Authority of New York and New Jersey proposed converting the main portion of the building into a restaurant and conference centre, but some architectural critics and historians opposed this move.

In December 2005, JetBlue, which occupies the adjacent Terminal Six, began construction of an expanded terminal facility, which will utilize the front portion of Saarinen's Flight Center as an entry point. The peripheral air-side parts of it have now been demolished to make space for a new terminal, which will have 26 gates and is expected to be complete by 2008.

Opposite: A vintage photo of the interior of the TWA Flight Center shows the beautifully sculpted concrete interior, complimented with hand rails and lighting that were also designed by the architect, Eero Saarinen.

FLIGHT WING 1
GATES 1-7
TWA

Opposite: The concrete structure of the building does not seem to include any straight lines. Each sweeping concrete curve marries perfectly with the next to create a beautiful swooping form.

Above: Externally, the building takes on the form of what some describe as a bird in flight. The lightweight pre-stressed concrete enables the structure to incorporate large glazed facades.

project data

- The TWA Flight Center was the first airline terminal to have closed-circuit television, baggage carousels, an electronic schedule board and baggage weigh-in scales.
- Idlewild Airport (now John F. Kennedy International Airport) was rare in the airport industry for having company-owned and designed terminals; other terminals included Worldport for Pan American World Airways and the Sundrome, which was occupied by National Airlines.
- Saarinen also designed Washington Dulles International Airport, which is now seen as a building of national importance.
- Four pre-stressed concrete domes make up the roof form, which is 15.2 metres (50 feet) high and 96 metres (315 feet) long.
- Not everyone liked the Flight Center, however – Peter Blake, editor of the *Architectural Record*, compared it to an enlarged Danish Modern salad bowl; while Ada Louise Huxtable, architecture critic for *The New York Times*, said, "The modern traveler, fed on frozen flight dinners, enters the city, not in Roman splendor, but through the bowels of a streamlined concrete bird."
- Saarinen died before the completion of his building, which is now a National Historic Landmark.

TEMPLE EXPIATORI DE LA SAGRADA FAMILIA BARCELONA, SPAIN

The Temple Expiatori de la Sagrada Familia is one of the most curious structures of modern times, and has been incredibly slow in materializing. The building has its origins in 1866, when an association was founded to raise funds for the construction of a new temple. The association purchased the site in 1881 and the foundation stone was laid a year later. Originally designed by the architect Francesc del Villar, the building was conceived as a traditional Gothic structure with vertical columns and pointed arches, along the lines of the great medieval cathedrals. A series of disagreements, however, quickly led to del Villar's replacement by Antonio Gaudí in 1883.

Influenced by a mix of Gothic, Moorish and turn-of-the-century Art Nouveau styles, Gaudí slowly adapted the Gothic form of the cathedral into the twisting, organic, almost tortured structure that is still under construction today. But, astonishing and romantic as it is, the building remains something of a conundrum for contemporary designers and builders. Part of the puzzle lies in the fact that Gaudí rarely worked in the traditional manner, and he produced far fewer drawings than one would expect for a project of this size. When Gaudí died in 1926 – he witnessed the completion of only one of the 12 bell towers – he took many of his design intentions with him. To compound the problem, many of the drawings Gaudí did leave behind were destroyed in the Spanish Civil War, along with a large number of models. Architects, engineers, sculptors and builders working on the cathedral today, therefore, often have very little to go on, and construction has limped along ever since his death.

It has long been known that Gaudí had worked within a system, but no one was ever quite sure what that system was or how he used it. Recently, however, academics have begun to understand Gaudí's design method, and they are now in a better position to work out what he would have done, or at least to make an educated guess. The reason Gaudí produced so few drawings is that he preferred to experiment through geometric shapes by suspending chains, ropes and sheets from his studio ceiling. For example, a piece of rope that hangs from both ends forms what is known as a catenary arch, a very stable and structurally sound form. Gaudí would photograph such forms, turn the photo upside-down and use the resulting image as a fundamental ingredient of his structural form finding. A close examination of Gaudí's work shows that other geometric forms, such as hyperboloids, hyperbolic paraboloids and double helixes, provide the key to understanding the Sagrada Familia.

These forms are well known to mathematicians and engineers, who can easily write the algebraic formulas for them. When these are inputted into a computer, the geometric shapes (or slices of them) can be manipulated in just the same way as Gaudí adjusted the equipment in his studio. Moreover, computer-generated forms can be superimposed onto the building elements that Gaudí actually built, so contemporary engineers can check to see if they are on the right track – very often, the built forms and digital/mathematical models correspond exactly. Once the engineers have worked out the underlying geometry for particular parts of the structure, the building almost designs itself.

This working method explains the recent rapid progress on the cathedral. Designs can be worked out and quickly prototyped (at real-life scale) in polystyrene. When the design team is happy, computer-controlled cutting machines reproduce the prototype in granite.

However, the design team also has to invent solutions, and can still be fine-tuning designs even after building work has commenced. The new 35-metre (115-foot) high Rose Window in the West Transept, which was designed by a team led by Professor Mark Burry of

project data

- Gaudí once said that "The patron of this project is not in a hurry."
- The building will, when complete, be a complex cluster of transepts, naves, towers and domes.
- Each of the three principal facades, featuring Christ's Nativity, Glory and Passion, is backed by four bell towers ranging from 90–112 metres (295–367 feet) in height.
- Six domes will sit atop the cathedral, the largest of which will rise 170 metres (558 feet) above ground level.
- The form of the Sagrada Familia is based on the structural possibilities of parabolic forms and leaning columns, derived from geometries that have an inherent mathematical purity and physical strength.
- Computer-aided design packages are proving invaluable to the present design team. Currently, building elements are being worked out with Catia, a 3-D modelling program developed by the French firm Dassault Systèmes for the aerospace industry.

Left: One of the very few original Antonio Gaudí drawings to survive, showing his vision for the final form and mass of the Sagrada Familia, the architect's greatest monument.

Opposite: The Nativity facade of Barcelona's Sagrada Familia. The building has the appearance of molten wax, but underlying the decoration is a robust and highly considered structural system.

the Royal Melbourne Institute of Technology (RMIT) in Australia, is a case in point. Here, the lower reaches of the window were actually being cut or put into place before the upper part of the window had been fully designed. This was feasible because all the designs within the Sagrada Familia are based on families of geometric rules – architects and engineers call this "parametric design" (designs that are based on parameters). The completed lower part of the window, therefore, established the rules within which the highest parts could be designed, and as the window progressed the fewer options there were. When designing the Rose Window, the team allowed for a construction tolerance of 10 millimetres (0.4 inches), which provided them with a small margin for error. As it turned out, this tolerance was superfluous.

The RMIT team has also designed the colonnade that wraps around the western side of the cathedral. There is almost no evidence of Gaudí's design intent for this part of the building, apart from a single photograph of a drawing the architect made in 1917. There is an ambiguity about Gaudí's drawing; many people imagine the columns as bone-like, but others see them as stretched sinews. Using the geometric preferences Gaudí exhibited in his built work, Professor Burry has created a set of columns that, he hopes, could be interpreted in both ways.

The Sagrada Familia is on course to being a fully enclosed volume by 2007/08, although there will still be two decades' worth of work before the building is capped by its 170-metre (558-foot) high dome.

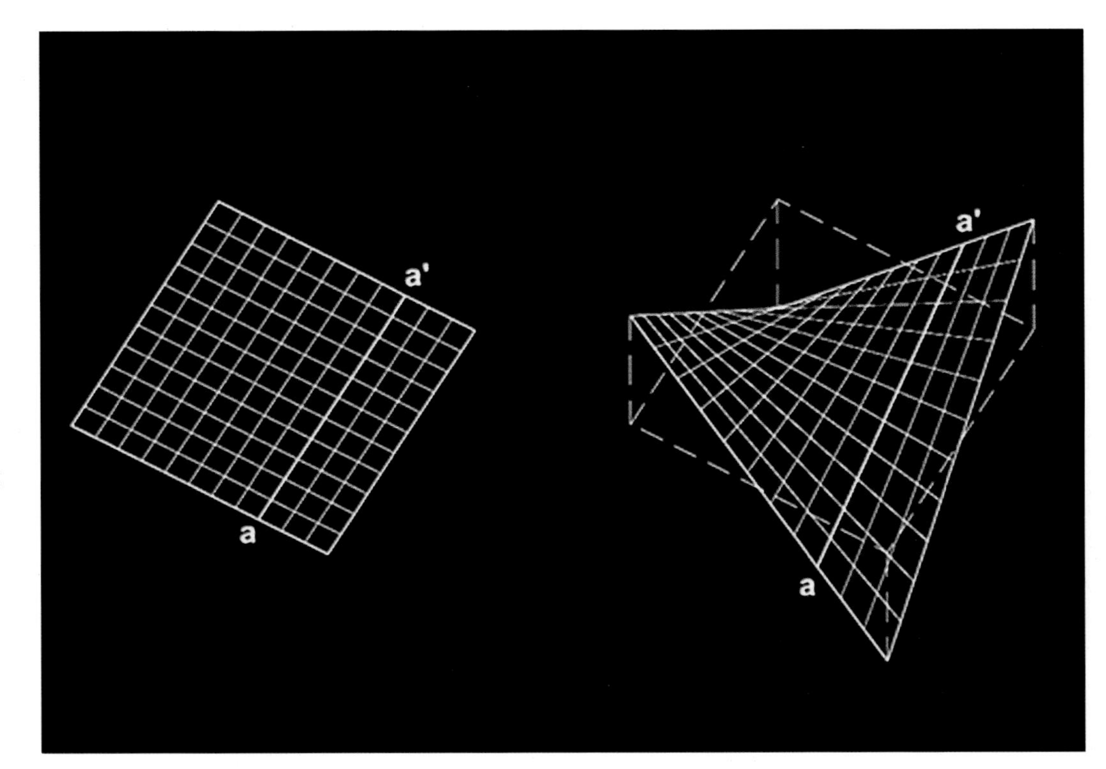

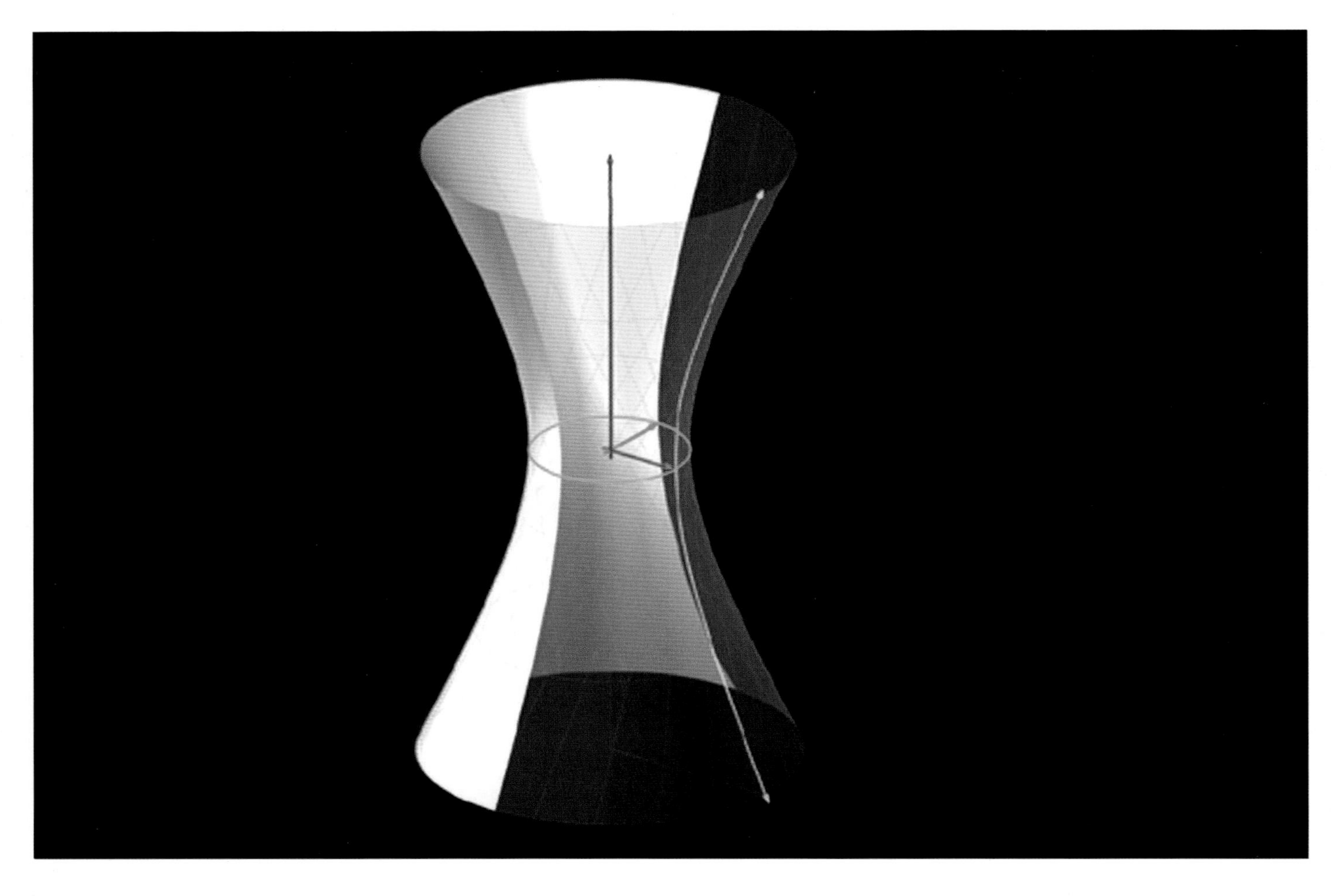

Above: These images show how complex lines are mapped out from fundamental geometric forms. A series of curved lines are created by distending a flat surface into the saddle form of a hyperbolic paraboloid.

Left: Similarly curved lines are generated by mapping the inner surface of a hyperboloid.

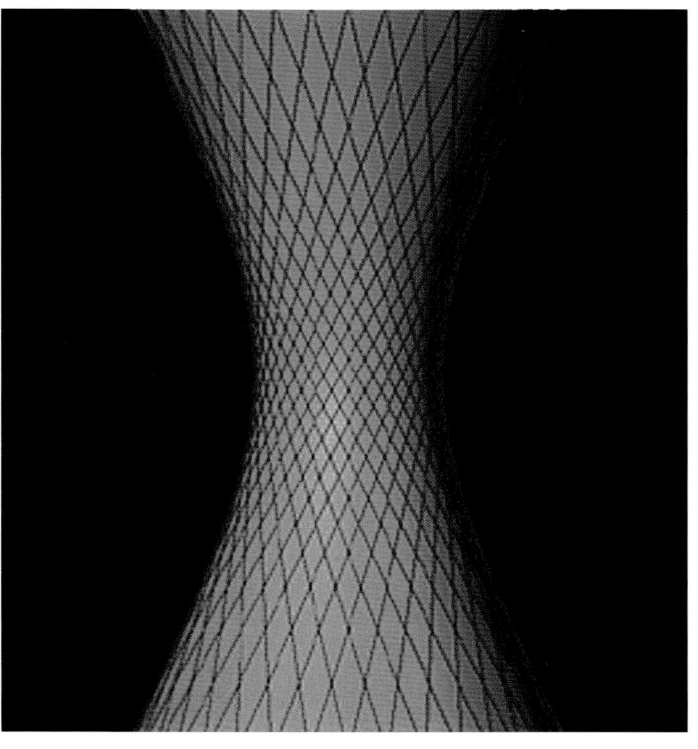

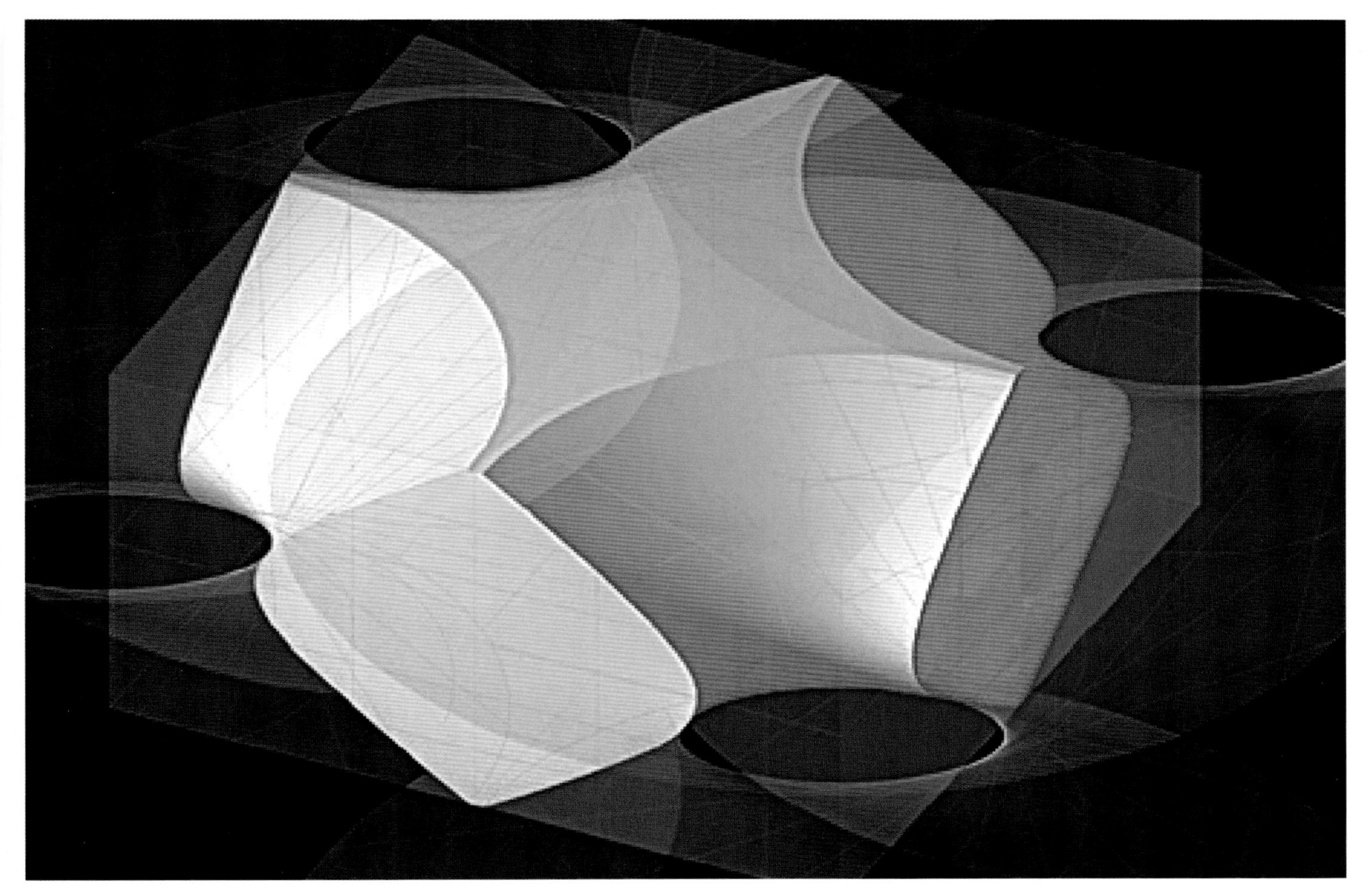

Above left: Modern designers can test computer-generated designs against what Gaudí actually built. Here, in yellow, digital forms are mapped on to the stone of Gaudí's work. There is a precise match.

Above: A computer-generated hyperboloid, one of the fundamental geometric forms which underpin the design of the cathedral.

Left: This computer-generated drawing shows a detail from the design of the new Rose Window in the West Transept of the building. Once approved, the three-dimensional computer model was fashioned in polystyrene, and then carved out of granite.

CENTRE NATIONAL D'ART ET DE CULTURE GEORGES POMPIDOU PARIS, FRANCE

Upon its completion in 1977, Paris had never seen a building like the Centre Pompidou before. In fact, the drama of this building, which looked more like a huge machine, impressed itself upon the entire world. Architects Richard Rogers and Renzo Piano had created a structure so different from any art gallery or museum before it that the normally verbose Parisians didn't know what to think.

They do now, though. The Centre Pompidou is one of the most popular modern architectural attractions in the world, drawing some 6,000 visitors a day: five times more than was originally estimated.

However, the design of the building was not derived for purely aesthetic reasons. When, in 1970, an international architectural competition was launched to create an arts and cultural centre according to the wishes of President Georges Pompidou, Rogers and Piano had wholly more pragmatic reasons for coming up with their design. The architects wanted to create a building with the ability to change to suit its requirements, with a flexibility that had not been seen before in the cultural sector. They would do this by designing an inside-out structure; removing the servicing and circulation requirements from the interior spaces, and freeing them up for artistic use.

Below: The building's exo-skeleton is both an overt visual statement and the means by which the structure is held up. Like high-tech scaffolding it supports the building and external escalators.

Opposite: A close-up detail of the facade shows the structural space frame (white) with the large blue air extraction pipes running from the internal air conditioning to external vents.

project data

- **Since its opening in 1977, the Centre Pompidou has received over 150 million visitors.**
- **The building was delivered on time and under budget in January 1977 at a cost of approximately £58.8 million. Another £40 million was required for the purchase of the land, construction of off-site facilities and general administration costs.**
- **The centre's exoskeleton is made up of 16,000 tonnes (17,637 tons) of steel, with some elements weighing as much as 10 tonnes (11 tons) each.**
- **The glass facade almost entirely covers the seven-storey building, using some 11,000 square metres (118,403 square feet) of glazing.**
- **The centre sits on 2 hectares (5 acres) of land in central Paris and its internal floor area over seven storeys is 103,000 square metres (1.09 million square feet).**
- **Richard Rogers and Renzo Piano have gone on to be two of the world's most renowned architects, each developing their own signature modern style.**

In addition, an external courtyard, or plaza, enabled the centre to hold both internal and external events within this dense urban area.

The team also wanted the building to hold no association with the historic character of its urban surroundings. It would be different in every way: scale, height, form, and expression; the building would meld with the city by way of its cultural attachment, rather than some contrived architectural similarity.

Many were surprised when these young perpetrators of high-tech architecture were presented the commission, but in April 1972, assisted by engineer Ove Arup & Partners (now known simply as Arup), construction work began.

The results are startling: a seven-storey building of sheer glass facades, with its "insides" on the outside; a rectangular glass box encased within a steel-framed skeleton onto which are hung colour-coded tubes, ducts, escalators and vents. The western elevation looking out over the plaza is dominated by transparent plastic tunnels with a red underbelly, which snake up the building and house escalators, while to the eastern side, giant blue, green and yellow ducts and tubes carry the air, water and electricity supplies, respectively. Again, these are placed outside the main columns, hanging dominantly over a narrow street.

These grand architectural statements almost completely removed the services and circulation areas from the interior of the building. Some heavy mechanical equipment is housed in the basement, and visitors don't enter the building by the external escalators, as the design would suggest, but via doors at the lower edge of the plaza. From these, access is through a double-height room that contains the reception, retail outlets and temporary exhibitions. Only here do visitors use an escalator, taking them to the street level on the north-west corner of the building, where a small lobby connects to elevators and the exterior escalator.

Work on the distinctive metal framework began in September 1974 and was completed just six months later. This external skeleton has 14 vertical steel tube columns cantilevered down either side (each 850 millimetres/33½ inches in diameter), creating 13 bays of 12.8 metres (42 feet) in width between them. Across the width of the building 45-metre (148-foot) long girders are attached to the columns by solid moulded-steel beam hangers, each measuring 8 metres (26 feet) in length and weighing 10 tonnes (11 tons): these spread the building's weight – its load stresses – evenly through the columns, while being balanced by tie-beams anchored on cross-bars.

The building's distinctive framework protrudes further out than the main column and girder frame. Outer tension-rods of 200-millimetre (8-inch) solid steel extend act in tension, pulling the cantilevered horizontal members in the opposite direction to the forces exerted by the weight of the floor span. This element is the "trick" that eliminates the need for supporting columns and means that, internally, each floor has an unobstructed width of nearly 50 metres (164 feet), with no columns, internal staircases or service cores.

Below: From the air, the building looks like some giant alien cuboid dropped into the traditional Parisian cityscape. Its unusual facade is like nothing else in the French capital; the building's mechanical services are built onto its exterior.

Opposite: At the building's highest level a glazed tunnel runs the length of the external facade, providing a dramatic walkway linked to the main building by enclosed bridges. Behind, one of the large white structural columns is visible.

RICHARD ROGERS' INSIDE-OUT ARCHITECTURE

The design of the Centre Pompidou came about by the architects' wish to blend the ideals of functionalism and high-tech architecture. Functionalism is the principle that a building should be designed entirely to suit its purpose; high-tech design involves the use of materials associated with the advanced industries of the 1980s and 1990s, such as space frames, metal cladding and composite fabrics and materials.

The Centre Pompidou and Rogers' Lloyds Building in the City of London are designed to be the perfect space for their function on the inside. So much so, that the architect has removed almost all of the structural elements and services – the lifts, escalators, heating pipes, air-conditioning ducts, generators and other mechanical plant – and placed them out of the way on the outside. In doing so, Rogers' created an architectural style all of his own, emphasizing the "mechanics of the building" in bold colours or shining steel. What had started out as a decision to rationalize the structure became a design signature that would see him recognized globally.

Ironically, Rogers didn't labour the point and his buildings don't feature inside-out services anymore. They do, however, almost all make bold reference to the structural elements of the building. Concrete is left exposed, while steelwork is highlighted in the bright primary colours first used on the Centre Pompidou. New examples of Rogers' architecture include the Welsh National Assembly building in Cardiff and Barajas International Airport in Madrid, Spain.

Finally, the frame is stiffened laterally to stop it falling over like a stack of playing cards, by cross-bracing along the long facades attached to the ends of the steel beam hangers. Stiffening in the end elevations is added by diagonal braces between lattice girders on both gable walls.

The building's vast glass walls are built 1.6 metres (5 feet) in from the columns and gable trusses. This is to ensure structural stability in the event of a fire inside the building, keeping flames and heat away from the steel frame. In addition, the frames of the glass walls have metal roll-down shutters, which are automatically activated by fire sensors, providing additional protection to the external structure from heat. These shutters are sometimes also used as shades from the summer sun.

Internally, the floor areas are completely open as per the architects' intentions. However, movable, bolted-together two-hour firewalls divide each level into two zones, and the ceiling support trusses can all be fitted with a bolt-on system of demountable mezzanines if required.

After almost five years' work, the Centre National d'Art et de Culture Georges Pompidou, to give the building its full name, was opened on February 2, 1977.

LOVELL TELESCOPE JODRELL BANK, CHESHIRE, UK

Radio waves constantly bounce around in space, many reflect off our atmosphere but those that penetrate it are often virtually "burnt out" by the time they reach Earth. In order to decipher these waves scientists have to concentrate them to a single point of focus, where an antenna, similar in principle to a television aerial, captures the waves and turns them into an electrical signal. This method of collection, or concentration, is achieved with the use of radio telescopes, and one of the largest, oldest and most famous is the Lovell Telescope at Jodrell Bank, near Manchester in the United Kingdom.

Its 76.2-metre (250-foot) diameter dish is shaped in the form of a paraboloid. Radio waves bounce off the concave surface and are reflected toward a centrally mounted antenna, from where they are fed back to a control room for scientists to analyse. The work of these scientists enables us to track moving objects and discover new astronomical phenomena many light years away in the night sky.

But the Lovell Telescope isn't some new technological advance in our quest to understand the cosmos: it was built by consulting engineer Charles Husband and scientist Bernard Lovell between 1950 and 1957. Lovell initially had some success in capturing radio waves in the late 1940s with a 66-metre (216½-foot) diameter dish telescope fixed permanently in one position, pointing directly upward. Advancing these technologies, he and Husband devised plans for a new telescope that could be manoeuvred to point at any part of the sky.

Lovell and Husband's new telescope had to be redesigned to make the surface of the dish much smoother even as contractors were setting up their cranes to start assembling it. This surface is the most important part of any radio telescope: any unevenness will distort radio waves. Its quality determines the ability of the telescope to pick up radio waves of shorter wavelengths. Wavelengths range from several metres to a few millimetres,

Left: The Lovell Telescope towers over its rural surroundings. Today, upgrades mean that the telescope's dish has a near perfect surface, allowing it to read a much greater range of wavelengths.

Opposite: A historic aerial image of the telescope shows well the circular tracks on which it rotates, as well as the construction of the supporting steel framework. Motors in the arms allow it to tilt through 180 degrees.

and imperfections on the dish should ideally be no more than one-twentieth of the shortest wavelength the telescope is designed to receive.

Lovell and Husband's original design was to have used a dish constructed of open-wire mesh with 5-centimetre (2-inch) gaps in it, meaning that it would work at the comparatively long wavelengths of 1–10 metres (3–33 feet). However, during its construction, scientific advances overtook the scientists' theories; in 1951 radio astronomers made the first detections of a 21-centimetre (8¼-inch) emission from hydrogen atoms in the Milky Way. Lovell's dish would have to be perfect to within 1 centimetre (0.4 inches) to stand a chance of reading the hydrogen atom emission.

The wire-mesh dish was discarded in favour of a more accurate, solid steel surface, made from 7,100 welded steel panels, each 2 millimetres (0.08 inches) thick: while the supporting structure of the bowl was completely redesigned to take the extra weight.

The telescope, named simply Mark 1, began trials in the summer of 1957 and was soon pressed into service tracking the Soviet Union's Sputnik 1 satellite, it being the only piece of equipment on the planet capable of picking up radar signals from the satellite's carrier rocket.

From the beginning, the 89-metre (292-foot) high telescope was designed to be able to point in any direction apart from down. The 1,500-tonne (1,653-ton) telescopic dish rotates, powered by electrical motors on a set of circular railway tracks with a diameter of 107.5 metres (353 feet), while the dish, supported on either side by two steel frame towers, can also be tilted at any angle from horizon to horizon, again using electrical power. The two motions are independent: the telescope can travel at nine degrees per minute in horizontal rotation and six degrees per minute through vertical. As radio waves bounce off the 5,270-square-metre (56,726-square-foot) dish they are collected by a radio receiver in the focus box. This is cooled to a few degrees above absolute zero, a trick that isolates the very weak signal from outer space from the electronic noise of the receiver itself.

Between August 1970 and November 1971 the Lovell Telescope underwent an upgrade, and a new reflecting surface was fitted above the old reflector. The new, smoother surface meant that the telescope could operate at the shorter wavelengths of 6 centimetres (2⅓ inches) or more. Jodrell Bank staff named the refurbished telescope Mark 1A. This telescope operated efficiently until very recently and, on its thirtieth anniversary in 1987, it was renamed the Lovell Telescope in honour of its creator.

In 2002 the Lovell Telescope underwent its most recent upgrade. The most important single modification was once again the addition of a new surface for the dish. Constructed from galvanized-steel panels, accurate to less than 2 millimetres (¾ inch), the telescope's new surface is now five times smoother than before. This has been achieved using a holographic profiling technique to set each individual panel on the dish into an overall parabolic surface with far greater precision than was possible even a few years ago. The steel panels are attached to the backing structure using self-tapping screws: this eliminates the thermal distortions, which were common with the welded surface joints used on previous surface skins.

The telescope is now 50 years old and in its refurbished state it can detect new minute radio waves emitted by low-luminosity pulsars and new wavelength lines from interstellar molecules, thus enhancing our knowledge of cosmic chemistry.

project data

- In total, the Lovell Telescope at Jodrell Bank weighs 3,200 tonnes (3,527 tons): the dish itself weighs 1,500 tonnes (1,653 tons).
- The dish's total surface area is 5,270 square metres (56,726 square feet), of which 4,560 square metres (49,083 square feet) is used for collecting radio waves.
- Bernard Lovell worked on radar systems during the Second World War, before designing antenna transmitters and then dish telescopes at Jodrell Bank for his research with Manchester University.
- Lovell's first dish-shaped radio telescope was a 66-metre (216½-foot) diameter fixed bowl supported by scaffold poles and steel cable that lay on the ground pointing straight up.
- The largest single-dish telescope in the world is at Arecibo in Puerto Rico and is run by Cornell University of the United States; it is a fixed 305-metre (1,000-foot) diameter dish lying in a natural hollow in the hills and is only able to see a restricted area of sky.
- The largest steerable radio telescope is 100 metres (328 feet) in diameter; it is based in Effelsberg near Bonn, Germany, and is operated by the Max-Planck-Institut für Radioastronomie.
- The Lovell Telescope was damaged in storms during January 1976; diagonal bracing girders were added soon afterwards to stabilize it.

Opposite: In this construction shot from the 1950s, cranes, which are built onto a large temporary scaffold that supports the telescope's structure during construction, lift the framework of the giant bowl into position.

Right: A crane builds the primary support structure for the telescope. The scale of the project is illustrated by the size of the car parked alongside the framework.

駐車場
PARKING

YOKOHAMA FERRY TERMINAL YOKOHAMA, JAPAN

Foreign Office Architects (FOA) won the international competition to design a new ferry terminal for Yokohama, the second largest city in Japan, in 1994. The commission catapulted the small London-based practice into the limelight and set in motion its rise as one of the stars of twenty-first century, computer-orientated architecture.

FOA's design created not just a terminal but also a new piece of outdoor public space in a city literally crammed to bursting with buildings. FOA treated the terminal as a landscaped surface, both inside and outside, with its roof acting as an extension of the urban realm.

The 70-by-430-metre (230-by-1,411-foot) terminal is not what you would immediately term a building: its designer calls it "landform architecture". Located inside a flat rectilinear protrusion, which juts out into the harbour are the arrival and departure facilities, with restaurants, shops and meeting rooms; below them, on the lower-most level, is a giant parking garage for cars and coaches; while, above, a landscaped park and a series of pathways unfold across the roof space. This unusual structure is so different from normal buildings that visitors to the park could be blissfully unaware of the bustling ferry terminal beneath if it were not for the gigantic ferries moored at its side.

The building rises only 15 metres (49 feet) above water level at its highest point, the peak of the highest grassed mound. The park includes a 50,000-square-metre (538,200-square-foot) wooden deck and lawns that all rise and fall in a seemingly random pattern. The space is designed to be interesting enough to revisit again and again, like a city park, and in complete contrast to conventional harbour structures, such as piers, which encourage travel back and forth in a straight line only. Architect Zaera-Polo explains, "We wanted to make a pier where you can walk in on a certain path and walk out on a different path. We developed this looped diagram, in which we were chaining all the parts of the computer model. Then we assigned to every line of the diagram a surface. We were interested in playing with the ground."

The result is a multi-surfaced public space that undulates and twists, creating intimate corners and wide promenades. Sloped areas are perfect for relaxing, while extensions of the giant structural girders break through, creating covered spaces to retreat to from the weather.

However, this external park space has not been designed as a separate roof-top garden but instead entirely in conjunction with the terminal's interior circulation areas, seamlessly linking the passage of public- and passenger-flow to and from the terminal, above and below "deck". Zaera-Polo explains, "We started with certain principles and later combined and changed them. The changes are never visual or aesthetic; they are always technical or practical. The lumps and slopes all correspond to the activities required below in the belly of the terminal. And, in keeping with this theme, there are numerous entrances into the terminal, the slopes descending inside with the wooden decking continuing to remind users that this is a continuous journey from exterior to interior."

Opposite: The main arrivals and departures hall of the ferry terminal is spanned by a continuous concertina of heavy steel panels. This unusual ceiling is both an aesthetic and structural feature.

Below: From high above, the ferry terminal seems almost like a flat rectilinear extension to the harbour. It is only at ground level that the low-slung building can be seen as one with multiple floor levels.

project data

- The Yokohama Ferry Terminal consists of 48,000 square metres (516,668 square feet) of space: 17,000 square metres (182,986 square feet) of terminal facilities including check-in, customs, luggage handling; 13,000 square metres (139,930 square feet) of conference space, restaurants, shops and assembly hall; 18,000 square metres (193,750 square feet) of transportation facilities, including parking, pick-up and drop-off and bus parking.
- The budget for the construction of the terminal was 23 billion Yen (approximately £132.5 million).
- The ferry terminal accommodates 53,000 passengers a year.
- Vertical movement is managed with sloping floors and elevators. A total of 10 ramps connect the three levels – park, arrivals/departures, and car park.
- The girders, running the length of the building are composed of 1.2-metre (4-foot) high box girders with steel plate thicknesses of 6–40 millimetres (0.24–1.57 inches).
- The wood used for the 50,000-square metre (538,196 square feet) park decks is Ipe, a Brazilian hardwood so dense that it doesn't float. It was the wood used for Coney Island Pier in New York.

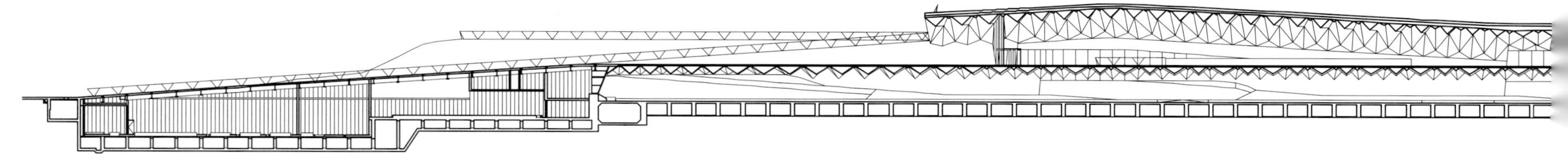

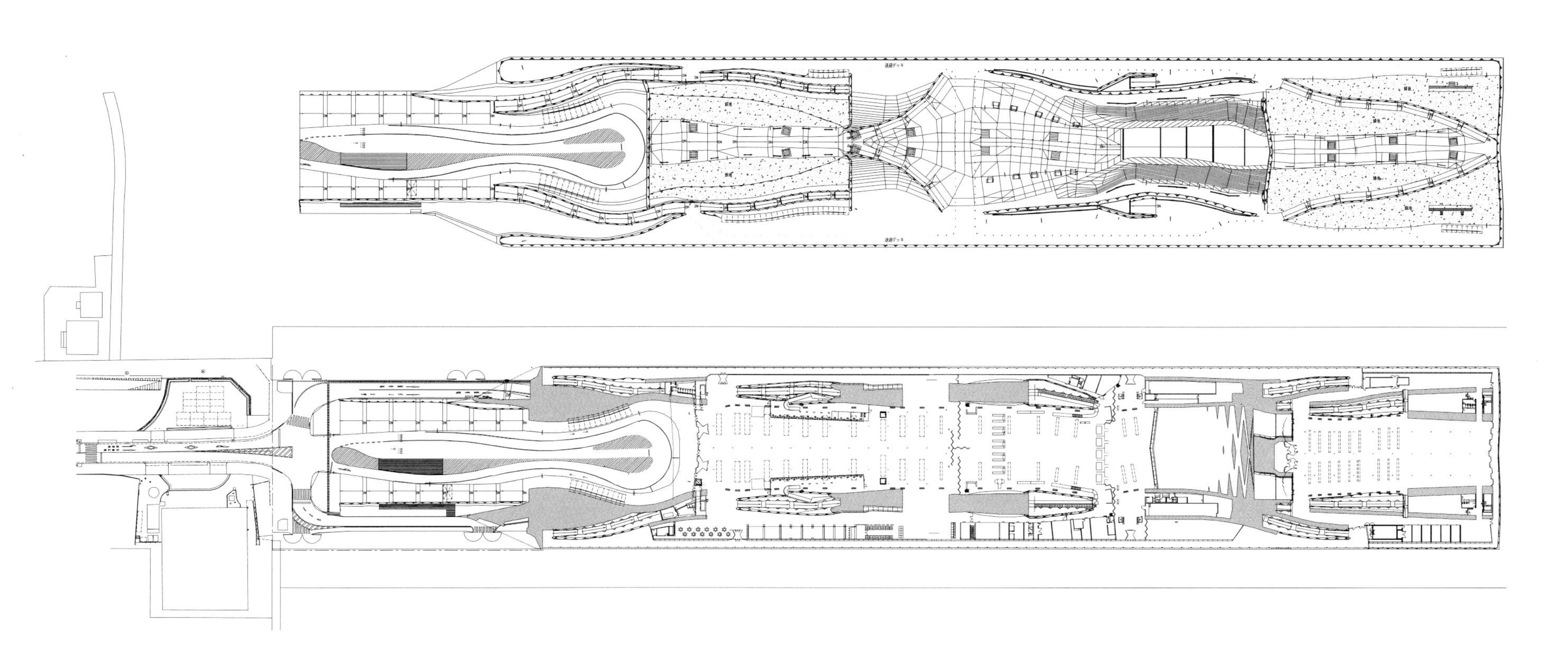

Opposite top: The public park and pier undulate across the top of the ferry terminal. In the foreground, the main entrance to the terminal includes a turn-around point for vehicles.

Opposite bottom: A site plan illustrates how the terminal juts out into the harbour.

Above: Two plan views – the highest park level (**top**) and the main arrivals and departures level (**bottom**).

Right: Viewed from the end of the building that faces out to sea, the different levels of the terminal can be seen, in context with a cruise liner to the building's right.

Below: A section through the terminal includes details of the concertina structural steel ceiling.

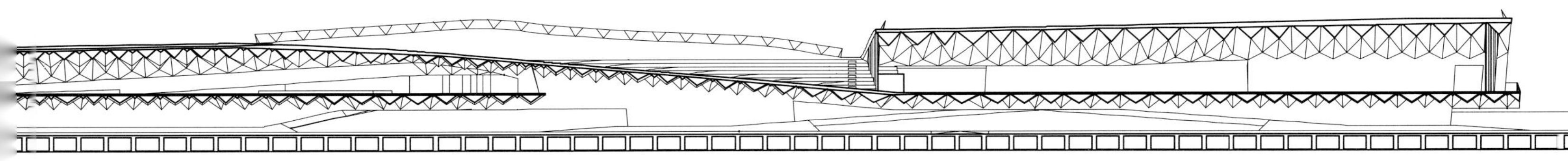

Moving from the top to the very bottom of the structure, over 600 hollow steel pile foundations were driven into the uneven harbour bed and filled with concrete. Resting on these massive foundations, the body of the terminal is a complex asymmetric assembly of folded steel. Triangular elements operate as beams, but they are packed together to form an undulating ceiling running across the width of the building, which is supported on huge longitudinal girders. This is graphically displayed in the main Arrivals/Departures area, where the strong folded-metal ceiling spans the space with no intermediate supports. This ceiling dominates the space and the eye is drawn to its asymmetric qualities: however, as with the other elements of the structure, these qualities are not purely aesthetic. The regularity of the beams corresponds to the positioning of the piling and girders that operate as support stanchions. At the extremities of the structure, the folded-steel beams pass over the girders and cantilever out by up to 14 metres (46 feet) at the sides, to form covered service areas.

This new type of building design demanded manufacture and assembly techniques more akin to factory conditions than those of the building site. Girders and folded-steel cross members were manufactured and prefabricated before being brought to site in factories in Japan, China and South Korea and then delivered by sea. Because of the different stresses exerted on parts of the building, the folded steel was constructed from three different thicknesses of sheet steel – 2.3, 3.2 and 4.5 millimetres (0.09, 0.13 and 0.18 inches), respectively. In areas where the thickest sections were still deemed too weak, the folded steel was bolstered with diagonal members fixed to its rear. This design work provided a finished folded-steel structure – much of which can be seen – that looks identical everywhere.

Digital design tools were the key to the entire project, from the calculation of the steel-beam thicknesses to the spatial layout of the park. Computers allowed the architect to visualize the scheme and make design changes easily. As such, FOA prefer designing with Computer-Aided Design to using physical models, because the digital medium allows them to integrate more information and make changes quicker and later in design, producing an organization of higher complexity. The result is a dramatic and altogether unique building.

Left: Steel and wood are the predominant materials used internally and externally on the terminal. Here, a walkway from the departures floor ascends to the upper park level, with the materials continuing from below to above.

SYDNEY OPERA HOUSE SYDNEY, AUSTRALIA

The construction of the Sydney Opera House was one of the longest contractual sagas of the twentieth century. Sadly, architect Jørn Utzon became embroiled in the wrangling of Australian political parties and withdrew from his project in 1966, nine years after construction had started. The building was completed in 1973 without him. However, 26 years on, the rifts had healed and he has since been involved in the building's renovation programme, which includes reinstating elements of his original design that had been left out.

Thankfully, the political infighting at the time of the building's construction didn't affect its overall external design, and, sitting on Bennelong Point in Sydney Harbour, it is one of the most awe-inspiring architectural works of the twentieth century.

Utzon, a Danish architect, won an architectural design competition for the commission to design the opera house in 1957. His original design was remodelled over and over until he and his engineers, from Ove Arup & Partners, solved the problem of how to build the structure's most distinguishing feature, its roof sails.

These sails, or shells as they are often referred to, were originally a series of parabolas supported by pre-cast concrete ribs. However, the engineers were unable to find an acceptable method of constructing them. From 1957 to 1963, when work on the podium on which the sails would sit was already underway, the design team continued to struggle with schemes using parabolas, circular ribs and ellipsoids, before a workable solution was found. Eventually, using some of the first computerized structural analysis techniques, the team settled on a design that saw the sails created from sections of a sphere, like the segments of an orange.

There are 10 sails in all: two sets of three facing the harbour; each set also has a rear sail facing inland; and there are a pair of smaller sails under which a restaurant is housed. The two largest groups of sails contain the concert hall and opera theatre and the other three theatres are located on the sides of the sail groupings. The form of the sails was chosen to reflect the internal height requirements of the performance spaces; rising from the low entrance areas, over the seating areas and up to the high stage towers. Their design, pre-cast concrete ribs and roofing panels, enabled all of the sail elements to be built on-site in a special concrete factory.

The shells were constructed by Australian company, Hornibrook Group, who pre-cast 2,194 concrete ribs and 4,000 roof panels. This method allowed the roof tiles to be prefabricated in sheets on the ground and adhered to the roof panels, instead of being stuck on individually at height. Ove Arup & Partners' site engineer supervised the construction of the sails, which used an innovative adjustable steel-trussed erection arch to support the roofs before their completion.

The 1,056,006 white and cream tiles covering the sails were imported from Sweden. Despite their self-cleaning nature, they are subject to periodic maintenance and replacement, and, when protesters climbed the opera house and daubed "No War" on them in 2003, the repair bill was over £40,000.

In 1963 Utzon moved his entire office from Sweden to Sydney and began designing the interiors of the opera house in earnest. However there was a change of government in 1965, and the new ruling party declared that the project now fell under the jurisdiction of the Ministry of Public Works. When Utzon presented the

Opposite: The sun glints off some of the one million off-white tiles that cover the 10 sails of the Sydney Opera House. This sail covers the entrance to the theatre venue: the one to the rear and left is the restaurant.

Right: An aerial view of the opera house shows the site well, with two sets of larger sails – the concert hall to the front and theatre behind – and the small restaurant building to the rear.

Minister for Public Works a schedule setting out the completion dates of parts of his work the minister withheld permission for the construction of innovative plywood prototypes for the interiors.

This and a lack of payment for his work, eventually forced Utzon to quit early in 1966. He left the project with its sails partially complete and the interiors of the building designed only to a concept stage. His position was taken over by architect Peter Hall, from the New South Wales Department of Public Works, who became largely responsible for the interior design.

Hall instigated a raft of changes. He clad the gigantic podium, on which the sails stood, down to the water's edge to create a large outdoor paved space. The construction of glass walls to the interiors were sanctioned, as opposed to Utzon's planned prefabricated plywood mullions. His plywood corridor designs and his acoustic and seating designs for the interior of both halls were also scrapped. Hall even changed the use of the two halls: the major hall, which was originally to be a multi-purpose opera and concert hall, became solely a concert hall. The minor hall, originally to be used for stage productions only, became an opera and theatrical venue. This completely altered the interior layout, and stage machinery, already designed and fitted inside the major hall, was ripped out and thrown away.

The opera house was formally completed in 1973, at a cost of just over £40 million. This was considerably more than the estimate made in 1957 of approximately £1.37 million and 10 years later than the original completion date. Today, however, the arguments of the past are forgotten and over 200,000 people take the guided tour of the opera house annually. It is often dubbed one of the modern architectural wonders of the world.

project data

- The Sydney Opera House covers 1.8 hectares (4½ acres) of land. It is approximately 183 metres (600 feet) long and 120 metres (394 feet) wide at its widest point. It is supported on 580 concrete piers sunk up to 25 metres (82 feet) below sea level.
- The original Sydney Opera House architectural competition in 1956 attracted designs from 233 architects in 32 countries.
- Jørn Utzon was awarded £5,000 for his winning design in 1957.
- Over 10,000 construction workers were employed during the construction of the opera house.
- The Concert Hall Grand Organ is the largest mechanical organ in the world; with 10,154 pipes, it took 10 years to build.
- In May 2003 Jørn Utzon was awarded the prestigious Pritzker Prize – the Nobel Prize for architecture.
- The recently refurbished Utzon Room is the first Utzon-designed interior at the opera house.
- It was originally estimated that the opera house would take four years to build. It eventually opened 17 years after Utzon won the design competition.
- The highest roof shell on the opera house is 67 metres (220 feet) above sea level, the equivalent of a 22-storey building.

Opposite top: The glazed end elevations of the buildings contrast with the solid sail structure and create a beautiful picture when the building glows from within at night.

Opposite bottom: Illuminated dramatically, the sails of the opera house cast a surreal image across the waters of Sydney Harbour. The building's unique form makes it instantly recognisable.

Above: Set in context with the city's other famous landmark, the Sydney Harbour Bridge (see page 110), the opera house is an imposing structure greeting sailing vessels as they float into the harbour.

PHILIPS PAVILION BRUSSELS WORLD'S FAIR 1958, BELGIUM

Swiss architect Le Corbusier is renowned as one of the originators of modern architecture, or the International Style, and his designs and buildings are cited by many contemporary designers as their inspiration for becoming architects. He lived from 1887 until 1965. One of his final built works was the Philips Pavilion at the Brussels World's Fair in 1958.

At these fairs, large corporations often used pavilions as large display stands on which to advertise their new technologies or products. Dutch electronics company Philips commissioned Le Corbusier two years prior to the fair for this purpose but, rather than requesting a traditional pavilion, the company asked for something that would be viewed as a work of modern art, which would utilize the company's advanced new sound and light technology.

The company gave the architect free reign to design and build the physical structure and to orchestrate audio and visual artworks within it. Le Corbusier took to designing *Poème Electronique,* a futuristic multimedia display featuring images, coloured lighting and abstract music: this was all to be housed within an enclosure that he dubbed the "stomach". The structure had a main auditorium with twisted paths leading to and from it, like a stomach, and warped, curving walls on which to project the colours and images. Internally, there was to be an auditorium, where up to 500 visitors could be seated to watch the show being projected on all the walls around them.

With Le Corbusier immersing himself in the creation of *Poème Electronique,* the actual detailed design of the building fell to Iannis Xenakis, a Greek architect who worked for him. He took Le Corbusier's vague "stomach" analogy and came up with a series of conjoined hyperbolic parabaloids – curved planes generated entirely from straight lines – that would form a tent-like pavilion.

However, as with any mould-breaking design, building the desired structure proved less than plain sailing. Xenakis's design, a tensile structure of steel cables strung from steel posts, to form the hyperbolic parabaloids, didn't provide solid, acoustically insulating walls. Le Corbusier liked the shape of the pavilion, but he required complete sound insulation from exterior noise for his show, and so a solution had to be found that would allow for more substantial walls.

The solution was devised by Hoyte Duyster, chief engineer on the project. He utilized Xenakis' wire cables and devised a method of hanging pre-cast concrete panels from them to create a solid sound-absorbing structure. Because Xenakis' hyperbolic parabaloids are generated by straight lines, the concrete panels, each 50 millimetres (2 inches) thick and 1.5 square metres (16 square feet) in size could be prefabricated easily off-site using simple sand moulds that matched the curvature of the pavilion.

On their transportation to the site, the panels were attached to the cabling, which was stretched taut between a framework consisting of 400-millimetre (15¾-inch) thick reinforced-concrete ribs and a base plate sunk into the ground. The panels were first supported by movable scaffolds and then hung from the cables to create the skin of the pavilion. Painted silver, the structure took on a "space-age" floating feel, belying its heavy construction.

The use of hyperbolic paraboloids was a daring structural challenge in itself but Le Corbusier was more interested in creating a piece of "total art". He was often preoccupied with what was going on inside the pavilion, insisting, for example, that the music for the pavilion be composed by Edgard Varèse, a well-known composer and a pioneer in the field of electronic music and the use of non-instrumental sounds, rather than his clients' preferred choice of the more famous but less radical British composer, Benjamin Britten.

Once Le Corbusier had got his client's consent, and Varèse had been commissioned, the architect left him to compose a musical piece of his choosing, without giving him any guidance as to what the pavilion would be like or anything that would be happening within it. This complete disassociation with the pavilion and visual components of the Le Corbusier's presentation allowed Varèse complete

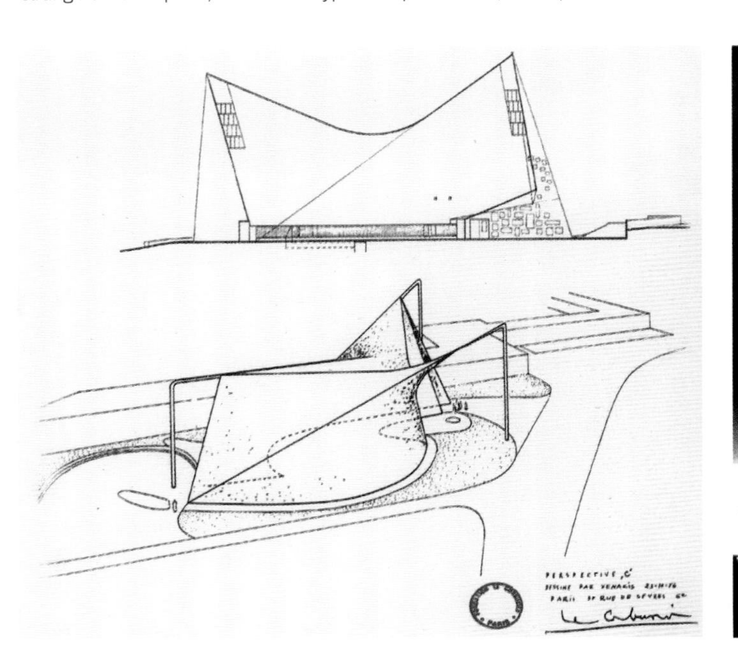

Far left: Le Corbusier's original concept sketches for the pavilion.

Left: A range of seemingly random images, all chosen by the architect, were projected onto the internal walls of the pavilion. Strange music also accompanied the visual show.

Opposite: This bizarre structure looks awkward and yet beautiful – as though it is constructed from some kind of fabric draped over a simple triangular frame. It is, however, a complex facade of curved concrete panels hung from steel cables.

project data

- Howard Taubman of *The New York Times* called the pavilion "the strangest building at the fair ... the sounds that accompany these images are as bizarre as the building itself."
- Two of Le Corbusier's most memorable buildings are the Unite d'Habitation in Marseilles (1946–52) and the Chapel of Notre Dame du Haut in Ronchamp, France (1955).
- Le Corbusier's eight-minute film for the pavilion was made up of seven sequences: Genesis, Matter and Spirit, From Darkness to Dawn, Manmade Gods, How Time Moulds Civilization, Harmony and To All Mankind.
- The Philips Pavilion was demolished on January 30, 1959. Like most world's fair buildings, it was a never meant to remain standing beyond the duration of the fair.
- The pavilion had 425 speakers attached to its walls to play Edgard Varèse's composition for Le Corbusier's *Poème Electronique.*
- The curvaceous silver pavilion was designed using straight lines to form hyperbolic paraboloids.

freedom to experiment. The results are startling. His eight-minute composition consists of a combination of electronically-generated sounds and real-life recorded noises, which seemed to many like random sounds and strange voices collected together in no particular arrangement. In the pavilion, different sound sequences were played through particular sets of the 425 speakers to create harmonies and climaxes dependent upon where visitors stood or sat. The effect was described by critics as "moving music", in which sounds would flow across the space, reverberating off the walls to further heighten the intensity of the composition.

Le Corbusier's film to accompany the music was an eight-minute looped composition that would be projected onto the pavilion walls. Still photographs, shown in pairs and highlighted by changing washes of coloured light, purveyed Le Corbusier's view of humanity. They were abstract and difficult to decipher, and included such diverse subject matter as tribal art, babies' faces, animals, machinery, comedy actors and even an atomic mushroom cloud. Charlie Chaplin and the mushroom cloud were shown next to each other in an attempt to highlight the absurdity of modern warfare.

The pavilion was one of the most visited at the fair, attracting nearly two million people. However, the architecture was harshly criticized. Italian architect Ernesto Rogers said, "Where the result should have been a fluid sequence of convexities and concavities, there are disturbing elements for reinforcing .... It is not a fulfilled architecture; it is not a clear composition ... it is only the indication of new architectonic dimensions."

The music's atmospheric impact was the most talked about element of Le Corbusier's amalgamation of architecture, film and sound. Varèse's score, while not enthusiastically received by the public, influenced an entire generation of avant-garde composers with its use of electronic music.

PHAENO SCIENCE CENTRE WOLFSBURG, GERMANY

The Phaeno Science Centre in Germany is a completely unique structure. Highly sculptural, structurally inventive and aesthetically daring, this building represents a significant piece of image making for the city of Wolfsburg.

Designed by Zaha Hadid Architects, who won an international competition, the building is supposed to be "a mysterious object, giving rise to curiosity and discovery". Containing a wide range of science exhibits, interactive demonstrations and areas for experiment, the centre was conceived as a place to excite people about the possibilities of science and to explain the principles behind subjects such as DNA. The architects tried hard to respond to this theme, designing an object that appears almost like a spaceship ready for take-off, or a peculiar globule of geology ripe for exploration.

Constructed from 27,000 cubic metres (953,496 cubic feet) of concrete and 5,000 tonnes (5,512 tons) of steel, this structure is unusual in that it is almost a single, coherent whole – architecture and structure are one and the same, like a piece of moulded plasticine. Also, the science centre is not a building of floors and walls; instead, it is a sculpted object of interlinked planes, vaults, niches, ramps and voids that appear almost as a landscape. Indeed, the architects have tried to take notice of the landscape of the surrounding area, integrating pathways and surfaces into the building itself. In some ways, it is as if the building has grown out of the ground.

This put the structural engineers, Adams Kara Taylor, in an interesting position. In fact, when they were appointed to the design team the engineers could not be absolutely sure that they could do what the architects wanted. However, with the help of analysis software, the engineers managed to pull it off. This project was also the product of a particularly close collaboration between architects and engineers. "Hadid wants every element to have a specific architectural and visual purpose; we try to give everything she wants in the building a structural purpose," said Adams Kara Taylor. "The design leaves no scope for redundancy; all the elements work together. So the walls and slab combine to make a continuous shell and the capacity of every element, whether concrete at the lower level and steel above, horizontal or vertical, is used to the full."

The bulk of the building is raised off the ground by 6–7 metres (20–23 feet), and supported by a series of concrete cones, which double up as access points, shops and kiosks. The structure works in such an integrated way thanks to the power of three-dimensional computer modelling and the technique of "finite element analysis" (FEA). FEA is a mathematical technique developed in 1943 to help engineers forecast how structures will perform once built. By recreating structures as a grid set over a series of nodes (points of particular structural relevance, such as joints) engineers

Below: A site plan of the Phaeno Science Centre in Wolfsburg, Germany. The building was designed as part of the urban landscape; its form was driven not only by its function, but by the fact that it grows out of its site.

Opposite: Inside the Phaeno Centre. The building was not designed as a set of walls, floors and ceilings, but as an assembly of different planes. As a science centre, the building itself pushed the boundaries of what is technically possible.

project data

- The Phaeno Science Centre was conceived in 1998, and a design competition in 2000 was won by London-based firm Zaha Hadid Architects.
- The centre cost £55 million (79 million Euros).
- The building contains 12,000 square metres (129,167 square feet) of space (plus 15,000 square metres (161,459 square feet) for its underground car park).
- 27,000 cubic metres (953,496 cubic feet) of concrete and 5,000 tonnes (5,512 tons) of steel were used in the construction of the centre.
- The Science Centre opened to the public on November 24, 2005.
- In 2006 the building was shortlisted for the United Kingdom's Stirling Prize, an annual award for the best building designed by a British architect.

can spot areas of weakness or stress and adjust the design to eliminate future problems. FEA (undertaken with a computer program called Sofistik) was especially important for the design of the Phaeno Science Centre, largely because the design would have been more conservative without it. In other words, Sofistik allowed the design team to test its ideas in advance and be as bold as possible, without leaving anything to chance. The building is so successful, structurally and aesthetically, that it has appeared as a case study on a graduate design course at Harvard (course literature describes the project as "an extreme in which it is difficult to tell where the architecture stops and engineering begins").

Part of the success of the project also lies in the use of self-compacting concrete, a form of concrete with chemical additives that allow it to settle on its own, leaving a very smooth finish. When built, the science centre was the largest building in Europe constructed from this form of concrete; without it the complex forms of the building would have been more difficult to achieve.

Opened in November 2005, the centre contains 250 exhibits in 7,000 square metres (75,347 square feet) of display space. The building has been well received both in Germany and internationally, and has won a number of awards.

Below: Natural light is admitted into this building through oblique windows cast into the concrete of the structure.

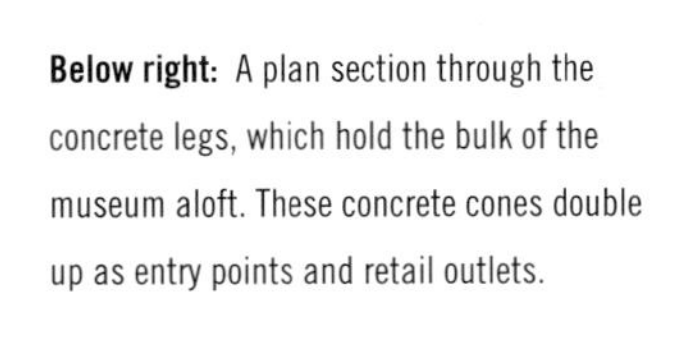

Below right: A plan section through the concrete legs, which hold the bulk of the museum aloft. These concrete cones double up as entry points and retail outlets.

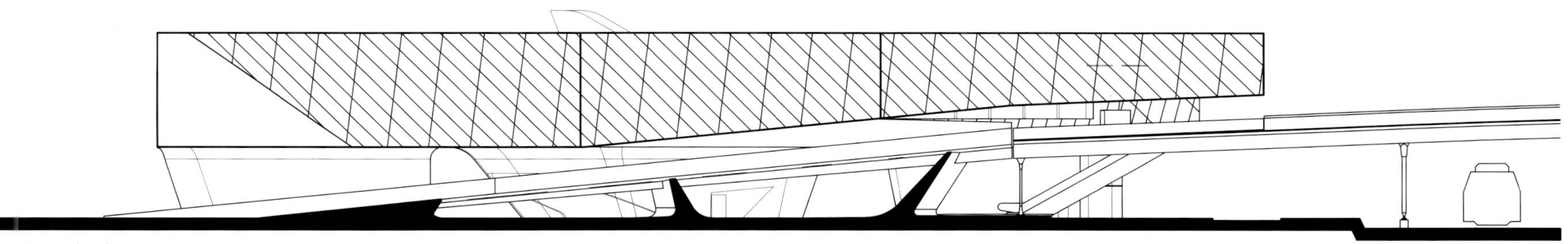

Elevation East

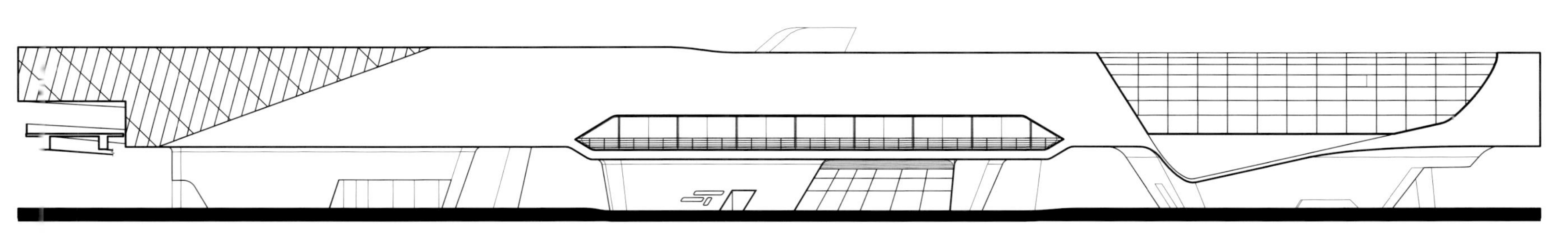

Elevation North

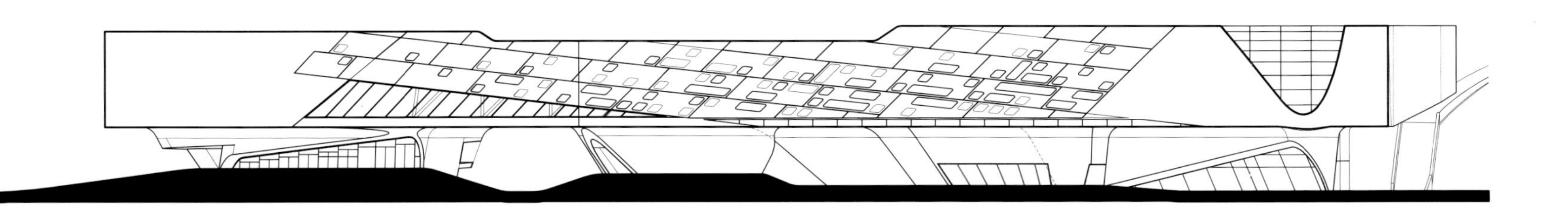

Elevation South

Opposite top: Prior to being fitted out with exhibitions and display cases, the Phaeno Centre appears like a stage set for a science-fiction drama – a spaceship, even.

Above: Elevations of the Phaeno Centre, which crouches on the ground like a spaceship ready for take-off. Computer modelling, especially the technique known as "finite element analysis", was essential in the making of this structure.

COMPUTER MODELLING

Buildings like the Phaeno Science Centre would not be possible without developments in computer technology, which now allows designers to create virtual buildings and test them before actually moving to the construction stage. Traditionally, structures have been drawn in pencil and their structural integrity tested through a mixture of mathematical rules, industry norms and personal experience. Architects and engineers began to experiment with computer-aided design (CAD) in the early 1980s but it was only in the late 1990s that computer-modelling designs in three dimensions became more mainstream. In this sense, architecture lags behind other industries, such as automotive and aeronautical design, which put computers at the heart of the design process much earlier.

There is now an extraordinary range of computer-modelling tools available to design teams – many of which were not even designed for the construction industry (often, they were originally conceived for the animation or film industries and architects have adopted them for their complex modelling abilities). When these programs are linked to computer-controlled production machinery or rapid prototyping machines, which can recreate virtual models as actual objects, the results can be spectacular.

Today, it is possible to build something of almost any shape because computers are fast enough to calculate the complex geometries in seconds. Computers, with the right programming, can also predict how people might move around a building, how fire will spread, how long the structure will survive when on fire, how wind will flow, how light will fall and even what a building will sound like. What they can't do is make aesthetic judgements – for that, we still need people.

ESPLANADE MARINA BAY, SINGAPORE

The Esplanade performing-arts complex, designed by an Anglo-Singaporean architectural team to be one of world's best-equipped facilities, is Singapore's principal cultural centre. Opened in 2002, the building contains five performance spaces, including an 1,800-seat concert hall and a 2,000-seat theatre. However, its most eye-catching feature is its oddly textured roof, giving rise to the building's local nickname of "the Durian" for its similarity to the exotic fruit.

Designed by British firm Michael Wilford & Partners, with DP Architects of Singapore, this structure is composed of a pair of complex enclosures that protect the performance venues inside. Essentially, Esplanade is a "buildings within buildings" environment, where the domes shelter the performance spaces beneath them – acoustically as well as environmentally.

This approach, simple in conceptual terms, proved immensely difficult to put into practice. The architects wanted people within the enclosures to be able to see out (especially at night) and people outside to see in, but constructing domes of glass would have been highly impractical. Singapore's latitude lies close to the equator and the strong year-round sunshine would have caused a glass structure to overheat quickly. Instead, the design team created a glass envelope covered in a metal skin. This skin is composed of thousands of shading devices, angled so that the sun's rays do not penetrate the interior too intensely, while providing views out at the same time. This design tactic actually benefits from Singapore's geographical location – being equatorial, the position of the sun does not change as much as it does in northerly or southerly latitudes, so the building's shading system does not have to cope with dramatic seasonal variations in the direction of sunshine. The sunshades could therefore be fixed, and the design team did not have to consider movable systems. The shading could be modulated to shield the building's interiors from the low sun angles experienced at dawn and dusk, and from its high angle at midday.

Another complication was that the two "domes" are not uniform in shape; in fact, they are highly complex forms that wrap around the performance venues (each of which has a different shape and size) as closely as possible. To explore and finalize the forms of the enclosures, architects and engineers employed computer techniques more commonly seen in the design of ships' hulls and cars. Using what are known as "NURBS" surfaces (Non-Uniform Rational B-Splines, where a "spline" is a free-form curve) engineers were able to conjure up a completely unique structure that would have been impossible with more traditional lines, arcs and curves. Within a computer model, engineers from German firm MERO constructed a series of "weights" and "control points" that allowed them to push and pull the virtual surfaces of the enclosures until the form fulfilled the design requirements. MERO's computer models ended up being extremely large, with thousands of points and line elements spaced out over what was called a "rhombic grid".

These computer-generated efforts were well worth it – they allowed the design team to plot the exact position, size and orientation of the sunshades, as well as providing the templates from which the sunshades would be cut. Furthermore, the computer work allowed a certain amount of rationalization to take place; at the British Museum, every one of the triangular pieces of glass in the roof of the Great Court is unique (see page 200) but just 25 cutting patterns were needed to produce the sunshades covering the complex surfaces of Esplanade's domes.

Left: The Esplanade performing arts complex in Singapore, affectionately known as "the Durian" for its physical similarity to the exotic fruit.

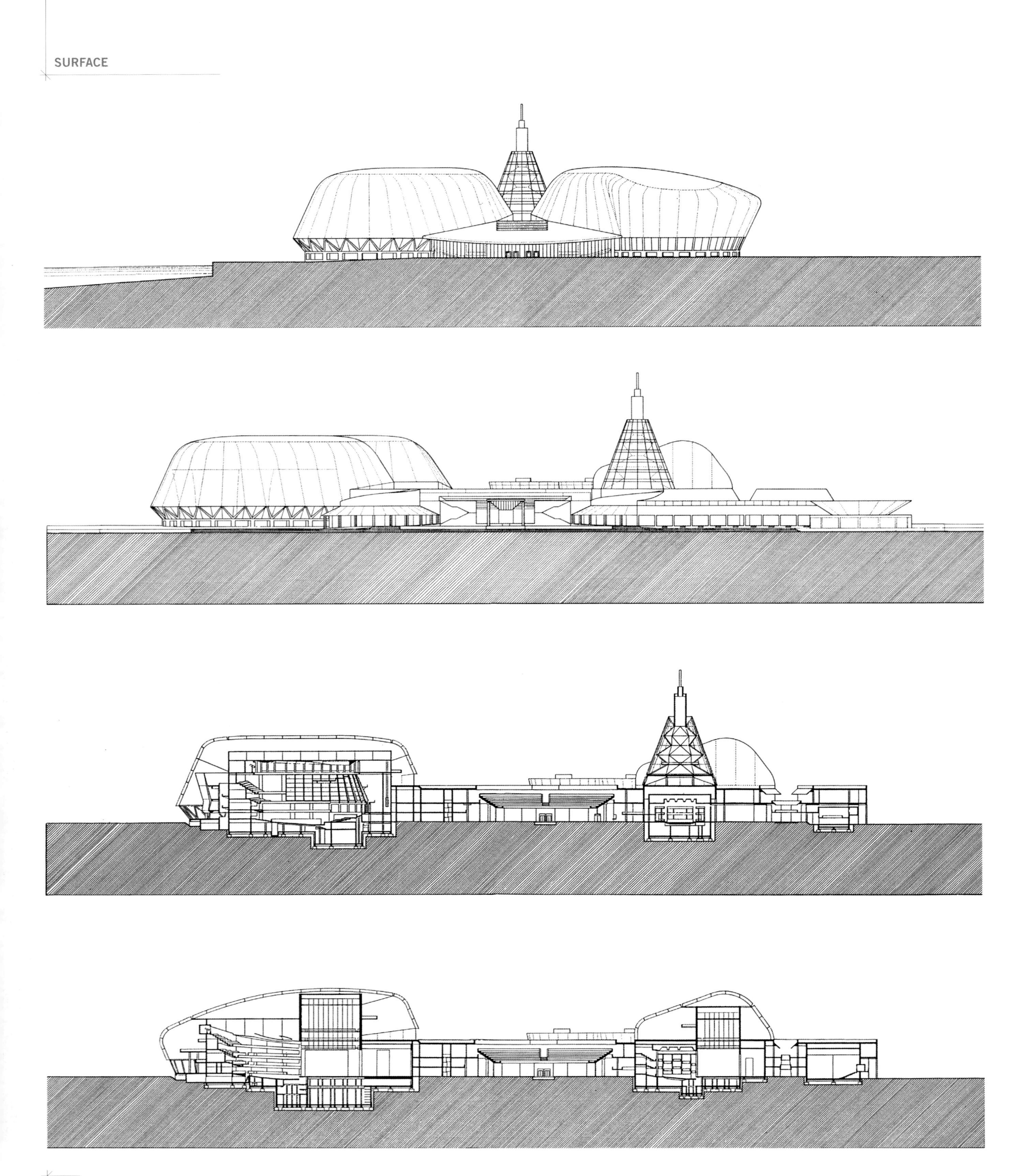

project data

- Singapore's Esplanade was conceived in the 1980s. Designs were presented to the public in 1994; the ground-breaking ceremony was conducted on August 11, 1996; the foundations were completed in 1998; the structure was completed by February 2001; the complex was formally opened on October 12, 2002.
- The building cost S$600 million (Singapore dollars) to build.
- Esplanade comprises five performance venues: the 1,800-seat Concert Hall, the 2,000-seat Lyric Theatre, the 850-seat Medium Theatre, the 450-seat Adaptable Theatre and the 250-seat Development Studio.
- The entire building covers 80,500 square metres (866,495 square feet).
- The project involved an international team including DP Architects (Singapore), Michael Wilford & Partners (UK), acoustics consultants Artec Consultants (USA), cladding consultants Atelier (Germany), cladding contractor MERO (Germany) and theatrical design firm Theatre Project Consultants (UK).

Opposite: Elevations and sections of the "Durian", illustrating its two principal domes and the cultural spaces they cover.

Right: Protected by carefully arranged sun-shields, this cultural building is able to admit daylight in a tropical climate without overheating.

Opposite: Inside the Esplanade centre, the acoustic and lighting systems are just as technically complex as the building's outer covering. Highly variable acoustic mechanisms allow the concert halls to stage a wide range of musical performance.

Left: The louvres on the outside of the building's domes allow filtered views of the outside, allowing theatre-goers to feel that they are neither in a goldfish bowl nor sealed off from the outside.

Below: A plan of the principal spaces within the Esplanade cultural complex.

Each aluminium sunshade is composed of a rhombus, folded along its shorter diagonal to form a "triangular pyramid". The sunshades are fixed to the steel grid that holds the glazing in place.

The mechanics of the performance halls are just as sophisticated as the skin of this cultural centre. A crucial part of the client's brief was that the building could be used for a wide range of music performance, including Asian and Western music. The acoustics of the performance halls, therefore, had to be flexible enough to allow an audience to fully appreciate the sound of, say, a solo violin and a group of percussionists. The Concert Hall is particularly well equipped, acoustically. It contains three adaptable acoustic canopies over the concert platform, allowing sound to be absorbed and reflected in a way appropriate to the music being played. Also, a set of massive "reverberation chambers" (equivalent in volume to the size of the hall itself) can be opened up to alter the acoustics of the space. There are even 1,000 square metres (10,764 square feet) of acoustic banners hanging in the hall, which can be adjusted to fine tune the sound of the music.

The Esplanade theatre complex is a significant addition to Singapore's architecture, and a bold and unusual form for a country more usually associated with high-rise buildings. In fact, Esplanade has some very tall architectural neighbours, so its roof had to be considered a "fifth facade" – that is, as well composed when viewed from the top as it is from street level.

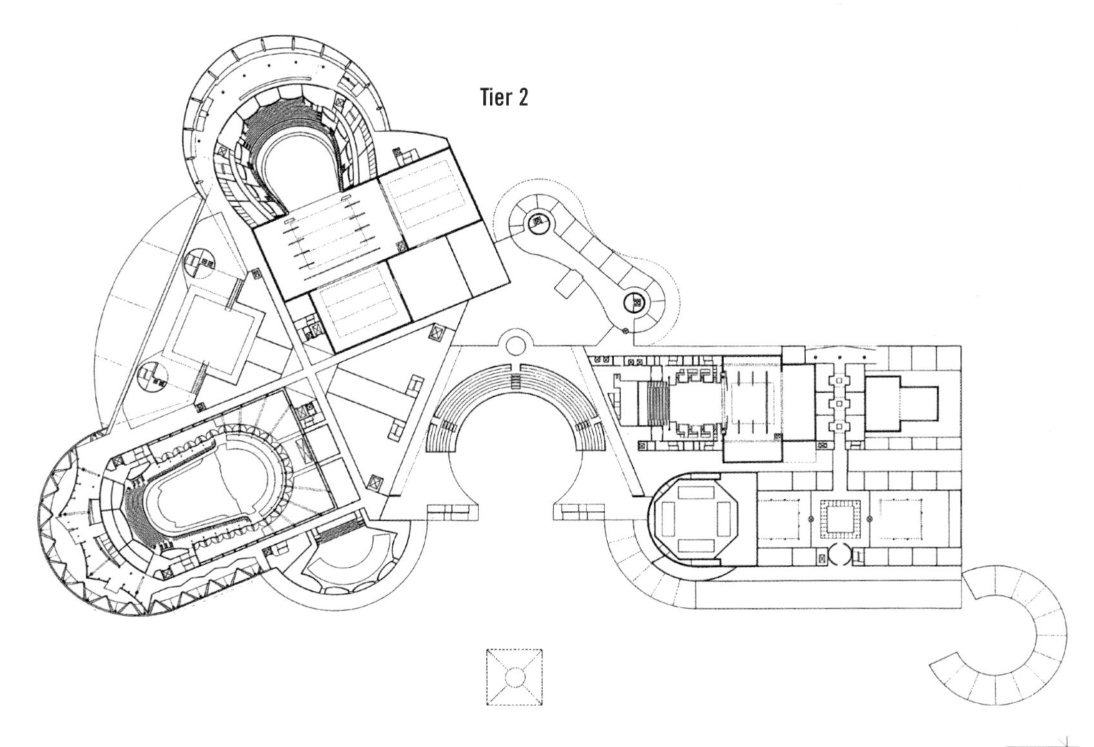

ATOMIUM BRUSSELS, BELGIUM

Atomium, an extraordinary steel and aluminium structure in Brussels, represents the crystalline form of a nine-atom molecule of iron, magnified some 165 billion times. Built as the centrepiece of Belgium's 1958 International Exhibition, this sculptural form rises 102 metres (334½ feet) above the Heysel Plateau.

The structure was opened on April 17, 1958 after three years of construction. Designed to reflect the possibilities offered by new technology, Atomium was a difficult design and construction undertaking. Designed by engineer André Waterkeyn, the structure was conceived as a cube balancing on one corner – the nine spheres representing the eight corners of the cube and the central point. Pivoting the structure in this way allowed the diagonal through this giant crystal to act as a vertical shaft, around which everything else could be supported. This explains Waterkeyn's description of the structure as an example of the "centred cubic system". But a cube of this immensity could not be supported by a single point alone, so three "bipods" were added to the design to provide stability.

The structure is, in fact, extremely stable. Partly, this is due to the immense concrete foundation, which weighs 454 tonnes (500 tons) and penetrates the ground by 17.4 metres (57 feet) with 123 piles. The structure itself is made of tubes of steel up to 12 millimetres (½ inch) thick, while the three bipods weigh 91 tonnes (100 tons) each. Moreover, scale models of the structure were subjected to wind-tunnel tests in the Belgian Ministry of Transport, as, although how wind flows around a single sphere could easily be calculated, it was not known how nine connecting spheres would behave in a high wind. As it turned out, three months of tests proved to the engineers that they had little to worry about. A series of further tests during construction, comparing actual stresses with those that were predicted in the design phase, proved that the structure was sound.

The actual dimensions of the structure also proved problematic at the design stage, because Atomium had to be a fair representation of an atomic structure, while being capacious enough to provide for the comfort and safety of visitors. Waterkeyn also needed the connecting tubes (which represent the forces of attraction between the nine atoms) to have the right compositional and aesthetic relationship with the spheres, so the final solution was a compromise between the shape of an iron molecule, the size of adult persons, the management of crowds, and the cost and practicality of construction.

Waterkeyn originally aimed to build the spheres with a diameter of 20 metres (65⅔ feet), but this was eventually scaled back to 18 metres (59 feet). The connecting tubes come in two sizes – those reaching into the central sphere are 3.3 metres (10¾ feet) in diameter, while the tubes

Left: The Atomium, Brussels, Belgium. Designed as the main attraction of an exhibition in 1958, this structure has become emblematic of Brussels.

running between the outside spheres are slightly smaller, with a diameter of 2.9 metres (9½ feet). This decision was taken purely for aesthetic reasons. It was always the intention to reduce the size of the connecting tubes to as small a diameter as possible; the steeper the gradient of the tubes, the narrower they could be in section (the perimeter tubes are set at a steeper angle than those joining with the central sphere, hence they could be smaller and still retain plenty of headroom).

In spite of the fact that all the spheres and their connecting tubes are large enough to accommodate people, only six spheres are actually part of the visitor experience: the base sphere, the three lower spheres, the central sphere and the uppermost sphere (which contains a restaurant and viewing platform). Circulation is managed through a system of escalators, stairs and a central lift. The lift rises through the vertical core at 5 metres (16.4 feet) a second, and is capable of taking 400 people to the top of the structure every hour. The three outer-upper spheres are the only ones without any sort of vertical support structure; it is these that are closed to the public.

The spheres are clad in aluminium tiles, configured as spherical triangles (a template that was arrived at by drawing circles around a sphere). Importantly, the design of the cladding system takes into account the different rates of expansion of steel (which provides the structure) and aluminium. Ignoring this differential would have led to cracking in the cladding. Atomium's windows are made of plexiglas, the lines of which follow the triangular pattern set up for the cladding system.

Originally designed as a temporary structure (as was the Eiffel Tower), Atomium came to be so highly regarded that it is now a permanent addition to the Belgian landscape. In March 2004 it closed for an extensive refurbishment programme, designed to scrub the structure up and restore its original gleam. Atomium re-opened on February 18, 2006.

project data

- Atomium was built by 15,000 people over a period of three years.
- The structure was the centrepiece of the Brussels International Exhibition, held between April 17 and October 19, 1958; almost 40 million people visited the exhibition.
- The structure represents a molecule of iron, composed of nine atoms joined by forces of attraction; these forces are represented by the 20 connecting tubes.
- Just six of the nine spheres are open to the public; the interiors of these spheres were designed by architects André and Jean Polak.
- Atomium is 102 metres (334½ feet) high; the tubes connecting its outer spheres are 30 metres (98½ feet) in length; the tubes connecting to the central sphere are 23 metres (75½ feet) long.
- Each sphere that can be visited contains two floors.
- The upper sphere contains a restaurant capable of seating 140 people; the viewing platform below can accommodate 250 people.

Left: Recently renovated, the Atomium sparkles like the science-fiction structure it was conceived as. Waterkeyn's ambitious construction, built over three years, was only intended to be temporary, but has lasted half a century.

SERPENTINE PAVILION 2002 LONDON, UK

Perhaps the smallest structure to be included within this book, the 2002 Serpentine Pavilion in London's Kensington Gardens is also one of the most magical. The design took initial reference from a solid white box that was bisected again and again, cutting out triangular shapes to form a seemingly unpredictable pattern. The result was a structure that would seem impossibly unstable, yet which was perfectly balanced.

Designed by renowned Japanese architect Toyo Ito and Cecil Balmond, deputy chairman of engineering firm Arup, the pavilion looked as though its structure was pieced together from a jigsaw of random triangular chunks of white steel. In reality, the design was the extrapolation of a mathematical algorithm devised by Balmond and his team at Arup's Advanced Geometry Unit.

The theory of the design is difficult to explain. Imagine drawing a square on a piece of paper with its base parallel to the bottom of the sheet. Then, draw another square of similar size on top of the first but tilt the base of this one at a slight diagonal angle. The drawing now looks like a somewhat chunky, lopsided star with eight points. Where the sides of the two squares bisect, triangles are created. This was the very beginning of the design for the pavilion. Balmond's team fed raw data into a computer, instructing it to draw these squares continuously. Using an algorithm-based program, the computer produced an infinite pattern of spiralling squares. The designers stopped the computer at the moment they saw the pattern they wanted and then used it as a guide to create the surface of the structure: the pattern of squares was wrapped around an imaginary box that represented the space within the pavilion, and the triangulated structure was born.

The pavilion was made up of a series of welded sections that combined to form a skeleton of primary members and secondary stabilizers. Together, they ensured that the structure stood up, while also forming the pattern. The stronger primary members carried the weight of the pavilion and supported the roof: the secondary stabilizers sat at angles to the primary members providing bracing for them to stop them falling over. Into this structural skeleton were inserted box-section panels: these were bolted to the framework and sealed at their edges, creating the solid elements in the walls and roof of the pavilion.

For the theoretical design to work, the engineers had to divide the pattern up into segments, each of which would be welded or bolted together to form a piece of the "jigsaw". The slenderness of the steel members and their positioning within the complex structure meant that there could be no margin for error. Even the size of welds were taken into account and reduced to minimize their impact on the finished pavilion.

Structurally, the biggest challenge for the designers and constructors of the pavilion was how to ensure that none of its thin supporting members buckled. Due to the pavilion's complete lack of linear – vertical and horizontal – geometry it was difficult to assess the loads imposed on different parts using conventional methods. The AGU team developed special re-iterative computer analysis techniques (software repeating an action to infinity – in this instance overlaying squares at slightly different angles, creating the pattern for the pavilion's structural frame) in order to prove that the structure wouldn't buckle and collapse.

The structural sections and panels were all manufactured off site, carefully labelled and then delivered and assembled using a large crane. When the walls were complete a "table" scaffold was built inside the structure. Then the roof elements were craned onto it and into their exact positions. Operatives bolted the many parts together, creating a roof that was able to fully span the pavilion. Finally, the solid panels and glazed elements were inserted to complete the pavilion's construction.

The roof panels varied in size and weighed between 5 and 10 tonnes (5.5 and 11 tons). They stretched over the 309.76-square-metre (3,334-square-foot) space with no internal support. The largest wall panel measured 20 metres (65½ feet) long by 4.5 metres (14¾ feet) high; including the base on which the structure sat, it was 5.35 metres (17⅔ feet) high.

The crux of the design was the belief of both Ito and Balmond that the structure of buildings should not be restricted to a simple rectilinear framework. Both men describe the work that they do as "animating structure" – taking something that could be boring and regular and creating something exciting instead. Balmond says, "Since geometry is the life-line of structure, its animation enlivens a piece of construction to be something other than the dumb frame."

The resulting white-painted steel structure was riddled with holes and spaces. The structure was thick: the 550-millimetre (21⅔-inch) depth of the steel members being what gave them their strength. It also created a feeling that visitors were entering into a once-solid space, rather than simply wandering into an enclosed area.

Below: A digital image showing the concept behind the design of the Serpentine Pavilion. A series of straight lines cut through the square plan at different angles: these were used to create a structural frame.

Opposite top, bottom left and bottom middle: The Serpentine Pavilion's pristine white facade features solid, glazed and open portions, creating a structure with seemingly no ordered or coherent design rationale.

Opposite bottom right: Inside the pavilion, a café is dappled by sunlight shining through the random spaces in the dramatic roof.

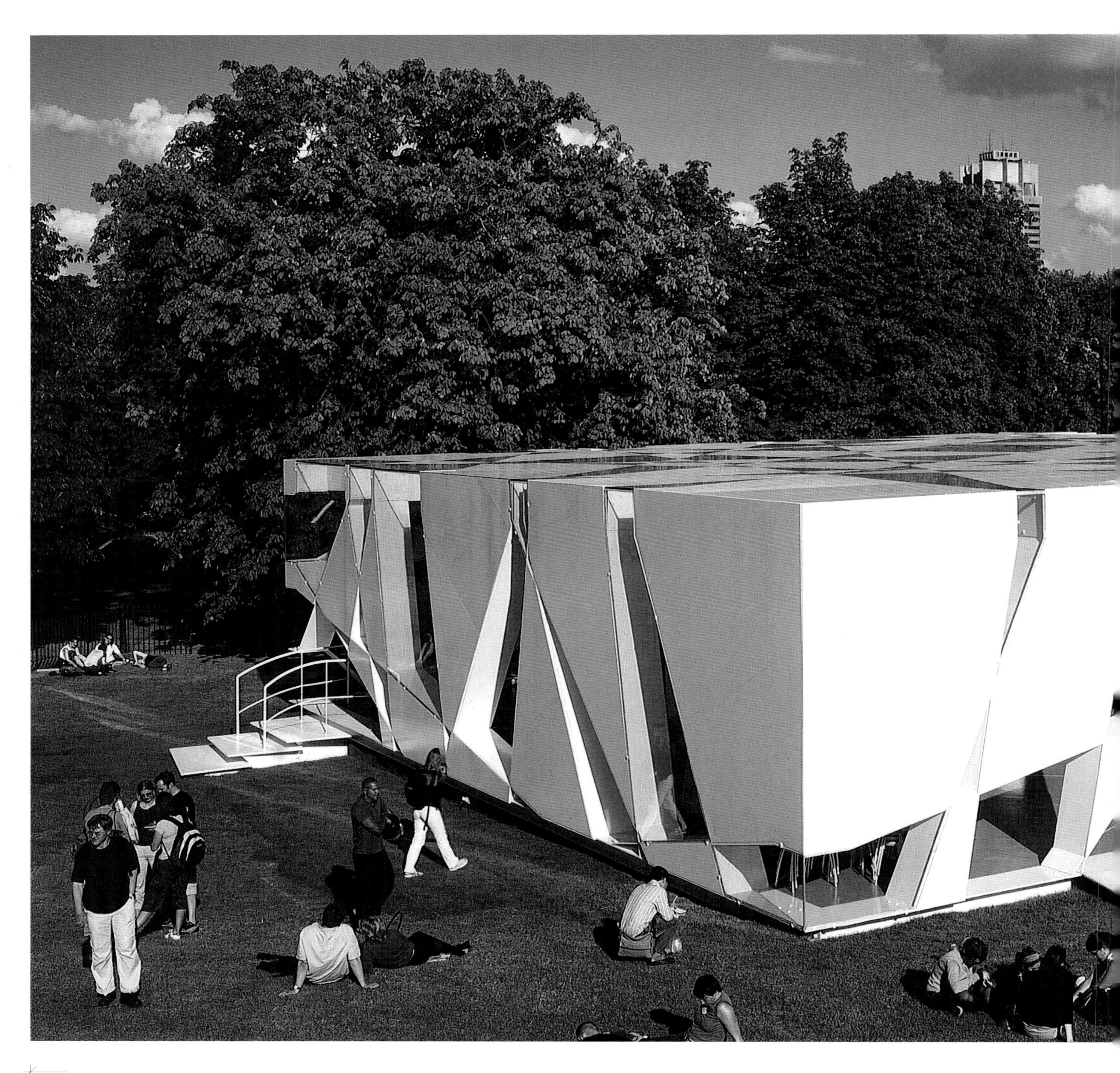

project data

- The pavilion measured 20 metres (65⅔ feet) in length on each of its four sides, by 5.35 metres (17⅔ feet) high.
- The concept for the structure of the pavilion was created using advanced mathematically based software, which reproduced a pattern of spiralling squares.
- Each year the Serpentine Gallery commissions an architect who has never worked in the United Kingdom before to design a pavilion. World-renowned architects including Daniel Libeskind, Rem Koolhaas and Oscar Niemeyer have all designed pavilions for the gallery.
- This pavilion and all of the others built are designed and constructed in just six months. They are then used by the gallery to stage events over the summer before being sold to recoup their cost.
- The pavilion is now the on-site marketing suite for the company developing London's Battersea Power Station project.
- The pavilion was used as a café and outdoor conference and party space.
- Toyo Ito has since used similar techniques to create a bizarre facade for a store for leather goods retailer Tod's in Tokyo.

Left: The pavilion sits next to the historic Serpentine Gallery in London's Kensington Gardens. This structure occupied the site during the summer of 2003. Each year a new pavilion is designed by a famous architect who has never before worked in the UK.

FRAUENKIRCHE DRESDEN, GERMANY

Imagine a construction race spanning three centuries: a stone Baroque church in Dresden, Germany, first built in the mid-eighteenth-century, and then entirely reconstructed in our own era. Who can build it the most effectively? Actually, the skill of long-dead German stonemasons proved a match for their contemporaries and the power of advanced three-dimensional modelling programs.

The Frauenkirche (the "Church of Our Lady") was completed in 1743 and possessed, until its destruction by Allied bombing in 1945, one of northern Europe's best examples of a large stone dome. The church was an architectural and engineering masterpiece – its 96-metre (315-foot) high, 10,886-tonne (12,000-ton) bell-shaped dome of solid stone had often been compared for its ingenuity to Michelangelo's dome for St Peter's Basilica in Rome. In addition, the Frauenkirche's organ, built by celebrated organ-builder Gottfried Silbermann, had been played by Johann Sebastian Bach, while Richard Wagner's Love Feast of the Apostles was actually written for the Frauenkirche.

Dresden was subjected to a massive bombing raid on February 13, 1945 and the Frauenkirche burned for two days before collapsing. The rubble of the Frauenkirche lay undisturbed for four decades until German practice IPRO won the contract to piece it all back together as a monument to reassembling the country itself. Reconstruction began in 1994 and the church was officially reconsecrated on October 30, 2005.

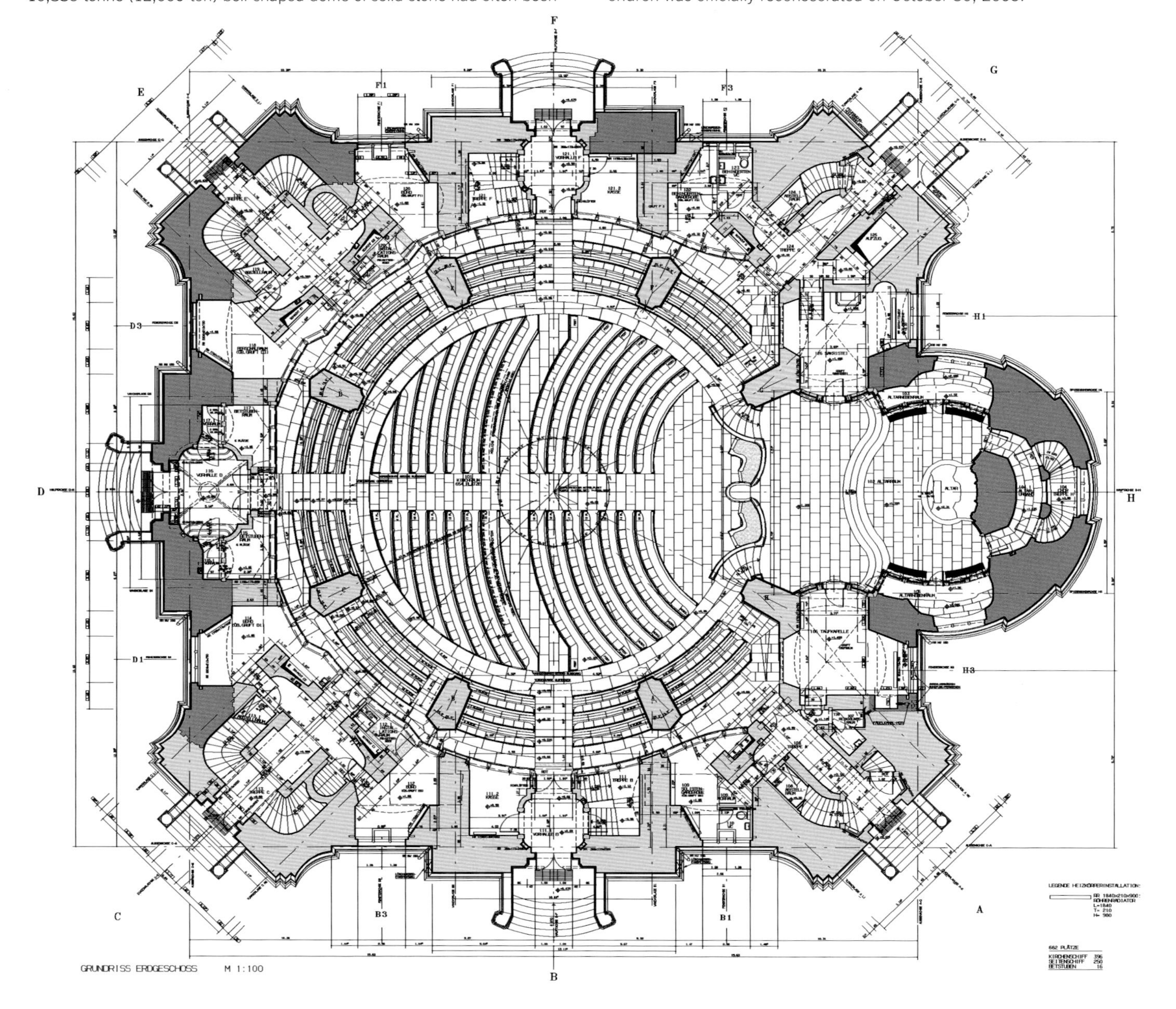

project data

- The original Frauenkirche was built by George Bähr between 1726 and 1743. The church was destroyed during a bombing raid in 1945 and a new foundation stone was laid in 1994. The crypt was completed in 1996 and the church reopened in 2005.
- The reconstruction project cost about 180 million Euros (US$217 million); the funds were raised internationally, largely from private donations.
- The replica orb and cross which sits on top of the dome was made in the United Kingdom as a peace gesture – it was, in fact, made by the son of one of the British pilots who took part in the bombing raids.
- The church's most distinctive feature was its 96-metre (315-foot) high dome, the Steinerne Glocke or "Stone Bell". According to eyewitness accounts of 1760, the dome was hit by cannonballs during the Seven Years War (1756–63) and they simply bounced off.

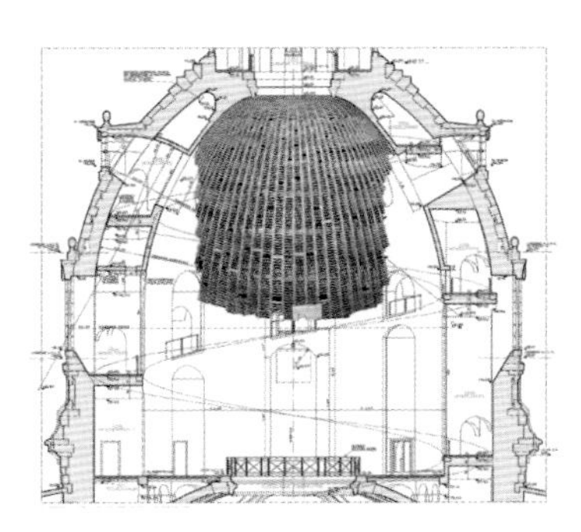

Opposite: A plan section of Dresden's Frauenkirche, built in the eighteenth century and rebuilt after being bombed in the Second World War. The contemporary builders reused as much of the original material as possible.

Above: Drawings of the dome and a portal of the church, illustrating the complexity of the original Baroque design and the conditions in which modern stonemasons had to work.

Right: The reconstructed Frauenkirche, completed in 2005 after lying in ruins for 50 years. The original stonework can clearly be seen against the lighter, recently cut stone.

Left: The Frauenkirche before the Second World War. By the 1930s, however, a structural problem with the church had begun to manifest itself; a new structural system, joining the dome with the main body of the church, was built into the new incarnation of the building.

Below left, middle and right: Under a protective canopy, the timber formwork of the church's dome is assembled, providing a foundation on which to lay the stone.

Opposite left: A section through the centre of the church, showing the complexity of the dome structure.

Opposite right: The precision with which the Frauenkirche was reassembled can be appreciated when you compare this image with the photograph on page 251.

Without the advanced computer-modelling program Catia, this architectural jigsaw – which has reused thousands of the original stones (perhaps 44 per cent of them), including some from a Gothic structure discovered beneath Baroque wreckage – would have taken a lot longer. But even the backing of this sophisticated software, the workhorse of French aerospace company Dassault, wasn't enough to give the team of architects complete comfort. "It was clear from the beginning that the only way we were going to reconstruct this church was through a 3-D model," said architect Christoph Frenzel at a lecture at London's Royal Society for the Arts. "It looked an absolutely insurmountable task from the start, and we couldn't be absolutely sure we were up to it."

The main problem was that there were only a handful of architectural drawings available, so knowledge gaps had to be filled by transposing the views of thousands of photographs onto what could be known for certain. Thankfully, because so many people had posed for wedding photos outside the church, there was an abundance of photographic material available, especially of the doors. Old purchase orders were also studied, which often provided information about the quality of the mortar and the details of paint pigment. Finally, the evidence of the stones themselves was invaluable – masons' marks often gave a clue about where a stone would have fitted, and larger forms could be generated from small fragments. In one case, an entire staircase was modelled from the lines of a single stone tread.

In the early stages of the project, two procedures went on in parallel – the site was cleared and useful-looking stones were scanned, labelled and catalogued, while, at the same time, the team constructed a virtual model of the church, known as a wireframe. Once the wireframe looked right, virtual copies of the stones were slotted into the computer model. New stones were then fitted around the old ones. According to the design team, the reconstituted church is no more than 10 millimetres (0.39 inches) different from the original building.

Crucially, though, computer modelling has allowed the modern team to put right what eighteenth-century architect George Bähr got wrong. The point where the square base of the church supports the different geometry of the dome had always been weak; indeed, authorities had closed the church in 1938 because of problems with cracking and damp. A new structural system has been deployed at this point, but the church is, in all other respects, intended as a faithful reproduction. Around one quarter of the building is formed from the original fabric, while the new sandstone was taken from the same quarry as the original building material. Of course, due to the fact that the older stones have been weathered (and burnt), the surface of the Frauenkirche clearly differentiates between old and new – this will be a feature of the building for some years to come.

But the project has proved a sharp reminder, if any were needed, of the declining art of stonemasonry. "This hybrid process [of stonemasonry and computer modelling] has given us a lot of respect for the original architects and builders. I just wish we could go back and follow them around from site to site to learn something more of what they knew," said Frenzel.

Some academics have wondered about the authenticity of the reconstructed church, especially because it was pieced together using modern techniques and some of the stones are not necessarily in their original places. In this sense, the "memory" of the building has been misplaced, they say. However, American former statesman Henry Kissinger, honorary director of fund-raising body Friends of Dresden, described the rebuilding of the church as symbolic of international peace and reconciliation: "The rebuilding of Dresden's Frauenkirche demonstrates an international commitment to overcome the cruelties of war and to build bridges among nations."

Opposite left: The reconstructed church looks every inch an original Baroque building. The truth is that modern surveying and computer modelling techniques played a key role in bringing this symbol of Dresden back to life.

Opposite right: A view upwards through a stone stairway, spiralling its way through the Frauenkirche.

Right: The Frauenkirche, "The Church of Our lady", was re-consecrated on October 30, 2005, and instantly became a symbol of reconciliation between Germany and the UK.

05
POWER

SOME structures are designed to do more than sustain their own weight – they generate power, they hold back the sea, they move. Occasionally, these structures are built in the public eye and perform celebrated roles, such as the Thames Barrier and the Hoover Dam. Often, they are structures invisible to all but specialist audiences, such as a particle accelerator or a nuclear power station. Inevitably, the scale of these achievements is awe-inspiring and they demonstrate how human beings can change the course of nature with a single, mammoth intervention. However, it is not just the size of these undertakings that is impressive. It is also the logistical inventiveness, the structural cunning, the lateral thinking and the sheer bravado that inspires wonder.

ITAIPU DAM

PARANÁ RIVER, BRAZIL/PARAGUAY

The Itaipu Dam straddles the Paraná River, which delineates the border between Brazil and Paraguay. Built between 1971 and 1982, the dam is made up of a number of six different dam types, such is its span. Including the massive earth- and rock-fill sections on its eastern flank, the dam is over 7.7 kilometres (4.8 miles) in length.

The vision for this colossal structure took shape in the 1960s when Brazil and Paraguay thrashed out a deal called the Act of Iguaçu, which was signed on June 22, 1966; construction works began in earnest in February 1971. Initially, work was focused on building the gigantic earth- and rock-fill dams that would eventually assist in holding back water from the 1,350-square-kilometre (521-square-mile) reservoir that would be formed.

The rock-fill dam to the right of the main concrete dam structure, when viewed from downstream, is 1,984 metres (6,509 feet) long and has a maximum height of 70 metres (230 feet). Some 12 metres (39 feet) wide at its crest, the dam thickens rapidly as it descends. It has a clay core with rocks piled on either side to create a structure with a volume of 12.8 million cubic metres (452 million cubic feet). Stretching out from this, farther away from the original course of the river, is an earth-fill dam some 2,294 metres (7,526 feet) in length. This massive mound of clay has a maximum height of 30 metres (98 feet) and a volume of around 4.4 million cubic metres (155.4 million cubic feet). To the left of the main

Left: A number of sluice gates on one section of the dam allow millions of litres of water to flood from the reservoir into the river below. To the right, the colossal reinforced wall of the dam is over 60 storeys high.

project data

- The name Itaipu was taken from an island that existed near the construction site; it originates from the Guarani language and means "singing stones".
- In 2000, the Itaipu Power Plant produced about 93,428 gigawatt-hours – a new world record, supplying 24 per cent of Brazil's power and 95 per cent of Paraguay's power.
- The total volume of concrete used in the construction of Itaipu would be sufficient to build 210 football stadiums of the size of Rio de Janeiro's 95,000-capacity Maracanã stadium.
- The iron and steel used on the project would be enough to build 380 Eiffel Towers.
- The height of the main dam (196 metres/643 feet) is equivalent to the height of a 65-storey building.
- Brazil would have to burn 434,000 barrels of petroleum a day to obtain the same energy production as Itaipu provides.
- The volume of earth and rock excavations at Itaipu was eight and a half times greater than that of the Channel Tunnel (see page 102) and the volume of concrete used was 15 times greater.
- The American composer Philip Glass has written a symphonic canata named Itaipu in honour of the structure.
- The dam cost US$12 billion to build.

DAM DESIGN

There are two main types of dam in common use today: gravity and arch. Gravity dams rely on their sheer weight and mass to hold back the water and resist the pressure to overturn, slide or be crushed. They are constructed using concrete, rock, earth or a combination of these materials. The foundation of a gravity dam has an extremely wide cross-section to provide a stable footing; as the dam wall rises it becomes narrower, as the water pressure drops away.

Arch dams gain their stability with a combination of arched construction and gravity action. This type of dam is normally used in narrow gorges with steep side walls composed of sound rock. While the gravity dam relies on its weight to hold back the water, the arch dam is engineered to redistribute the forces upon it into the rock walls it is built against. This is done by building a curved reinforced-concrete dam wall. The water pressure, which is greatest at the centre of the dam wall, is not simply held back by the concrete, but redirected along the line of the curve and dissipated into the canyon walls that the dam is connected to.

Timber and metal dams were experimented with during the early years of the Industrial Revolution. Both had their uses, especially in areas where other suitable materials were not easily available, but neither could be built to the colossal size of earth and concrete dams, so they are no longer used on projects of any significant size today.

Opposite top: This construction image of the dam reveals the original size of the river, the flow of which was diverted to create the 1350-square-kilometre (521-square-mile) reservoir. The scale of the project can be gauged from the two-lane traffic bridge spanning the river in the foreground.

Opposite bottom: Illuminated in an eerie green glow, the main dam, which houses the turbines, is a dramatic spectacle – one visited by countless tourists each year.

Above: An historic shot of the giant sluice gates in operation, as work continued on the dam's completion below the main reinforced concrete walls.

dam and spillway is another earth-fill dam, measuring 872 metres (2,861 feet) long and 25 metres (82 feet) high.

As these gravity-based dams were being constructed, temporary works took place to divert the Paraná River from its natural course in order that the main dam could be built upon the dry river bed. Huge steel sheet piles were driven into the ground and a passageway excavated. Then, on October 14, 1978, the river poured through the diversion channel and work on the main dam could begin.

While the earth- and rock-fill elements of the dam are conventional "gravity-based" systems, the main concrete dam wall is a reinforced-concrete dam, constructed in three distinct sections. A 1,438-metre (4,718-foot) long solid concrete buttress dam, with a maximum height of 81 metres (266 feet) and a base width of 54 metres (177 feet), curves around to link the spillway gates with the central section of the dam wall. The main central section is constructed as a hollow gravity dam, some 187 metres (614 feet) wide at its base and 196 metres (643 feet) tall. Sluice pipes allow water to pour through this part of the dam to power the 20 massive turbines. Finally, a third section, to the right-hand side of the main dam, is 146 metres (479 feet) wide at its base and up to 162 metres (531 feet) high; this, too, has sluice pipes.

The construction of these concrete elements required the speedy manufacture of vast quantities of high-grade concrete: in all, some 12.6 million cubic metres (445 million cubic feet) of concrete were required. On a conventional construction project, tests of the concrete's strength are carried out at intervals of seven and 28 days; however, due to the large quantities concerned, the concrete on the Itaipu project couldn't wait that long. Instead, a concrete manufacture plant and laboratory was constructed on site. At this plant, two crushing complexes produced 2,430 tonnes (2,679 tons) of aggregates per hour: while six concrete complexes, each with a capacity of 180 cubic metres (6,357 cubic feet) per hour, churned out concrete for transportation and placement via two monorails, seven aerial cables and 13 tower cranes. In all, over 40,000 people worked on the construction of the dam, which was completed on October 13, 1982.

From the time the gates of the spillway were completed and closed, the 170-kilometre (106-mile) long reservoir took only around one month to fill to capacity. The Itaipu Dam started producing hydroelectric power on May 5, 1984. Initially, only two turbines were powered up, but, gradually, up to 1991, 18 were brought into service, and now the hydroelectric plant supplies around 20 per cent of Brazil's power and over 90 percent of Paraguay's power.

The last two turbines, which will bring the total to 20, are expected to start operations before the end of 2007, increasing the capacity of the plant from 12,600 megawatts to 14,000 megawatts. This increase in capacity will allow for 18 generation units to remain running all of the time while two stay down for maintenance.

FALKIRK WHEEL FALKIRK, UK

The Falkirk Wheel is not actually a wheel at all. However, it is the first ever rotating boat lift to be built in the world, and the first new boat lift to be built in Britain since the Anderton boat lift in Cheshire was completed in 1875. It is a grandiose exercise in engineering that reconnects the canals of east and west Scotland for the first time in 70 years and provides a fully navigable waterway between Edinburgh and Glasgow.

The wheel connects the Forth and Clyde Canal with the Union Canal. In the past, when canal travel was at its peak, boats had to navigate a staircase of 11 locks, which descended 35 metres (115 feet) over a distance of 1.5 kilometres (0.9 miles). Today, this distance, which is relatively small yet was once a huge undertaking for floating vessels, can be surmounted in just a few minutes.

Designed by architectural practice RMJM, with significant input from Arup and Butterley Engineering, the wheel is part of the Millennium Link, an £84.5 million regeneration scheme, which included the renovation of 121 structures, including bridges, aqueducts and locks, along the 110-kilometre (68-mile) route between Scotland's two most famous cities, Edinburgh and Glasgow.

At a cost of £17 million, the Falkirk Wheel was the most ambitious element of the entire scheme. The wheel is actually a rotating beam that has two sets of arms, each extending 15 metres (49 feet) beyond a central axle that is 25 metres (82 feet) long. The arms, some 35 metres (115 feet) in diameter, hold two huge rectangular tanks, or caissons, each capable of carrying 300 tonnes (331 tons): these caissons (also known as gondolas) are the vessels that carry boats up and down the 35-metre (115-foot) change in level between the two canals.

The design team explored a number of different methods of creating a boat lift, including a simple balanced lift; a counterweighted circular basin; an oval wheel; and even a rolling egg design, in which boats and crews would have been sealed within a spheroid as it toppled from high to low water.

However, the rotating beam design was eventually arrived at as the team formulated the design of the 100-metre (328-foot) long aqueduct that approaches the lifting device. The aqueduct's dramatic support columns' circular top sections gave rise to the idea of circular motion for the lift and the "wheel" was born. The flat-bottomed caissons are, in effect, an extension of the aqueduct, simply slung between the arms of the wheel. However, a system of gears enables them to rotate in a completely stable fashion, keeping the caissons upright as the wheel turns through 180 degrees. This is of paramount importance, not only to allay any fears of the people using the wheel, but also because if water were to spill from one caisson it would change its weight and disrupt the balance equilibrium, causing the wheel to malfunction seriously.

The drive mechanism for the wheel consists of a series of 10 hydraulic motors mounted in the last aqueduct support. It takes just 22.5 kilowatts to power the electric motors, which consume just 1.5 kilowatt-hours of energy in four minutes.

Perhaps the most challenging problem on the project was that of providing a waterproof seal at the connection of the wheel and the aqueduct. The lock-gate seals used a solution proven in the design of airlock doors in the tunnelling industry. The seals at each end of the caissons and on the canal gates of the aqueduct and the basin below it are totally watertight. The gates themselves form an extremely tight seal and are held shut by the pressure of the water that they are holding back. To release the seal and open the doors, hydraulic pressure is provided from an external self-aligning hydraulic link that automatically connects each time a caisson docks in the aqueduct or canal basin.

At the base of the wheel, a similar system is used within the dry well, which isolates the lower caisson and arm from the canal basin. The dry well stops the arms and caisson being immersed in water on each rotation, a factor that would, if it happened, make the lower caisson buoyant and create drag on the arm, each action potentially unbalancing the counterweight of the upper arm.

These complicated solutions would have been of no use whatsoever if the structure of the wheel were not designed properly, as each individual element of the 270-tonne (298-ton) arms moves through a full 100 per cent range of stresses between tension and compression in each rotation. The curved forms were manufactured by hand by Butterley Engineering and the whole construction was assembled in the workshop before being disassembled and delivered to site.

In all, 12 pieces make up the curved box beam arms, a three-part axle and multi-section caissons. The steel thickness used in the caissons ranges from 10–50 millimetres (0.4–2 inches), depending on the stresses involved, and some 15,000 bolts were required to slip through 45,000 holes drilled into the steel sections of the flange plates to securely fasten the sections together.

Building and installing the wheel on site meant using a 1000-tonne (1,102-ton) crane. The entire wheel had to be suspended on an adjustable temporary rig so that it could be aligned with the aqueduct to an accuracy of 10 millimetres (0.4 inches). The operation was carried out smoothly, thanks to careful pre-planning and practice assembly.

The Falkirk Wheel was opened on May 24, 2002 by Queen Elizabeth II, as part of her Golden Jubilee celebrations.

Below: The original concept sketches for the built wheel: these rough drawings were then turned into a structure, the likes of which cannot be seen anywhere else in the world.

Opposite: A most unusual and also ingenious piece of engineering, the Falkirk Wheel dominates the rural landscape in which it is set. The visitor centre and operations building behind is dwarfed by the giant rotating arm of the structure.

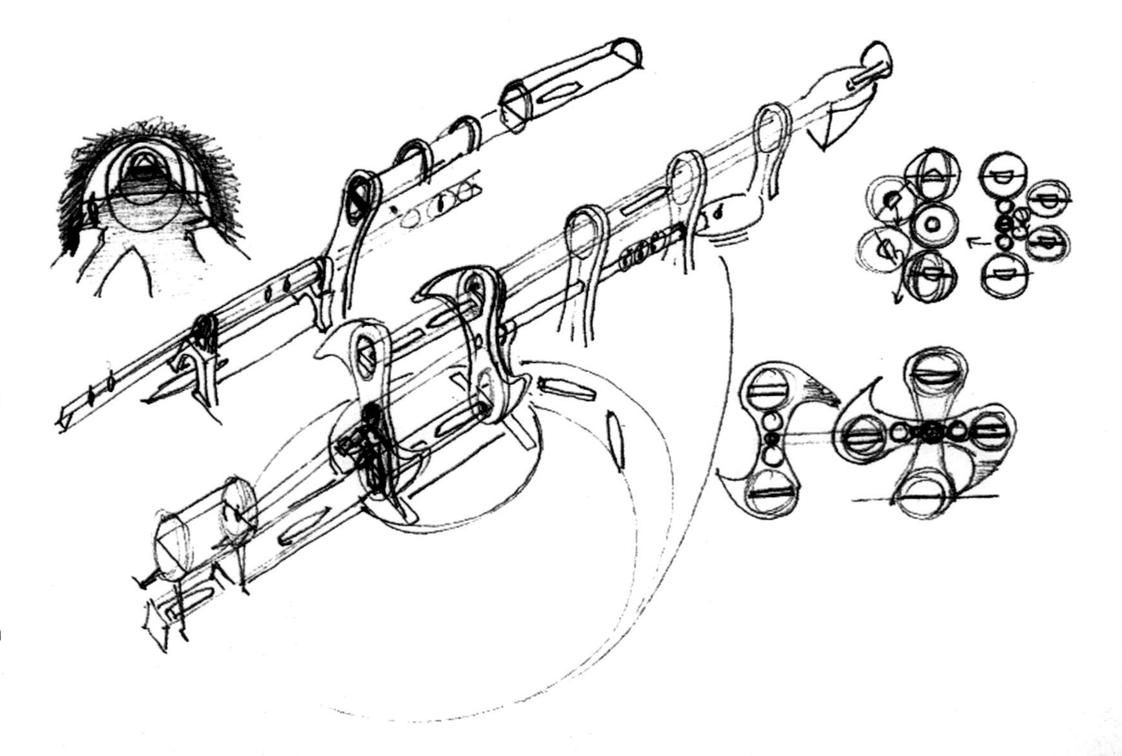

Left: The giant aqueduct is supported on reinforced concrete pillars that seem to grow out of the Scottish hillside. The circular loops of the aqueduct actually inspired the form of the main wheel itself.

Right and below: Concept design sketches, created by the architect of the project, show alternative ideas for transporting boats from high to low water levels. These included a giant water-filled "egg" that would tilt over from an upright position while boats floated on water inside and counterweighted systems operating using massive cables, and giant caissons, similar to those on the completed wheel.

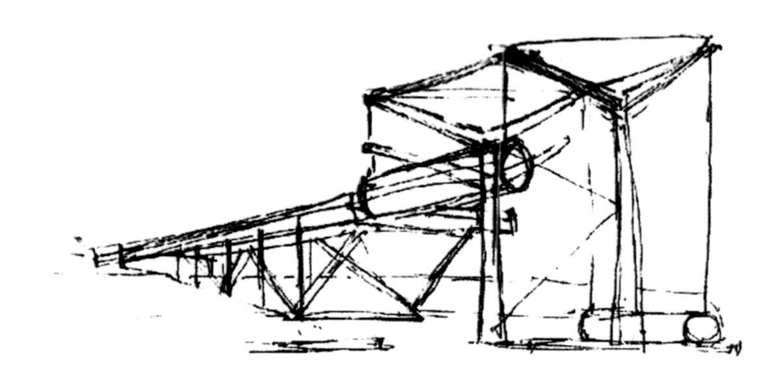

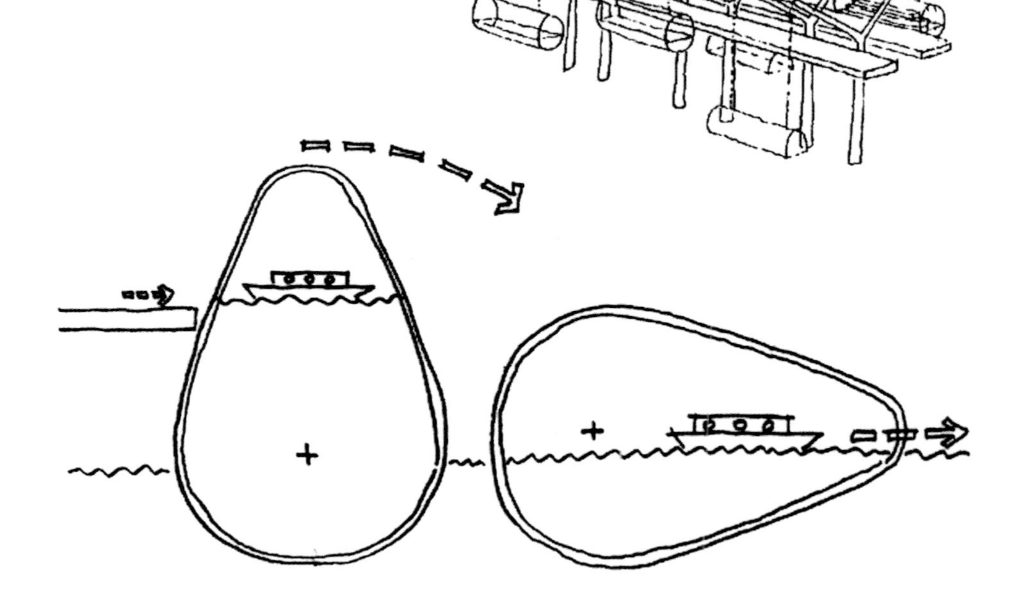

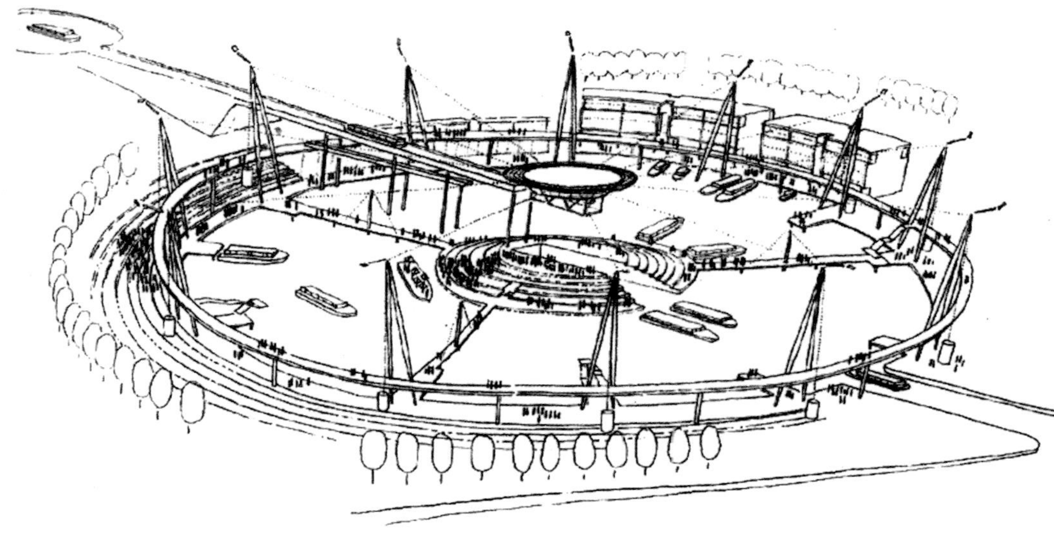

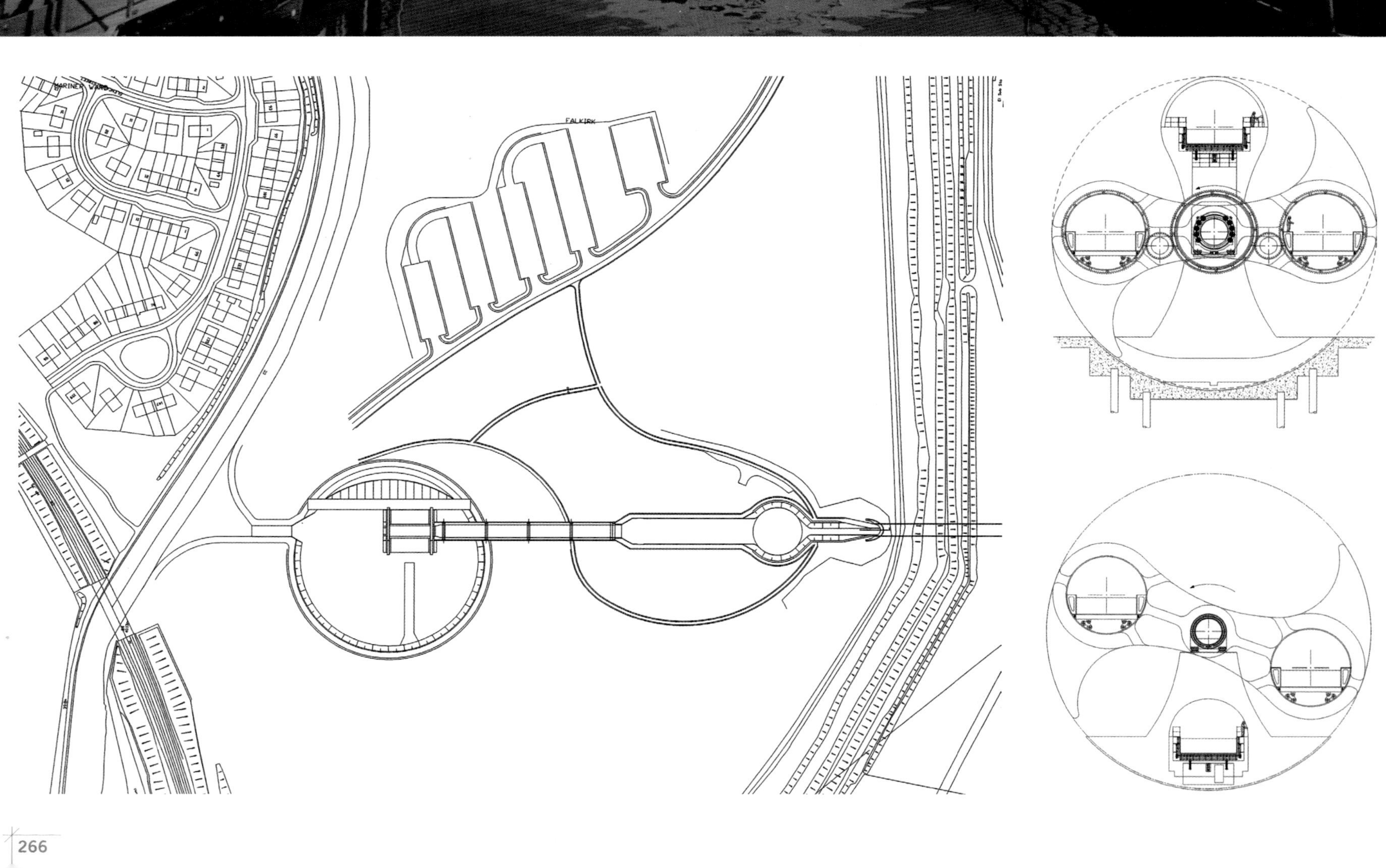
FALKIRK

Opposite top: The view from a boat as it travels from the aqueduct and into the wheel. In the foreground, the gates of the caisson are open to allow the barge to sail into it.

Opposite bottom left: A plan view of the site shows the higher canal level to the right, including a widened section and small circular basin. Moving to the left, the slim viaduct comes to an end at the wheel caissons, which stand over the larger circular canal basin to the left. Boats exit on to the lower canal to the far left.

Opposite bottom right: Images showing sections through the wheel at each of its rotating arms: (**top**) at the arm that connects to the aqueduct; and (**bottom**) at the extreme end of the boat lift.

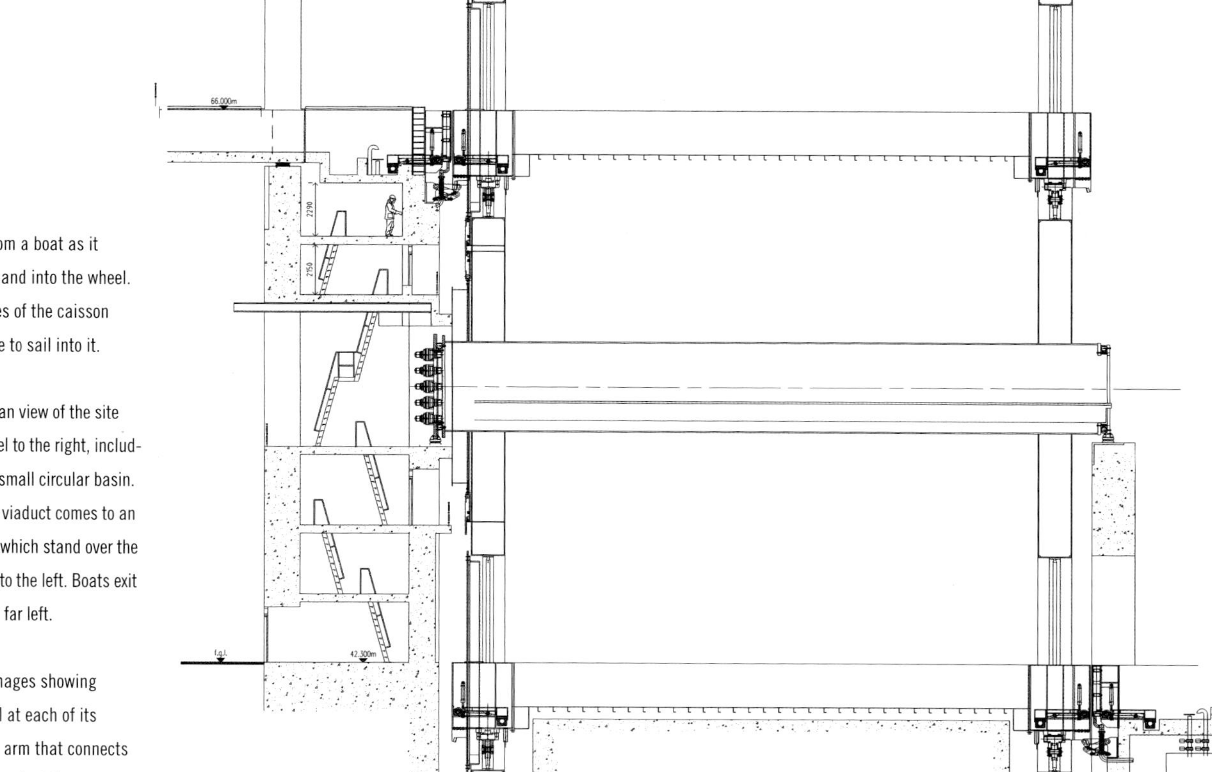

project data

- The Falkirk Wheel took 22 months to build and was designed to last for 120 years.
- It cost £17 million, while the entire canal restoration project totalled £84.5 million.
- The wheel can raise boats and 600 tonnes (661 tons) of water up the 35-metre (115-foot) elevation in under four minutes.
- The wheel takes about 15 minutes to rotate; it used to take eight hours to go from one level to the other via a series of 11 locks.
- The two caissons can carry up to four boats each.
- The mechanism is so well balanced that the energy required to operate the 10 hydraulic motors is less than that needed to boil two kettles.
- The construction programme of the wheel had to be timed around both fish- and bird-breeding seasons on the canals.
- The project also included a new 100-metre (328-foot) long aqueduct and a 168-metre (551-foot) long tunnel – the first new canal tunnel built in Britain for a century.

Above: A section through the wheel illustrates its size. Some six flights of steps to the left, allow for maintenance: the diameter of the main axle is nearly as tall as two of these flights.

Left: The wheel in half rotation, lowering a tour party boat into the canal basin.

ASWAN HIGH DAM RIVER NILE, EGYPT

The Aswan High Dam is both an engineering wonder and an ecological offender. Conceived in the 1950s to generate electricity and to tame the River Nile's propensity to flood, the dam has also prevented vital nutrients from travelling downstream. Indeed, much of the nutrient-rich deposits that would ordinarily have flowed into the Nile Delta now fall to the bottom of the vast reservoir that has built up behind the dam, leading to fears that the reservoir will eventually silt up.

The River Nile is of vital importance to Egypt, and always has been. The principal source of the country's water, the river is used for the irrigation of crops and transport. However, seasonal variations in rainfall much farther south can cause the river to rise and fall dramatically and catastrophic flooding has always been a risk – indeed, the Nile traditionally overflowed its banks on an annual basis. Simultaneously, the vast volume of water that flows northward to the Mediterranean has always represented a potential source of power. The construction of the dam, therefore, constituted a chance to control water levels and install hydroelectric generators. When completed in 1970, the dam produced half of Egypt's power.

The High Dam was not, in fact, the first attempt at taming the Nile. A smaller dam (called the Low Dam) was constructed by the British in 1902. This dam proved insufficient, however, and its height was increased twice before the decision was taken to build a much larger structure 6 kilometres (3.7 miles) upstream (that is, to the south). The construction of this larger edifice was politically and diplomatically controversial, and the dam soon became a Cold War bone of contention. The Egyptian government eventually obtained financial and technical support for the dam's construction from the Soviet Union. Construction started in 1960 and the dam was completed a decade later at a cost of around US$1 billion.

It was an awesome undertaking. The dam is 114 metres (364 feet) high and extends 3,830 metres (12,566 feet). At its base it is 980 metres (3,215 feet) wide and 40 metres (131 feet) wide at its top. This mega-structure contains 44.3 million cubic metres (1.56 billion cubic feet) of building material and holds back a reservoir that can accommodate 169 billion cubic metres (5.97 trillion cubic feet) of water. This reservoir, named Lake Nasser after the Egyptian president Gamal Abdel Nasser, who died in the year construction ended, extends for 500 kilometres (311 miles) and is up to 35 kilometres (22 miles) wide. The power is produced by a dozen 175-megawatt generators, which, when the dam began producing electricity in 1967, allowed many villages throughout the country to be connected to the power grid for the first time.

Before the dam was built, a considerable number of archaeological projects were conducted, including the removal and relocation of ancient

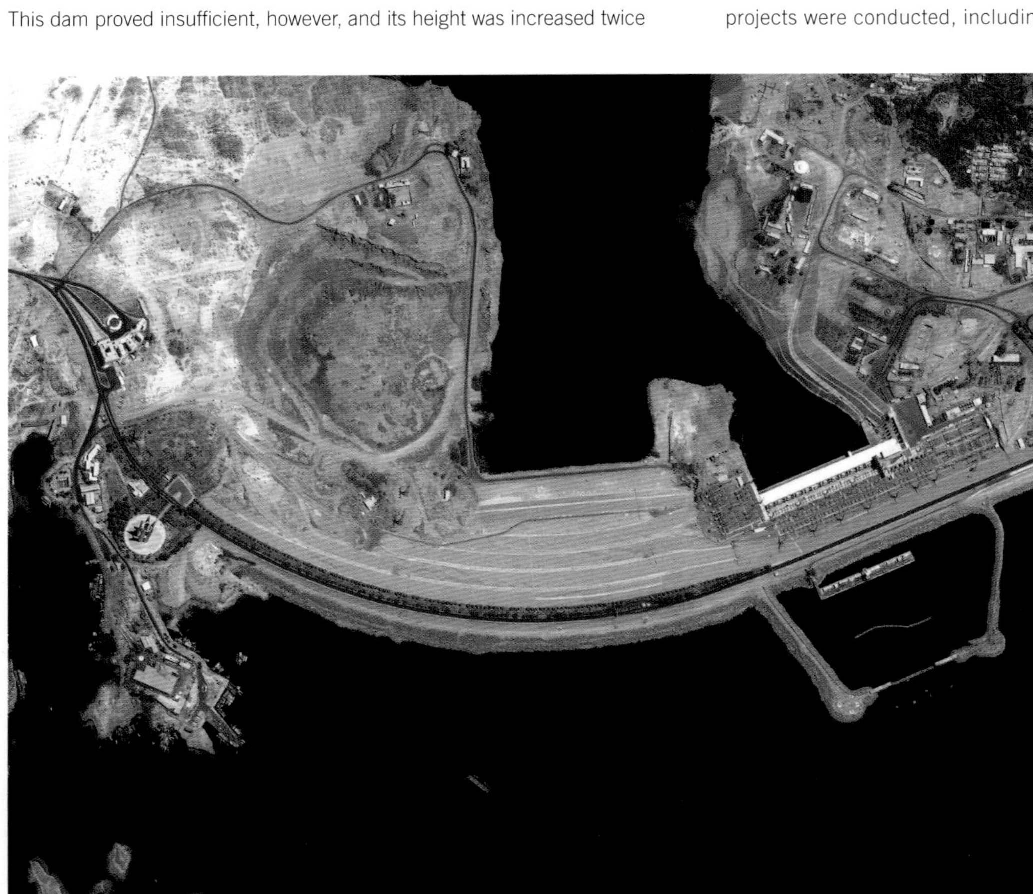

Left: Aerial view of the Aswan High Dam, Egypt, showing the Lake Nasser reservoir to the south.

Right: The dam controls the flow of the Nile so well that much of the river's silt falls to the bottom of the reservoir. The fertility of agricultural lands and the Mediterranean Sea has declined as a result.

monuments that would otherwise have been submerged under the waters of the new lake. Many people were also displaced (some sources say up to 90,000) from their homes in southern Egypt and Sudan. Furthermore, because part of the reservoir (about 17 per cent) would lie within Sudan, a Nile Water Agreement covering water use and extraction had to be reached between Egypt and Sudan before construction work could start. The agreement was signed in 1959 and is still in force.

Composed of enough granite, sand, concrete and clay to regulate what was once an unpredictable and even dangerous river, the dam has certainly done what was intended. The dramatic changes in the river's height and volume can now be controlled while water is available in abundance for irrigation. This means the danger of catastrophic flooding can be avoided, while a constant stream of water is available in the event of a lack of rainfall to the far south (which once led to drought and famine). However, there is a downside. The silt that would normally flow to the Nile Delta now sinks to the bottom of the reservoir and there are fears that the delta itself is being eroded because it is no longer being renewed by river deposits. Indeed, Nile mud was traditionally used for the manufacture of bricks, but this natural and constantly replenished resource is no longer available. Furthermore, the nutrients carried by the silt are having to be replaced by artificial fertilizer, and some observers believe that even fish in the Mediterranean have suffered because Nile silt is not enriching the water with silicate, phosphate and other minerals.

The Aswan High Dam is an immense engineering and political achievement. Reaching down through the silt and sand of the Nile's riverbed to rest on the granite beneath, this massive undertaking is as good a demonstration as any that daring infrastructure projects can affect the course of nature. Unfortunately, such projects can also have unintended consequences.

project data

- The Aswan High Dam, built near the Egypt–Sudan border, was built in two stages between 1960 and 1970.
- The dam's 12 generators produce around 2 gigawatts of electricity every year.
- Lake Nasser, the reservoir formed by the creation of the dam, crosses the border into Sudan; a water-use agreement was signed between Egypt and Sudan in 1959. The water agreement was based on the average flow of the Nile in the first half of the twentieth century. Egypt was allocated 55.5 billion cubic metres (1.96 trillion cubic feet) of water; Sudan got 18.5 billion cubic metres (653 billion cubic feet).
- Up to 11,000 cubic metres (390,000 cubic feet) of water can pass through the dam every second; emergency spillways can let a further 5,000 cubic metres (176,600 cubic feet) of water pass through.
- The older Aswan Dam, built by the British in 1902 and modernized in 1960, sits 6 kilometres (3.7 miles) north of the High Dam, and also generates electricity.

Opposite: The construction of the dam appears almost like a project of the ancient Pharaohs. Like the pyramids, the Aswan High Dam has become part of Egypt's identity.

Above: During construction, the Aswan High Dam became embroiled in Cold War rivalry. Originally, the dam had the support of the Western powers, but it was eventually built with help from the Soviet Union.

Right: This image illustrates the power of the water that is directed through the dam, which is a major producer of Egypt's electricity.

Far right: The dam, an impregnable wall of masonry anchored deep within the bed of the Nile, is the picture of engineered strength.

PALO VERDE NUCLEAR GENERATING STATION

SONORA DESERT, ARIZONA, USA

The Palo Verde Nuclear Generating Station is the largest nuclear power facility in the United States and one of the largest in the world. Comprising three separate nuclear reactors, and built between 1976 and 1988, the Palo Verde plant produces power for more than four million people in the states of Arizona, California, New Mexico and Texas.

Located in the Sonora Desert, west of Phoenix, Arizona, Palo Verde had a complex and lengthy birth. Planned in 1973, construction on the power plant began in June 1976 with a staggered schedule that had the three units coming into operation approximately two years apart. Ultimately, Unit 1 achieved commercial operation in January 1986, somewhat behind schedule; Unit 2 began operating on schedule eight months later; and Unit 3 began generating power commercially in January 1988, ahead of schedule.

It was a mammoth undertaking, involving contributions from 40,000 people – more than 8,000 of whom were employed on the construction site at the peak of activity in June 1983. Indeed, no description of Palo Verde is possible without resorting to superlatives and mind-bogglingly large numbers. For example, enough concrete was used in the construction of this power plant to build a highway between Phoenix and Los Angeles, while three times as much steel was used here as in the construction of the famous ocean liner *Queen Mary II*. The construction cost of the power plant was US$5.9 billion.

At the heart of Palo Verde is a set of three Pressurised Water Reactors (PWRs), one of two types of nuclear power generator used in the United States (the other being the Boiling Water Reactor). In a PWR, power is generated in the following manner: within the domed containment building, the nuclear fuel in the reactor – often called the core – heats water which is pumped under high pressure (preventing the water from boiling) through thousands of alloy pipes in giant heat exchangers known as steam generators; the high temperature of these pipes heats non-radioactive water outside the tubes, which is used to create steam, which in turn spins the turbine-generator assemblies to create electricity.

Quite apart from the science behind the nuclear technology, the engineering of even the steam generators is extremely complex. At the end of 2003, engineering and construction company Bechtel (which originally built the plant) replaced the two steam generators installed in the domed containment building of Unit 2. Extracting the original generators and replacing them with newer and larger versions (approximately 23 metres/75 feet tall and weighing 726 tonnes/800 tons) meant cutting through two concrete walls and working in incredibly cramped conditions. "It's kind of like working in a space capsule," said Bechtel's project manager at the time. "You don't have the luxury of throwing more and more people at the problem ... You don't want grinding sparks flying around or dropped tools falling into other work areas. Getting the right people in the right places at the right time is a multi-layered chess game." Even planning the installation of the new equipment took nearly a decade. The generators were manufactured by a specialist company in Milan, Italy, over a period of three years. Once complete, they were shipped to Arizona via the Panama Canal and transported northwards through Mexico.

The two steam generators in Unit 1 were replaced in 2005 and the steam generators in Unit 3 were due to be replaced in 2007.

With the replacement of steam generators and other equipment upgrades, the output of each unit has been increased by approximately 90 megawatts – strengthening Palo Verde's position as the largest power producer in the United States. With the new equipment, each of the three units is capable of producing approximately 1,340 megawatts. Of the three nuclear reactors on the site, Unit 2 is the largest and most powerful. Together, the generators far outstrip the generating capacity of any other nuclear plant in the country, and they produce around one third of the power used in Arizona. Even before the improvements, in 2002 the plant produced 30.9 billion kilowatt-hours of electricity — making Palo Verde the only American power plant to generate more than 30 billion kilowatt-hours in one year.

One of the unusual things about the Palo Verde complex is that, unlike most nuclear power plants, it is far from any ocean, river or lake, which are normally used as water sources for nuclear power plant cooling towers. Instead, Palo Verde uses recycled sewage effluent from Phoenix – recycling more than 20 billion gallons of waste water every year, which is processed at the plant's own water reclamation facility and stored in a nearby man-made reservoir covering 80 acres. Palo Verde is the only nuclear power in the world that obtains its cooling water in this manner.

Over recent years the United States authorities have taken steps to bolster security at the Palo Verde complex should there be a significant terrorist threat, by drawing up plans to deploy the National Guard in times of crisis. However, the concrete, domed containment buildings that hold the primary nuclear components have been engineered to withstand significant external forces, including the impact of a commercial aircraft.

In November 1987 the United States National Society of Professional Engineers selected Palo Verde for its Outstanding Engineering Achievement Award.

project data

- **The Palo Verde Nuclear Generating Station is located on a 1,640 hectare (4,050-acre) site near Wintersburg, approximately 80 kilometres (50 miles) west of Phoenix, Arizona.**
- **Approximately 2,300 people are employed at the site.**
- **The site contains three nuclear power plants which each have an initial licence for 40 years of operation. Unit 1 is currently licensed to run until December 2024; Unit 2 has a licence until December 2025; Unit 3's initial licence expires on March 2027.**
- **More than 611,600 cubic metres (21.6 million cubic feet) of concrete, 102,512 tonnes (113,000 tons) of steel and 7.6 million metres (25 million feet) of wire and cable were used in the construction of the power plant.**
- **Over 4.74 million cubic metres (167.4 million cubic feet) of earth were excavated during the construction programme.**
- **The Palo Verde complex is owned and operated by seven electric utilities, the largest being Arizona Public Service (with a 29.1 per cent share); APS is also the plant's licensed operator.**
- **According to the Nuclear Power Institute, if all the electricity used by one American citizen in their lifetime were generated by nuclear power, the nuclear waste produced by that individual would fit inside a soft-drinks can.**

Opposite: Completed in phases during the 1980s, the Palo Verde Nuclear Generating Station is the largest of its type in the US. It is a sprawling complex, the size of a town.

Right: Located in Arizona's Sonora Desert, the power station comprises three separate nuclear reactors. They are cooled by recycled sewage effluent from Phoenix.

Below: Each nuclear power plant at Palo Verde is a monolithic assembly of steel and concrete. These immense structures are due to carry on functioning until at least the 2020s.

TROLL A GAS PLATFORM NORTH SEA, OFF NORWAY

Oil and gas platforms are some of the largest man-made structures, although like the icebergs that they share the oceans with, most of their structure is hidden beneath the waves. And, with the accolade of the tallest and heaviest man-made structure ever to be moved on the planet, the Troll A gas platform is a true giant among giants.

Troll A is located 174 nautical miles off Norway's west coast in Troll, Europe's largest offshore gas field, which holds an estimated 1.3 billion cubic metres (45.9 billion cubic feet) of gas. With these huge reserves to be tapped – 60 per cent of all the gas on the Norwegian continental shelf – the platform has been designed to last 70 years; it is anchored to the seabed, toughing it out against all that the North Sea can throw at it.

The platform is one third of the US$5 billion Troll Gas Project, which includes two 91-centimetre (36-inch) pipes to transport the gas back to the shore and an onshore processing plant at Kollsnes on the Norwegian Coast. In total the project took five years to complete, starting in 1991.

The vast majority of Troll A's structure is the concrete gravity base on which the gas platform sits. This is 369 metres (1,211 feet) tall and weighs 656,000 tonnes (723,000 tons). In comparison, the platform, or deck, complete with all accommodation and drilling equipment, weighs only 22,500 tonnes (24,800 tons).

The bottom section of the concrete base was constructed in a dry dock in Stavanger on the coast of Norway. It consists of 19 reinforced-concrete cylinders, 40 metres (131 feet) high, cast in a linked cluster. This massive structure was then floated to a nearby fjord, where the gigantic hollow concrete legs were built on top of it while the whole structure floated in the water.

Below: One of the few times that the true size of the gas platform could be appreciated was as it was towed from its construction site in a Norwegian Fjord out to the gas fields. Here a flotilla of tugs work in unison to ensure it travels out to sea in as smooth a fashion as possible.

Opposite: Once it had been delivered to the site the platform was sunk to the seabed, leaving only a relatively small proportion of it exposed above the waves.

TROLL A
31/6 STATOIL
TROLL A
31/6 STATOIL

Left: Maintenance workers carry out tasks deep under the sea but within the confines of one of Troll A's 300-metre (984-foot) high reinforced concrete legs.

Opposite top: Out at sea the platform includes a multi-storey living accommodation and workspace block (to the left) with a heli-pad on top, as well as the mass of gas extraction equipment, cranes and a tall exhaust for burning off excess gas.

project data

- Gas began flowing from Troll A to shore on October 1, 1996. Production is expected to last for 70 years, yielding 1.3 billion cubic metres (45.9 billion cubic feet) of gas.
- The Troll Gas Field covers 750 square kilometres (290 square miles), with vast reservoirs of reserves up to 1,400 metres (4,590 feet) below sea level.
- In 2006 musician Katie Melua played a concert some 303 metres (994 feet) below sea level in the base of one of the platform's concrete shafts to mark Troll A's tenth anniversary.
- The amount of concrete used to build the platform's gravity base would be enough to construct foundations for 215,000 ordinary houses.
- The massive concrete gravity base cost US$500 million to build.
- 15 Eiffel Towers could be built with the 100,000 tonnes (110,000 tons) of steel used in Troll A's construction.
- From the highest point on the platform to the base, sunk 36 metres (118 feet) into the seabed, Troll A is 472 metres (1,549 feet) tall.

The method used to construct the tall concrete legs was slip-forming. This is a relatively new advance in concrete construction that uses formwork (a mould) that is moved very slowly by hydraulic jacks as the concrete is poured. Initially, the formwork is filled with concrete, which is given time to start to set, then the form is inched upward by a few centimetres every 10 minutes while being constantly filled with concrete. By the time the concrete is exposed below the formwork, it has set hard enough to withstand the pressure of the load above it. The construction of the base was started in July 1991 and completed in December 1994; 245,000 cubic metres (8.7 million cubic feet) of concrete were used.

The steel deck structure was constructed at the nearby Aker Stord dockyard between August 1992 and December 1994. The two elements were then brought together in January 1995, while the structure was still within the calm waters of the fjord. Measuring 170 by 51 metres (558 by 167 feet), the deck was floated on barges into position over the base, which had been lowered to just 6.5 metres (21 1/3 feet) above water level. With it sitting in exactly the correct position, water was gradually pumped from the hollow chambers in the base legs and they rose, lifting the deck 30 metres (98 feet) above the water.

Once all works to the deck had been completed, the platform was ready for its journey out to the gas fields. Ten of the world's largest tugs were employed for the 174-nautical mile journey, which took one week to complete.

While the structure is massive, its slender legs present only a relatively small amount of resistance against the waves and sea currents. When the platform arrived at the gas fields, the more solid bottom layer of concrete cylinders was gradually filled with water and sunk onto the seabed and then sunk a further 36 metres (118 feet) into the seabed to provide a stable base. Troll A was now finally ready to begin drilling for gas in pockets in the earth's crust up to another 1,000 metres (3,280 feet) below the seabed.

TO FLOAT OR NOT TO FLOAT

Oil- and gas-rig platforms are some of the largest movable man-made structures in the world. The Petronius Platform in the Gulf of Mexico stands 610 metres (2,000 feet) above the ocean floor. It could claim the title of the world's tallest building, although only 75 metres (246 feet) of the structure is above water.

Petronius is a compliant tower design. This means that it is fixed to the seabed via a relatively narrow tower that allows for lateral movement. Other fixed platforms, such as Troll A, are built on anchored concrete caissons or steel jacket legs. Steel jacket piles are driven into the seabed, while concrete caissons, which are usually huge hollow legs, are built at shore, floated to their destination and then filled with water, sinking them to the seabed. Fixed platforms are economically feasible for installation in water depths up to 600 metres (1,970 feet).

Floating platforms enable oil exploration to be carried out in much deeper oceans. Semi-submersible platforms have legs that are buoyant enough to make the rig float but which are heavy enough to keep it upright. They can be towed between oil fields and used in depths of up to 1,800 metres (5,900 feet). Similarly, Tension Leg and Spar platforms both float. They are tethered to the seabed using tensioned tethers and mooring lines, respectively; the former provides a stiffer connection and lessens lateral movement.

Left: The Thunder Horse Oil rig is the largest semi-submersible oil platform in the world. Its legs are buoyant enough to float and yet of sufficient weight to keep the rig upright in the water. This floating structure is tethered to the seabed using long cables.

DINORWIG POWER STATION LLANBERIS, UK

Dinorwig Power Station is perhaps Britain's best-hidden secret. Being literally buried within a mountain, the only signs of its existence on the surface are two large lakes and a visitors' centre.

Situated near Dinorwig, on the edge of the Snowdonia National Park in North Wales, the power station is a 1,728-megawatt pumped storage hydroelectric scheme. It utilizes the force of vast amounts of water falling from a high reservoir, through turbines, into a lower reservoir, to generate power. The project was conceived to create an extra power source in times of high demand and provide an alternative in case of National Grid failure. It also had the beneficial effect of landscaping an abandoned slate quarry, which is now the lower reservoir, named Llyn Peris.

The power station itself is located deep inside the mountain of Elidir Fawr. High on top of this windswept peak is Marchlyn Mawr reservoir, from which water is drained in order to turn the turbines. The construction of the project began in 1974 and took 10 years to complete. At the time it was the largest civil engineering contract ever awarded by the British government. Some 12 million tonnes (13.2 million tons) of earth had to be moved from inside the mountain to create 16 kilometres (10 miles) of tunnels, some as wide as major roads, and enormous caverns, the largest of which is the 51-metre (167-foot) high, 180-metre (591-foot) long machine hall.

The power station's engine room comprises six 288-megawatt generator/motors coupled to reversible turbines. Each generator has 12 electromagnetic poles, each weighing 10 tonnes (11 tons). When spinning, these poles produce a terminal voltage of 18 kilovolts. Weighing a huge 450 tonnes (496 tons) each, the generators can start and synchronize with one another to reach full load in around 75 seconds. When synchronized they can generate an 1,800-megawatt load in approximately 16 seconds. This is far faster than powering up a conventional fossil-fuel power station, which takes up to 12 hours to start from cold or 45 minutes to get to full capacity if they are on "hot" standby mode.

In order to excavate the mountain, engineers and geologists had to assess the differing types of ground conditions that they would come across and develop methods of digging or blasting through the mountain, and supporting and securing it. The main caverns, access tunnels and high-pressure tunnels, the lower half of the high-pressure shaft and the diversion tunnel are all excavated from a rock type called the main Cambrian Slate Belt, which is made up of differing types of slate. The upper works were excavated from a mix of grits and slates.

Left: The power station operates using water transferred between two reservoirs. This image shows the man-made dam of Marchlyn Mawr, the higher of the two bodies of water.

Opposite: The extent of the worked-out quarry, in which the power station is built, can be seen here. To the bottom right of the picture, the outlet from the turbines hidden within the mountain is visible.

The layout of the power station's caverns was dictated by the need to maintain structural stability within the mountain: to do this, rock excavation had to be limited and rock pillars and walls in key locations had to be retained, while hollowing out caverns in less structurally fragile areas.

As well as the careful control of excavations, workers installed rock-reinforcement dowels, 3.7-metre (12.1-foot) long bolts and 8-metre (26¼-foot) rock anchors to stitch together adjacent blocks of slate within the rock mass. Heavy supporting elements, such as steel arch ribs and pre-cast concrete linings, were also installed, and drainage holes and channels were dug to prevent the build up of water pressure within open rock faults.

A sprayed concrete called Shotcrete was also used extensively throughout the tunnel and cavern complex to maintain the integrity of excavated surfaces. This was applied to the walls and ceilings using a high-pressure hose system in thicknesses ranging from 25-300 millimetres (1–11¾ inches). Shotcrete sets quite quickly to produce a solid covering layer; however, in critical areas the Shotcrete was also reinforced with a steel mesh.

The largest tunnel is the plant access tunnel, measuring 8 metres (26 feet) wide, 7 metres (23 feet) high and 711 metres (2,333 feet) long. It was designed for transportation of the largest piece of equipment in the power station, the 420/18 kilovolt generator-motor transformer. This tunnel also serves as the main access route for vehicles, personnel and plant to all areas of the cavern complex.

Externally, in order to accommodate the amount of water needed to operate the turbines, both lakes needed to be enlarged into reservoirs. A dam was built at Marchlyn Mawr to increase the holding capacity of the reservoir to 7 million cubic metres (247.2 million cubic feet) of water. Llyn Peris also needed enlarging, but this was achieved more easily by excavating the huge amounts of slate quarry waste from the lake, than by constructing dams.

During full operation of the power station the water level in Marchlyn Mawr falls and rises by up to 34 metres (112 feet). When the valves are opened water falls down 6-metre (20-foot) diameter pipes at a rate of up to 60 cubic metres (2,119 cubic feet) per second. As it passes through the turbines there is an enormous surge in pressure. To counteract this, another shaft 65 metres (213 feet) long and 30 metres (98½ feet) wide has been built to a surge pond high upon the mountain. Water rushes up this shaft to the surge pond, which is 80 metres (262 feet) by 40 metres (131 feet) and 14 metres (46 feet) deep, before sinking back down as the pressure subsides.

The plant runs on average at between 70 and 80 per cent efficiency. This means it uses between 20 and 30 per cent more electricity than it actually produces: the majority of this electricity is expended on pumping water back up to the Marchlyn Mawr ready for reuse. However, Dinorwig is designed to provide bursts of power by responding to sudden surges in electricity demand. The alternative would be to be to produce excess capacity using conventional power stations, which would mean releasing around an extra 140,000 tonnes (154,324 tons) of carbon dioxide into the atmosphere per annum.

project data

- The hydroelectric generating system is buried deep inside Elidir Fawr, in a man-made cavern that is large enough to house St Paul's Cathedral.
- Cables taking electricity to the National Grid are buried for approximately 10 kilometres (6 miles), rather than using pylons, in order to preserve this area of outstanding natural beauty.
- Dinorwig Power Station has 16 kilometres (10 miles) of underground tunnels; its construction required 10 million tonnes (11 million tons) of concrete and 4,500 tonnes (4,960 tons) of steel.
- Dinorwig Power Station is the largest scheme of its kind in Europe.
- When operating at maximum output, as much water passes through the tunnels at Dinorwig as the population of London uses in a day.
- When the extra power is not needed the turbines are reversed and water is pumped back to Marchlyn Mawr, ready to use again.
- The main vertical ventilation shaft, or chimney, for the internal power station is 255 metres (837 feet) high by 5 metres (16 feet) in diameter.

Opposite top: Construction of the surge pond and its giant surge pipe is illuminated by large flood lamps. As water enters the lower reservoir in great volumes any excess is forced up this pipe to relieve pressure.

Opposite bottom: An aerial view of Llyn Peris. The outflow of the power station can be seen to the left.

Left: The main transformer hall is a vast cave within the heart of the mountain. Its size and shape are almost entirely dependent on the strength and stability of the layers of sub-strata in which it has been excavated.

HOOVER DAM COLORADO RIVER, ARIZONA/NEVADA, USA

The Hoover Dam, which extracts enough power from the Colorado River to serve 1.3 million people annually, is a monument to statistics. When it was completed in 1935, the dam was the tallest in the world and until 1948 it was the world's largest hydroelectric producer. There is enough concrete in this giant structure to build a road right across America from San Francisco to New York.

Built to tame the flood-prone Colorado River and to provide irrigation water for surrounding agriculture, the dam was a triumph of engineering and construction prowess. The project involved diverting the river through tunnels carved into the walls of the forbidding Black Canyon, digging through 35 metres (120 feet) of sediment to the bedrock below and casting 6 million tonnes (6.6 million tons) of concrete to provide a new land-bridge between Arizona and Nevada. All this was done in just five years.

Originally called the Boulder Dam, the Hoover Dam was, however, a long in time coming. First conceived around 1905, it was not until the early 1920s that serious thought was devoted to the project. A decade was then spent conducting geological studies and reaching a settlement on how irrigation water and power would be distributed to the surrounding states. As a massive government-sponsored project, the dam was designed by a large team of federal employees led by civil engineer Elwood Mead, who died just prior to the opening of the dam and lent his name to the newly created lake. To soften the highly functional aesthetic of the structure, architect Gordon B. Kaufmann was recruited to the team. It was Kaufmann who introduced the Art Deco elements to the dam.

The Hoover Dam is an arch-gravity dam: the formidable volume of water contained by Lake Mead is held back by both the sheer weight of the structure and the inherent strength of its curved shape. It is thought that the vast bulk of the dam is sufficient to keep the waters back by itself, and that the curve, which transfers the forces of the water into the rocky walls of the canyon, is almost superfluous.

In spite of its monolithic bulk, this concrete dam was not built as a single, homogenous structure. It couldn't have been, because when the constituent elements of concrete (Portland cement, aggregate, sand and water) are mixed together they generate heat, and if the entire dam had been poured at once, it would have taken 125 years to cool. Worse than that, the temperature differential created by cool surfaces and a hot interior could have caused catastrophic cracking.

This problem was partly solved by building the dam incrementally: in units 1.5 metres (5 feet) high, cast as slabs up to 135 square metres (1,500 square feet) in area. Each slab was left to cool for 72 hours before further layers were added. Cooling was further aided by embedding a series of steel pipes within each slab. River water was then passed through the pipes to give the concrete its first cool, followed by iced water supplied by a specially built refrigeration plant nearby. Once the temperature had been reduced sufficiently, the pipes were cut and pressure-filled with cement grouting. In this way approximately 122,300 cubic metres (4.3 million cubic feet) of concrete were poured each month.

The dam rose gradually as a series of trapezoidal columns between June 1933 and May 1935. This was thanks, in large part, to the skill and timing of the crane operators who controlled the dump buckets that transferred the concrete from the mixing plants to where it was needed. Because a relatively dry mix of concrete had been specified (calculated to provide a strong end product), the crane operators had to work fast and accurately to prevent the concrete from drying in the buckets. Consequently, the crane operators were among the highest paid workers on site.

Far left: The construction of the Hoover Dam led to the creation of Lake Mead, whose waters pour through four intake towers in order to generate electricity.

Left: A contemporary photograph of the newly completed Hoover Dam, showing the structure and the rising waters of Lake Mead.

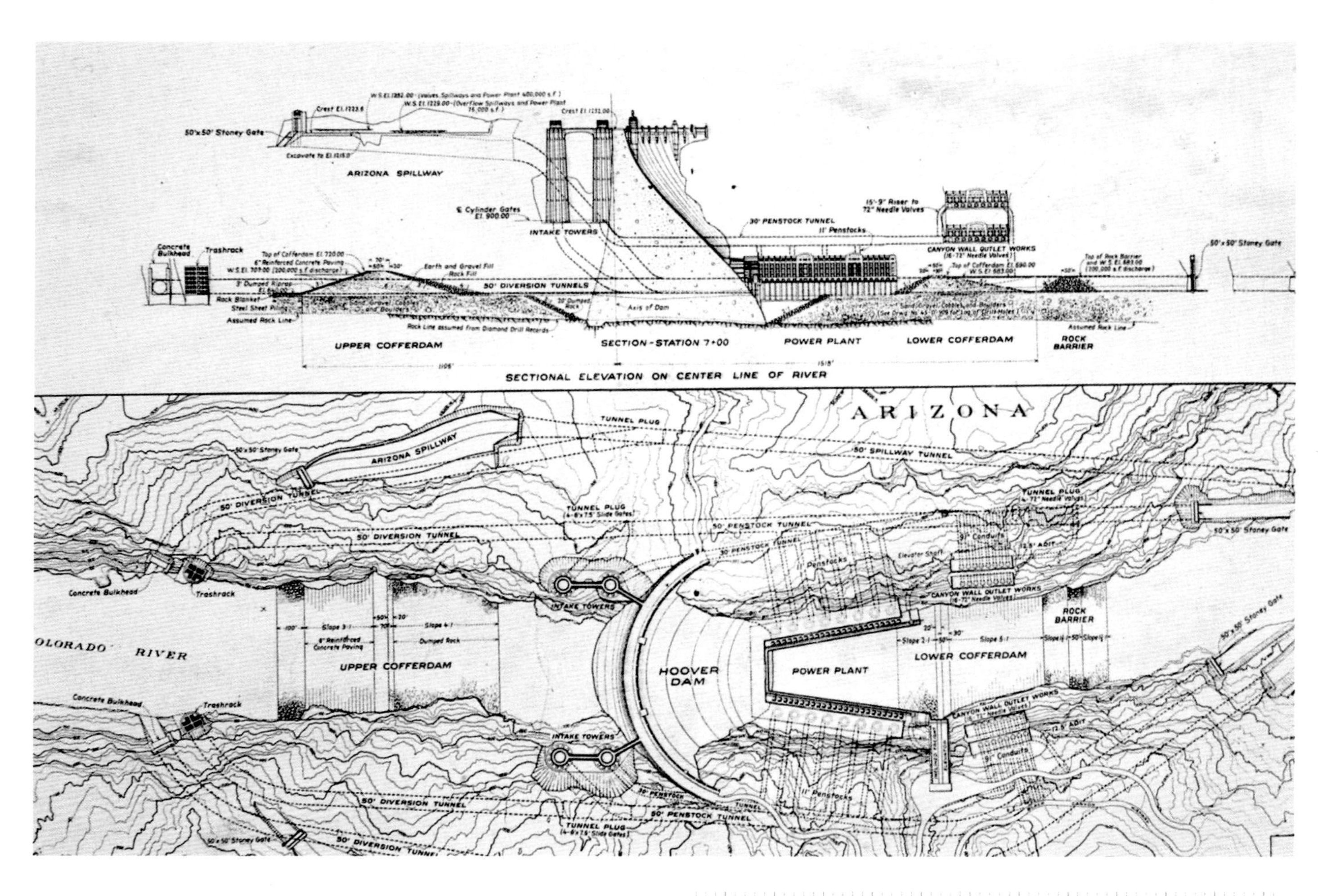

Left: This drawing illustrates the rationale for the location of the Hoover Dam – a steeply inclined canyon, with swift-flowing waters. If necessary, the dam could expel water at the rate of 14,160 cubic metres (500,000 cubic feet) per second.

Opposite: The dramatic downstream face of the dam, with the power plants at its base. This wall of concrete is 221 metres (725 feet) high.

Once poured, rubber-booted workers (known as "puddlers") agitated the concrete with shovels and pneumatic vibrators to remove air bubbles.

The danger with amassing such a large structure from so many individual slabs was the issue of hairline cracks. The solution was to cast a series of grooves along each side of each slab, so that every unit interlocked like a megalithic Lego set. Once the slabs had cooled, cement grouting was forced into any gaps that had been caused by the contraction of the concrete, thus bonding the entire structure into a single object.

The structure was built by 21,000 people (with an average of 3,500 people on site at any one time) and was the first structure to exceed the masonry mass of the Great Pyramid of Giza, according to the United States Department of the Interior. In 1984, the American Society of Civil Engineers designated the dam as a Historic Civil Engineering landmark.

"Ten years ago the place where we are gathered was an unpeopled, forbidding desert," said President Franklin D. Roosevelt upon dedicating the dam on September 30, 1935. "In the bottom of a gloomy canyon, whose precipitous walls rose to a height of more than a thousand feet, flowed a turbulent, dangerous river. The mountains on either side of the canyon were difficult of access with neither road nor trail, and their rocks were protected by neither trees nor grass from the blazing heat of the sun. The site of Boulder City was a cactus-covered waste. The transformation wrought here in these years is a twentieth-century marvel."

project data

- **The Hoover Dam rises 221 metres (726.4 feet) from bedrock to the roadway along its top and weighs 6 million tonnes (6.6 million tons).**
- **The dam sits on, and between, extremely hard and durable volcanic rock.**
- **During the dam's construction, the Colorado River was diverted through four 15-metre (50-foot) diameter tunnels, two on each side of the river, cut through the walls of the canyon.**
- **After being poured, the concrete was cooled using 937 kilometres (582 miles) of pipework that was embedded within it and circulated iced water.**
- **The dam contains a total of 17 turbines, which provide around 4.8 billion kilowatt-hours of energy every year.**
- **Lake Mead, the large body of water that was formed by the creation of the dam, covers 640 square kilometres (247 square miles). At the base of the dam, this water exerts a pressure of 219,700 kilograms per square metre (45,000 lbs per square foot).**
- **Contrary to legend, nobody is buried inside the dam. Figures vary, but around 100 people died of industrial accidents during the construction of the dam.**

5M WIND TURBINE MORAY FIRTH, UK

Unlike most structures in this book, the 5M turbine is not a unique structure: rather it is a manufactured product and therefore capable of being replicated many times. Designed and produced by German energy company REpower Systems AG, the 5M is said to be the largest wind turbine in the world. This three-bladed rotor, with a diameter of 126 metres (413 feet), could (if turning constantly) power 4,500 homes.

This turbine was actually designed for offshore wind farms, where wind is generally stronger and less obstructed – and the turbines are out of sight and therefore less likely to attract objections from people worried about impositions on the landscape. The first 5M, however, was built on land as a prototype. Completed toward the end of 2004, the prototype was installed at a site in Brunsbüttel in Germany's Schleswig-Holstein, adjacent to a nuclear power station. First, a foundation was laid comprising 1,300 cubic metres (46,000 cubic feet) of concrete and 180 tonnes (198 tons) of steel. The five-section tower was then constructed to a height of 120 metres (394 feet), followed by the installation of the 290-tonne (320-ton) nacelle (containing the electrical and mechanical systems behind the turbine, to which the rotor blades are attached), followed by the rotor assembly.

The installation of the rotor blades is the most demanding stage of the construction process, and can be done only when there is virtually no wind. Each rotor blade weighs 18 tonnes (20 tons) and measures 61.5 metres (202 feet) in length. The three blades are fixed to their hub, then the entire assembly, which is known as the "star", is hoisted by a heavy-lift crane to the top of the tower.

For such a vast assembly, it is amazing that it moves at all, but under normal operating conditions the rotors turn 7–12 times per minute. The optimum wind speed for the operation of the turbine is 13 metres (42½ feet) per second, but the 5M will begin turning at speeds as low as 3.5 metres (11½ feet) per second. The turbine is designed to cut out, however, in wind speeds higher than 25 metres (82 feet) per second (30 metres/98 feet per second for the offshore model) to prevent the rotor from becoming damaged.

In spite of being such a heavy object, the manufacturer says that the turbine is, in fact, relatively light for its size. The tower is actually hollow, allowing access and providing a casing for the power systems; the rotor shaft, too, is hollow. Significantly, the rotor blades are made from a glass/carbon fibre hybrid, and the cowling that protects the nacelle from the elements is made from glass-reinforced plastic (GRP).

Two 5M prototypes have been installed in the North Sea 25 kilometres (15½ miles) off the coast of Scotland. This "demonstrator project", part of a 41-million-Euro energy initiative called DOWNViND, began in 2006 and is due to last around five years. The project is taking place in the Beatrice oilfield in the Moray Firth and the two turbines, anchored to the seabed in around 44 metres (144 feet) of water, will supply power to the Beatrice Alpha oil platform. The prediction is that, when fully in operation, the turbines will provide 70 per cent of the platform's electricity needs via an undersea cable.

The turbines were shipped in pieces from the German port of Bremerhaven to Nigg in Scotland, where they were assembled. The 900-tonne (992-ton) turbines were then transported to the Beatrice oilfield on a crane barge, manoeuvred into position and fixed to structures pinned to the seabed. This pair of turbines is testing the idea of large-scale, sea-based wind farms. If the turbines perform reliably, they could pave the way for a wind farm of up to 200 units, costing £1 billion.

Left and opposite top: The 5M turbine, serviced by a giant floating crane, being fixed to a platform anchored to the bed of the North Sea.

Opposite bottom left, middle and right: The giant 5M turbine is assembled on land before being floated out to sea off the coast of Scotland, to generate power for a North Sea oil platform.

project data

- The 5M turbine, so-called because it is designed to generate 5 megawatts of power, is said to be the largest wind turbine in the world.
- At its prototype site in Germany, the 5M could generate 17 gigawatts of electricity every year, enough to power 4,500 three-person homes.
- Each of the turbine's three rotor blades weighs 18 tonnes (20 tons); the prototype blades were made by LM Glasfiber in Denmark.
- The 5M rotor has a diameter of 126 metres (413 feet); each blade is 61.5 metres (202 feet) long.
- The "head weight" of the turbine (the nacelle and rotor) is approximately 400 tonnes (440 tons).
- The 5M is to be manufactured in onshore and offshore versions; the offshore version is equipped with a helicopter landing platform on top of the nacelle.
- The hub of the onshore model is 120 metres (394 feet) high; the offshore model is set around 90 metres (295 feet) above the water's surface.

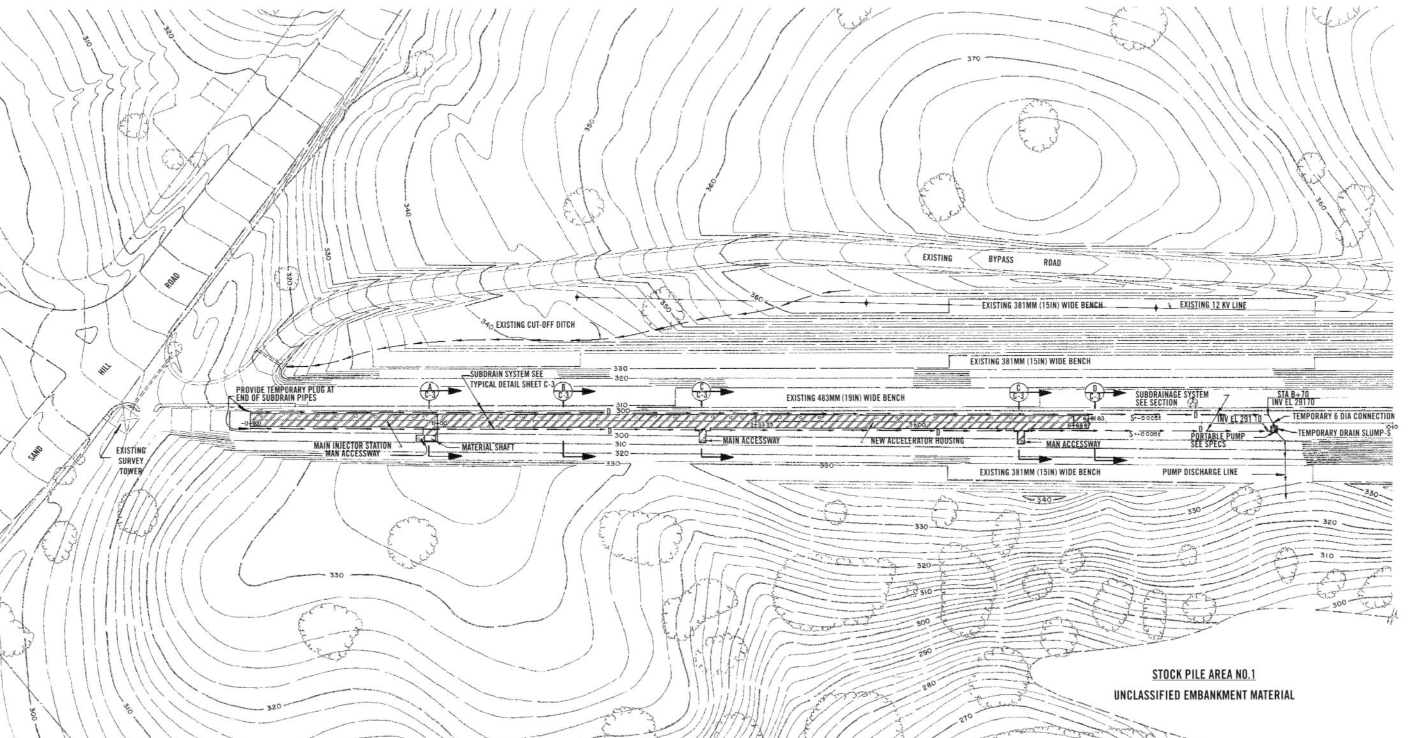

Above: The Stanford Linear Accelerator Center, said to be the world's longest and straightest building, lies across the Californian landscape with little regard for its topography.

Left: A plan drawing and contour map of the SLAC complex, a uniquely straight object within an undulating landscape.

Opposite left: The SLAC facility, around which cluster a variety of scientific buildings, runs underneath a highway, seen towards the top of this picture.

Opposite right: The group of buildings around one end of the SLAC development is the size of a small town.

LINEAR ACCELERATOR STANFORD LINEAR ACCELERATOR CENTER, MENLO PARK, CALIFORNIA, USA

The linear accelerator ("linac") at Stanford Linear Accelerator Center (SLAC) is a 3-kilometre (1.86-mile) long piece of equipment that, since it was completed in 1966, has been at the cutting edge of particle physics. This building-machine is found in Menlo Park, California, and is the world's longest linear accelerator and the straightest object on the planet. It certainly has to be straight – its role is to propel sub-atomic particles at extraordinarily high speeds (almost the speed of light) through a copper pipe in order to study their behaviour and detect the existence of their constituent elements when collided. It was here that curious sub-atomic particles such as the "charm quark" and the "tau lepton" were discovered in 1974 and 1975 respectively. In the four decades since the linac was built, four researchers have been awarded Nobel prizes for research carried out at SLAC.

There are two types of particle accelerators: linear, or "linac", accelerators; and circular, or "synchrotron", versions. SLAC has a linac machine, which means it is a long and straight piece of equipment. In a circular accelerator particles are spun around and around (like a weight at the end of a piece of string) until they reach speeds high enough to be of interest to the scientists. At SLAC's linac, particles are produced at one end, through the actions of an electron gun (in which a laser strips electrons from a semi-conductor's surface) and then accelerated via a series of electromagnetic pulses to a 3,629-tonne (4,000-ton) detection device.

At its simplest the linac is like a combination of a standard television and a kitchen microwave oven, scaled up to an unimaginable size, power and accuracy. Any television (or computer monitor) produces electrons that are accelerated, steered and detected (on the screen), and the linac works in a similar way. Here, though, the particles are propelled along their 3-kilometre (1.9-mile) journey by pulses formed from microwaves generated by machines called klystrons, situated 7.6 metres (25 feet) away.

The linac is a copper pipe assembled from more than 80,000 disks and tubes, almost like a gigantic tube of Polo mints, the electrons flying down the hole in the middle. A complex series of jacks is used to ensure that this copper assembly remains perfectly straight.

Building work on the site began in 1962. At its simplest, the complex consists of the accelerator assembly (located in a tunnel), the klystron building found at ground level, and the detector assembly – a multi-layered piece of kit the size of a six-storey building that sits at the end of tunnel. The accelerator tunnel was built using the "cut and cover" (or "cut and fill") process: a trench is dug, the infrastructure is built inside and then buried. It was exactly this method of construction that was used to build the world's first section of underground railway line – stretching between Paddington and Farringdon in London – in the 1860s. At SLAC, however, concrete was used for the walls, base and roof of the tunnel instead of brick. Once the accelerator tunnel was complete, the roof structure of the klystron gallery, which houses the microwave generating equipment, was built. Water pumping stations were built along the length of the tunnel to cool the accelerator, which can reach temperatures of 80°C (176°F) when in operation.

Construction work was completed in 1966 and its first high-speed electron beam was generated a year later. In 1968, scientists uncovered the evidence for the sub-atomic particles called quarks.

In October 1964, during construction, the fossilized remains of a Paleoparadoxia, a marine mammal that lived 10–20 million years ago, were discovered. The fossil is now on display at the site.

Construction here has never really stopped and other pieces of equipment continue to be added in order to help conduct experiments into cosmic phenomena, such as the nature of matter, its origins and the application of particle physics to medicine, science, power generation and manufacturing. Recent experiments have led to innovative ways of vastly improving the performance of particle accelerators. Scientists have, for example, added a plasma chamber to the accelerator tunnel, giving the electrons passing through 3,000 times more energy than usual.

SLAC is not the only facility looking for answers to these questions. In 2007, for example, the "Large Hadron Collider", a 27-kilometre (16.8-mile) circular accelerator was being fitted out 100 metres (328 feet) under the French–Swiss border. This facility, like SLAC in California, will continue to look for evidence of particles that are presently only theoretical – including the presence of anti-matter.

project data

- **The Stanford Linear Accelerator was built between 1962 and 1966 in California.**
- **The acceleration tunnel at SLAC runs underground for 3 kilometres (1.86 miles).**
- **Built to detect sub-atomic particles and test the theories of physicists, SLAC's linac has been instrumental in the discovery of particles, including the charm quark and tau lepton.**
- **The particle accelerator produces electrons and propels them through a chamber close to the speed of light.**

THREE GORGES DAM YANGTZE RIVER, YICHANG, HUBEI PROVINCE, CHINA

The Three Gorges Dam is the largest hydroelectric dam in the world. The project has been the source of much political debate concerning its impact in terms of both humanitarian and environmental damage to the vast area that the construction site and reservoir cover. However, purely as a feat of engineering there are few that rank as great as this in the last 100 years.

The dam is 2.3 kilometres (1.4 miles) in length and stands 181 metres (594 feet) high. It spans the mid-section of the Yangtze River at Sandouping in the Hubei province of China. The Yangtze is the longest river in Asia; it flows for some 6,211 kilometres (3,859 miles) from high on the Tibetan plateau to the East China Sea near Shanghai.

Structural work to the dam was finished in May 2006. However, generators are still being installed and commissioned, and they are not all due to become fully operational until 2011. When the reservoir, which began filling in June 2003, reaches its full capacity, its surface will be 175 metres (574 feet) above sea level: this is in contrast to the river's original height of 65 metres (213 feet) above sea level. The reservoir will then be 660 kilometres (410 miles) long and cover an area of 1,084 square kilometres (419 square miles). It will hold 39 billion cubic metres (1.4 trillion cubic feet) of water.

This vast water resource will eventually flow through thirty-two 700-megawatt turbine generators. Some of these are already operating; they produced 49.1 billion kilowatt-hours of power in 2005. The first turbine came into operation in July 2003. By 2008, 26 will be in operation and the Chinese government has plans to install six further turbines underground. When these become operational in 2011 the hydroelectric production will reach its peak, at 100 billion kilowatt-hours per annum.

The idea of damming the Yangtze had been tossed back and forth by Chinese leaders for nearly a century: construction of a dam was first proposed in 1919, by Dr Sun Yat Sen. Since 1954, Chinese and foreign scientists and engineers have often been employed in the planning and design of a dam project, but until 1992 political arguments always prevented physical work from actually starting. Then, despite opposition from one third of the Chinese government's delegates, the government gave the go-ahead for the construction project to begin.

Preparation work started soon afterwards in 1993. First the Yangtze had to be redirected to leave the dam site dry. To do this, new channels were blasted and dug around the site to alter the course of the river, and three coffer dams – temporary enclosures within the river, which were pumped dry – were built

project data

- At more than five times the size of the Hoover Dam, the Three Gorges Dam is the largest in the world.
- The Yangtze River is the third longest in the world, flowing for 6,211 kilometres (3,859 miles) across China.
- The dam is 2.3 kilometres (1.4 miles) long and reaches a height of 181 metres (594 feet).
- The reservoir formed behind the dam will be 660 kilometres (410 miles) long, have an average width of 1.1 kilometres (0.7 miles) and hold a colossal 39 billion cubic metres (1.4 trillion cubic feet) of water. When full it will be visible from the moon.
- The dam will generate electricity equivalent to about 45.4 million tonnes (50 million tons) of coal per annum, so reducing emissions of sulphur dioxide and carbon dioxide.
- Some parts of the project, including a bridge, were demolished and rebuilt when certain concrete structures were found to be unstable.

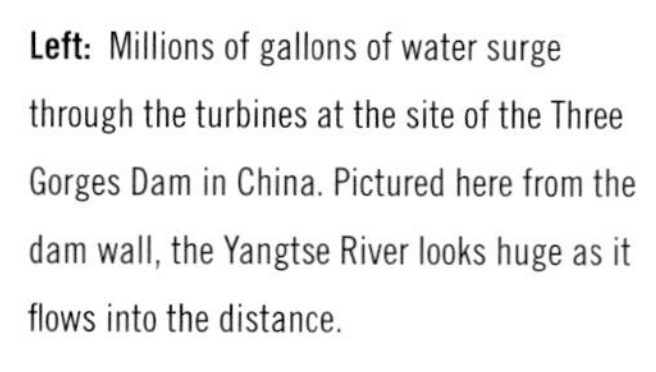

Left: Millions of gallons of water surge through the turbines at the site of the Three Gorges Dam in China. Pictured here from the dam wall, the Yangtse River looks huge as it flows into the distance.

Opposite: A satellite view shows the dam and massive 10-lock system used to transport ships above and below the dam. Here, the surging water from the turbines (lower left) is dwarfed by the rest of the structure

Opposite: Three Gorges extends away from the dam wall for over 645 kilometres (400 miles). Many villages and even towns were flooded to create the giant reservoir.

Below left: Two large ferries, moored side by side, are dwarfed by the walls of one of the system of giant locks that enable them to navigate the Three Gorges Dam.

Below right: The dam was a massive undertaking, many years in the making. Some say it was necessary; others believe it to be a giant folly of the Chinese government, intent on demonstrating its construction might.

on the site of the proposed dam. These coffer dams were demolished on the completion of the main dam to allow water to start flooding against its massive concrete wall.

The new reinforced-concrete dam and all associated works have consumed 26.43 million cubic metres (933.37 million cubic feet) of concrete. This phenomenal amount of material was mixed and poured according to a specially devised computerised supervision and control system for concrete production, conveying and placement, which was developed to achieve optimal work and efficiency rates.

The project required this type of sophisticated monitoring and production techniques due to the colossal undertakings involved. Some 102.59 million cubic metres (3.62 billion cubic feet) of stone and earth were excavated and 29.33 million cubic metres (1.04 billion cubic feet) were redistributed at required dam sites. Over 281,000 tonnes (310,000 tons) of metal structures were erected; these covered anything from tower crane supports to fixtures for the turbines and steel-framed buildings. Over 354,000 tonnes (390,000 tons) of reinforcing bars were fabricated and placed within the concrete walls of the dam.

Two sets of giant locks have been built to aid shipping. Each has five levels, through which ships pass in manoeuvres that take up to four hours in total. The locks are 280 metres (919 feet) long by 35 metres (115 feet) wide; they have been designed to raise and lower 10,000-tonne (11,000-ton) barges, which regularly ferry goods up and down the river, a distance of up to 113 metres (371 feet), which is the maximum difference in water levels on either side of the dam.

Supporters of the dam's construction point out its benefits, stating that it will greatly reduce the risk of flooding along the Yangtze, which in 1954 killed 30,000 people and left one million homeless. It will also provide a proportion of the clean power required to fuel China's economic growth and create a much easier passage along the river from Yichang to Chongqing for larger ships, creating new industry and jobs.

These arguments are countered by those opposing the dam. They believe that the dual cost of human resettlement and environmental damage is enormous. Chinese officials estimate that the reservoir will partially or completely flood 13 cities, 140 towns, and 1,352 villages across 11 provinces. More than 1.3 million people are being resettled and over 23,800 hectares (58,800 acres) of fertile farmland will be lost.

Environmentally, the project is already having a devastating effect on endangered species, such as the Chinese River Dolphin and Chinese Sturgeon. The reservoir has flooded nest sites of the rare Siberian Crane and even destroyed areas inhabited by Giant Panda and tiger. Ecologists also predict that silt carried by the river will build up rapidly within the reservoir and impede the power generation capabilities of the dam. Farther downstream, riverside communities could be devastated as their lands are washed away due to the lack of silt. In addition, some 1,300 archaeological sites are being frantically excavated in order to save historical relics. However, archaeologists believe that many more relics will be submerged by the rising waters of the reservoir.

FARNBOROUGH WIND TUNNELS FARNBOROUGH, UK

Located on the site of the former Royal Aircraft Establishment (RAE) in Farnborough, Hampshire, England, this series of wind tunnels dating from the first half of the twentieth century made a significant contribution to what are now considered classic examples of aircraft design. The forms of the Spitfire, Tornado, Harrier and Concorde were developed here, and one of the wind tunnels, later equipped with a rolling road surface, was eventually used to test Formula 1 racing cars.

The old RAE site was sold to a private developer in the 1990s but, thankfully, all five of these historic wind tunnels are to be preserved and the hope is that three of them will become more than just tourist attractions and can still make their way as scientific and engineering instruments.

The largest and most visually impressive wind tunnel on site is the 7.3-metre (24-foot) diameter "low speed" facility, built in 1935 and closed in 1996. This is a vast, sculptural object of concrete (with mahogany propellor blades) that is large enough to put full-scale aircraft through their paces, as well as other large objects including helicopter rotor blades, radar aerials and architectural elements designed for buildings. It has also been used for parachute testing and assessing the behaviour of coniferous trees for the United Kingdom's Forestry Commission. It was here that the Spitfire, Hurricane, VC10, Trident and BAC111 aircraft were tested, as were the vertical-take-off-and-landing components for what was to become the Harrier jump-jet.

This wind-tunnel facility, contained in what is known as Building Q121, comprises a vast concrete shell, into which the 7.3-metre (24-foot) propellor is set. It is such a well-balanced mechanism that the gigantic propellor can be turned by hand. When in operation, the propellor sucks air through the testing area and pushes it around a circuit, generating speeds of up to 185 kilometres (115 miles) per hour. This does not sound particularly fast, but in aeronautical terms low speeds are crucial, and matters of stalling, turning and manoeuvring at very low speeds are important aspects of aircraft design. Aircraft can be placed on sophisticated balance mechanisms fixed to the ground, or alternatively suspended from gantry cranes and lowered into place in front of the mouth of the tunnel. The tunnel also contains a "forced ventilation system", which extracts air through holes cast into the bell-shaped mouth that leads up to the propellor.

It is a mammoth structure, so perfectly modelled for performance that its aesthetics are entirely suggestive of immense power. In fact, so powerful is this building-machine that the propellor blades are protected by a net of steel cable, similar to an anti-submarine net, preventing anything but very small debris from damaging the machinery should the test rig fall to pieces.

Building R133 contains a visually less impressive but far more potent piece of kit. Again, this is an "inhabitable machine", yet it is configured more like a spacecraft. Known colloquially as "the Flask", this transonic tunnel is far smaller than the facility described above. Just 2.4 by 1.8 metres (8 by 6 feet) in section, this wind tunnel was built in 1942 and can generate wind speeds of 1,610 kilometres (1,000 miles) an hour. The Flask was instrumental in testing the aerodynamics of Concorde. Running at temperatures up to 50°C (122°F), the Flask could operate at speeds of Mach 1.2 or below. A smaller 61-by-46-centimetre (2-by-1½-foot) transonic tunnel, which shared some of the facilities of the Flask, could generate speeds of Mach 1.4.

This is much more a piece of machinery than a building and, when in use, immense steel doors were pushed into place along railway tracks and bolted into place to completely seal the tunnel off from the outside world. Inside, aircraft models approximately 1.8 metres (6 feet) long would be secured to a central fin and subjected to immense airspeeds and varying atmospheric pressures. Curiously, because this facility was designed and built in the pre-computer age, airflow was ascertained in a basic but highly effective manner. The fins on which models were secured were covered in fine chalk powder, which would erode where airflow was most intense: engineers could therefore study an actual picture of the way that air flows across the surfaces of aircraft models, in much the same way as if you blew air over a fine layer of sand laid out on a table. Airflow tests on scale models of Concorde were conducted in exactly this manner.

project data

- **The wind tunnels at what was once known as the Royal Aircraft Establishment are now owned by Slough Estates, a commercial developer who is redeveloping much of the site as Farnborough Business Park. As well as continuing to host the biannual Farnborough Air Show, the site will provide 160,000 square metres (1.7 million square feet) of office space.**
- **Three of the five tunnels on site are intended to be re-used commercially, including the 7.3-metre (24-foot) low-speed tunnel built in 1935.**

Far left and left: Scale models of aircraft (including Concorde) undergoing tests in Farnborough's transonic wind tunnel.

Opposite: A helicopter rotor assembly positioned in front of the blades of Farnborough's 7.3-metre (24-foot) mahogany wind tunnel. This tunnel has been used to test everything from aircraft to the flexibility of trees.

Unfortunately, this test facility was decommissioned in 1994 and is unlikely ever to run again. The brine tanks, which contained cooling fluid, have been drained and, because of the effect of stress cycles and the enormous amounts of energy needed to run these tunnels, the site's owners estimate that it would be commercially unattractive to bring them back into working order. "It is unlikely to be economic to operate in view of its high power consumption and cooling load and high on-going maintenance costs," says the Farnborough Air Sciences Trust, which aims to preserve the tunnel as a piece of engineering heritage. "The tunnel is not only of historical significance because of the projects carried out in it but also because the equipment is highly specialized and has significance from an engineering point of view."

In some ways, in spite of the age of these machines, it a waste of potential. The Flask could subject models to wind speeds of Mach 1.2 in a wide range of pressures from 0.25–3.0 atmospheres. However, this sort of work is being challenged increasingly by computer modelling, which is now becoming sophisticated enough to begin to simulate the conditions in a live wind tunnel.

Below: Construction of the 7.3-metre (24-foot) turbine at Farnborough in the 1930s. This peculiar structure would become one of the UK's primary aircraft testing facilities.

Right: The completed 7.3-metre (24-foot) wind tunnel. The six-bladed fan is so finely balanced it can be turned by hand.

INDEX

U

V

W

Y

Z

PICTURE CREDITS

The publishers would like to thank the following sources for their kind permission to reproduce the pictures in this book.

1: AKG, London **3:** Barbara Burg + Oliver Schuh/Palladium Photodesign **4 from top left to bottom right:** 1 AA World Travel Library/Alamy, 2 Gaphotos/Alamy, 3 Wilford Schupp Architekten GMB / EujinGoh, 4 Jean-Pierre Lescourret/Corbis, 5 AFP/Getty, 6 Jim Zuckerman/Corbis, 7 Dominic Burke/ Alamy, 8 Angelo Hornak/Corbis, 9 Sciencephotos/Alamy, 10 Galen Rowell/Corbis, 11 Tibor Bognar/ Corbis,13 AROS, 14 Hulton Archive/Getty, 15 Richard Bryant/Arcaid/Corbis,16 BP PLC. **6:** Dirk Radzinski/AKG London **7:** Chade Ehlers/Alamy **8:** Aflo Foto/Alamy **12:** Free Agents Limited/Corbis **13:** Louie Psihoyos/Corbis **14:** Tibor Bognar/Corbis **15:** Jim Zuckerman/Corbis **16:** Jon Hicks/ Corbis **17:** Pictor International/Alamy **18:** James Sparshatt/Corbis **19:** AA World Travel Library/ Alamy **20:** BDP **21:**t Duncan Hale-Sutton/Alamy, b Richard Klune/Corbis **23:** Rudy Sulgan/Corbis **24:** r Bettmann/Corbis, l Time & Life Pictures/Getty **25:** Henry Westheim/Alamy **26:** Hulton/George Marks/Getty **27:** Private Collection **28:** Robert Essel/Corbis **29:** JL Images/Alamy **30:** Xiaoyang Liu/ Corbis **31:** Xiaoyang Liu/Corbis **32:** Private Collection **33:** Gueorgui Pinkhassov/Magnum Photos **34:** Louie Psihoyos/Corbis **35:** Louie Psihoyos/Corbis **36:** Juergen Effner/Corbis **37:** Wendy Connett/ Corbis **38:** Roger Ressmeyer/Corbis **39:** Craig Lovell/Corbis **40:** b Bettmann/Corbis, t Bettmann/ Corbis, br Ralf-Finn Hestoft/Corbis **43:** Dominic Burke/Alamy **44:** Foster and Partners **45:** r Acestock/Alamy, l Foster and Partners **46:** Rufus F. Folkks/Corbis **47:** AKG London **48:** Barry Lewis/ Corbis **49:** Jon Hicks/Corbis **50:** Hulton Archive/Getty **51:** Hulton Archive/Getty **52:** Bettmann/ Corbis **53:** Hulton Archive/Getty **54:** b Bettmann/Corbis, t Hulton Archive/Getty **55:** Underwood & Underwood/Corbis **56:** AROS **57:** AROS **58:** AROS **59:** AROS **60:** Ted Spiegel/Corbis **61:** Bill Ross/ Corbis **62/63:** Richard Cummins/Corbis **63:** Bora/Alamy **66:** Charles E. Rotkin/Corbis **67:** Jean-Pierre Lescourret/Corbis **68:** Jean-Pierre Lescourret/Corbis **69:** G P Bowater/Alamy **70:** Information Based Architecture **71:** Information Based Architecture **72:** Simon Reddy/Alamy **73:** Sharon Lowe/ Alamy **74:** Robert Harding World Imagery/Alamy **75:** Jon Arnold/Alamy **76/77:** Roger Ressmeyer/ Corbis **77:** Keck Observatory **78:** Roger Ressmeyer/Corbis **79:** Roger Ressmeyer/Corbis **82:** Aflo Foto/Alamy **83:** Chris Wilson/Alamy **85:** b Murat Taner/Corbis, c Time & Life Pictures/Getty, t Honshu-Shikoku Bridge Express/Honshu-Shikoku Bridge Expressway Company Limited **87:** tl Tom Carrol/ Alamy, r David R. Frazier Photolibrary Inc/Alamy, bl Time & Life Pictures/Getty **89:** Angelo Hornak/ Corbis **90:** Wilkinson Eyre **91:** Wilkinson Eyre **92:** AP Images/PA Photos **93:** Time & Life Pictures/ Getty **94:** Bettmann/Corbis **95:** br AKG London, tl Bettmann/Corbis, bl AP Images/PA Photos, tr Topham Picturepoint **96:** Rijkswaterstaat **97:** b Arthur Gebuys/ Alamy, t Rijkswaterstaat **98:** Arthur Gebuys Alamy **99:**l Barbar Burg & Oliver Schuh/Palladium Photodesign, b Barbara Burg & Oliver Schuh Palladium Photodesign, **100:** Barbara Burg & Oliver Schuh/Palladium Photodesign **101:** Hulton Archive/Getty, Barbara Burg & Oliver Schuh/Palladium Photodesign **104:** Roger Bamber/ Alamy **105:** Gaphotos/Alamy **106:** Stephane Compoint **107:** Foster and Partners **108:** Foster and Partners **109:** b Foster and Partners, r Stephane Compoint **110:** Mary Evans Picture Library/Alamy **110/111:** Dallas & John Heaton/Corbis **112:** Theo Allofs/Zefa/Corbis **113:** AA World Travel Library/ Alamy **114:** Robert Harding World Imagery/Alamy **115:** Skyscan/Corbis **116:** t Alamy Images / Aerofilms, b /David Ball **117:** Simon Wilkinson/Alamy **118:** Fredrik Olsson/Oresundsbron **119:** Mollers Design Studio APS **120:** l Mollers Design Studio APS , r Stig-Ake Jonsson/ Oresundsbron **121:** c Oresundsbron, t /Pierre Mens/ Oresundsbron, b /Miklos Szabo/ Oresundsbron **123:** World Pictures **124:** Danny Lehman/Corbis **124/15:** Danny Lehman/Corbis **126:** t Corbis Images, b Danny Lehman/Corbis **127:** H. N. Rudd/Corbis **128:** Foster and Partners **129:** Dominic Burke/Alamy **130:** Alamy **130/1:** Dominic Burke/Alamy **131:** Foster and Partners **132/3:** David R. Frazier Photolibrary, Inc./Alamy **134:** AM Corporation/Alamy **135:** b Robert Harding World Imagery/Alamy, t Jan Stromme/ Alamy, tr Galen Rowell/Corbis, tl Charles Derleth Papers, Water Resources Center Archives, University of California, Berkeley **138/9:** Roger Viollet/Topham Picturepoint **139:** rc Hulton Archive/Getty, br Hulton Archive/Getty, t Roger Viollet/Topham Picturepoint, rc Roger Viollet/Topham Picture Point **140:** Francesco Venturi/Corbis **141:** Francesco Venturi/Corbis **142:** Grimshaw **143:** James Cheadle/ Alamy **144:** r Marc Hill/Alamy, l Derek McHattie/Alamy, c Gerry Penny/Corbis, b Grimshaw **145:** Grimshaw **147:** b L. M. Peter/ AKG London, t /Florian Profitlich/AKG London **148:** tl L. M. Peter/ AKG London **148:** bl McCanner/Alamy **148/9:** Juergen Henkelmann/Alamy Images **150:** Roger Viollet/ Topham Picturepoint **151:** The Bridgeman Art Library **152:** Herzog & de Meuron **153:** Blickwinkel/ Alamy **154:** b Maximilian Weinzierl/Alamy, t Herzog & de Meuron **155:** t Glyn Thomas/Alamy, b Herzog & de Meuron **156:** b Martin Siepmann/Alamy, t Herzog & de Meuron **157:** tr /Interfoto/Alamy, cr Interfoto/Alamy, l Stefan Obermeier/Alamy, br Herzog & de Meuron **158:** Bernard O'Kane/Alamy Images **159:** Aga Khan Trust for Culture **160:** Aga Khan Trust for Culture **161:** Aga Khan Trust for Culture **162:** Edward Cullinan Architects **163:** Richard Learoyd/Edward Cullinan Architects **164:** Edward Cullinan Architects **165:** b Roger Bamber/Alamy, t Edward Cullinan Architects **166:** Arup **167:** b Arup, t Associated Press/PA Photos **168:** AKG London **169:** AKG London /Ullstein Bild **170:** AKG London **171:** AKG London **172:** Masato Ikuta/Paul Andreu © ADAGP, Paris and DACS, London 2007 **173:** Shinkensiku-Sha/Paul Andreu © ADAGP, Paris and DACS, London 2007 **174:** b Paul Andreu, t /Kawashaki Heavy Industries © ADAGP, Paris and DACS, London 2007 **175:** Paul Andreu / Masato Ikuta © ADAGP, Paris and DACS, London 2007 **176:** c SIAT Architektur + Technik/ Barbara Burge & Oliver Schuh/Palladium Photodesign, b SIAT Architektur + Technik/ Barbara Burge & Oliver Schuh/Palladium Photodesign, t /Siat Architektur + Technik/Barbara Burge & Oliver Schuh/Palladium Photodesign. **177:** b Barbara Burge & Oliver Schuh/Palladium Photodesign, t SIAT Architektur + Technik Barbara Burg & Oliver Schuh/Palladium Photodesign **178:** Barbara Burge & Oliver Schuh/ Palladium Photodesign **179:** Barbara Burg + Oliver Schuh/Palladium Photodesign **180:** Rubens Abboud/Alamy **182/3:** Tibor Bognar/Corbis **182:** Hulton Archive/Getty **184:** Andrew Holt/Alamy **185:** Tim Ayers/Alamy **187:** t Alex Bartel/Alamy, b Frans Lemmens/Getty **188:** t Popperfoto/Alamy, b John Walton/Empics/PA Photos **189:** Arup **190:** Arup **191:** Arup **194:** Ian Dagnall/Alamy **195:** Roger